MW01518789

Disability Rhetoric

Critical Perspectives on Disability

Steven J. Taylor, Beth A. Ferri, and Arlene S. Kanter, *Series Editors*

Books in the Critical Perspectives on Disability series, launched in 2009, explore the place of people with disabilities in society through the lens of disability studies, critical special education, disability law and policy, and international human rights. The series publishes books from such disciplines as sociology, law and public policy, history, anthropology, the humanities, educational theory, literature, communications, popular culture studies, and diversity and cultural studies.

Disability
Rhetoric

Jay Timothy Dolmage

SYRACUSE UNIVERSITY PRESS

This research was supported by an Insight Development Grant from the Social Sciences and Humanities Research Council of Canada.

∞ The paper used in this publication meets the minimum requirements of the American National Standard for Information Sciences—Permanence of Paper for Printed Library Materials, ANSI Z39.48-1992.

For a listing of books published and distributed by Syracuse University Press, visit our website at SyracuseUniversityPress.syr.edu.

ISBN: 978-0-8156-3324-2 (cloth) 978-0-8156-5233-5 (e-book)

Library of Congress Cataloging-in-Publication Data
Dolmage, Jay.
    Disability rhetoric / Jay Timothy Dolmage. — First Edition.
        pages cm. — (Critical perspectives on disability)
    Includes bibliographical references and index.
        ISBN 978-0-8156-3324-2 (cloth : alk. paper) — ISBN 978-0-8156-5233-5 (e-book) 1. People with disabilities.   2. Rhetoric—Social aspects.   I. Title.
    HV1568.D65 2014
    305.9'08014—dc23   2013039624

Manufactured in the United States of America

The cover image of this book is a photograph of a sculpture by the Japanese artist Haroshi. The sculpture is called *Screaming My Foot*. The image shows two feet pointing in opposite directions. The feet are sculpted out of dozens of multicolored broken skateboard decks, glued together. It seems like the legs are broken off around the calf, and you can see splinters in the wood where the legs stop. Sculpture by Haroshi. Photograph by Taro Hirano. Reproduced with permission of the artist and photographer.

For Matt Dolmage

talk
with two sets of hands, two mouths
one of mine
and one of yours
     this is all of language
one person's word has to touch another person's word
the touch is language, not the words

you have to pause to talk
you can put all of the meaning in the talk . . .
     or
     you can put most of the meaning in the pause
     in the patience, the moment
     and this is like eating dessert
     first

Matt—who talks to me in toasters, birds, horns, wide-wale
     corduroy, the wind of passing trains,
the texture of
each
syllable
Matt—who talks to me in applause, laugh tracks, dishes,
     shoulders, over glasses,
through the perfectly broken speakers of an old keyboard

this poem takes 6 'C' batteries

I remember your hand on mine
shifting gears and pressing elevator buttons
     and instantly it's not a memory
              so long as I count the gears and floors out loud

writing on your computer
my job sometimes was to press the space bar—you'd grab my hand
that space is the best character
it's there between the subway platform and the subway car
between 6:59 and 7:00

between the clouds and the sun
between trying and helping

I can write the words . . .
but I forever miss you in
and I'm so glad to see you in
and look at all the friends we invited in
the space between.

Jay Timothy Dolmage is Associate Professor of English at the University of Waterloo. He is the founding editor of the *Canadian Journal of Disability Studies* and has published award-winning articles in *Rhetoric Review, Cultural Critique, College English, Disability Studies Quarterly,* and other journals.

Contents

Illustrations

Disability
Rhetoric

Prothesis

History is useful insofar as it reminds us of the variousness and mutability of human behavior.
—Sharon Crowley, "Let Me Get This Straight"

Get the story crooked!
—Hans Kellner, *Language and Historical Representation*

I WILL BEGIN THIS BOOK with three moments, three spaces.

First, here we are in Periclean Athens, following the Ten Years' War. Many Athenians have been wounded and disabled. The city must be rebuilt. A huge festival is held to celebrate Hephaestus, the Greek god of metallurgy, a god with a physical disability, his feet twisted and pointed in opposite directions. In this "new" Athens, there will be a need for craftspeople like Hephaestus—everyone will have to get to work. There is also a shift toward new bodily values. Hephaestus becomes the figure for new forms of ingenuity and production, but he also *embodies* these values. He embodies these values through the rhetoric of *mētis*.

Second, here we are after World War II, as former soldiers return to their home countries. They are injured too. Their countries also badly need them to rebuild, or to kick-start postwar industries. The creation of new prosthetic technologies allows many of these wounded veterans to work. These technologies also address, perhaps incompletely, some of the emasculating and stigmatizing effects of disability in these cultures. Again, bodily values shift.

Third, here we are today, perhaps even reading this text online. Technologies such as the scanner, text messaging, voice recognition software, optical character recognition, and even e-mail, first developed for people with disabilities, are now an integral part of our discursive and communicative world. Body values have shifted again, to the degree that we may even fantasize that bodily difference can be eradicated by technology. Technology is supposed to make the body obsolete, right? Or at least technology will allow us to choose our bodies, heal them, perfect them? Yet so many of the technologies that suggest to us that we are perfectible, that intensify our dedication to norms, have been invented specifically because we are not perfect or normal. Bodies continue to change, as do attitudes about them, and the rhetorical entailments of these bodily transformations continue to be negotiated.

These changes, shifts, and transformations are at the center of contemporary disability studies. A "futuristic" disability studies will not be about eradication of disability, but about new social structures and relations, made possible by new rhetorics. This book will offer avenues for this important critical work.

This will be a rhetorical study, and this is a rhetorical text. Rhetoricians focus on the uses of language for persuasive ends. While some recognize rhetoric only in a pejorative sense—as the intentional misuse of language to mislead and obscure meaning—rhetoricians also recognize the ways that rhetoric shapes not just utterances or inscriptions, but also beliefs, values, institutions, and even bodies. One simple way to define rhetoric is to say that it is the study of all of communication. But more specifically, rhetoricians foreground the persuasive potential of all texts and artifacts, questioning the sedimentation of meanings, recognizing the constant negotiations between authors and audiences, and linking language to power. Gerard Hauser has suggested that rhetoric is "communication that attempts to coordinate social action" (1986, 2). Rhetoric can be seen as an operational, discursive means of shaping identity, community, cultural processes and institutions, and everyday being-in-the-world. Rhetoric not only impacts all of those variables in our lives that are not given and thus subject to opinion and persuasion; rhetoric also works to whittle away our sense that any part of our lives could ever truly be set and certain.[1]

---

1. George Kennedy even goes so far as to say that rhetoric "in the most general sense may perhaps be identified with the energy inherent in communication" and is biologically

I see rhetoric as the *strategic study of the circulation of power through communication*. Following this definition, this book will focus on the central role of the body in rhetoric—as the engine for all communication. Aristotle famously suggested that rhetoric is "the faculty of discovering in any particular case all of the available means of persuasion" (1991b, 1). A central argument of this book is that the body has never been fully or fairly understood for its role in shaping and multiplying these available means. In each of the above snapshots or moments in history, when cultural ideas about the body and its potential shift, rhetorical possibilities transform and expand also. This book is about searching for these rhetorical shifts, looking for meaningful bodies, and interrogating the entailments of these changing values. Further, I hope to impel *further* shifts in our understanding of disability and the rhetorical body. In so doing, I will argue for a critical alliance between disability studies and rhetoric. Disability studies would mandate that rhetoricians pay close attention to embodied difference; in return, rhetorical approaches would give disability studies practitioners means of understanding the debates that in part shape these bodies. Rhetoric needs disability studies as a reminder to pay critical and careful attention to the body. Disability studies needs rhetoric to better understand and negotiate the ways that discourse represents and impacts the experience of disability.[2]

I will begin by investigating the role of disability in rhetorical history. I will dwell mainly in the sphere of my first historical snapshot, the classical world. My goal is not to write the definitive account of disability

---

prior to speech (1992, 23). Diane Davis disagrees with the pure biological essentialism of Kennedy, and instead argues for an "always prior rhetoricity, an affect*ability* or persuad-*ability* that is due not to any creature's specific genetic makeup but to corporeality more generally, to the exposedness of corporeal existence" (2011, 89).

2. As Melanie Yergeau and John Duffy write in their introduction to a special issue of *Disability Studies Quarterly* devoted to rhetoric, "Rhetoric functions as a powerfully shaping instrument for creating conceptions of identity and positioning individuals relative to established social and economic hierarchies. A function of the rhetorical scholar is to identify such powerfully shaping instruments and their effects upon individuals, including disabled individuals" (2011, n.p).

rhetoric, or to exhaustively catalog the presence of disability in ancient history. But the effort to locate and engage disability generates fuel for critical reorientations. In this effort to uncover the extraordinary body, I feel we are forced to productively reconsider and redefine rhetoric: its definitions, canonizations, operations, and values. So this book tells several important stories about the rhetorical body—not all stories, not the *most* important stories, certainly not well-known stories, and definitely not stories that can be easily confined to these pages. In fact, these stories have been chosen because their bodies have considerable momentum, power, and multiplicity that exceed the restraint of being written. I am looking for spaces and moments in rhetorical history in which tension around the body is most pronounced, so that I can amplify and recirculate this tension. Doing so, I hope, also shakes the foundations and shifts the structure of this history. Further, in situating disability as uniquely rhetorical, this book should challenge cultural meanings that surround disability, as it situates disability itself as positively meaningful and meaning-making.

I will show that tension around the body exists, first, because efforts to define rhetoric have so often denied and denigrated the body; second, because this denial has always been laughably impossible; third, because modern body values and anxieties have always been mapped back across history; and finally because studying any culture's attitudes and arguments about the body always connects us intimately with attitudes and arguments about rhetorical possibility. That is, to care about the body is to care about how we make meaning, to care about how we persuade and *move* ourselves and others.

Yet in doing the recovery work, locating and engaging disability in rhetorical history, I have come to understand that disability has a rhetorical push-and-pull not just wherever we might recover disabled bodies, but also when we find any supposedly "abnormal" body—foreign, raced, feminized, sexualized, diseased, aging. Disability is often used rhetorically as a flexible form of stigma to be freely applied to any unknown, threatening, or devalued group. In these ways, the "abnormal" or extraordinary body is highly rhetorical. So we need to look for it actively and engage the rhetorical body in our historiography. If we follow this impulse, we would reclaim stories from the margins and from apocrypha, as I have tried to do in reclaiming disability in rhetorical history. But a differently embodied historiography does not just find new stories; it offers new ways to circulate these stories, in order to generate new ontologies, new phenomenologies, new rhetorics. .

In this book I will argue for a critical reinvestigation of several connected rhetorical traditions, focusing on the embodiment of rhetoric. I will argue that rhetoric has ignored the body. Also, I will suggest that this ignorance is reinforced by a fear of imperfection, a fear about the boundaries around our own bodies, and a fear of the strange bodies of Others. The rhetorical history we have chosen often conforms to modern schemes of ability and disability, but this history and the epistemology it reifies can both be challenged. Reexamining rhetorical bodies, and resituating the disabled body in particular, I will suggest that we might claim new models of communication and artistry. Throughout this book, I will also attempt to apply disability rhetoric to contemporary questions. I will shuffle disability rhetoric's multiple histories, its modern applications, and its generative possibilities.

I understand rhetoric as the strategic study of the circulation of power through communication. Further, I believe that we should recognize rhetoric as the *circulation of discourse through the body*. When we do so, we will expand our available means of persuasion. Where we do so, we will find the conflict and variation that impel any rhetorical endeavor.

Mētis Methodology

The engine and the theme of this work is *mētis* (pronounced MAY-TISS). *Mētis* is the rhetorical concept of cunning and adaptive intelligence. *Mētis* demands a focus on embodied rhetoric and, specifically, demands a view of the body and embodied thinking as being *double and divergent*. Unlike the forward march of logic, *mētis* is characterized by sideways and backward movement. *Mētis* is the rhetorical art of cunning, the use of embodied strategies, what Certeau calls "everyday arts," to transform rhetorical situations. In a world of chance and change, *mētis* is what allows us to craft available means for persuasion. Building on the work of Detienne and Vernant, and Certeau, I argue that *mētis* is a way to recognize that all rhetoric is embodied. It is not enough to rebody theory—doing so simply incorporates untroubled bodily norms in an unchallenged realm of abstraction. Developing the concept of *mētis*, I will show how embodiment forms and transforms in reference to norms of ability, the constraint and enablement of our bodied knowing.

I will use disability studies theory throughout this work, exposing the tropes and stereotypes about disability that shape the stories our culture holds on to. I also will use disability studies to critique held views about the phenomenology of embodiment, and I will propose new models and metaphors that more fully theorize the body's attachment and reliance, its vulnerabilities and adaptations. Filtering rhetorical theory through disability studies, I will focus on the meaningfulness of bodily difference. In this new light, more inclusive theories of rhetorical ability can grow.

I will exercise my own *mētis* as I retell mythical stories and revisit several sites of rhetorical history.[3] I believe that the job of the rhetorical historian is not *just* to reconstruct a persuasive narrative from a corpus of artifacts and from piles of pages. I say this is not the *only* the job of the rhetorical historian, because this storytelling is something any historian does, however self-consciously. What I hope to show is that the action of a *mētis* historiography, a *mētis* rhetoric, is also to layer a rich variety of meanings, array the stories that are most contested, and offer double and divergent means of engaging these stories so that readers might find their own rhythm at their own pace.

David Zarefsky writes about the "four senses" of rhetorical history: the history of rhetoric, the rhetoric of history, the historical study of

---

3. In this spirit, I will generally also use footnotes as a space for sideways and backward digression. I will treat the footnote, as Frederic Jameson does, as a "lyrical form" allowing for the "release of intellectual energies," but also as a place where I can fully give over space to other voices and other stories (1985, 9). I do not generally intend to use footnotes for "supporting evidence" or data, though I acknowledge that footnotes are often used in this way. The footnote will not be used primarily to support my own arguments, but rather to make space for parallel, contradictory, or more fully elaborated others. When I offer a list of other authorities, I do so not primarily to shore up my own argument, but because I imagine that you (like me) might be curious to look elsewhere, and might very well learn more from leaving this book than you would from staying in it.

rhetorical events, and the rhetorical study of historical events. This book consistently focuses on the rhetoric(s) of history: "the inventional and presentational practices of historians" and the ways that "historians argue not only about history; they also argue from it, using historical premises to justify current actions and beliefs" (1998, 28). Concurrently, as much as this concurrence is possible, this book also takes up the rhetorical study of historical events, through which "the historian views history as a series of rhetorical problems, situations that call for public persuasion to advance a cause or overcome an impasse" (ibid., 30). So the double move here is to view the ways that others have used history, and to engage in new approaches to its reexamination.[4] *Mētis* is represented as backward and sideways movement—this book moves backward in order to create parallel histories and to recognize our interpretive biases.

While the settings and chronologies change, this text is always also about the role of disability, of the body, and of rhetoric in contemporary culture, and through all of our possible futures. In this way, I engage what Janet Atwill labeled the "pragmatic genre" of historiography: the idea that "history is written to be 'used'" (1993, 102).[5] Any rhetorical history is also a reflection of a desired future and a critique of a version of now. James Berlin has famously championed this pragmatic approach: "In telling us what happened, the historian is telling us what ought to happen now and tomorrow. . . . The historian then owes it to us and to herself to tell us where she stands so that we can know whether we want to stand with her" (1994, 127). My hope is to position my history with feet facing sideways and backward.

4. Janet Atwill (via Lyotard) might label this the "syntactic genre" of rhetorical history, the analysis of the relations between expressions. Such an approach is said to "foreground the construction of both author and audience" through the writing of history (1993, 108).

5. Similarly, James J. Murphy defines rhetoric as the "systematic analysis of human discourse for the purpose of adducing precepts for future discourse" (1983, 3). Clark and McKerrow argue that, "through rhetoric, history is created anew in the process of each revision. Our understanding of the past depends on the historian's selection of a mediated reality and the further mediation of that reality through a narrative that bespeaks its 'presence' in our own time" (1998, 46).

I am deeply invested in uncovering disability across history, and I do this so that I might complicate held and normative stories about rhetoric, writing back toward the past(s), but also as I argue for a new view of embodiment that can be useful, practiced. I will champion *mētis* not just as an interesting idea from the past, but as the rhetoric that best empowers bodily difference now. My *mētis* historiography then wants to look like an extraordinary body: double, divergent, flawed, incomplete, surprising, in need of others. Hans Kellner urges all historians to "get the story crooked!" He suggests that this entails "looking at the historical text in such a way as to make more apparent the problems and decisions that shape its strategies" (1989, vii). In his words, "the straightness of any story is a rhetorical invention" (ibid., xi). I would suggest that this is also a creation in service of the straight body—and this straight and normal body is itself a fantasy. To get these stories crooked, we should also shift our view to bodies that exceed and challenge norms and affirm that history comes from the body's crookedness, too.

In defending what she calls "constructionism" in history, Sharon Crowley echoes my own sense of the virtue of *mētis* historiography. She argues that "history is useful insofar as it reminds us of the variousness and mutability of human behavior. Constructionism prefers difference to identity; it reads the particulars of history rather than its general sweep; and it situates historical events in cultural constructs that may seem exotic and/or foreign to today's readers" (1994, 16). This strikes me also as an approach distinctly suited to disability studies. Thus, following from Crowley's definition of "constructivist" history, I will focus on stories through which the body itself is rhetorically negotiated and constructed and in which this body retains difference and mutability. In this way, this book itself embodies disability rhetoric.

Resisting Normativity and Memorialization

The field of disability studies emphasizes the idea of the social or cultural construction of disability, while *also* insisting on the materiality of disability. Using a disability studies filter to view rhetoric, I recognize the emancipatory potential of new stories in both the "material" and the social sphere. Disability, in this light, is bodily and rhetorical—two concepts that are tightly united. I situate rhetoric as the function of power within language, and I connect it to the body because the body is what has been traditionally defined and (thus) "disciplined" by rhetorics of disability, while at the same time our bodies speak. Creating, as well as uncovering, new stories and alternative traditions—different bodies—is thus a powerful move. As James Berlin has said, "Rhetorical histories are important [because] they explore the relationship of discourse and power, a rhetoric . . . being a set of rules that privilege particular power relations" (Berlin et al. 1998, 12). As I read for disorder and variousness, I also hope to show the ways that we read history as a normative text and how this history (our story of history) has privileged the "normal" body.

The term *normate* has been developed in the field of disability studies to connote the ways normalcy is used to control bodies—normalcy, as a social construct, *acts* upon people with disabilities. Rosemarie Garland-Thomson defines *normate* as "the constructed identity of those who, by way of the bodily configurations and cultural capital they assume, can step into a position of authority and wield the power it grants them" (1997a, 8). Rhetorically, normalcy functions not to define itself, but to mark out what it is not. Understanding this negative capacity is of utmost importance because, as Douglas Baynton has written, "disability has functioned historically to justify inequality for disabled people themselves, but it has also done so for women and minority groups . . . the *concept* of disability has been used to justify discrimination against other groups by attributing disability to them" (1997, 33).

As Lennard Davis and other disability studies scholars have pointed out, the categories of normal and abnormal, able and disabled are invented and enforced in service of "a certain kind of society" in service of particular ideologies (1995, 9–11). John Duffy writes that rhetorics are "the ways of using language and other symbols by institutions, groups, or individuals for the purpose of shaping conceptions of reality" (2007, 15). Thus, the "certain type of society" or ableist "reality" that Davis alludes to has been created, and is maintained, rhetorically. In the next chapter, I will investigate the concept of normativity in greater detail. But it is important to foreground the idea that disability in history always highlights particular power relations, relations that affect everyone. Normalcy in the "modern world" is also a useful fiction that marks out unwanted elements while reinforcing the hegemony of the dominant group. Yet ideas of normalcy have changed over time. Davis suggests that "disability was once regarded very differently than it is now," and he mentions Greek society as an example (1995, 9). As Harlan Hahn writes, there has been a noticeable "failure of prior investigations to discover any positive features of the aesthetics of disability" (1988, 27). Yet Hahn has also shown that many cultures have, historically, valued disability in ways that seem foreign to us now (ibid., 30). Thus, I think that it is important, in telling new stories about disability, to examine the roots of disability in Western civilization and elsewhere—in order to fully understand the connection between our history and changing ideas about normalcy. This provides space to understand disability as more than just the ongoing antistrophe of normalcy.

My investment in uncovering disability, and in at times endorsing constructivist and pragmatist approaches, however, should not be misinterpreted as a belief in the triumph of history itself, nor should it be recognized as a reinvestment in the power of memory to "heal" past oversights and wrongs. In Judith Halberstam's *Queer Art of Failure*, the author argues for three virtues of this "queer art": resist mastery, privilege the naive or nonsensical, and suspect memorialization (2011, 12–15). Elaborating on this third premise, Halberstam writes that "while it seems commonsensical to produce new vaults of memory about [for example] homophobia or racism, many contemporary texts, literary and theoretical, actually argue against memorialization," advocating for "certain forms of erasure over memory precisely because memorialization has a tendency to tidy up disorderly histories" wherein memory "reads a continuous narrative into one full of ruptures and contradictions, and it sets precedents for other 'memorializations'" (ibid., 15). Page duBois, in *Out of Athens*, makes a similar argument. She advocates for a reading of ancient Greece in which we "identify the snags, the acts of resistance, barely visible in the historical record" and in which we are "attuned to resistances and countertransferences" that provide models for contemporary use. Instead of worrying solely about a politics of historiography moving backward, taking contemporary understandings of the mind, of society, of norms, and using them to read antiquity, we could also free ourselves to transfer political movements and moments in the other direction, when useful (2010, 115).[6]

Such reading and writing, even as it resists its own authority, also puts the lie to the straight and normative history from which extraordinary bodies have been erased. In this way, the "failure" of this historiography is also critical and generative. This history might be seen to fail because we are not offered a *single* certainty. Thus, we may be left with *nothing*. Yet we also may unleash many uncertainties, and, on their sunlit side, many possibilities.[7]

In later chapters, I will more fully address the overlaps between queer theory and disability studies. But then—and now—I will argue that this queer "art of failure" is also ideally suited as a disability studies methodology, precisely because even though it is important to revisit the ways disability has been erased and the ways people with disabilities have been minimized or eradicated throughout history, we know that there is no perfect history to replace the flawed or failed one. Further, the attempt is not to correct or cure history, but rather to highlight and preserve its unevenness and elisions. Disability historiography cannot be a normative mission; disability history should move like disability itself, understandable and unique *because* of its imperfections, suspect of any normative impulse.

Mythical History

One caveat: myths belie arguments about reality. Myths cannot be read as static and reliable catalogs of attitudes, but can be viewed as something more important: an inventory of and impetus for arguments about cultural values. Because so much of the "material" of this book is

---

6. There are also parallels between Halberstam's method, duBois's method, my own *mētis* mythological historiography, and Carla Freccero's concept of a "fantasmatic historiography"—one that "argues for an eccentric relation between events and their effects" (2006, 4). Freccero, like Halberstam, warns that "writing the history of those without one is a fantasmatic activity that describes an impossible wish" (ibid., 81).

7. Another phrasing for this idea comes from musician Leonard Cohen: "There is a crack in everything, that's how the light gets in" (1992, n.p.).

mythological, there is a danger that I will further mythologize disability—and deny its material experience. Yet I hope to respond to this danger by carefully revealing the rhetorically constructed facets of disability as well as its ineluctable and productive materiality.

Another caveat: at times in this book, I will compress, juxtapose, and juggle eras and locations. This is intentional—and the purpose might be, at different times, to put a narrative together in a strange or jarring way. Another purpose might be to show the ways that others have achieved this same shrinking and shuffling of distinct and discrete aspects of the rhetorical tradition. For instance, when I speak of Plato, I also often invoke Plato*nists*. I do so to mark the distinction between what Plato may have actually said or believed and the ways that Plato has been taken up in the philosophical and rhetorical tradition—how he has been reinterpreted and spoken for by others.[8] The same can be said of the relation between Aristotle and Aristotelians, or the synecdochic relations between the actual thinkers of the Sophistic period, such as Gorgias, and the agglomerative group known as "the Sophists," as well as later neo-Sophists, and so on.

Yet another caveat, and probably not the last: in much of this book, I will be tangling and untangling myths from across locations and traditions—from Greek myth to the many myths of King George VI of England, to the mythical worlds of contemporary film, literature, performance, comics. In doing so, I allow and speak to—without fully refuting or agreeing to—the idea that "myth is not a medium of historical record for times beyond our grasp" (Dowden 1995, 44). That is, "however usefully myth may illustrate common attitudes [about a specific time and place], allegiance to it for this

---

8. As Ellen Quandahl has argued, "The Plato of rhetoricians did not write the same texts as did the Plato of, say, logicians or ethicists." The rhetorical tradition, in her estimation, cannot see the ways that Plato acknowledged the "power of contextual or contingent elements in rhetoric" (1989, 347). So I will make an effort to distinguish in this book between Plato and Platonism, and when I invoke Platonism, I may allude to a wide range of Platonists—from Plotinus and the neo-Platonists of the third century, to early Christian neo-Platonists, to the Cambridge Platonists of the seventeenth century, to a range of modern neo-Platonists like Goethe and Jung.

purpose [of historical record] is far from steadfast" (ibid., 45). Myth does not always or even often offer an authoritative historical record—luckily, this is not what I am looking for. Instead, as Froma Zeitlin has suggested, "myths often address those problematic areas of human experience that resist rational explanation, and they explore and express the complexity of cultural norms, values, and preoccupations" (1996, 124). In short, myths can offer important rhetorical evidence, and must be read rhetorically.[9] To the degree that myths "fail" as historical evidence, they succeed as rich rhetorical artifacts.

Kathryn Bond Stockton writes that "I can only think beside the terms of history. . . . I use these dynamics to think about how to horizontalize history by putting texts outside of it by its side . . . to reveal that *it* grows sideways and outside itself." History contains an infinitude of possible meanings and readings, and history also "grows itself from the side" by way of the fictions that sit beside it now but may later be inside it. Myth is a great example of this sidewaysness: myths are ways for a culture to "grow itself from the side" as rhetorical means of making sense of realities; yet these myths later become part of history itself, as we see of ancient Greece and of rhetorical history. Thus, history grows itself "from what is to the side of it" (2009, 9).[10] And what is to the side of much of

9. Stephen Gencarella has also similarly argued that "to recognize the folkloric aspects of rhetoric's origin" is "not merely to highlight esoterica" but to "illustrate a yet-untapped aspect of pre-modern speculation for our postmodern condition" (2007, 253). Revisiting these myths and folklore reveals (and reflects) the "mutability of historical discourse" and challenges set origins and truths (ibid., 254).

10. Stockton also advocates for the virtue of what she calls "delay." She borrows from Derrida to suggest that "the structure of delay . . . in effect forbids that one make of tempo-ralization . . . a simple dialectical complication of the present as an originary and unceas-ing synthesis" (1976, 413; quoted in Stockton 2009, 15). Stockton tropes delay as a form of arrested development, but also as caution, care, an understanding of the danger of closing down meaning—and also as a temporal rhetoric—calling meaning into the time of *kai-ros*. Stockton suggests that children are also delayed by parents—who want them to stay children. And she catalogs a range of ways that queerness is delayed or is structured as delay. But in our culture there is also the diagnosis of delay through IQ and other tests that pathologize anything but "normal" development. In fact, children are so comprehensively

history is myth. And the rhetorical apparatus for sideways reading and writing is *mētis*.

To read myth in this way, one must also challenge the idea that myths themselves are predictable, one-dimensional. Lévi-Strauss famously suggested that "mythical thought always progresses from the awareness of oppositions toward their resolution" (1979, 221). Eric Havelock writes that the performance of myth—the oral, repeated iteration of the myth—committed stories to the "cultural encyclopedia" (1982, 123). Indeed, the performance of myth was said to lull the audience into near hypnosis.[11] Yet Laura M. Slatkin writes that *The Odyssey* "continuously repositions itself with respect to a tradition made up of alternative narrative possibilities. . . . [E]ach performance/composition must necessarily reflect, and participate in, the evolution of possible alternatives to the version it actually presents" (1996, 226). Slatkin suggests that each myth "embodies, in its many weavings, its reversals, its twisting of time, a *mētis* of its own" (ibid., 237). John Peradatto concurs, reading specific passages from *The Iliad* as "*mētis* at its best: a story about *mētis*, achieved by *mētis*" (1990, 47).

Clearly, despite our own largely rote reception of the role of myth—as a vehicle for the transmission of static cultural knowledge (even if this knowledge cannot be trusted now)—we can recognize it as a rhetorical arena. Specifically, it is the embodied nature of myth that grants it this indeterminate and contested nature. As Peradatto shows, there is often a subtle and cunning interaction between the role of the characters in a myth and the role of the poet or narrator, whose presence in front of an audience belies the role of the listener in codetermining the end of any story (ibid., 46). The bodies within the stories also challenge norms. Lévi-Strauss famously suggested that the "plot" of myth was always linear and predictable. But Klaus-Peter Koepping offers a clear repudiation of this

---

measured and charted for size and other more nebulous markers of development by age that the entire medical enterprise around children is structured to hurry to locate delay. However, reclaiming delay as a very useful interpretive strategy might also work to call into question its medicalization.

11. And, according to Susan Jarratt, "the present [was] seamlessly interwoven into the past" (1991, 33).

thesis as "plainly fallacious or at least unproved." Koepping points specifically to the role and rhetoric of bodies in myth, where "anomalies and ambiguities [and] the paradoxes of life within set boundaries of language and custom do not admit true resolution but rather need [ever-varying, contextual] expression" (1985, 197). In this way, myth becomes an embodied vehicle, as it is a site for the rhetorical body.

Recognizing this change and evolution allows me to suggest that cultural ideas about disability also change, as they are told through myth. Susan Jarratt writes that despite the "official" view that Greek myth was rote and didactic, there is evidence that myth was a site of conflict that "rhetoric would eventually be formed to negotiate." Mythical discourse, in her view, "is capable of containing the beginnings of . . . public argument and internal debate" (1991, 35). Of course, locating this "beginning" with Homer (as she does) is a move that I will not agree with. Yet I do want to suggest that mythical meanings have always required rhetorical reading and interpretation. More specifically, Lillian Eileen Doherty argues that the "interpretation [of mythology] is [always] an exercise of *mētis*" (1995, 4). I will suggest that mythology (even much before Homer) has always contained a rhetorical engine and specifically manifests and requires *mētis*. Amber Jacobs argues that "myth transmits secrets as well as narratives, and these secrets become entrenched in and determine social organization and practice" (2007, 73). Recalling my definition of rhetoric as the circulation of power through communication, it might be suggested that this range of circulation Jacobs alludes to—from secret transmission to social entrenchment—can best be understood as rhetorical.

Maria Torok suggests that "if [myths] provide food for understanding, they do so much less by what they say than by what they do not say, by their blanks, their intonations, their disguises" (1994, 1:94). This nicely speaks to my own definition of rhetoric and of *mētis*. In reading myths and cultural stories for their blanks and intonations, I hope to illustrate the rhetorical centrality of *mētis*. I also hope to continually call up the similarity between the corpus of "history" and the body itself: as also partial; as disguised and cunning; as contingent and contested as it is certain.

Finally, my alliance between rhetoric, myth, *mētis*, the body, and disability is not opportunistic; it is not a retroactive accretion. As Nicole

Loraux (1995) shows in her interrogation of Plato and Platonism, these very things—myth, *mētis*, rhetoric, and the body (in particular the feminine, diseased, abnormal body) must be concealed, denied, and cast out in order for the *logos*, for reality, to take form in the Western philosophical tradition. These things are placed together in their denigration, compared to one another, allied, invoked multiply. Yet as Loraux also shows, in myth, "all this returns" incessantly, and every form of separation is also a form of reception (2000, 111). I bring these elements together expressly *because* they ghost all of our understandings of philosophy, of rhetoric, of meaning-making.

I situate rhetorical history as the study of the negotiations that orbit any history. These constellations of value and their variable gravities are exactly what we *should* be looking for—and we should be asking questions not to set the universe in order, but to better understand ourselves by locating those things we disagree, worry, and wrestle about most vehemently.

The body of history has been shaped to look like an idealized human body: proportional, inviolable, autonomous, upright, forward facing (white, and masculine). But if you find the *rhetorical* body, you find tension, trial, and trouble. Find the body in history, and you need rhetoric not just to uncover strata of evidence but also to parse the investments and arguments of the historical record. Then, writing *from* bodies we would do history differently, not just by recognizing "other" bodies, but also because our histories and rhetorics might more closely represent the difference and diversity of our bodies themselves.

Chapter Overview

In chapter 1, "Disability Studies of Rhetoric," I begin by breaking down the function of norms, means, and ideals as rhetorical categories that structure our understanding of the body and its available means of persuasion. I locate a crucial tension around norms of ability in Greek antiquity, arguing that disability was an important yet unsteady representational system used to define rhetoric. I then create an interchapter inventory of the disability myths that (most often negatively) shape and transmit cultural understandings of disability.

In the second chapter, "Rhetorical Histories of Disability," I create a background and a range of characters for a deeper exploration of antiquity. I explore classical debates about what makes the body significant, representable, and rhetorical. Classical Greece has been taken for granted as the "birthplace" of rhetoric. In this chapter, I respond to that selective legacy by questioning the norms of this origin story and repopulating it with its other bodies.

In chapter 3, "Imperfect Meaning," I begin by examining a key rhetorical debate in the field of disability studies around the "construction" of disability, asking to what extent disability has been or can be rhetorically constructed. The goal of this chapter is to explore the ways disability has been (and has not been) rhetorically understood, negotiated, and materialized. I investigate prosthetic rhetoric, or the idea of rhetoric itself as prosthesis. I also explore disability genres and ways-to-move with and through disability to make (imperfect) meaning. I again use an interchapter to outline a repertoire of disability rhetorics, responding to my previous inventory of disability myths with a range of tools for resignifying disability.

Chapter 4, "*Mētis*," builds from this foundation to more deeply introduce the concept of *mētis*. I suggest that we view *mētis* as not only a key disability rhetoric, but as a powerful means of reconceptualizing rhetorical facility and artistry. I argue that *mētis* is rhetoric and rhetoric is *mētis*. I also, therefore, have to question how and why the concept of *mētis* has been devalued. In chapter 4, telling the stories of Hephaestus, the Greek god of metallurgy who embodied *mētis*, I recombine versions of his story to show, and to critique, how his disability has been variously represented. I argue that the art of *mētis* locates rhetorical facility in the divergence of the body and mind[12] from the norm, in our doubleness and our ability to draw on cunning strategies, in fostering responsiveness to chance and

---

12. Throughout the book, I will refer to the body, the mind, the body *and* mind, or body/mind. In all of these iterations, I am allying the two, as you will see, and negating their division. I agree with Elizabeth Grosz, who wrote that "bodies and minds are not two distinct substances but somewhere in between those alternatives" (1994, xii).

change, and capitalizes on our ability to connect with and to become that which is Other.

In chapter 5, "Eating Rhetorical Bodies," the stories of the goddess Metis, eaten by her husband, Zeus, because her cunning intelligence threatens his authority, will allow me to illustrate how and why *mētis* has been suppressed—and why it must be recovered and utilized as a still-powerful challenge to normative rhetoric. In this chapter, though my analysis remains rooted in the ancient context, I also make an effort to show that *mētis* is a rhetoric that cuts across rhetorical bodies, traditions, and geographies. The legacy of *mētis* can creatively unfurl along a surprisingly different trajectory than the narrative we have inherited. I examine Helene Cixous's use of the Medusa myths, myths of the Egyptian goddess Maat, Trickster figures across a range of cultures, and finally Gloria Anzaldua's stories of *mestizaje*. I suggest that there are useful similarities across geographies and eras, all linked by *mētis*, and I also aim to inspire further connections and creative applications.

In the sixth and final chapter, "I Did It on Purpose," I apply the concepts and critiques of the previous five chapters to a contemporary cultural text, the site of a recent example of the mythical life of both rhetoric and disability: the movie *The King's Speech*.

1

Disability Studies of Rhetoric

Ideas about disability in the ancient world are part of our common consciousness.

—Martha Rose, *The Staff of Oedipus*

IN THIS FIRST CHAPTER I want to make two initial moves to align disability studies and rhetoric. First, I want to explore the rhetorical history of the disability studies concept of normativity. Then, I want to chart some popular and persistent disability myths.

I will begin by suggesting that, as historian Martha Rose writes, "ideas about disability in the ancient world are part of our [contemporary] common consciousness" (2003, 2). We have always had disability myths, and these myths have always been rhetorically significant and rhetorically contested. I would suggest that common contemporary ideas about disability are always prefaced by, always circumscribe, and always interact with our contemporary ideas of the norm. Our sense of what is normal conditions our dispositions toward history and toward rhetoric. Further, the imposition of narrow norms delimits our available means of persuasion, here and now. At times in this book, I may seem to be looking for the body at the "origins of civilization." But I am actually much more interested in establishing the body itself as the origin and epistemological home of all meaning-making. Or, more accurately, I am much more interested in establishing imperfect, extraordinary, nonnormative bodies as the origin and epistemological homes of all meaning-making.

Norm, Mean, Ideal

Disability studies is a coherent but interdisciplinary, multidisciplinary field of study, holding that disability is a political and cultural identity, not

19

simply a medical condition. Disability studies challenges the idea that disability is a deficit or defect that should be cured or remedied, disrupts the idea that an individual with disabilities can be defined solely through her disabilities, and critiques representations of disability as pitiable, inviting charity, to be compensated for, made invisible, or overcome. Although there are many different disabilities and many different communities of people with disabilities, and while perspectives on disability vary and are constantly contested, disability studies does provide a somewhat unified stance on disability—cognitive, physical, learning, mental, emotional, psychological, and so on—because of common ground in the experience of stigma, oppression, the fight for more positive representations, and the struggle for physical and intellectual access.

There are many different disabilities represented under the umbrella of disability studies. There are tensions created by this grouping. However, disability studies scholars often show how disability is represented as a catchall—people with physical disabilities are assumed to be cognitively disabled, and representations of physical disability often rely on reinforcement from suggestions of mental or physical deficit. These "groups" are also united by the experience of stigma and oppression. For these reasons, and only contingently and carefully, I am going to bundle learning disabilities and physical "impairments" together, for instance.[1] What is of interest is the rhetorical *use* of disability to Other, to reinforce normativity. Also important is the rhetorical action of re-representing. While the attribution of disability is used to shore up other stigmatization—for instance, categorizations of race and homosexuality have relied upon the attribution of biological inferiority—it is important to respond by critiquing the constructions of disability, rather than disavowing this attribution while allowing cultural meanings of disability to go unchallenged, and therefore actually reifying them. So I choose, here, to at once affirm disability as a shared and positive identity, while challenging the

---

1. There will be a lengthier discussion of the distinction between "disability" and "impairment" in the third chapter of the book. I will also discuss the agglomeration of disabilities through the "myth" of "disability drift" later in this chapter.

use of disability as a wide brush for the application of derogation. I will further define such disability studies methods here, directly, and as I use them throughout this text.

Just as there are many different disabilities under the umbrella of disability studies, there must be many rhetorics generated by disability rhetoric: already, there is a growing field of Autistic rhetorics, for instance (see Yergeau 2010, Rodas 2009, Yergeau and Duffy 2011, Yergeau and Heilker 2011, Broderick 2011) or rhetorics of mental disability (see M. Price 2011).[2] My goal here is not to cover all of this ground, but to make space and to structure occasions for others to move. This space- and moment-making entails shouldering and sharing some work, acknowledging that even with the diversity of possible disability rhetorics, there are some common forces that prescribe and restrain disability meanings. So, I will begin with what might be the rhetorical center of disability studies: the norm.

We might recognize the normal position, when we think about it, to be able-bodied, rational-minded, autonomous, polite and proprietary, and so on. In North America, the normal position is also middle to upper class, white, male, western European, preferably American, overconfidently heterosexual, right-sized, and so on. These norms change, but the presence of a desired, central, and privileged position persists. Below, I will more closely examine how modern norms have come to be understood and utilized—but a simple definition of the norm is that it acts as a noun designating culture's desire for homogeneity, and it also acts like a verb, in that this agenda is enforced. No person is immune from the power of norms—they are ubiquitous and fundamental. Norms also ensure their own systemic enforcement.

Normativity employs logics of both *ableism* as well as *disablism*. "Disablism" can be defined as "a set of assumptions (conscious or unconscious)

---

2. Indeed, the special 2011 issue of *Disability Studies Quarterly* devoted to rhetoric provides a powerful inventory of disability rhetorics: mapping disability genres, metaphors, tropes, visual grammars, architectures, economies, chronotopes, watershed moments. Importantly, the issue focuses not just upon negative rhetorical constructions of disability, but also on the rhetorical *creativity* of disability.

and practices that promote the differential or unequal treatment of people because of actual or presumed disabilities" (Kumari-Campbell 2009, 4). Disablism, broadly conceived, negatively constructs both the values and the material circumstances around people with disabilities. Ableism, on the other hand, positively values and makes able-bodiedness compulsory. As Siebers writes of the "ideology of ability," we (through vehicles like philosophy and rhetoric) have constructed ability as the key feature of what constitutes being human (2010, 22). Ableism renders disability as abject, invisible, disposable, less than human, while able-bodiedness is represented as at once ideal, normal, and the mean or default. Disablism constructs disability as negative quite directly and literally. Ableism constructs a mythical able-bodied norm, thus differentially constituting disability.

Disability studies scholars then use the term *normate* to designate the privileged subject position of the supposedly (or temporarily) able-bodied individual and the culture that valorizes this position. Normalcy is used to control bodies primarily through ableism. Garland-Thomson defines the normate as "the constructed identity of those who, by way of the bodily configurations and cultural capital they assume, can step into a position of authority and wield the power it grants them" (1996a, 8). A normate culture continuously reinforces the centrality, naturality, and neutrality of this normate position. As Jacques Stiker, a key historian of disability, has pointed out, "figuring disability as an anomaly to be made to disappear through integration into social conformity is to represent society . . . as a norm not to be transgressed, as a sort of universal capable of assuming, through annulment, all differences" (1999, 136–37). This assumption, importantly, is never complete. Simply, norms need outliers. In this way, normativity also controls bodies through disablism. Cultures demand normalcy and enforce norms, also marking out and marginalizing those bodies and minds that do not conform to norms of ability. Though the normate position in terms of ability is in many ways drastically different (and in some ways importantly similar) to other discourses of differentiation, the normate position can be understood as somewhat analogous in its logic to the concepts of whiteness or of heteronormativity: normate cultures mark out what is *not* normal, employing a logic of negation, even as they demand conformity. Disability studies challenges normalcy by disrupting the default alliance of disability and deviance and challenging the idea that social imbalance can be explained by biology.

In comparison to today, in Greek antiquity the norm was embodied in different but connected ways. Disability can still be recognized as a representational system in this ancient context. Indeed, the study of rhetorical history does well to focus on the work of normativity. Examining antiquity, we are asked to locate our own normative filters at the same time as we address the charged interchanges of the period, encounters that powerfully, seductively, and formatively invoke debate about what was normal, as I will show.

The term *normate* designates the subject position of the supposedly (or temporarily) able-bodied individual. The word also converts the idea of normalcy into an active process—norms *are* but they also *act*: we live in a culture in which norms are enforced, a normative society. It can—and has—been argued that in antiquity there was not a concept of normalcy per se. But as Lennard Davis writes, although the word *normal* appeared in English only in the mid-nineteenth century, "before the rise of the concept of normalcy . . . there appears not to have been a concept of the normal, but instead the regnant paradigm was one revolving around the word 'ideal.' . . . [I]n the culture of the ideal, physical imperfections are not seen as absolute but as part of a descending continuum from top to bottom. No one, for example, *can* have an ideal body, and therefore no one has to have an ideal body" (1995, 105). Yet Aristotle had more than one concept of ideality—he expounded on the idea of the mean, for instance. He outlined the idea of both an absolute mean, a method for measuring humans against one another, and a relative mean, a system for disciplining oneself (L. Davis 1995, 6–7). I would argue that the commingling of these imperatives results in a normative mandate—both to uphold the fiction of perfection and to generate the systematic self- and other-surveillance and bodily discipline of normative processes. Antiquity may have been in some ways normative in "our" sense, and "we" are also still quite classical in our adherence to bodily ideality, as well as its infinite algebra of self-judgment and other-comparison.

Importantly, the debate about the normal body and mind in antiquity (and, as I will later show, since antiquity) wraps around ideals for discourse—and this link is more than metaphorical. (Plato wrote and) Socrates said, in the *Phaedrus*, that "any discourse ought to be constructed like a living creature, with its own body, as it were; it must not lack either head or feet; it must have a middle and extremities so composed as to suit each other and the whole work" (1961e, 128). This idea of proportionally bodied discourse connects with Aristotle's concept of the mean from the *Nicomachean Ethics*:

> By the absolute mean, or mean relative to the thing itself, I understand that which is equidistant from both extremes, and this is one and the same for all. By the mean relative to us I understand that which is neither too much nor too little for us; and this is not one and the same for all. . . . And so we may say generally that a master in any art avoids what is too much and what is too little, and seeks for the mean and chooses it—not the absolute but the relative mean. (1985, 6–7)

The mean body, then, is the same for corporeality as it is for discursivity.

In this next short section, I may introduce some discomfort in the reader as I jump a few chronological barriers. My intention in doing so is to cover ground, but also to mirror a historical bunching and riffling that already exists, in order to show that classically and neoclassically, the bodily ideal is the foundational metaphor for proper speech and writing.[3] We have fused philosophers and eras, but the message we take away from the "seat of civilization" is that the speaker's body and his words must conform to a limited set of norms. Ideal bodies produce ideal communication, and rhetoric polices nonideal bodies, or else betrays them.

In the more narrow, normative classical tradition, those without the ability to speak and those without the ability to "control" their bodies have

---

3. See Brenda Jo Brueggeman's *Lend Me Your Ear* and her essay "Delivering Disability, Willing Speech," in which she reveals the power of the norms of proper speech, but also reveals how disabled bodies, "performing outside the typically narrowly prescribed boundaries of rhetorical "standards," perform successful political and persuasive discourse" (2005, 17).

been omitted from considerations of rhetorical capacity. The mean becomes codified as a normate position, and thus we get a picture of what bodies are allowed to be, to do, to look like, to express. The mean becomes naturalized, or perhaps supernatural, as the mean is connected to the virtuous soul. Recognizing aberrancy from the mean allows one to diagnose the flaws of the individual's very essence. Lennard Davis writes that, in the regnant paradigm revolving around the culture of the ideal, "physical imperfections are not seen as absolute but as part of a descending continuum from top to bottom. No one, for example, *can* have an ideal body, and therefore no one has to have an ideal body" (ibid., 105). The ideal, as Davis sees it, places perfection out of reach—and he suggests that therefore ideality was not made compulsory, was not enforced. What the individual was supposed to control was her or his relationship to the mean. It is true that, although Plato and Aristotle put forward a concept of ideality, in their definitions of pure virtue and the forms, they also had a qualified sense, a relative sense of the mean, what is called the relative mean. Aristotle, in particular, went to great effort to qualify and relativize the mean, as I have shown in my lengthy quote from the *Nicomachean Ethics*. Yet classicists have long fused ideality and the mean into a concept that looks and acts much more like "our" norm. That is, it functions to mark out those bodies that do not fit.

Davis's definition of this modern norm suggests that it arrives with the development of statistics, and he suggests that "rather than being assigned to a less-than-ideal body in the earlier paradigm [of the ideal], people . . . have now been encouraged to strive to be normal" (1995, 105).[4] Though this resonates with Aristotle's concept of the relative mean, Davis clarifies that the norm "is a kind of fiction, a created character" (ibid., 109). The norm, reliant as it at first was upon statistics gathered across a broad population, is similar to what Aristotle calls the absolute mean—a way

4. Davis explores how industrial capitalism figured this norm mathematically and economically through concepts like the bell curve. Of course, in our own late capitalist society, the math might be better understood through something like the Occupy movement's 99 percent. Our society could be seen as organized around a desire to be part of the 1 percent and our social structures designed to deliver privilege to this 1 percent, and yet regardless of how hard we strive, most of us will never share these privileges.

of measuring humans against one another. Davis argues that the norm is justified as a concept that would increase democracy and equality, because it purports to locate "every man" on a standard grid. The relative mean, on the other hand, is about one's personal behavior, bearing, presentation—one's composition. We have the innate potential to conform to our own relative mean.

Traditionally, in order for this logic of normativity to function, the male body had to remain relatively unmarked. This in turn relied on the supposed aberrancy of the female. Andrea Lunsford (1995), Cheryl Glenn (1997), Joy Ritchie and Kate Ronald (2001), Susan Jarratt (1991), and others have shown that the rhetorical traditions that have been chosen and taught in our modern milieu overlook—if not explicitly devalue—the female body. Aristotle famously wrote that female offspring is the first step toward "monstrosity"—"the first departure from type is indeed that the offspring should become female instead of male" (1944, 70). He states that "the female is, as it were, a mutilated male," establishing man as the baseline and women both as pure aberrancy and as responsible for all deviation (ibid., 68). We might also recognize this as one origin story for normativity.

This is true for women particularly, but the stigma of femininity is also applied to men. For instance, the orator Demosthenes was said to have been soft and lame, because he spoke with a stutter and had an overly feminine demeanor. Physical disability was mingled with femininity to discredit him—see his exchanges with Meidias in particular and Cicero's investigation of Demosthenes's self-education in *De Oratore*. This trend is consonant with the notion that, as Douglas Baynton has written, and as I have already once mentioned, "disability has functioned historically to justify inequality for disabled people themselves, but it has also done so for women and minority groups. . . . [T]he *concept* of disability has been used to justify discrimination against other groups by attributing disability to them" (1997, 33).[5]

---

5. The binary between the soul and the body is also used to support this masculinist view—Aristotle argues that "the rule of the soul over the body is natural, [which makes] the

Nancy Demand further explains some of these attitudes in her monograph *Birth, Death, and Motherhood in Classical Greece*, suggesting that "Greek medical theory supported the androcentric bias of Greek society by providing a rational (or rationalized) basis for the belief in the inferior nature of women [who] were held to be weaker, softer, more porous, and warmer than men. . . . [M]oreover, female physiology was seen as essentially incomplete" (1994, 32). Clearly, to today's reader, the "scientific" basis for this division seems laughable. And it is true that, in many ways, we cannot compare Greek "medicine" to contemporary medical discourse. Yet the contention that women were essentially, spiritually, and genetically "disabled" was seen as an unrepudiable fact, one that reached beyond the Greek context to influence medicine (and culture) across eras.

Of course, the normativity we now encounter is largely a product of more contemporary, post-Enlightenment science. We might define this medical rhetoric according to Foucault's concept of biopower. I refer here to Foucault's explanation of biopower in volume 1 of *History of Sexuality*: how power invests, distributes, and controls the body, and specifically how it controls entire populations of bodies. Biopower tracks the ways that power and knowledge become transformative factors on human life. In his words, there is a "tactical polyvalence of discourses" that can be linked to the "intensification of the body," "its exploitation as an object of knowledge and an element in relations of power" (1973b, 93, 107). The extension or systemization of biopower is biopolitics, the ways that definitions and valuations of life organize politics and economics.

Shelley Tremain provides a Foucauldian analysis of this process of medicalization: "The modern body was created as the effect and object of medical examination. . . . The doctor's patient had come to be treated in a way that had at one time been conceivable only with cadavers. The

---

male by nature superior and the female inferior; the one rules and the other is ruled" by the body (1944, 4). Finally, as Nicole Loraux suggests, "unless it meets the other, the masculine man has no body" (1995, 10). That is, we have long celebrated a Greek ideal in which the "disincarnated male model" is exalted.

passivity of this object resulted from the procedure of clinical examina-tion, where the investigative gaze fixed and crystallized as 'the body' that which it perceived" (2002, 35). Disability now extended beyond actual impaired bodies to become an operative and essential element driving subject-object dualism—any body subjected to the medical gaze becomes disabled to some extent, through its positioning as passive object, and through the oversignification of bodily deviation. An extension of this might be what Nikolas Rose identifies, in our contemporary advanced lib-eral culture, as an "emergent form of life" characterized by "vital risk and vital susceptibilities, demanding action in the vital present, in the name of vital futures to come" (2007, 7). According to Rose, the poles of health and illness are now confused; we have new rules and regimes for relational "biological citizenship" and for how we understand ourselves as "somatic individuals"; there are new somatic experts and expertise and new ways to capitalize on "biovalue" (ibid., 6–7). In short, Foucault's biopower has been become a biopolitics that has been further molecularized, intensi-fied, and capitalized upon. And thus we live in a very urgent and sophis-ticated culture of biologized and marketized normativity.

Understanding this capsulized rhetorical history then can allow us to further understand the disability studies concept of normativity. In short, the medicalized, post-Enlightenment norm has been conflated with the classical absolute mean and with the classical ideal. The norm now primarily allows us to see and schematize that which is abnormal, but also involves us *all* in an urgent health and ability market. This perhaps contributes to the opacity of the norm—as "a kind of fiction, a created character" (L. Davis 1995, 109). To maintain the ghostly status of the norm, we work hard to show what it is not. The norm is defined by medical phi-losopher Georges Canguilhem as "a polemical concept which negatively qualifies: the abnormal, while logically second, is existentially first" (1991, 243). As David Mitchell and Sharon Snyder suggest, "The able body [has] a *phantom* materiality" (2001b, 374). In this way, norms are what give (exces-sive) materiality to all bodies—once we have a culturally determined body, it is already somewhat disabled. In our contemporary culture, then, the panic around our abormalities multiplies.

To norm is to employ a logic of negation. Roland Barthes (1972), John Fiske (1987), and Patricia Williams (1997) have all written about this process of "exnomination" as it applies to race. As Jeffrey Melnick argues, "The practice of racial naming" always entails "the unnaming of whiteness itself as a racial identity" (2007, 265). Siobhan Somerville argues that "culture anchors whiteness in the visible epistemology of black skin" (2000, 21). Normativity also works through exnomination: an elaborate taxonomy of abnormality is created and applied. Ability is anchored and erected through the labeling of disability.[6] In this way, the classical concept of the ideal has been turned inside out, insofar as all bodies (and all discourses) are best known through their aberrations and errors. The individuating benefits of the relative mean also come somewhat detached from the body as each of us becomes part of a statistical mass. And what does this leave us with? We come away with a rhetorical tradition in which classical ideals are central and often invoked to disqualify bodies and voices. We also recognize the perpetual operation of the mean as a basis for comparing oneself to others as we police ourselves. Finally, we witness the incorporation and schematization of all three concepts—norm, mean, and ideal—into a contemporary normativity, a grammar premised on both the ideal and the mean at once, and propelled and powered by the rhetorics of science and medicine.

I should clarify that my purpose here is not to provide a detailed history of rhetorical norms, but rather to locate a definition of normalcy through the consideration of a few isolated examples that illustrate the conflation of the ideal, the mean, and the norm—especially in the uptake of classical rhetorical teachings. Rhetorical history—in this strange mixture of voices from antiquity and filters from our own time—does enforce bodily norms. These norms reach into the body and mind through discourse about who can learn, what rhetoric is and is not, via rules of

6. Here I am not trying to say that disability is like race or even that whiteness is like normativity. Instead, I am simply hoping to show that the logic and rhetoric of exnomination can explain aspects of both ongoing cultural processes.

oratory and prescriptions for delivery or writing, and via discourse about discourse.[7] All of this said, the aim of this book is to translate a limited sense of the *mean* (as a baseline used for identifying deviation) into a more inclusive sense of the available *means* of persuasion (an expanded repertoire of words, tools, and bodies as persuasive vehicles for achieving rhetorical goals).

7. Standards for discourse also function mainly by negation; we know much more about the man speaking poorly than we do about rhetorical facility—just as today writing teachers continue to focus on error. And it is the specter of disability that has always been used as an attribution of rhetorical Otherness or of arhetoricity. As such, it is important for disability studies to engage with this complicated history of normativity. This is a history that has always been *about* rhetoric (who can speak) as it has also always been rhetori*cal* (an invested series of arguments).

An Archive and Anatomy of Disability Myths

AS ROSEMARIE GARLAND-THOMSON writes, "Seeing disability as a representational system engages several premises of current critical theory: that representation structures reality, that the margins constitute the center, that human identity is multiple and unstable, and that all analysis and evaluation has political implications" (1997b, 19). With this in mind, I will pause here to create a quick overview of some of the myths of disability that are ubiquitous across cultures and eras and that condition our understanding of disability (and thus of all identity and all bodies). This investigation of disability myths is an extension of my interrogation of the logics of normativity. Each of these myths works to mark and construct disability as surplus, improper, lesser, or otherwise *other*—and none of them actually directly defines what "normal" is, except via an excessive exnomination. In this way, these myths reach into all bodies, yet they also very particularly structure roles for people with disabilities.

I call these myths, but I also situate them also as stereotypes and tropes. These may not be fully "mythological," in the rich rhetorical sense of myth I will try to put forward throughout this book. But these are myths in the manner of Roland Barthes's *Mythologies*: meanings are attached to these images, and they become routinized and easily consumed (1972, 92). Each one of these myths is also a *misplacement* of meaning. These are stereotypes because they are often narrow and inflexible and render simple understandings. They are tropes because they shape stories and emplot. They are rhetorical because they provide material for a wide range of expressions, whether through compressed analogies or longer narratives.

Regardless, these figures shape both stories and lives. As Joseph Shapiro has shown, "Disabled people have become sensitized to depictions of disability in popular culture, religion, and history. There they find constant descriptions of a disabled person's proper role as either an object of pity or a source of inspiration. These images are internalized by disabled and nondisabled people alike and build social stereotypes, create artificial limitations, and contribute to discrimination" (1993, 30).

I borrow for my taxonomy from several sources, including Shapiro. Rosemarie Garland-Thomson looks carefully and systematically at disability in literature, and Ato Quayson (2007) similarly offers a "typology" of representations.[1] Michael Norden, Paul Longmore, and Leonard Kriegel also look at disability stereotypes in film, television, and literature.[2] The chart is greatly indebted to Mitchell and Snyder's "Body Genres," which maps out an "anatomy" of the common characteristics found in disability portrayals across genres of film (2006, 188).[3] Disability studies scholar G. Thomas Couser describes the "preferred plots and rhetorical schemes" of disability in nonfiction or memoir (2001, 79). These rhetorical schemes or myths tell familiar stories about disability from an ableist perspective. The use of all of these myths in discourse, then, both borrows from and shapes cultural beliefs about disability in the everyday.[4]

Of course, this book will mainly focus on the ways disability can be positively and expansively represented and not on simple, negative dismissals. Yet sometimes these two polarities need to engage with one

1. In addition to her literary analyses, Rosemarie Garland-Thomson (2002) also suggests that there are four dominant visual rhetorics of disability: the wondrous, the sentimental, the exotic, and the ordinary or realistic.

2. See Norden 1994; Longmore 1985, 2005; and Kriegel 1987; among other surveys and sources for the analysis of disability stereotypes.

3. In turn, Mitchell and Snyder borrowed and revised this anatomy from Linda Williams's influential essay "Film Bodies: Gender, Genre, and Excess" (1991).

4. Importantly, echoing all of the other disability studies scholars who have surveyed these ideas, Couser suggests that these schemes appeal to audiences because they reaffirm commonly held ideas about disability. "What characterizes these preferred rhetorics," he writes, "is that they rarely challenge stigma and marginalization directly or effectively" (2001, 79).

another. In the field of disability studies, an understanding of these nega-tive myths offers shorthand for the ways that disability is narrowly repre-sented or depicted. These myths offer evidence of some of the most basic and omnipresent ways that disability is rhetorically shaped. I will work through many of these myths here to further illustrate how disability studies and rhetorical theory should intersect. It is worth noting that most if not all of these myths interact with others in the chart.

Also, it is important to state that although these myths engage in what might be called "negative critique"—the act of saying that disability is "not this, not this, and not this"—and though this litany may feel a bit rote to many disability studies scholars and students, or a bit trenchant to those who are new to the field, laying out these disability *wrongs* generates a range of possible awarenesses, critical tools, and disruptions.[5] The fact that disability is so naturally and habitually associated with negativity in our society means that we cannot neglect to question these natural hab-its, and we cannot forget that the pause, reflection, and reconsideration we might engender will themselves be critical *and* creative opportunities.[6]

5. I borrow from Elizabeth Povinelli's *Economies of Abandonment* for this description. Povinelli defends "negative critique" against the claims that such critique "lacks a direc-tion around which a practical politics could be built . . . is parasitical on a given normative world [and] reflects the precritical political positions of the author" (2011, 189). In response, she suggests that proposing a *not this* "makes a difference even if it does not produce a propositional otherwise" because it "makes the world unready-at-hand for those for whom it has worked smoothly" (ibid., 191–92). This should serve as an excellent model for the criti-cal work of disability studies, even when a focus is on "policing" ableism and normativity by arguing that disability is "not this" or that stigma, "not this" or that degraded position.

6. Tobin Siebers also suggests that a legacy of poststructuralism is what he calls "abso-lute critique, one in which the ability to run critique against itself is valued above all oth-ers"—the more radical the critique, the more emancipatory it must be, and this has resulted in the banishment of experience (*Theory* 293). But Siebers argues against this, suggesting that disability studies can be one place where bodily experience can augment a critique in service of emancipatory goals. Povinelli's "negative critique," in disability studies, mani-fests itself in the absolute triumph of experience: disability is "not this" way that normate culture represents it, because its lived experience is different; or, disability is "not this," because this representation or social structure is felt quite sharply and negatively within a

Fiona Kumari-Campbell and others might suggest that listing these disability myths characterizes the strategic position of examining *disablism*—which is "limited" to challenging negative attitudes and offering corrections that would only assimilate disability into normative culture (2009, 4).[7] But my suggestion, and my aim, in discussing each of these myths, is to relate them more broadly to logics of normativity and ableism, moving beyond cultural representations that are right or wrong, and linking these narratives to "genealogies of knowledge" (ibid., 5). I will first present the myths in brief form in a chart, then expand on each myth, and then undertake a lengthier "test" for these myths to end this interchapter.

Myth	Description	Example
Disability as Pathology	People with disabilities have been historically labeled, sorted, and arrayed on scales according to their deviation from standardized norms. In this way, perhaps the most prominent disability rhetoric is the medical model.	There is almost always a moment in a narrative in which the disabled character is "explained" by a doctor or nurse, who provides a sort of WebMD overview of their pathology. Disability rarely circulates in popular culture without a medicalized explanation and definition.
Kill-or-Cure	Just as a loaded gun shown in the opening scenes of a movie will eventually be fired, a disabled character	Lennie from *Of Mice and Men* is a large man with an assumed mental disability. Throughout the novel, death

---

particular body or set of bodies. Somewhere between "negative critique" and "absolute critique," then, disability rhetoric does its work, from upon a material but malleable substrate between the triumph of a body and the triumph of a theory.

7. Kumari Campbell suggests that disability studies approaches that only challenge disablism "produce scholarship that contains serious distortions, gaps, and omissions concerning the production of disability" because they essentially only try to reform attitudes or compensate, and fail to recognize the more nuanced and pervasive ways that disability is constructed (2009, 4).

Myth	Description	Example
	will either have to be "killed or cured" by the end of any movie or novel in which they appear.	follows the character: a dead mouse, not one but two dead dogs, all foreshadowing his eventual tragic death.
Overcoming or Compensation	The person with a disability overcomes their impairment through hard work or has some special talent that offsets their deficiencies. Shapiro calls this figure the "super crip."	In Homer himself, we are to recognize a blind man who is a "gifted" poet and seer, his great memory and his story-weaving capabilities making up for his defect.
Disability as Object of Pity and/or Charity	People with disabilities are represented as sad and impotent, a problem that can be solved via charity.	Dickens's Tiny Tim is the prototypical example from literature.
Physical Deformity as Sign of Internal Flaw	Describing the body of an individual and accentuating its foreignness, abnormality, or exoticness allow for insinuations of internal deviance or lack.	Leonard Kriegel argues that Captain Ahab from *Moby Dick* "is not merely crippled—his leg torn from his body by the white whale—he is crippled in the deepest metaphysical sense. His injury became his self-hood" (1987, 18).
Disability as Isolating and Individuated	The "emphasis on individual isolation as the overriding component of a disabled life" (Mitchell and Snyder 2001c, 198).	People with disabilities in film and literature most often live in hospitals and institutions, as though these are their natural habitats—they rarely have romantic relationships or enduring friendships and often are left alone at the end of the narrative, as Raymond Babbitt is in *Rain Man*.

Myth	Description	Example
Disability as Sign of Social Ill	Disability is symptomatic of a deviant society.	Perhaps the most abhorrent example of this myth was put forward by televangelist Jerry Falwell, who suggested that "AIDS is not just God's punishment for homosexuals, it is God's punishment for the society that tolerates homosexuals" (Press 2007, n.p).
Disability Is a Sign from Above	Disability can be "taken as a signifier of sacred or ritual processes" (Quayson 2007, 46).	This is one of the key tropes of the Bible and other religious literatures, as well as Greek myth. Note that in Falwell's attribution above, it is God who is punishing society.
Disability as Symptom of Human Abuse of Nature	As with the idea that disability is a punishment for an individual or social evil, disability is often used to reflect, even more "causally," humankind's degradation and neglect of the natural world and the environment.	We recognize this myth often in superhero comic books: looking just at the villains in *Batman*, there is a long list of baddies who have been disfigured because they have treated the environment poorly: Clayface, Two-Face, the Joker, Mr. Freeze.
Disability Drift and the Disability Hierarchy	Physical disabilities are equated with mental disabilities and vice versa.	For instance, a person in a wheelchair is also treated as cognitively or even psychologically disabled.
Disability Drop	This myth interacts with the push to cure disability, overcoming, and the idea that people with disabilities	In the film *The Usual Suspects*, Verbal Kint (played by Kevin Spacey) has a physical disability—he is labeled a

Myth	Description	Example
	are "faking" or embellishing their disabilities. Characters with disabilities "drop" the act of being disabled as part of the climax of a narrative.	"gimp." It turns out, however, that he is faking this disability and taking advantage of people's perceptions of his weakness. The film ends with a tracking shot of Kint walking away from a police station, scot-free, and his limp gradually disappears.

Disability as Pathology

People with disabilities have been historically labeled, sorted, and arrayed on scales according to their deviation from standardized norms. As a result of this, it became easier to justify their institutionalization and erasure, and this contributed to the medicalizing of disability through an array of scientific terms. In this way, perhaps the most prominent disability rhetoric is the medical model—abnormal bodies undergo a rhetorical accretion toward synecdoche, and an abnormal body becomes the sum of its dysfunctional parts. Through its sustained critique of the medicalization of bodies, disability studies allows the student of rhetoric to better understand the social construction of any body as—always, in part—a scientific or medical artifact.

Disability is then "owned" and controlled by the doctor or scientist; it is no longer a personal experience or a generative aspect of one's subject position. Science, medicine, therapeutic, and even pharmacological discourses and practices cast disability as a personal deficit or deviance to be cured. This myth of disability-as-pathology interacts with the trope of "kill-or-cure" (discussed below) as the only proper medical way to view disability is as something to be fixed or eradicated. As pathology, disability can also never be understood as something positive.

For example, there is almost always a moment in a narrative in which the disabled character is "explained" by a doctor or nurse, who provides a sort of WebMD overview of their pathology—if the doctor or nurse does not deliver this diagnosis directly, then it is parroted through another character or a voice-over. In the controversial film *Million Dollar Baby*, this happens the very first time we view the protagonist in a hospital bed after she has been paralyzed. One of the very first things she says is "I'm a C1 and C2 complete, means my spinal cord's so broke they're never gonna be able to fix it. Gonna be froze like this the rest of my life" (2010, n.p.). In *Rain Man*, when we are first introduced to the character of Raymond, a male nurse is in the room to explain him, pointing out that "he's an autistic savant . . . high-functioning. . . . There's a disability that impairs the sensory input . . . and how it is processed" (2004, n.p.) Just as it must be medicalized as soon as it appears in a film, disability rarely circulates in our culture without a medicalized explanation and definition, something that people also often demand: "What's *wrong* with you?"

One important point of interrogation for this myth is the analysis of shifting diagnoses. Disabilities such as Asperger's syndrome or bipolar disorder are relatively new phenomena, medically. Recent changes in their definitions have resulted in drastic changes in the lives of those diagnosed. These are not "mythical" disabilities by any means, but the experience of living with them is heavily mediated through discourses of medicine, psychology, and pharmacology. We also see that many of the diagnoses and treatments of Western disabilities have begun to shift to other parts of the world, and the impact that these diagnoses and their treatments have had on foreign cultures has been notable. Recognizing this impact allows us to view the ways that disability is culturally specific and culturally constructed through medicine and to understand how shifting medical markets might export forms of ableism and disablism across the globe.[8]

---

8. Conversely, as Marianne Kastrup, a doctor and the head of the Center of Transcultural Psychiatry in Denmark, has shown through her research on depression, "culture influences depressive symptomatology, explanatory models, help-seeking behavior, and societal response" (2011, 119). Just as the movement of the Western medical model might impact norms across cultures, so too will those cultures reshape the experience of disability.

Kill-or-Cure

Just as a loaded gun shown in the opening scenes of a movie will eventually be fired, a disabled character will either have to be "killed or cured" by the end of any movie or novel in which they appear. This death or cure will often seem to "redeem" a protagonist—the death will be sacrificial, or the cure will be credited to the hero. Adding some nuance to this formula, Mitchell and Snyder suggest that the "resolution" of disability in a comedy film will be humiliation, in a horror film obliteration, and in a melodrama compensation (2006, 188). Lennie's death in *Of Mice and Men* offers a canonical example.

Norden has also written about the "magical cure" theme in films—for instance, in the rock opera *Tommy*, the "deaf, dumb, and blind" lead character regains all of his abilities. In *Heidi*, the hero's friend Clara sheds her disability and jumps up and dances around at the end of the film. The "kill-or-cure" myth also inflects current abortion and euthanasia debates and contemporary genetic science: society views disability as something that must be eradicated in one of these two ways. Recall Maggie's medicalized explanation of her paralysis from *Million Dollar Baby*, cited above: she eventually concludes that because she cannot be cured, she should kill herself.

Of course, the tenuousness and expendability of the disabled body are not just mythological. As a recent article in the *Lancet* showed, disabled adults are four times more likely to be victims of violence than nondisabled adults (Hughes et al. 2012, 1621).

Overcoming or Compensation

In this myth, the person with a disability overcomes their impairment through hard work or has some special talent that offsets their deficiencies. Shapiro calls this figure the "super crip." In this myth, the connection between disability and compensatory ability is intentional and required. The audience does not have to focus on the disability, or challenge the stigma that this disability entails, but instead refocuses attention toward the "gift." This works as a management of the fears of the temporarily ablebodied (if and when I become disabled, I will compensate or overcome), and it acts as a demand placed upon disabled bodies (you had better be very good at something).

For example, in Homer himself, we are to recognize a blind man who is a "gifted" poet and seer, his great memory and his story-weaving capabilities making up for his defect. Dustin Hoffman's depiction of Raymond Babbitt in the movie *Rain Man* provides another analogue: Raymond is autistic, but is capable of remarkable mathematical calculations and feats of memory. I will discuss both of these examples in chapter 2.

Katie Rose Guest Pryal also writes about the trope of "creativity mystique," wherein mood disorders are correlated with creativity. This trope is "a product of the era of modern psychiatry, suggests not only that mood disorders are sources of creative genius, but also that medical treatment should take patient creativity into account" (2011, n.p.). Pryal shows how conservative scientific literature has begun to draw that correlation, but also how more fringe scientific and pop-scientific publications have begun to go so far as to suggest a causal link between mood disorders and creativity, or even "inverse-causation" wherein creativity causes mood disorders (ibid.). This research may greatly impact treatment options, but it also constructs mood disorders as phenomena that had better connect to genius. Emily Martin, in *Bipolar Expeditions*, also suggests that as we begin to see manic depression as an "asset," we may be constructing two kinds of mania: a "good" kind characterized by successful celebrities like Robin Williams and a "bad" variety "to which most sufferers of manic depression are relegated." The consequence is that "even if the value given to the irrational experience of mania increases, validity would yet again be denied to the "mentally ill," and in fact their stigmatization might increase" (2007, 220).

Disability as Object of Pity and/or Charity

Much of the language of disability relies on a semiotics of pity: myths of powerlessness that demand to be answered with charity. As Rosemarie Garland-Thomson shows, one of the key visual rhetorics of disability is "the sentimental." This visual rhetoric "produces the sentimental victim or helpless sufferer needing protection or succor and invoking pity, inspiration, and frequent contributions" (2002, 63). People with disabilities are represented as sad and impotent, a problem that can be solved via charity. The donator also extracts value from this exchange, feeling better about him- or herself, and more "able," through giving (see Shapiro 1993). Dickens's Tiny Tim is the prototypical example from literature. The Jerry Lewis telethon is one contemporary vehicle that most strongly reinforces this position, though Lewis was recently ousted from his spot at the helm. In the article "Infantilizing Autism," Jennifer L. Stevenson, Bev Harp, and Morton Ann Gernsbacher also show how highly visible and "successful" autism organizations currently rely on images of autistic children to evoke pity and inspire charity and this charitable giving is focused on a "cure" (2011, n.p.).

Physical Deformity as Sign of Internal Flaw

Describing the body of an individual and accentuating its foreignness, abnormality, or exoticness allow for insinuations of internal deviance or lack. As Longmore writes, "Physical handicaps are made the emblem of evil" (1987, 66). Leonard Kriegel argues that Captain Ahab from *Moby Dick* "is not merely crippled—his leg torn from his body by the white whale—he is crippled in the deepest metaphysical sense. His injury became his self-hood" (1987, 34). This "internal flaw" also often explains why a character behaves badly (see "Disability as Evil" also, immediately below). Whereas, traditionally, a "stigma" was a mark branded onto the skin (as was the custom with Greek slaves), or a mark indicating a history of disease or abnormality (according to the medical definition), more often we see physical signs of disability as indicative of mental or psychological problems, the outward "stigma" the product of an almost-hysterical transubstantiation from interior to exterior.

Disability as Evil

Often, in fiction, a character with a disability is evil because he or she is "mad at the world." In many cases, the evil or lack of the disabled figure is a way to establish the virtue and character of the nondisabled protagonist. The disabled character can be a repository of evil or can be a trick mirror that reveals weakness or strength in a more central character.

Shakespeare's Richard III is perhaps the best example of this trope, and we also recognize this stereotype working across nearly the entire canon of children's literature, which bulges with disfigured pirates and witches, outfitted with the requisite crutches and eye patches. Children are then encouraged to fear people with disabilities. For further discussion of Richard III, see my final chapter.

Disability as Good

Just as disability can be read as evil, disability can also be represented as pure goodness, through the creation of an equal but inverse one-dimensional character. Rhetorics of infantilization and paternalism often power this myth. The result of this myth is that people with disabilities are disallowed from being bad or fallible, and thus they cannot really be fully human—or if they somehow fail to live up to this standard, their failure is particularly pronounced.

Tiny Tim is an example of a character rendered as pure good. This allows him to serve as a litmus test for the good of other characters and also allows him to be an object of pity and charity. Another entailment of this myth is that disability has to be *profitable*—Raymond in *Rain Man* has a "good" disability because his brother can capitalize upon it (through gambling).

There is a binary relationship between disability-as-good and disability-as-evil as well: as soon as a disability is no longer profitable, curable, rehabilitable, infantile, and/or unassuming, it can be quickly made evil. "Good" disabled characters who grow up or make demands can quickly become evil. As Colin Cameron writes, "Resisting categorisation in terms of one stereotype (passive, uncomplaining victim) simply leads to being identified in terms of another (bitter and twisted)" (2009, 385).

Disability as Ethical Test

Both Couser and Quayson recognize that disability often "acts as some form of ethical background to the actions of other characters, or as a means of testing or enhancing their moral standing" (Quayson 2007, 36). How a protagonist treats these disabled figures then establishes the hero's ethos. Pat Thomson recognizes this as an "infuriating genre which might be deemed a 'second fiddle' book. In these, there is indeed a disabled character but they exist only to promote the personal development of the main, able-bodied character" (1992, 24). The role of the Beast in *Beauty and the Beast* is central to the plot of the story in that we can gauge Beauty's development of morality based upon her acceptance of the Beast. Circe in Toni Morrison's *Song of Solomon* and Boo Radley in *To Kill a Mockingbird* are also examples of this trope.

Disability as Isolating and Individuated

Mitchell and Snyder argue that an "emphasis on individual isolation as the overriding component of a disabled life" has "artificially extracted the experience of disability from its necessary social contexts" (2001c, 198). The result is that disability can be rendered as a personal tragedy, or even a punishment delivered to one individual, and not the product of either chance or of social processes. The impact of this trope on all of our lives is apparent—when we each inevitably experience pain or debilitation, even temporarily, we are expected to keep it to ourselves, lest we become a burden upon others. As Tanya Titchkosky puts it, even though more than one billion people worldwide have disabilities, the impulse for isolation mandates that they be seen tautologically as "a huge number of the unfortunate few" (2011, n.p).

People with disabilities in film and literature most often live in hospitals and institutions, as though these are their natural habitats—they rarely have romantic relationships or enduring friendships, and often are left alone at the end of the narrative, as Raymond Babbitt is in *Rain Man*. This belief that disability *should* be isolating is reinforced by, and also justifies, the "warehousing" of people with disabilities in institutions, segregated classrooms, sheltered workshops, and so on. The individuated approach, in education, stresses that an individual with a disability can receive accommodations that are both specific and temporary—accommodating students one by one also means that the entire educational paradigm resists widespread change.

Disability as Sign of Social Ill

In this myth, disability is viewed as symptomatic of a deviant society. In this case, the external evidence of difference is used as an analogue for an ill or evil that is not isolated to the individual, but reflects a social problem.

As Nicole Markotic suggests, "A character presented as 'less' than able is not only a moral marker of social ill but is also a physical embodiment of cultural blunders" (2003, n.p.). Perhaps the most abhorrent example of this myth was put forward by televangelist Jerry Falwell, who suggested that "AIDS is not just God's punishment for homosexuals, it is God's punishment for the society that tolerates homosexuals" (Press 2007, n.p.).

Disability Is a Sign from Above

Disability can be "taken as a signifier of sacred or ritual processes" (Quayson 2007, 46). This is one of the key tropes of the Bible and other religious literatures, as well as Greek myth, as I will explore in my discussion of Tiresias and Hephaestus in other parts of the book. Note that in Falwell's attribution above, it is God who is punishing society.

As a "sign," disability can also be connected to traditions of scapegoating or, in ancient Greece, the *pharmakon*. In this Greek rite, after a disaster (a famine, an invasion, a plague), a "cripple" was supposedly selected and expelled from the community. The disabled individual may not have necessarily been situated as the cause of the disaster, yet the death of this individual was seen as a way for the community to appease the gods, as a form of atonement or expiation. This tradition has been written about extensively by Burkert (1985) and Girard (1986), as well as Derrida (1981).

Disability as Symptom of Human Abuse of Nature

As with the idea that disability is a punishment for an individual or social evil, disability is often used to reflect, even more "causally," humankind's degradation and neglect of the natural world and the environment. That is, the disability stands not just as a symbol, but also as a real supposed consequence: cancer and other diseases can be viewed as a consequence of certain forms of pollution, as are some "deformities." Sometimes the causal relationship is "real"—but this often does not have to be proven for the disability to signify.

We are offered this myth often in superhero comic books: looking just at the villains in *Superman* and *Batman*, there is a long list of baddies who have been disfigured because they have treated the environment poorly: Clayface, Two-Face, the Joker, Mr. Freeze (in *Batman*); Lex Luthor,

Metallo, Parasite, Solomon Grundy (in *Superman*).[9] Of course, it is important to remember that these villains, in addition to their disabilities and disfigurements, also receive some superpowers as well. And although it is easy to look just at the ways environmental degradation leads to the disfigurement of the villains, the heroes' abilities and disabilities are also often connected to a debased physical world, and their superpowers very often mean they can control nature fantastically (or can build prostheses to allow them to do so).

As Franny Howes writes, "Disability is prevalent in comics but at the same time persistently erased, denied, and made invisible." Indeed, even when the arguments are not explicit, disability appears in comics in ways that argue against oppression, question narratives of cure, and locate the tension and the continuum between disability and ability (2013, 24). This tension also often tightly fuses the physical body and mind of both heroes and villains to the (equally susceptible and mutable) natural world. One other argument that this myth can make is that, in the words of Lawrence Buell, "all Americans [are] not . . . being poisoned equally"—or, in more inclusive terms, all humans are not being poisoned equally (2001, 5). (And then, maybe even more inclusively, all beings are not being poisoned equally.) We know that exposure to pollution is not evenly distributed in our world and often breaks down along class and race lines—and those who pollute are not always those who "suffer" from the effects of their polluting. In this way, the "myth" of environmentally caused disability can be a way to hold up certain bodies as ecocritical evidence, and/or we can take this myth and convert it into a powerful rhetoric to interrogate the manner in which discourses of the earth's defilement can mitigate or vitiate its contamination, but also how both discourse and disease enter real bodies. More simply, we need to recognize and understand disability myth and rhetoric as they operate in our relationships with the physical

9. Thanks to Franny Howes for sharing her considerable expertise on this subject and making all of these suggestions to me. Thanks also to Trevor Holmes, Lindsey Joyce, William Lakeman, Joe Gooden, Sarah York, Dale Jacobs, and Eir-Anne Edgar for their incisive thoughts on this issue.

world, how we talk about this world, what we do to it, and what it does to us. See Stacy Alaimo's excellent *Bodily Natures* (2010) or Mel Chen's *Animacies* (2012) for more on this.

Disability Drift and the Disability Hierarchy

In this myth, physical disabilities are equated with mental disabilities, and vice versa. For instance, a person in a wheelchair is also treated as cognitively or even psychologically disabled. Within the disability community, this has sometimes led to a problematic hierarchy of disability—wherein physical disabilities are situated as less stigmatizing than cognitive disabilities, and people are encouraged to make downward comparisons to others with supposedly more severe impairments. Disability "drift" also works to make the disability overpower all other facets of an individual's personality.

People often hold up Stephen Hawking as a positive representation of disability, as evidence that physical disability does not equate with diminished intellectual capacity. Hawking as a "super crip" proves this.[10] But this narrative, which argues against disability drift, also reinforces a disability hierarchy: physical disability is more desirable than mental or psychological disability. Mark Deal has written extensively about this hierarchy, looking at the attitudes of disabled people themselves toward other "impairment groups" (2003, 897). For this same reason, if we do see characters with disabilities in popular media, these people often are most acceptable if they come from further up the hierarchy—wheelchair users seem to be the most "acceptable" figures with disabilities. Yet these same people may often be infantilized and treated as though their disabilities are more than physical, creating a catch-22.

Disability Drop

This myth interacts with the push to cure disability, overcoming, and the idea that people with disabilities are "faking" or embellishing their disabilities. Characters with disabilities "drop" the act of being disabled as

10. See, for example, Helene Mialet's *Hawking, Incorporated* (2012).

part of the climax of a narrative. Ellen Jean Samuels (2006) has looked extensively at this phenomenon in film, literature, and culture, labeling it the "disability con" and linking it to persistent backlash against social assistance and entitlements for people with disabilities. Samuels examines the "disability con" primarily within Melville's work *The Confidence-Man* but also through nineteenth-century racial masquerade.

In the film *The Usual Suspects*, Verbal Kint (played by Kevin Spacey) has a physical disability—he is labeled a "gimp." It turns out, however, that he is faking this disability and taking advantage of people's perceptions of his weakness. The film ends with a tracking shot of Kint walking away from a police station, scot-free, and his limp gradually disappears. The viewer realizes that his disability has been an act and that he is actually the evil criminal ringleader Keyser Söze. Edward Norton plays a similar character in the movie *The Score*, pretending to be an intellectually disabled janitor. Johnny Knoxville of *Jackass* fame also fakes a mental disability in the movie *The Ringer*. In all of these examples, the character with a "fake" disability actually draws out and takes advantage of the stereotypical attitudes of other characters. But when the disability is "dropped," the idea that disability is in part "fake" is reinforced, and the challenge to the stigma around the disability loses much of its power.

The concept of "malingering" also infers that people might fake disability to get out of military service or criminal sentences or to gain something else, like welfare. It is important to note that the concept of "faking" disability or "malingering" is a key shaping myth in the creation and implementation of social services: "Policy makers have historically sought to forestall fakery by making both the process of determining eligibility and the experience of receiving benefits—so to speak—arduous. They fashioned what amounted to ceremonies of social degradation for persons seeking or getting assistance" (Longmore 2003, 240).[11]

---

11. In film we also see disability "drop" happening across an actor's career. After an actor has played a character with a disability, the next major role seems to be very notably able, as a form of "rehabilitation." In the film *Tropic Thunder*, this propensity becomes the basis for a joke—after Ben Stiller's character takes on a role that is seen as *too* disabled, his next role is as a Stallone-style action hero in the movie *Scorcher VI: Global Meltdown*.

The Disability Myth "Test"

The "Bechdel Test" was developed by graphic novelist and zine author Alison Bechdel (2008) in her series *Dykes to Watch Out For*, as a way to quickly determine how female characters are positioned in a movie. The premise is relatively simple, and thus the results are often particularly upsetting. Simply, there are three criteria: ask whether there is more than one major female character in a movie, then ask whether these female characters talk to one another, and then ask if they talk to one another about something other than a man. The first question is designed to investigate whether the film actually has a significant female presence, the second question furthers this first question, and the third interrogates the nature of the female characters' roles; together, they reveal whether the women in the movie are fully developed or just foils or love interests for the men. Do the women think for themselves? Is there an actual female community or social structure in the film? Are women subordinated or supplemental?

What happens when we begin to interrogate the depiction and rhetorical construction of disability in cultural texts in a similar way? The disability myths listed on the last few pages can all, in some way or another, be incorporated into this test. Without necessarily using the tripartite structure of Bechdel's test, we can instead try to identify as many disability myths as possible in a given text.[12] We might apply this rubric to

12. A disability test might also ask whether there is more than one character with a disability in the film—most often, the answer is no, because disability is seen as isolating and is also most often supplementary. Then we might ask if the characters with disabilities talk about more than their "problems" or "afflictions"? Do they talk at all? Are they seen as capable of forming romantic relationships, acting independently from the protagonists (in ways that do not cause tragedy), growing and changing as characters? We also might say that, in general, in films with more than one character with a disability, all of the characters with disabilities are together and rarely talk to other characters who are nondisabled. This is a way to reinforce the isolation of people with disabilities. So let me try another iteration:

1. Is there more than one character with a disability in the film?

2. If the answer to the first question is yes, do the characters with disabilities interact with nondisabled people?

a few popular movies and cable TV series from the past few years, just to try this out.

For instance, the 2011 film *The Iron Lady* immediately passes the Bechdel Test: in fact, the major male characters, after the first half hour or so of the movie, exist purely in relation to Margaret Thatcher, played uncannily by Meryl Streep (who won an Oscar for the role). Yet beyond these rather unconventional gender dynamics, this seems like a rather conventional disability story. Thatcher has dementia, and the film chronicles a "descent" further into this disease, mainly through her hallucinated conversations with her deceased husband.[13] The dementia definitely isolates her—and the dementia also subsumes any of the other reasons she may be isolated. She is neither killed nor cured—in fact, the dementia gets worse. The disease "explains" why she is so cold and critical toward

---

3. In this interaction, do the nondisabled people do more than care for the people with disabilities? And do the characters with disabilities do more than explain their symptoms and impairments to the nondisabled characters?

I am thinking here of documentaries like *Murderball*, or films such as *Girl, Interrupted* and *One Flew over the Cuckoo's Nest*, which each in some way collect people with disabilities "outside" of society, in exceptional circumstances and microcultures. Such films do answer the question "Is there more than one character with a disability?" but then go in the other direction. This may create some possibilities for valuing crip community, but also serve as ways of abjecting and justifying segregation.

Or another way to set up such a quiz that gets at the simple kill-or-cure logic would be:

1. Is there a character with a disability in the film?

2. Is the character still alive at the end of the film?

3. If the character is alive, is she or he still disabled in the same way she or he was at the beginning of the film, or has this character been cured, has their condition been ameliorated or overcome, or has it deteriorated significantly?

Another key question: are the characters with disabilities in a film or television show played by actors with disabilities? Almost all the time, the answer to this last question is no.

13. The fact that Thatcher is so reliant on her husband's advice and approval, even after he has died, can be read as undermining her agency. If the third question in the Bechdel Test is actually designed to determine whether the female character has an autonomous role that is not subordinated to her relationship with a man, then *The Iron Lady* functionally fails this part of the test.

her doting daughter (even though there could be myriad other reasons for the degeneration of this relationship that preclude her dementia). It also seems to explain why she is disaffected and aloof toward all she meets (even if this might simply be her general affect). In this way, by narrating the film through her dementia, disability drifts back into the entire character study and life narrative, and we can begin to understand it more critically.[14] The dementia could be seen as either a symptom of a social ill or a sign that Thatcher is being repaid for her political sins. Yet the dementia also humanizes her, softens this iron lady so that the audience may find it difficult to retain their previous attitudes toward her. Although her conservative politics essentially wiped out state support systems in England, this character invites a charitable rereading. For some audiences. Certainly, many would resist this softening. But because the film filters its retrospective lens through her dementia, the audience is at least strongly invited to let pity drift back across Thatcher's entire life and political career.[15] Applying a disability rhetoric "test" to the film, then, we recognize disability being mythologized through pity/charity, isolation, and evil.[16] We recognize disability being used as the sign of a social ill,

14. *The Iron Lady* is also a "biopic"—in chapter 3 I will examine the biopolitical dimensions of recent iterations of this genre, and I will also analyze them as forms of epideictic rhetoric.

15. It might be suggested that certain parts of her political career, particularly her rise to power and her popular "success" in the Falklands War—elements of her career that lend themselves to heroic montages in the film—are not overwritten by her dementia in ways that other, later, parts of her career are in the film. This allows her heroism to "stand alone" and to be "reliably" narrated. This, however, also allows the film to conform to the genre rules of the tragedy, the falling action triggered by her disability. There may be an (intentional or unintentional) selection of which parts of her career can be unambivalently narrated and which need the filter of her dementia to be viewed charitably.

16. It is particularly interesting and ironic that Thatcher is shown having access to quite a bit of private care. This lies in direct opposition to the cuts to public supports for people with disabilities that she authored. Thus, the film suggests not only that disability is isolating, but also that the individual is responsible for her or his own "care"—which is not a social concern. The opening scene from the film also shows Thatcher out on the streets, trying to buy groceries. The scene suggests that she herself is tremendously vulnerable out in the public,

and we witness the ways that disability can drift across other facets of a person's personality—the "pure goodness" of disability as a concept or myth inflects the legacy of Margaret Thatcher, allowing us to at least partially forget who she really was as a politician.[17]

Of course, *The Iron Lady* both is exemplary of the usefulness of a disability rhetoric "test" and also extracts and displays its limits. Using the test and its tools can get us quickly to the representational heart of the film, allowing us to recognize a range of rhetorical possibilities that rely on disability. Yet, on the other hand, texts always exceed our desire to solve them. Another way to say this: even if a text actually does want to represent disability in a purely negative, simplistic manner or use disability as a tool of dissimulation, in many ways it will fail.

Aside from this acknowledgment, and through it, I will continue to try to apply the test. One of the foremost critical successes of the past five years has been the TV series *Breaking Bad*. There were ostensibly four major characters with disabilities in the show. Moreover, these characters are neither seen as automatically bonded together by their experiences nor seen as isolated from one another. The first and most "obvious" disabled character is Walter White Jr., the son of the series' "hero." The show's website identifies him as being "born with cerebral palsy" but also, in the same sentence, as a "typical high school kid" (2011). Walt Jr.'s character is

---

in modern England. This too is ironic—it suggests that she should be locked up for her own safety, but it also totally reverses the idea that Thatcherism has been and continues to be a tremendous threat to the public, perhaps especially to the immigrants that she thought were "swamping" England, and with whom she now must communicate to buy her milk.

17. Of course, Robert McRuer (2013) and many others would strongly challenge this tendency to forget Thatcher's political legacy, particularly in this current era of austerity measures and neo-Thatcherism in the UK and elsewhere. Yet at the same time, we would not necessarily want to see a film that uses disability to render her purely evil, nor would we necessarily want to see a film that elides the fact that Margaret Thatcher truly does suffer from dementia, nor would we really want this dementia to render her as a heroic, overcoming, figure—which *The Iron Lady* seems to resist doing. In many ways, *The Iron Lady* is a terrific intertext for the final chapter of this book, which examines *The King's Speech*, and I will refer back to *The Iron Lady* in that section of the book.

indeed quite well rounded, and instead of trafficking many stereotypical disability myths, he twists them. He creates a website to raise donations for his father, who has cancer, making his dad extremely uncomfortable, as the last thing Walt Sr. wants is to be viewed as an object of pity and charity—but then he does not want any attention at all, really, considering that he is moonlighting as a large-scale drug manufacturer. It is worth noting that R. J. Mitte, who plays Walt Jr., has cerebral palsy himself, which is notable mainly because there are almost no actors with disabilities on TV or in the movies.[18]

We also see that Walt Sr.'s cancer disables him at different times throughout the series.[19] Walt Sr.'s disability, because it is a persistent presence, though his level of actual "impairment" oscillates, troubles traditional representations of illness as disability. Illness is most often narrated clearly in the direction of either kill-or-cure, and much less frequently through the ambivalent and unpredictable, temporary polarities of debility and recovery that Walt experiences. Further, though Walt might seem to be "bitter" about his cancer, this bitterness translates into a sustained anger and into planned and deliberate action—the "bitterness" is not disabling, but rather it shakes him out of his routine and onto another radical path. And it is worth noting that this action is in part a necessity: he also

18. The series creator, Vince Gilligan, has said that he intended for Walt Jr. to be a strong character, one who does not follow the common disability trope of inviting pity from others or of pitying himself. Gilligan supposedly based the character on a college friend who had CP. (Mabe 2011, n.p.). This said, Walt Jr. does function as narrative prosthesis in a few connected ways. He is an "ethical test" for his father, and thus propels the plot. When Walt Sr. believes he is going to die from cancer, he justifies starting a lucrative career making meth through the belief that he needs to provide for his son's care after he himself is gone. This reasoning makes the entire plot not just believable, but much more appealing than if Walt Sr. were just greedy. This said, as the series has developed, the question of Walt's ethics has become much more nuanced, and we are invited to question what his true priorities and motivations are; the simple story of a man-gone-bad to provide for his disabled son sublimates into a range of other more difficult possibilities.

19. You could also suggest that Walt Sr.'s meth-cooking sidekick Jesse Pinkman's crystal addiction is also a disability in a similar way, impermanently impairing but persistent.

needs to find a way to pay for his cancer treatments. The provenance and morality of Walt's actions are openly in question, but Walt's character is not subordinated to his illness, cancer does not make him bitter and withdrawn or bitter and purely evil, nor does cancer make him a better person, a medicalized "warrior," or a reflective philosopher.

The third major character with a disability is Walt Sr.'s brother-in-law Hank, the Drug Enforcement Administration agent who has also been pursuing him (though Hank does not know that the drug kingpin he pursues is his own brother-in-law until halfway through the final season. In season 4, Hank has been shot and can no longer walk. Here it is worth quoting disability media critic S. E. Smith at some length, as she writes about a key episode:

> We're seeing Hank after the shooting, Hank in recovery, Hank at home. We're not quite sure what is going to happen with Hank and where they are going to take his character, although I have high hopes, because *Breaking Bad* seems the most willing to actually do its homework with disability, and to try and do a good job with it. Whether this is a temporary disability, or a permanent one, right now, we are seeing Hank in a very vulnerable place. Hank is in the adjustment period. Acquired disabilities can bring up some strong emotions as people transition between different bodily states, identities, beliefs about their own worth and value. . . . We are uncomfortable in solidarity with Hank, who is clearly trying to navigate this new situation and to, yes, *adjust* to the changes he's experiencing, to his new body, to a radically different life than the one he knows. . . . The ways that people deal with the adjustment period are immensely variable, and I'm looking forward to seeing how it's handled here. One of the problems with limited depictions of disability on television is that any appearance is taken as an authoritative one, which puts shows like *Breaking Bad* in a tough position because their decisions for characters may be mistaken by viewers and critics as definitive statements on disability. . . . If Hank is depressed, which he appears to be, that's clearly because of the character, not because the writers and creators think that disability is depressing, or even that the adjustment period is depressing for all people, although depression is

not uncommon. What they're depicting here is true to many lived experiences, and I hope that their record of careful research and thoughtful handling of disability carries through, and that Hank's journey continues to be true to the actual experiences of people who share that disability, or who have experienced similar injuries. (2011, n.p)

Clearly, *Breaking Bad* is a space for genuine rhetorical negotiations of disability.

Hank is at times represented as desexualized by his disability—but in the episode "Half Measures" he loses a bet to his wife when she suggests she can get him aroused in a minute and he believes she can't. He does seem depressed to be disabled and finds physical therapy tremendously difficult, but, as Smith argues, his "bitterness" seems to be a genuine aspect of his personality, not something that his disability has introduced. The disability sometimes seems to dissuade him from doing any further detective work, yet at other times affords him the time and space to reconsider new angles on open cases. When Hank does want to do undercover work, he enlists Walt to be his driver, and this irony creates incredibly tense moments in the series. Further, because Hank's insurance will not pay for all of his medical bills (just as Walt's insurance would not pay for the best treatment for him), this plot point situates the series quietly in the very middle of contemporary contradictions of biopower: there is no shortage of medical and therapeutic interventions available, all positioned as matters of life or death, yet all marketed out of the reach of the social support system. Walt begins secretly using his drug money to pay for Hank's treatments too. The irony is thick: in this day and age, you have to sell illegal drugs to be able to pay for the drugs that keep you vital or alive, to pay for the therapies that ameliorate your suffering or facilitate your autonomy. To be "successfully" disabled in late capitalism, it helps to be a meth millionaire.

The other clearly disabled character, however, is less three-dimensional. Hector "Tio" Salamanca is himself a former drug kingpin and the uncle of several drug cartel members. He communicates through facilitated means, ringing a bell when a nurse or assistant points at a letter of the alphabet. This facilitated communication is a major plot device throughout the series, and Tio's ability to manipulate people's expectations of him shows evidence of "strategic ignorance," a concept I will explore in more detail in chapter 3. Tio knows what is going on around him quite well; he just can't speak in a conventional way. But he also *won't* ever speak to police, and he holds a grudge very well, enabling and authorizing his nephews to hunt down Walt Sr. and Hank. Later, these nephews are the ones who shoot and paralyze Hank. By the explosive conclusion to the very last episode of season 4, Tio is dead. The way that he dies provides interesting justification for applying something like the Bechdel Test to disability texts. The simple question we can and probably should ask of any disability text is, was the character killed or cured?[20] Far too many films—from *Dark Victory* in 1939 to *Million Dollar Baby* in 2004—convey the message that living with a disability is simply not an option and end not just with the death of a disabled character, but with the message that this death is a mercy, maybe even a victory.[21]

20. This is such a prevalent device that when a film like *The Station Agent* (2004) places a disabled character played by Peter Dinklage on a set of train tracks at night, wandering drunkenly, the inevitability of his death feels so palpable that it is experienced by the viewer before it happens—and when we see he is still alive in the morning, we are left in a perhaps-ironic yet still deeply disturbing emotional space. It is hard to feel relief, because the surprise of the character's survival seems only to highlight so many other filmic disability deaths.

21. In fact, if you look at Clint Eastwood's entire oeuvre as a director, you see that disability almost always plays a role in the end of his movies, not just in *Million Dollar Baby*, where Eastwood himself pulls the plug on the hero, who insists she cannot live with a disability. In *Gran Torino*, Eastwood plays the hero, a failing old man, who basically commits a kamikaze suicide at the end of the film to make the world safer for his young neighbors. In *Mystic River*, perhaps the most confounding of all of his films, a mystery is solved at the end of the movie when we are asked to retrospectively understand that the "deaf boy did it" simply because he was mad at the world because of his deafness—even though the character (and this motive, which we are expected to accept unquestioningly) has not been developed at all in the entire movie. Mary Johnson's excellent book *Make Them Go Away: Clint Eastwood, Christopher Reeve, and the Case against Disability Rights* (2003) further examines Eastwood's battle against the Americans with Disabilities Act in his own business life, linking his filmic representations to his personal politics).

Because when characters with disabilities die, we often see that they die not in subtle ways, but spectacularly. In *Breaking Bad*, Tio is used as a human bomb to kill the show's villain. This reveals the essentially *instrumental* nature of Hector's disability and of many disabled characters: he or she can literally be used as a weapon on a villain, as the "nuclear option" for the text's plot. Of course, throughout *Breaking Bad*, many more "answers" to a disability test are also very much—and very interestingly—unanswered.

Dis Ex Machina

This leads me, finally, to a concept I will call disability *ex machina* (or *dis ex machina*). *Dis ex machina* signals one highly prevalent but underexamined species of disability myth in popular culture, and it leads directly from the concept of kill-or-cure that I have also been exploring. In this myth, disability is more than just a central theme or affective presence, more than just something that is assigned to a character; disability is instead (or also) a type of plot or narrative device, a structure *and* an action. I will offer a slightly more extended analysis of *dis ex machina* to conclude this chapter, adding it to my inventory of disability myths, but also linking it to a broader range of disability signification that I will expand upon throughout the book.

The original definition of *deus ex machina* in Horace's *Ars Poetica* referenced the "god in the machine," used in Greek tragedy—gods literally appeared in a play to resolve the plot artificially (1926, 191). The actors who played the gods in these plays were either lowered or raised onto the stage mechanically. Horace warned against this plot device, popularized (and overused) by Euripedes and others. More contemporary examples of deus ex machina include *The Lord of the Flies*, resolved when a ship appears on the horizon to save the deserted boys. The Harry Potter series is lousy with gods in machines, and one example of this is the saving grace of a sword in a hat, delivered to Harry by nothing less than a phoenix in *The Chamber of Secrets*.

Dis ex machina is a play on this lazy rhetorical convention, because disability is often used at the end of a film or book to wrap things up. For instance, Hector in the TV series *Breaking Bad* literally becomes the human bomb that explodes to end a season and a story line, killing the antagonist. I have already said enough about the *dis ex machina* of death: contemporary texts continue to mass-manufacture this plot device. Cure narratives and "disability drop" also function as forms of *dis ex machina*— the cure of the character with a disability, or the revelation that she or he was faking it, functions to conclude the story, solve the crime, wrap up the loose ends. Yet at times *dis ex machina* can be more subtle.

In Julian Barnes's auspiciously titled *The Sense of an Ending*, the 2011 Booker Prize–winning novel, when the narrator, Tony, discovers that a child born to his best friend and his ex-girlfriend's mother was disabled, we are somehow supposed to be able to understand exactly why this best friend committed suicide.[22] The novel is most commonly read as a "mystery," and the revelation of a disabled child offers one solution to the mystery. Of course, there is more going on in Barnes's book than just a mystery, as you might guess from the title.[23] As the narrator's best friend says at one point early in the novel, "History is that certainty produced at the point where the imperfections of memory meet the inadequacies of documentation" (2011, 18). This book is all about senses and gestures, refractions, circular paths through memory. Thus, even the *dis ex machina* at the end of the book holds a subversive note. That we are led to believe that the narrator can now understand his friend's suicide—he killed himself because he had an illegitimate child with an older woman, and this child was disabled—may very well be a mirage or even a critique of the impulse toward that easy assumption. At every turn, as he tries to

22. At this point, it would be totally fair to ask why I am analyzing so many winners and front runners and critical darlings. Isn't it a bit problematic to only look at these highly "successful" films, thus reifying this canon? Yes, its problematic, and this problem will continue as I continue to analyze the "heroes," heroic texts, and heroic spaces of intellectual history. But this is in part what I feel I have to do: I need to shake the centrality of our placement and the surety of our interpretations of these texts to make space within them (and in every direction away from them) for other meanings.

23. As Barnes would be fully aware, the book shares a title with Frank Kermode's 1967 book of literary criticism, a book that attempted to connect the ways we imagine the end of fictions and the ways we imagine the end of the world (or the ends of our own lives).

understand his past, Tony is told he does not get it. He even suggests that this could be written on his grave stone: "Tony Webster—He Never Got It." The reader thus cannot trust the narrator's sense of the ending, and thus cannot have a solid sense of any ending. The rhetorical power of this uncertainty then begins to expand: Is Tony suffering from dementia? Does this dementia exemplify the imperfection of any form of memory? Does "the sense of an ending" ask us to read back across all of the ways that we think we ourselves "get it"?

Sometimes *dis ex machina* is employed bluntly: Heidi's friend Clara jumps up and dances around; the disabled character explodes. And *dis ex machina*, like other disability myths, not only gives us ways to read cultural texts, but also structures social institutions and attitudes. As I have explored elsewhere, one way to view the *dis ex machina* in a film like *Million Dollar Baby* is that it tells people that if they become disabled, they will *want* to die—and it tells their caregivers to help them do so. Failing to question the flaws in the machine in the conclusion of *Million Dollar Baby*, the movie was taken up by the public as an argument for the "right to die," or the right to assisted suicide, in the wake of the Terry Schiavo case.[24]

But also and at other moments, or through other valences, *dis ex machina* is imperfect and opens up as many meanings as it closes down. Alice Hall has written about the open-ended narrative structures in Faulkner's fiction, suggesting that "the representation of physically and developmentally disabled characters enable [*sic*] him to explore alternative narrative spaces and forms of sensory perception in his fiction but also to explore what literary techniques can achieve" (2012, 49). In Faulkner, the "fragmented body disrupts . . . aesthetic closure" (ibid., 45). The open-endedness of Faulkner's novels or of *The Sense of an Ending* also speaks to a trend that we can read also back through the past few years' worth of popular films. From *Lost in Translation* to *No Country for Old Men* to *Shame* to *Inception* (not to mention the TV series *The Sopranos*), the "open

---

24. See Dolmage and DeGenaro (2005). For more on the Schiavo case, see M. Johnson 2006.

ending" is en vogue. The prevalence of open endings in films and novels could be understood as a victory for uncertainty, a strike against the neatness of tropes and conventions, a willingness to retain (or even embrace) subtleties and weaknesses of signification.

Often, the ending is left open *because* of disability: in Scorcese's *Shutter Island*, or 2011 Oscar-nominated films *Take Shelter* and *Martha Marcy May Marlene*, the ending is left open because we do not know whether the lead character is "crazy," and the scenes at the very end of the film accentuate or introduce this doubt.[25] In this way, the very meaning we are to take away from the film is toggled by the rhetorical construction of disability—every moment of the film needs to be read backward, critically, to parse whether the character's psychological "abnormalcies" add up to a diagnosis or rule it out, and this diagnosis would then reframe the entire action of the film.[26] This manifestation of *dis ex machina* is the very opposite of the simple and lazy forms we often see, even if disability is also here used as a plot or narrative device, instrumentally. That is, the simple way to look at the role of *dis ex machina* is that disability, when it appears, will readily and apparently signify, using the language of disability myth. The more complex role situates disability itself as always a rhetorical process and allows the machine to manufacture a range of possible meanings instead

25. I use the term *crazy* here advisedly—the specific "mental disability" of the character is undiagnosed in the film, also perhaps intentionally, because the goal seems to be to construct a somewhat stereotypically "crazy" character, and "accuracy" does not matter so much as the gesture toward the character's supposed unreliability.

26. This is not exactly a new device in film. And it is worth noting that when the device is used, almost always the film's narrator is rendered unreliable by disability: in *Memento* the narrator has antiretrograde amnesia, in *Fight Club* the narrator is schizophrenic, and in *Taxi Driver* we might consider Robert DeNiro to have post-traumatic stress disorder (though I should perhaps be more hesitant in diagnosing and labeling). Looking a bit further back, we see *dis ex machina* in the canonical *Cabinet of Dr. Caligari*. The epilogue of this film reveals that the lead character, through whose eyes we see the action of the movie, is a patient in an insane asylum—the entire plot is thrown into doubt. Joan Crawford, as the protagonist of *Possessed*, also narrates the events of the film, and we later find out these are paranoid hallucinations.

of one simple one. The audience may be placed into the role of diagnostician, but the audience also recognizes diagnosis for what it is—often dangerous, subjective, even frustrating.

The key "lesson" here is that disability representation can never really be narrowed down to a "test" or an inventory of tropes or myths. This moves us from looking for what is simply noxious in a representation to looking for what is anxious, from locating straight stigma to feeling for curved subtlety. We can object to *dis ex machina* because it explodes the reality effect of a given representation, or we can celebrate the idea that disability exposes the rhetoricity of reality, both in the text and in the bodies of its actors and audiences.

Conclusions

Rosemarie Garland-Thomson (1999) explains that to read disability through the "representational system" she references, and that I have tried to map through my chart of disability myths, is also to recognize the hegemony of the norm. As I hope I have shown in this chapter, "normal" is the myth that sublets all other disability myths within its broader real estate. Subsequently, the myth of the norm is also what renders disability myths imperfect, faulty. Disability itself is not necessarily mythical—but because it is read through reference to an invisible and impossible norm, disability has had a very unsteady representational power. As Tanya Titchkosky has argued, "Texts never just get it right or get it wrong insofar as they are also a 'doing'—right or wrong, texts are always *oriented social action*, producing meaning" (2007, 21).

So it is important to view each of my charted myths as more than just textual features but also as somewhat less than realized and sedimented attitudes.[27] None of these myths of disability "works" transparently or

---

27. As Garland-Thomson reminds us, even Aristotle understood that literature and poetry are normative: "Literary representations depend more on probability—what people take to be accurate—than on reality." Garland-Thomson accesses Aristotle's *Poetics* here to make a point about the presence of disability stereotypes in literature: how we produce "perceptual categories that may harden into stereotypes or caricatures when communally shared or culturally inculcated" But it could also be said that Aristotle was arguing that

efficiently. When these myths surface in narratives or in social life, they most often signal a breakdown in meaning. These figures are "shorthand" in all of the ways that word might metaphorically and ironically describe them. Hopefully, I have begun to show where meaning multiplies in the holes and gaps and errors.

In *The Sense of an Ending,* Tony Webster "never got it." In this spirit, then, a fitting epitaph for this chapter might be this: Disability Rhetoric—Never Get It.

---

literature is where we *negotiate* "what we take to be accurate" and where, just as some stereotypes "harden," others crumble or sublimate (1996a, 11).

2

Rhetorical Histories of Disability

> The disabled body changes the process of representation itself. Different bodies require and create new modes of representation.
> —Tobin Siebers, *Disability Theory*

Normate Antiquity

TO BEGIN THIS CHAPTER, I will offer a compressed overview of disability in antiquity. This overview is important historically and for the "narrative" of this book. But my hope is not just to start telling a story here, but instead to establish, through this quick scan of the role of the body in antiquity, a lexicon and a critical repertoire that is much more far-reaching. This compression is intended to simplify, to make a vast expanse of time accessible, but also to create density and force. My hope is to explain and illustrate the ubiquity and impact of normativity as the orbit around which all embodied rhetoric swivels and the foundation upon which any body becomes intelligible. In this *rhetorical* version of antiquity, you will recognize many disability myths operating, but I also hope to begin telling the story of a rhetorical history in which disability signals much more than stigma and disqualification.

Homer, the mythical seer Tiresias, Oedipus, the great orator Demosthenes, Paris's killer Philoctetes, Croesus's deaf son, and others form our view of disability in antiquity. These men overcome their disabilities, or compensate for them with poetic genius, or bear them as punishment; therefore, they both adhere to and perhaps provide archetypes for some of the most prevalent modern myths about disability. Further, Aristotle's *Generation of Animals*, the Hippocratic Corpus, and even the plays of Aristophanes act as catalogs of disability, functioning much as the *Diagnostic and Statistical Manual* does today, delineating a range of abnormal bodies.

Robert Garland, the author of *The Eye of the Beholder*, one of only three book-length studies of disability in the classical period (see also M. Rose 2003; and Haj 1970), suggests that "disability would have been familiar to many" in ancient Greece—either through the birth of a "defective infant" or through aging (1985, 11, 21). Bad plumbing, malnutrition, young mothers, war, and even violent sports would have been factors that led to injury or disease and then to disability. In Garland's view, the roles available to the disabled, rhetorically and otherwise, were severely limited. That his book is entitled *The Eye of the Beholder* is ironic, but also symbolic. *He* is the "beholder," and his biases are readily apparent. Garland's eye looks for the "compensation" the disabled make (ibid., 42), or for the "natural kinship" between people with disabilities (ibid., 63), or for the "rich empathy" that they inspire in others (preface). He gives his chapters titles like "Survival of the Weakest," "Half-Lives," and "Deriding the Disabled." His history canonizes the view that, as disability theorist Harlan Hahn writes (and as Hahn also disproves), disability has always symbolized "loss, repugnance and personal tragedy" (1988, 31). Yet Garland's research suggests that in the ancient world, the question of "normalcy" was central. Garland notices that, even in ancient Greece, the exclusion and isolation of different bodies were ways to "re-affirm the unity" of the hegemonic group (1985, 82). Rhetoric provided an arena for this reaffirmation and its troubling.

As mentioned, in Homer himself, we are to recognize a blind man who is a "gifted" poet and seer, his great memory and his story-weaving capabilities making up for his defect. Dustin Hoffman's depiction of Raymond Babbitt in the movie *Rain Man* provides a modern analogue: Raymond is autistic, but is capable of remarkable mathematical calculations and feats of memory.[1] Homer was blind, but he had an amazing memory. The connection between the disability and the compensatory ability is

---

1. His gift is then used by his brother, Charlie (Tom Cruise's character), for Charlie's personal gain.

intentional, and this perpetuates the idea that a person with a disability will always have some remarkable skill or talent. In the field of disability studies, much work has been done to reveal the ways that such depictions of disability work to manage the fears and projections of the supposedly nondisabled audience. The effect is that the general public does not have to focus on the disability, or challenge the stigma that this disability entails, but instead refocuses attention toward the "gift." In Greek myth, Tiresias is also given a gift from the gods to compensate for having been blinded—his gift is omniscience, a talent that he uses to resolve disputes between the sexes and to foretell the future.[2] The stereotype that disability is a punishment interacts with the demand that people with disabilities compensate for or overcome their difference. The message is that people with disabilities deserve to be disabled, and then also deserve to be disadvantaged, unless they can efface their difference, a difference that, if it is not overcome, reinforces the cultural fear of disability. One way to digest disability is to believe that a lack is erased by something extraordinary. This works as a management of the fears of the temporarily able-bodied (if or when I become disabled, I will compensate), and it acts as a demand placed upon disabled bodies (you had better be very good at something, preferably classical piano or brain-contorting mathematics). The stories we tell ourselves about disability then translate such hopes and imperatives into action.

In addition to the examples I included above, scholars have noted that there is at least one example of a rhetorical oration written in this period

---

2. In her 1958 monograph *Hermaphrodite*, classicist Marie Delcourt writes that the "most striking case" of transsexuality "is that of the soothsayer Tiresias, born a boy (and later becoming a woman), who was to become a man, fabulously old" (1961, 33). Upon interrogation, our reception of the myths of the sex-shifting "blind seer" Tiresias might reveal as much about our own modern interpretive biases for disability as they do about the attitudes toward such characters at the time of the myths' telling. As Martha Rose writes of the stories of Tiresias, such "myths and tales reflect truths *and* anxieties about sight and blindness [as well as other disabilities] from the ancient world" (2003, 2). That is, myths were (and are) sometimes used to reflect societal values, but also sometimes to exorcise, reimagine, or negotiate. I will return to these myths later in this chapter.

specifically for a speaker with a disability. The speech is recorded in *Lysias* 24. This speech concerns whether the speaker is eligible to receive a pension. Martha Rose, in interpreting the speech, cautions that we assume neither that Greeks had a form of welfare specifically for people with disabilities nor that the speaker in *Lysias* is made to "prove" that he is disabled. She stresses that the court simply ruled on a person's ability to make a living and gave those who could not some monetary support (2003, 98). We might be led to read this speech as an argument about what "counts" as disability and the ways in which a society must respond with charity, a textbook ableist response. In this way, the speaker would also be performing his body. Yet Rose cautions against this reading. Rose also, through such examples, argues that there are many more stories about disability to be found in our study of antiquity; importantly, she also argues that the stories we already have should be reinterpreted in order to avoid reinscribing our own ableism.

Expanding on Garland's and Rose's histories, rhetoricians Brenda Jo Brueggeman and James Fredal focus specifically upon the ways that rhetoric recognized, and shaped, disability in the period—but they seem frustrated by what they discover. There is a tone of resignation when they write: "Rhetoric [was] the cultivation and perfection of performative, expressive control over oneself and others. Deformity at once prevented any rhetorical achievement, while at the same time it symbolized the problem with rhetoric as a deceptive and sensuous art" (1999, 131). This tone of resignation seems to stem from the sense that there could and should be other stories about disability in rhetorical history and in history generally.[3]

---

3. It is actually quite interesting that, in both Fredal's and Brueggeman's other work, they both challenge their own assumption. To begin with, they both engage with the problem of speech. Brueggeman has argued that it is historically difficult to separate rhetoric from speech—but that we should consider rhetoric's much broader relation to the body as more than a mouthpiece (1999, 199). Fredal argues, similarly, that were we to shift to a "new map" of body rhetoric and away from this emphasis on speech, "what we [would] gain most is a broader perspective on the possibilities for human expression and meaningful interaction, and so a broader understanding of how, at the beginning of Western thought,

We have been asked to accept that disability was the opposite of rhetorical facility. The truth is that, as Leslie Fiedler suggests, it is all too easy to believe that "the strangely formed body has represented absolute Otherness in all times and places since human history began" (1996, xiii). We can be easily persuaded that, wherever abnormality was, it was stigmatized. The tradition we have accepted also demands that we accept these assumptions, that we enforce them. Over time, the tradition of *using* constructions of disability to mark excess has silenced disabled bodies as it has stifled the female body, the foreign body, the raced body, and so on. Naturally, with a definition of rhetoric as, simply, oratory and the use of the "controllable" body for persuasion, people with disabilities can be easily ignored. When the calculus of rhetorical ability always factors upon a normal body or an invisible body, marking a body's difference and excess disqualifies it from expression. So we need to question our choices about what counts as rhetoric and who counts as a rhetorician. All of rhetoric is connected to the negotiation—the enforcement, the transgression, the resignification—of bodily and intellectual norms, of embodied meanings. Yet a close examination of rhetoric in antiquity allows us to recover many overlooked examples of people with and without disabilities weaving disability rhetoric, and thus to challenge the idea that "abnormal" bodies can or should be silenced. This recovery then also allows us to construct new models of expressive power for people with disabilities across eras and geographies.

My suggestion in this chapter is not that our rhetorical predecessors were necessarily discriminatory, but instead that we can expand our ideas about who our rhetorical teachers might be, and what types of intelligence they might valorize, as well as what forms this intelligence might take in body and mind (always together) in action.

---

human self-fashioning and refashioning took place on rhetorical terms" (2006, 32). Cynthia Lewiecki-Wilson (2003) both echoes Fredal and challenges his exclusions when she suggests that rhetoricians must look at the expression of those who cannot verbally speak, yet communicate through other avenues. Just as Fredal successfully challenges the omission of the body, we must further challenge the continued omission of disabled bodies—representing rhetorical possibilities that seem too easily left behind.

In my introduction I mentioned Judith Halberstam's concept of the "queer art of failure" and the premise that we must be suspect of memorialization: "memorialization has a tendency to tidy up disorderly histories."[4] Alternatively, Halberstam argues that "forgetting becomes a way of resisting the heroic and grand logics of recall and unleashes new forms of memory that relate more to spectrality than to hard evidence, to lost genealogies than to inheritance, to erasure than inscription" (2011, 15). Many scholars, particularly disability studies scholars, would argue that "forgetting can easily be used as a tool of dominant culture to push the past aside in order to maintain the fantasy and fiction of a just and tolerant present" (ibid., 82–83). But "in fact we can never really put the past back together again in the way that memory promises" (ibid., 83). We never *get it*. With this in mind, "forgetfulness can be a useful tool for jamming the smooth operations of the normal and the ordinary" (ibid., 70).

I suggest that we begin to look for neglected stories. But when we do this searching, which requires that we shake up the methods and the archives of the historian, we should put history back together not as we found it—as a smooth and celebratory space shaped by the victors, normative, clean, and straight—but as a tenuous and temporary collage. Let's try on a forgetting of the forward march of history and its heroes, a forgetting of the rigid rules and reified resources of the historian. Most of all, let's forget the historical refrain ensuring us that disability is arhetorical and remix that sentiment to force a creative, untidy overlap between disability and rhetoric.

We can wield this forgetting strategically, as a way to address the active elision of the body from rhetorical history. For instance, Elizabeth Grosz, challenging a long tradition, from Plato to Descartes and beyond, suggests that philosophy cannot admit it has a body. I would echo Grosz

---

4. A very literal example of this was the unveiling of the 1997 Franklin Delano Roosevelt memorial in Washington, DC. The statue depicted FDR without his wheelchair or crutches. In this case, disability activists protested so loudly that another statue was created, with FDR seated in his wheelchair, and this other depiction was added to the original memorial (see Crutchfield and Epstein 2000; and Ott 2005).

by arguing that we have accepted a historical narrative in which rhetoric, similarly, denounces the body, overlooks its phenomenological and persuasive importance, and lifts discourse from its corporeal hinges. In Grosz's words, "The body has remained a conceptual blind spot [sic] in both mainstream Western philosophical thought and contemporary feminist theory" (1994, 3). The body then becomes "what is not mind . . . implicitly defined as unruly, disruptive, in need of direction or judgment, merely incidental . . . a brute givenness which requires overcoming" (ibid., 3–4). Throughout this book, I will argue that rhetoric has a body—has bodies. Further, I will show that it also matters *which* bodies we align with rhetoric. Rhetoricians and philosophers have always been engaged in an argument over the bodies that matter—who gets to speak, who shapes rhetorical interaction, how we read bodies. But for those who have made Plato and Aristotle the center of a canon and the architects of an epistemology, the body is a distraction or, worse, a deterrence to clear thought. We believe that the focus of the "great philosophers," clearly, was on the mind and its powers.

Ironically, we might actually view the rhetorical moves of Plato and Aristotle as being hypermediated by the body—whether through Socrates's desire for Phaedrus in that famous dialogue, his sense of his own bodily difference (specifically his snub nose) that comes across in many of the dialogues, or Aristotle's obsessive categorization of deviancy in *On the Generation of Animals*. As Richard Enos points out, Plato was himself a junior Olympic champion, Socrates was honored by Athens for his accomplishments as a soldier but was also described as disabled, and Aristotle was uniquely sensitive to his own physical limitations.[5] A more complex view of Greek history reveals that, for these philosophers, the obsession with the mind does not always (or perhaps ever) fully divert attention from the body. Yet this is not the view we have chosen to

---

5. Thanks to Richard Enos for his thoughtful comments on this matter when he reviewed a very early version of this chapter. Also, note that, in contrast to his dialogues that seem to denigrate the body, in the *Republic*, Plato explicitly advocates for the training of *both* the body *and* the mind (1894, 402e).

canonize. We may conflate Aristotle and Plato, we may mix their many voices and evolving views into a composite, and we may drastically simplify our view of Greek thought, but I will show that it is largely true that, despite a close acquaintance with bodily difference, expression, and training, we have chosen to focus on classical denials of the body, and we have erected a rhetorical tradition that also valorizes the split between the mental and the physical. It can also be argued that the body we invoke when we think of antiquity is idealized and made "normal."

For instance, women were seen to inhabit inferior and lacking, or monstrously different, bodies, and this difference ruled every aspect of their being, even their soul. In this way, any departure from the bodily norm is seen as potentially "crippling" all other capacities, even the soul. The "crippled" or feminized body was supposedly incapable of philosophical thought and is also blamed for any corporeal distractions. Femininity and disability, then, are classically intertwined. Disability and disease become key metaphors in this history of thought—a history that we have selectively inherited and interpreted.

In the *Phaedo*, Plato lectured that "we shall continue closest to knowledge if we avoid as much as we can all contact and association with the body" (1961d, 111). As Kristen Lindgren points out, this fear of the body was attached to a fear of disease—"any diseases which attack us hinder our quest for reality" (ibid.; Lindgren 2004, 146). The body has been seen as "a distraction for philosophers and an unfit subject for philosophy" (Lindgren 2004, 146). This abjuration of the body has always been connected to the perceived weakness and vulnerability of the body—of particular bodies, specifically feminine, diseased, or otherwise "abnormal." There is a classical view that, if the body disables thought, the feminine body is particularly disabling and disabled. This all comes together, then, as nothing short of a *canon* of rhetorical history. It is now canonical to say that femininity and disability both equated with arhetoricity. Throughout this work, I will explore this canon across a spectrum of eras and bodies, from Demosthenes to Margaret Thatcher.

It is important for me to specify that I do not see rhetoric itself as necessarily an ableist force—in fact, quite the opposite. Instead, I argue, from a disability studies perspective, that certain stories have been neglected, but that we can now read such stories as a challenge to a view of rhetorical history that reinscribes normative ideas about communicative facility and about which bodies matter. I will analyze the function of such norms and make an effort to disrupt our acceptance of an ableist view of rhetorical history. I will argue that exclusion has been imported into the classical world, and we have been left with a narrow view of the role disability may have played in the period. An emphasis on rhetorical embodiment, when coupled with this disability studies perspective, offers ways to interrogate how our ideas about bodily norms have conditioned our experience of rhetoric and offers ways to analyze how and why, and to what effect, we have projected our visions, feelings, and experiences of rhetoric into this narrow, nearly fictional world, invested in a particular kind of body, imprisoned in the geometry of the norm. We may never fully escape this normative conditioning, but we can engage in the ongoing work of critical realignment. The first step is to recognize the *canon* of bodily denigration and then to begin shaking it, both from within the specific rhetorical histories we have chosen and from without.

Mythologizing Sex, Sexuality, and Disability

One key vector for this realignment, as I have already shown, is at the intersection of sex, sexuality, and disability. For instance, the mythical stories of Tiresias and Hermaphrodite, which I will not explore in great depth here, but that I do explore deeply in other work, intrigue because of the mythical overlap of disability, "deviant" sexual difference, and gender ambiguity. Queerness both reinforces and plays off disability, and vice versa. This not only impels mythical meaning, but also challenges us to redefine the ways that we approach sex, sexuality, and disability as mutually constitutive concepts. In his book *Crip Theory* (2007), Robert McRuer aligns queerness and disability, and the result is a repositioning of signs and bodies, a rethinking of queer theory, and a paradigm shift within disability studies. It is counterintuitive to many that anyone would *want* to align with disability *or* queerness. And, historically, these identity categories have been defined against yet through one another: homosexuality or nonnormative sexuality as some terrible disease or genetic flaw, people with disabilities as sexually inappropriate, over or undersexed, as "freaks." For instance,

Margrit Shildrick argues that disability's "exclusion from the very notion of sexual subjectivity is so under-problematized that it is taken almost as a natural fact" (2009b, 116). Yet just as mythical (and real) bodies are characterized as queer, improperly gendered, and disabled in order to denigrate or abject them, so too does the act of queering, confusing, and disabling cultural stories generate new consequences for all embodied subjects, each unable to comply with norms of a given civilization or chain of signification. Instead, disability studies could push us to see the "plasticity of the erotic" by valuing the ways that disability disorganizes economies and anatomies of desire (ibid., 130). For these reasons, the stories of Tiresias and Hermaphrodite might serve to mythologize gender, sex, and ability norms in positively subversive ways. While these myths can be read for their ableist biases, they can also, as McRuer suggests, *queer* and *crip* culture by revealing the myth of normalcy, the lie of categorical homeostasis, and the easy classification of bodies and desires.

The different versions of the story of Demosthenes, or the varying myths of Tiresias or Hermaphrodite, for example, do illustrate how our chosen versions of history constrain or deflect our attention away from bodily difference, but they also should remind us of the ways that the imposition of a bodily ideal results in a tension that underlies the very idea of the body—a potentially combustible heat generated from the push-and-pull between discursive or narrative suggestions and embodied realities. These myths and stories are all incomplete, shifting, and variously invested significations (they are rhetorical), each inspired by and driven by disability. Sex and sexuality are equally and similarly mythological (as they are equally if not always similarly material). That is, these categories also appear in and fuel the generation of normative myths. These myths then might similarly support the imposition of norms across eras and cultures, or we might redirect them rhetorically toward subversive ends.

As Jennifer Terry has argued, in writing histories of homosexuality, we are confronted with the fact that queer experience and identity have been overwritten by "pejorative labels, medical diagnoses, and penological categorizations" (1994, 280). Queerness is "inscribed within the clinical and pathologizing mechanisms that brought the deviant subject into being and induced it to speak" (ibid., 280). In this way, queer historiography is like disability historiography: it also confronts absences, and it has also been powerfully spoken for in ways that abject, pathologize, and objectify.[6] So Terry advocates for deviant historiography, cognizant of the ways that queerness and sexual "abnormality" have been written and searching "not only for how [deviant subjects or bodies] are produced and policed [by dominant discourses] but for how they are resistant and excessive to the very discourses from which they emerge" (ibid., 286).

One simple way to begin this study is to look at the ways that, in Greek art, the "Other" body was most often depicted with abnormal genitalia. As J. Michael Padgett has shown, "Negative naturalism was deployed in [vase-painted] depictions of male dwarfs, hunchbacks, and other physically aberrant people, who were routinely represented with genitals that were, at best, natural and nonideal or, at worst, grotesquely enlarged" (2003, 43). As Padgett shows, these figures were often shown to be Metics or foreigners as well. There was certainly an easy sexual symbolic shorthand that allowed artists to rhetorically position bodies as physically and racially or ethnically other.[7]

Yet sexual difference was much more often symbolically rich, complex, even positive, especially in the case of sexual "mixture." Scholars such as Nicole Loraux have also suggested that while there are many examples of an "imaginary bisexuality . . . envisioned only from the standpoint of the body" in the ancient context, this "strictly corporeal notion of bisexuality" that envisions these bodies as "blocked . . . a type of short circuit" while locking the mind into a stereotypical "ossified vision" of bisexuality as

6. Disability historiography is like queer historiography in some cases, when these parallels respect the boundaries and unique goals of both; disability historiography is in fact consonant and consubstantive with queer historiography in some spaces and times; and at other times disability scholars absolutely fail to recognize the ways they center heterosexual normativity even when challenging other forms of ableist normativity, while queer theory often neglects or refuses to acknowledge vectors of ableism and disablism, even when such acknowledgment seems obvious and useful.

7. Of course, this shorthand continues to be used. See Strage's *Durable Fig Leaf: A Historical, Cultural, Medical, Social, Literary, and Iconographic Account of Man's Relations with His Penis* (1980); and Robyn Wiegman's *American Anatomies* (1995).

monstrosity, "the Greeks . . . have also understood that a double register [for sex]—that of metaphor, for example—offers the mind more possibilities than does the simultaneously disparate and overly homogeneous
notion of monstrosity" (1995, 7). In this "enlarged" perspective on sex,
sexual mixture is not simply inversion, and sexual difference is not easily
binarized. If sex is seen as, for instance, a mixture of the physical and the
metaphorical, then the normalcy, purity, symmetry, and oppositionality
of masculinity and femininity can be questioned.

First of all, while our culture commonly reads "improper" sex and
sexuality as *also* disability, as evidence of bodily or mental aberrancy, classical perspectives are much different. In his "Origins of Human Sexual
Culture," largely an archaeological study, Timothy F. Taylor suggests that:
"Biological capacity (the allowances of the body) and identity roles within
a community can change during a typical life history. Obviously, overly
reductive biological classifications that assert the categorical and objective
existence of just two types of person, which one either is or is not, ignore
this important process of becoming and transforming that is so typical
of human beings" (2007, 86). Taylor provides a rich and broad corpus of
examples in his 1997 *The Prehistory of Sex* (a book with the telling sub-
title *Four Million Years of Sexual Culture*).[8] Yet despite such rich and varied
examples, the traditional, historical reading of sexual difference posits
that gender ambiguity or sexual anomaly was strictly policed and stigmatized, that sex and gender transition was arrested whenever possible.
Taylor suggests that these "naturalist assumptions" can be "effectively
refuted" by "archeological data" (ibid., 70). Thomas Laqueur would also
argue that in the classical world, sex was seen as transitional—he argues
that, in antiquity, there was not a binarized sense of sex; sexual difference

---

8. Notable examples include North American indigenous cases of "two-spirited"
individuals and the Scythian *enarees* that Herodotus describes, with both examples providing the possibility of cultural (that is, horseback riding), social (drugs and feminizing
"agents" such as horse urine), and rhetorical (dress, gesture—*habitus*) factors impelling or
impacting *desired* biological movements between sexes/genders (T. F. Taylor 1997, 84). Contemporary commentators have been quick to interpret these cases as evidence of a small
group of people "suffering from a condition" (ibid.).

was just a matter of degree within what he calls "the one-sex body" (1990, 207). Gender difference, on the other hand, because it was more strictly governed by social norms, was more "real." That is, social roles were seen as dictated by eternal truths. Biology was viewed as much less certain and unchanging. Because nature revealed a wide range of bodily possibilities, what we would call "biological" sex was seen more flexibly at this time. Our contemporary ideas about the difference between sexes were largely the invention of Enlightenment science and are not a product of (or really applicable within) the classical world. I hope to suggest that we can read and write, rhetorically, with this transition in mind, recognizing movement and transition between bodily possibilities. This should be seen as the "natural" extension or incorporation of a *mētis* rhetoric.

For instance, in Roger Graves's summary of the stories in Apollodorus, Ovid, and Pindar, he juggles the varying versions of the myths of Tiresias, revealing the many stories of his metamorphoses. In one take, the originally male Tiresias's sex is changed because he sees two serpents in the act of coupling, and when the female attacks him, he kills it: "Immediately he was turned into a woman, and became a celebrated harlot" (1955, 2). Not only is the male Tiresias punished for stumbling across a sexual scene, but Tiresias is made a harlot—the transition between sexes is sexual*ized*. In this take, "seven years later he happened to see the same sight again at the same spot, and this time regained his manhood by killing the male serpent." In another version of the story, Aphrodite turns Tiresias into an old woman because he does not judge her the winner in a beauty contest (ibid., 11). In these stories Tiresias could be seen as a failure as a man. Yet these failures set into motion alternative corporealities and social roles.

As for Tiresias's blindness, the stories become even more tangled, and, importantly, the myths remain sexually charged. First, the stories are about sexual roles and norms—from questions of pleasure to questions of life and death. Second, they are charged insofar as sexual "polarity" runs along an alternating current. In one story, a young male Tiresias is blinded by modest Athena, because he sees her naked—when "one day he accidentally surprised her in a bath [and] she laid her hands over his eyes and blinded him, but gave him inward sight by way of compensation" (ibid., 98; see also Plutarch and White 1996, 15). In another story, Zeus and Hera argue over who receives more pleasure from lovemaking, men or women. Tiresias decrees that "if the parts of love-pleasure are to be counted as ten; Thrice three go to women, only one to men" (Ovid 1717, 320). Hera is so enraged that she blinds him.

Despite this blinding, Tiresias's story is often one of compensation and of overcoming: after he is blinded, Athena cleans his ears so well that he can understand the notes of birds and follow the divine symbolism of their songs and their flight (Apollodorus 1921, 3.6.7). In another story, Zeus, to compensate for what Hera has done to Tiresias (blinding him), grants him the power of prophecy. He later uses this gift to predict that Narcissus will "live to a ripe old age, provided he never knows himself" (Graves 1995, 286); also to reveal to Queen Iocaste that her husband Oedipus has killed his own father and married her, his mother (ibid., 11); also to give Odysseus advice about sacrifices and to prophesy his fate—he will not die peacefully of old age (Homer 2000, xi).

The important emphasis in many Tiresian myths is chronological: Tiresias's power of ornithomancy is allowed because of his sexual and ability transition. He changes sex and/or he becomes blind, but then he develops the ability to parse bird songs for their sacred meanings and/ or the ability to see the future. He also has a special, somewhat magical staff that helps him get around—in one story he also has a slave to lead him (Sophocles and Griffith 1999, 910–11). As with the ornithomancy and prophecy, the magic staff is *prosthetic* in a simple sense: it allows for the overcoming of or compensation for his disability. These aids and extraordinary abilities function to temper the stigma of *his* disability, without negating the stigma of disability more broadly. Here, the prostheses do not figure into a holistic sense of his embodied self—as a human who, like all of us, incorporates various tools and aids in order to interact with the world and with others. Instead, the suggestion is that people with disabilities have other *super* abilities (and if they do not, they *should*), like the ability to commune with animals,[9] and that with the aid of technology it

___

9. Here it is worthwhile to recall the earlier discussion of the possible alliances between disability studies and animal studies; that argument for alliance reinvokes this very classic

can seem as though *they are not disabled at all.* The effect is an erasure of disability—it is not acceptable; one can be seen positively only when disability disappears (see my chart of disability myths).[10]

Rather than choosing any one interpretation from the above readings of the myths of Tiresias, I prefer to think that together, they generate possibility from their tension. That is, I would argue that just as the meaning of Tiresias is currently contested, it was contested in antiquity (and likely before that "era" and across other spaces). In fact, Tiresias's

---

ableist message—that, in a negative sense, people with disabilities are allied with animals as both are less than human or that disability belongs to an animal world. Of course, the contemporary alliance between disability studies and animal studies radically repositions this relationship.

10. Robert Garland comes at disability another way: he suggests that the stories of Tiresias's compensation and overcoming hide not the possible positive value inherent in disability, but simply temporarily mask the unequivocal negativity of having a disability. In doing so, Garland strips disability of all possible positive social value. Striving for an improbable halting of signification, Garland writes that those who delivered the myth of Tiresias as "seer" would not have suggested that the blind were actually employed in "poetry, music and seercraft" in ancient society. He argues that people with disabilities "more likely relied on charity as their disability disqualified them from work" (1995, 34). In Garland's version of the Tiresias myth, he is arguing against the story's implicit representation of the character's power, based on the assumption that no person with a disability could hold a socially valued role. Of course, in countering such representations, we can swing the emphasis back the other way. For example, Martha Rose wrote that "the Greeks did not perceive of a category of physical disability in which people were a priori banned from carrying out certain roles and compartmentalized into others" (2003, 2). The ableist reading of this history holds that it was impossible to have seen disability as positive, and this historiography also writes a script for the disabled body to perform. Yet these scripts often conform to stereotypes from our own time and therefore might be revised. For instance, Garland's statement directly clashes with Martha Rose's point—in her reading of *Lysias,* discussed in the first chapter—that charity was not rewarded by the courts based upon physical ability or disability as "impairment." One would not have to perform one's body before the courts to qualify for charity, as the "cripple" in Lysias's speech is said to have done, defending his right to receive a small pension in front of the courts. Instead, one was judged based on one's ability to work, with a disability or without, and certainly the Lysias speech reveals this.

constant metamorphoses—from man to woman and back to man again, from sighted to blind to superhearing—are a metaphor for the push-and-pull of symbolic forces upon the cultural *idea* of disability, of sex, of the body and its tenuous boundaries, and the myths were a site for this contestation. In this chosen tradition (and in others), sex and disability could be read to impel rhetoric from its very center.[11]

In *Hermaphrodite* classicist Marie Delcourt writes that Tiresias represents a "kind of *successive androgyny*" through the "psychological aura" of which "we can approach the ideas which the Greeks associated with bisexuality" (1961, 34; emphasis in the original). Delcourt suggests that "in the folklore of all nations there is a danger in the sight of snakes copulating" (ibid., 37). On the other hand, "in the classical world and elsewhere, serpents confer the gift of prophecy" (ibid., 38). In some versions of the story of Athena's granting Tiresias the gift of superhearing, serpents clean Tiresias's ears. Delcourt's intention, in shuffling the order of cause and effect in her interpretation, is to suggest that the changes Tiresias undergoes were *both* punishment and reward. That is, "if the explanations which the Ancients found for the prophetic gift on the one hand, for the change of sex on the other, are interchangeable . . . [we should] relate both to another and wider explanation in which each can find a place" (ibid., 39). Her explanation is that "the legend of Tiresias seems to be a Greek interpretation of the artificial androgyny of the shamans" (ibid., 42).

This link, in some ways, diminishes the symbolism of blindness; it turns blindness into a metaphor instead of revealing it as a common condition that Tiresias simply lives with and adapts to, as many Greeks

---

11. The *Tiresias Project*, a community dance performance in which "disabled artists came together to explore the beauty of [their] bodies, perform[ing] defiantly [their] place in the loss and richness of a sensuous encounter," was based in (very small) part on a much earlier version of this chapter. Petra Kuppers, who was one of the leaders of the performance, wrote that the goal was to "claim Greek gods with a sarcastic eye" because "disabled people and our fascinating bodies, senses, and minds live in Greek mythology. In the *Tiresias Project*, we extend that lineage, and use our own disabled bodies to reshape myth" (2011, 213). I can think of no more perfect rhetorical revisiting and reinvigoration of these myths.

may have done. Martha Rose suggests that blindness would have been so common in the ancient period (imagine our world without glasses), that it would not have much significance—"some blind people were venerated; some were castigated; most went about their business." It follows that more extreme stories of blinding have survived: "stories about ordinary people with vision fading from cataracts are not the stuff of legend" (2003, 80). For this reason, we might proceed with seeing "blindness" as a symbol, while we keep in mind the interaction between myth and reality—indeed, the connection between myth and body, a rhetorical connection, is essential to this discussion.

The symbolic connection most marked for Delcourt is between the positive value of "seeing" and the possibly positive valuations of the ambiguously sexed body. As Luc Brisson suggests, figures with successive dual sexuality (sex that changes over time, rather than "hermaphroditism"—see discussion of terms below) are often seen as "mediators" (2002, 115). In the *Encyclopedia of Homosexuality* (1990), Warren Johansson comments on this phenomenon, suggesting that the association of shamanism and divination with the symbolic exchange of sex has been historically and geographically widespread. "Are we rash in thinking that bisexuality [successive or dual sexuality]," Delcourt asks, "had a positive value, bound up with human aspirations to perpetual life" and to shamanic knowledge? (1961, 42). Once this question has been asked, of course, once we stumble upon it, we are all given the gift of a different kind of "vision."

One thing remains static in all of the tellings of Tiresias's story, regardless of the order of sex changes or where on a sexual continuum the character lands, regardless of the sequence of the loss and gain of "sight," and that is Tiresias's long life. Tiresias lives to be positively ancient. Tiresias lives on even longer when we begin to reconsider this mythology as a contestation that has bearing on our modern conceptions of gender, ability, and embodied meaning.

Similarly, the ongoing mythology of Hermaphrodite impels this meaning. Marcel Detienne and Giulia Sissa, in *The Daily Life of Greek Gods* (2000), in tracing the etymology of Hermaphrodite as an embodied symbol, explore the meanings behind Hermaphrodite's lineage. As a symbolic compound, Hermaphrodite is sometimes seen as the child of Hermes and

Aphrodite. Both of Hermaphrodite's parents were gods who represented sexuality and virility—and *mētis*. Joseph Russo suggests that theirs was an "ambivalent *mētis*"—"one of thieves and lovers" as opposed to "the positive *mētis* of Athena and Hephaestus, one of strategy and craftsmanship" (2008, 263). The more impassioned, unpredictable *mētis* of Hermes and Aphrodite was denigrated because it was affiliated so closely with the desires of the body. Aphrodite, for her part, was the god of marriage and making love (*aphrodisiadzein*), and in her path creatures were "impelled to intermingle their limbs and bodies" (Detienne and Sissa 2000, 230). Aphrodite embodies erotic power (ibid., 37). Her body is formed from an actual sperm, and her son is Priapus, he of the "great tool" (ibid., 237). The authors suggest that Aphrodite is also highly ambiguous, even before she merges with Hermes. She is sometimes represented as a black goddess with a poppy in one hand, an apple in the other, representing death and life at once (ibid., 163). There are also sculptures of a bearded Aphrodite, which can be read as confusing, except that her role as god of making love links her forever to the phallus (and the beard is the outward sign of this cloaked part)—lovemaking governed at the time by an intense phallocentrism.

Yet Hermaphrodite challenges the gonadal basis/bias of subjectivity by (forever) meaning something else. The figure of Hermaphrodite tiptoed along the wafer-thin edge between myth and reality. Delcourt writes that "androgyny is at the two poles of sacred things. Pure concept, pure vision of the spirit, it appears adorned with the highest qualities. But once made real in a being of flesh and blood, it is a monstrosity" (1961, 45). The other conflict, of course, is that Hermaphrodite both blurs and reinforces the distinctions between male and female. For instance, Hermaphrodite's cult members celebrated a feast on the fourth day of every month at which men and women exchanged clothes (ibid., 47). Yet we are also led to believe that Hermaphrodite symbolized sexual union between men and women, thus reinforcing their polarity, and that the exchange of clothes at the festival was a celebration of male virility transposed onto a female body, or at best a carnivalesque catharsis and immediate reintegration into the old masculine economy. Still, unquestionably, the figure of Hermaphrodite played an important role in the symbolic order of sex and sexuality in

Greek life: images of the deity were painted on the walls of many private homes (New 1993, 114).

As the stories of Tiresias and Hermaphrodite show us, the ambiguously gendered body, which is "unintelligible" in the normative matrix Judith Butler outlines, is thus (verb) *disabled*. I hope that this connects with Butler's argument that it is equally important to examine "how and to what end bodies are not constructed" (1993, 16). We can follow the "sedimented" as well as the radically transitive constructions of the intersex as well as the disabled body, *as* they connect with the very rhetoric that would reject and abject them. To do so is to recognize not just the subversive potential for remythologizing, but also to generate discursive, rhetorical, and physical bodies that resist signification, bodies that will not be fully sexed or normed by discourse, and will thus be empowered.

When I use the term *disabled* here, I gesture both to pejorative disablism and to the idea that disability can be a positive thing. For instance, the myths of Hermaphrodite and Tiresias offer the possibility of a positive value for intersexuality or transsexuality. We might see Hermaphrodite as the symbol of intersexuality, a union and confusion of sex and gender, the figure of the *concept* itself. Indeed, one key argument for studying the classical myths of Hermaphrodite is that more "modern" conceptions of intersexuality have been so influenced by this mythology. As Morgan Holmes writes, "What people understand the term 'hermaphroditism' to mean [today] is both vague and variable, depending on the degree to which one associates it with classical mythology, contemporary 'chicks with dicks' pornography, circus sideshows and spectacles, or any combination of these." Holmes continues, distinguishing hermaphroditism from intersex: "Briefly stated, intersexuality refers to a physical and/or chromosomal set of possibilities in which the features usually understood as belonging distinctly to either the male or the female sex are combined in a single body" (2008a, 32). The medical term *genital ambiguity* offers up only confusion and uses the very spectacle of this confusion to ground perceptions that there are indeed two "normal" sexual states. Holmes suggests that the ambiguity is rendered by "the prejudice of the expert viewers" of these bodies, who infer through this diagnosis that "intersexed genitals do not look like *anything*" (ibid., 33).

As Holmes explains, intersex "shares some [political and cultural] features [with] transex and transgender [but] also has some distinct features that have rendered problematic any easy alliances" (ibid., 45). Holmes explains: "While an intersexed body may confuse the boundaries of sexual definition for those who hold a biologically grounded definition of it," as might LGBTQ (lesbian, gay, bisexual, trans, queer) identities, intersex does not automatically connote a movement from one set gender or sexuality to another by choice or by medical intervention (ibid., 46). Further, intersexuality has been so comprehensively grounded in the realm of medical "disorder" that it should be seen as connected to disability in important ways. Of course, other nonnormative sexes and sexualities have been pathologized. As Butler writes, because trans people have been "understood" through the diagnosis of gender identity disorder, trans people are also caught in a paradox in which "it is possible, necessary, to say that the diagnosis leads the way to the alleviation of suffering, and it is possible, necessary, to say that the diagnosis intensifies the very suffering that requires alleviation" (2006, 295). Yet the "case" of intersex remains distinct: whereas "abnormal" sexual preference or performance has been traditionally pathologized psychologically (with attendant physical interventions), intersex has been pathologized at the very physical, "gonadal" level first (with attendant and always interwoven psychological intervention). Despite this, Holmes suggests that "with a few notable exceptions disability studies have not taken account of intersexuality. . . . [M]eanwhile, the medical presupposition that intersex characteristics are inherently disabling to social viability remains the taken-for-granted truth" (2008a, 1).

Mētis asks us to move beyond simple amalgamations of physical and sexual Otherness and suggests that there were also ways that sex and sexuality impelled rhetorical meaning, rather than very simply connoting abjection. As Loraux suggests, "The mixture of the sexes was a Greek question" (1995, 8). As such, it was a rhetorical question. As such, it should still also pose and impel a series of distinctly rhetorical questions.

Enabling Rhetoric

As I hope the myths of Tiresias and Hermaphrodite begin to illustrate, there is a theoretically tenuous yet insistently material link between our conceptions of the ancient world, our sense of rhetorical history, and our ideas about (and actions upon) contemporary bodies. That is, though I would never suggest rhetoric was born in Greece, a rhetorical History has been. Likewise, norms are eminently culturally variable—but contemporary Western norms are also inflected by classical ideas. I ask you to accept, critically, my own anachronistic, geographically limited revisions, as I challenge the canonicity of this very emphasis on our Greco-Roman lineage. My suggestion is not that this is *the* history, but that it has conditioned our experience of rhetoric and disability, just as we have projected our visions, feelings, and experiences back into this narrow, nearly fictional world. In order to trouble this history in subsequent chapters, I will examine, critique, and revise disability myths. I will look for new stories from Athens and elsewhere. I will examine the idealistic, and normative, idea of the emergence of rhetoric. I will show some of the ways that our chosen versions of rhetorical history efface bodies and erase bodily difference. I will argue that the imposition of a bodily ideal results in constraint of rhetorical facility. Bodily denial and discipline generate a tension that underlies all rhetorical discourse and all discourse about rhetoric. This denial impacts all bodies, now.

Building on the work of historians such as Martha Rose, Jacques Stiker, James Fredal, Brenda Jo Brueggeman, and others, this project is about *enabling* rhetoric. I rely upon disability studies for the language and critical concepts, the myths and images that would allow us to critique the rhetorical tradition, allowing us to see that we have canonized it as a normate, normalizing force. Further, we have carried rhetorical tools forward and backward through this history, selecting myths and stories that constrain the possible meanings disability can embody or drive. From antiquity to the very present, disability has been seen as something simple to trope and frame. In this way, rhetoric has been used to mark out and stigmatize disability, thus providing us with limited means of interpreting and understanding the role of people with disabilities in rhetoric and in society. Yet as Harlan Hahn has written, "Humans have always exercised the right to make choices about the anatomical features that they consider desirable or interesting, and, at times, these options have included rather than excluded women and men with disabilities" (1988, 30).

The dominant message that we have about classic rhetorical oratory is that it was a sphere for only the most able-bodied—we link this with ideas about delivery that connect only with very narrow interpretations of the rhetorical body. Cicero wrote that the best oration has a "middle quality"; its "form" and "complexion" have "fullness" but are "free from tumor" (1955, 251). The voice is plain but not without nerve and vigor. A good speech/speaker has the "complexion of beauty . . . diffused throughout the system of the blood" (1955, 251).[12] Extending the idea that words have a physiognomy, James Wilson and Cynthia Lewiecki-Wilson suggest that we might see language as an "address interpellating the body" (2001, 2). Just as the body is constructed by discourse, discourse has an ideal body. Wilson and Lewiecki-Wilson argue that certain bodies are made subservient by rhetoric itself (ibid., 6). It is from the material of this suggestion, and the potential of its subversion, that I want to forge a definition of embodied rhetoric.

The subservience of the body to rhetoric, suitably, is mostly about silence. It is also about subtext, maybe it is about denial, certainly it is about misdirection. We might begin with James Fredal's assertion that Western, particularly post-Platonic and post-Aristotelian, rhetorical theory has "altered the medium [of rhetoric] from the body to the word" (2006, 127). In his calculation, "writing redefined speech in its own image," and denies, or struggles to make transparent, the body: disappearing delivery; ignoring practice, action, performance (ibid., 134).[13]

12. Within the field of composition and writing studies, very bodily ideas about "flow," "cohesion," and "voice" carry similar metaphors, and also construct a normal and normate embodiment for rhetoric. These narrow views must be challenged. As Merleau-Ponty suggested, words have a physiognomy—we behave *toward* them (1965, 235). We also behave *within* the constraints they create.

13. Yet on the other hand, there is a common argument, articulated in phenomenological philosophy but also in studies of embodied rhetoric like those of Hawhee and Fredal, that bodily delivery has the presence that the written text lacks. To study performance or delivery or physical education is to place the body back in the rhetoric. This seems to echo Plato's argument, perhaps most clearly expressed in his *Phaedrus* (1961d), that speech is superior to writing—that speech is alive. Such an argument is reinvoked by historians Walter Ong (1982) and Eric Havelock (1982), who suggest that the invention of writing led to

abstraction and disembodiment. Ong suggests that "oral memory differs significantly from textual memory in that oral memory has a high somatic component" (1982, 67). The oral word, he argues, "never exists in a simply verbal context, as a written word does. Spoken words are always modifications of a total, existential situation, which always engages the body" (ibid., 68). Words are "alone in a text," they "lack their full phonetic qualities" and their "extratextual content"; they are disembodied (ibid., 101). Only speech is alive.

I would worry about erecting such a binary, such a strict point of bifurcation. As Derrida writes in his critique of Husserl, there is a pronounced bias that "the word is a body that means something only if an actual intention animates it and makes it pass from the state of inert sonority (*korper*) to that of an animated body (*leib*)" (1973, 81). In this way, phenomenology has actually (according to Derrida) made speech bodily and writing a nonbody (and a nonpresence). It is against such beliefs, deeply held in Western philosophy, that I argue. As Derrida writes, "In every reading there is a *corps-a-corps* between reader and text (1984, 126). In "Plato's Pharmacy," Derrida also critiques the idea that only in speech is rhetoric real. Plato, he says, argued that "logos committed to writing is without its father" (1998, 77). Writing, for those who have read Plato literally, "substitutes the breathless sign for the living voice" of speech (ibid., 91). Writing is therefore death.

I would argue that Plato (or rather Platonism) performs a double effacement—Plato suggests that writing has no breath, but not in order to locate physicality in speech and thus argue for its superiority. For speech to be True, it also must denounce the body. As Derrida sees it, speech, for Plato, "emanates from the interior, from absolute proximity to meaning" (1973, 75). When words have been spoken, the speech itself vanishes (as does the body), and meaning stands alone. We are to believe that for Plato, if writing does belong to the *phusis* or the physical, it is to the dead body (1998, 105). Speech belongs to immortality, to the soul.

Derrida argues that writing is "errancy as such, mute vulnerability to all aggression" (ibid., 124). Writing "has a blindness to do with it . . . hasn't a damn sight to do with it" (ibid., 135). He argues that "only out of something like writing . . . the strange difference of inside and outside can spring. . . . [O]ne would then have to bend [*plier*] into strange contortions what could no longer even simply be called logic or discourse" (ibid., 103). There are traces of stereotypical constructions of disability in this discourse—writing is vulnerable and oblivious. Yet there are also traces of the affirmation of that which *springs* from disability, those meanings that our imperfect bodies unconventionally traffic.

In Jasper Neel's analysis of Plato and Derrida, he urges his reader to "pull down the tapestry and reveal Plato in the game with the rest of us where writing tells him what he thinks he knows, not the other way around" (1988, 29). Plato's *Phaedrus*, according to Neel, is "a divided, diseased inscription" (ibid., 56), not just because it is conflicted, but also because all texts are conflicted, a very contagious disease. He pushes this biometaphor when he suggests that "any living creature ought to be constructed like a discourse, with its own language, as it were; it must lack either a pre-existing sign system or group of sign users; it must have an infinite series of differences so that it can come to know itself through

Central to this chosen tradition, then, is a fear of the body and of bodily difference that has limited our ability to recognize and communicate with and from our own bodies. Beyond these delimitations of bodily possibility, we also see bodies pejoratively associated with rhetoric in order to subordinate the material possibility of persuasion and gild the transcendent "truth" of a fixed "Real." When one needs to malign rhetoric, it is aligned with the body. Susan Bordo claims that "Plato imagines the body as an epistemological deceiver, its unreliable senses and volatile passions continually tricking us into mistaking the transient and illusory for the permanent and the real" (1993, 3). Indeed, this is one of the dominant views of Plato perpetuated by a long line of Platonists.

I use the term *Platonist* here to mark the distinction between what Plato may have actually said or believed and the ways that Plato has been taken up in the philosophical and rhetorical tradition—how he has been reinterpreted and spoken for by others. I allude here, as well, to a wide range of Platonists—from Plotinus and the neo-Platonists of the third century, with their focus on transcendence and divine intellect, to early Christian neo-Platonists, to the Cambridge Platonists of the seventeenth century and their strong belief in the priority of the mind over matter, to a range of modern neo-Platonists like Goethe and Jung. The unifying thread between these thinkers is a disavowal of materialist epistemologies. Therefore, it is no surprise that we now see Plato as a philosopher against the body, regardless of his actual views. This perspective comes

---

differing from itself and thus be whole by being part" (ibid., 30). This statement succinctly sums up the twist I want to give to the normative body rhetoric of antiquity, the normative body rhetoric we have canonized. Neel directly reverses Socrates's statement that "any discourse ought to be constructed like a living creature, with its own body, as it were; it must not lack either head or feet; it must have a middle and extremities so composed as to suit each other and the whole work" (1961e, 128), a quote that I discussed in relation to the norm, the mean, and the ideal previously. But in this reversal, Neel seeks not to transfer the demand for ideality, for proportion and presence, for a normative body, from speech to writing, or from discourse to the body, or body to discourse. Both Neel and Derrida spin and recharge this famous declaration, demanding the transience and the continual play of difference of embodied signification.

across most strongly in his condemnation of the Sophists and their teach-ing of rhetoric, and so Platonists have focused on his denunciations of the body, aligning this with his denunciation of rhetoric. After tightly delimit-ing the role of the body epistemologically, Plato seems to use the body to discount rhetoric altogether.[14]

Interestingly, as Richard Enos has argued, it is quite possible that Plato's denunciation of the Sophists was unpersuasive in his time: he "failed to convince his immediate audience of the shortcomings of sophistic rhetoric" (1993, 101). Yet this denunciation has been quite con-vincing in the intervening centuries. Plato's philosophical position, arguing for idealized truths and essences, clashed with the Sophistic philosophy of contingency and *kairos*, the usage of abstraction and con-traries (particularly associated with the Sophist Gorgias). The Platonic push-and-pull between the "essence" of the written versus the spoken word also came to accent this denouncement. The result, according to an enduring Platonist tradition, was that rhetoric was denounced as bodily, and therefore inferior to philosophy, which is connected to the soul. Rhetoric was thus saddled with an excess of corporeality, the stigma of being bodied.

This view can perhaps be most easily inferred from a quick reading of Plato's *Gorgias*, the text that we have come to read as his key denun-ciation of rhetoric. Socrates suggests that politics concerns itself with the good of the soul, rhetoric (and sophistry) with the pleasures of the body (1961b, 464b–465d). Therefore, rhetoric is not only inferior to political and philosophical applications of the intellect, but also capable of doing harm—inducing "misery" and "wretched[ness]" (ibid., 479e306, 473a1).[15] The suggestion is that the philosopher will enable humanity, the rhetori-cian will disable. Indeed, we are led to believe that the flesh is capable only of deception. In this normative logic, as the male has been set against

14. And, of course, Plato needs to use rhetoric—he needs to be rhetorical—to make his denunciation of the body convincing.

15. In the *Phaedrus*, Plato could be seen to change positions slightly, suggesting that certain forms of more "scientific" and therefore "noble" rhetoric might be acceptable (see D. White 1993; Ramsey 1999; McAdon 2004; and Solmsen 1983 for a range of readings).

the female, the body is used to mark rhetoric out, as being everything that philosophy is not: confused and confusing, broken, bodied. This logic then leaves little expressive capital for the body. And this is not some historically distant memory to us today—we must still control and belittle our bodies; to be *bodied* too much or too "abnormally" is still to be in danger of disqualification.

Plato may have *used* the stigma of the body to denounce rhetoricians, and thus we have selected a history that minimizes the role of the body, that retains and internalizes much of this stigma. This occurs first in our selective rereading of the classical period. And this rereading carries through to medieval rhetoricians such as Saint Augustine, who championed the intelligible over the sensible (see Mazzeo 1962), to renaissance humanists and Enlightenment rhetoricians who prioritized the mind over the body, and even through to contemporary pop philosophy (and serious philosophy) that prizes the transcendence of the body through technology. The body undergoes a general submersion through the narratives that we have accepted.

But I will suggest that we might respond to this oppressive legacy by using our bodies significantly and making rhetoric significantly bodied. In other words, rhetoric can reclaim the body. In further words, the extraordinary body can be *the* body of rhetoric.[16]

I want to suggest that we should pay attention to the embodied delivery of the spoken text, and we should pay attention to the fusion of physical and rhetorical training, but not in order to suggest that these are the only venues where the body is engaged, comes alive. Even in the image, act, and performance of writing (perhaps as much so as in any other somatic medium), the body is present.[17] Likewise, rhetoric has a body. Rhetoric always extends into and issues from our experiences of embodi-

16. The use of the word *extraordinary* here, and elsewhere, constitutes a nod to the work of Rosemarie Garland-Thomson and her book *Extraordinary Bodies: Figuring Physical Disability in American Culture and Literature* (1996) foundational in disability studies.

17. As Lewiecki-Wilson writes, "We have an impoverished language for conveying the rhetoricity inherent in embodied life" (2003, 157). In many ways, we fail to direct critical attention to either the rhetoricity of the body or the body of rhetoric. I would echo N.

ment. Rhetoric, as a tool and an art and a way to move, mediates and is mediated by the body.

At this point, I want to put forward three theses about bodily rhetoric. First, the body is rhetorically invested, inscribed, shaped; second, all rhetoric is embodied; third, because of the rhetorical construction of the body, and rhetorical invention *by* the body, all bodies must be read through a normative matrix, a means of understanding the doubly constructed/constructing force of the disabled body. I will elaborate.

One: the body is invested rhetorically. The body has always been a rhetorical product or experiment, even as bodies have always been insistently material. All meaning issues forth from the body, but communication also reaches into the body to shape its possibilities. Sharon Crowley writes that, rhetorically, "no body is disinterested" (1999, 363). Embodiment, in this sense, is always a mode of persuasion. The body is also always invested with cultural meanings. Bodies practice culture.[18] But cultures also practice embodiment. As Certeau says, "There is no law that is not inscribed on bodies" (1984, 165). Further, as we saw through our discussion of means and ideals, rhetoric enforces bodily norms. As Lennard Davis argues, "Language usage, which is as much a physical function as any other somatic activity, has become subject to an enforcement of normalcy" (2002, 104). Rhetoric converts fear and misapprehension of the body into linguistic and performative practice.

Two: rhetoric is always embodied. The body can be seen as rhetorical equipment, a rhetorical instrument, *and* a rhetorical engine. The body is rhetorical—it communicates and thinks.[19] Bodies are always present in and through signification.

Katherine Hayles, who writes that (despite its denials) philosophy does have a body, that it is normative, and that it is always clashing with our ("actual") embodiment (1999, 85).

18. This cultural investment is perhaps most thoroughly theorized by Bourdieu, who wrote of the *habitus*, dispositions organized and structured by a dynamic normativity: the ways bodies reproduce the regularities of past practice while adjusting to the demands of present contexts.

19. Expanding Crowley's point about bodily investment, we could look to Giulia Sissa who writes that "the body stands in front of you not as an insignificant instrument

Three: Judith Butler also investigates the materiality we ascribe to bodies and suggests that all bodies are read through a gendered matrix. I hope to show how this gendered matrix is also a *normative* matrix of ability, relying upon and reinforcing constructions of disability as material otherness. As Elizabeth Grosz points out, for instance, female knowledge is *different* because there have always been such "sexually differential forms of body thinking" (1994, 37). Thinking has always been represented as masculine, and thus as the nonpresence, nonimplication of the body (ibid., 39). The very markedness of other bodies encourages us to think around or over them, or allows them to be thought *of*, represented, but not to think. The important lesson to learn from this is not to repeat this elision, but rather to recognize that these other forms of knowing, situated within bodies, can be claimed, as we constantly examine the normativity of the everyday.[20]

It is this expanded definition of embodiment, and of rhetoric's role in producing bodies, and the fact of rhetoric's production *by* bodies, and by bodies always in reference to norms, that is at the heart of my exploration of disability and rhetoric. This is not an effort to simply mark the negative impact of norms. The body of rhetoric always *both* constrains and enables. Performance theorists write of the expressive power of "whole" bodies

---

of the enunciation but as its meaningful context" (1999, 161). Although this might be read to reinforce what James Fredal asserts when he writes that "words could never exhaust the expressive power of the speaking moment produced and felt not by mouths or minds, but by whole bodies," I would rather construct the concept of rhetorical embodiment as always including words, mouths, hands, minds, bodies, technologies, in dynamic interaction— whether one is speaking or signing or writing, always as we compose our thoughts, as we think *through* this composition (2006, 4).

20. Echoing this contention, feminist philosopher Iris Marion Young argues that the "body" of philosophy or of rhetoric always both constrains and enables, and it is always involved in the production of normalcy. In her words,

"Experiences of moving, perceiving, interacting with others, manipulating tools, thinking through problems and expressing oneself are always conditioned and constituted by social structures of constraint and enablement, as well as by forms of representation of persons, as both normal and deviant. The subject of disability herself is constituted as varying and culturally constituted lived body" (Young 1990, xiii).

as a way to argue for a more full recognition of communication, beyond just written texts. Disability studies shows that there is no such thing as a whole body—but also that normative references to wholeness are part of the matrix within which bodies are made intelligible. I would warn against conceptions of rhetoric or communication that seek to sidestep the body, even though these sidesteps may be the result of an unavoidable pull within the dance of normativity. That is, we should not just affirm the body. We should affirm the disabled body. And as we affirm the disabled body, we should understand the power of bodily norms to undercut or spin this affirmation. To affirm the disabled body is to affirm embodied rhetoric. Conversely, to deny disability is to misrepresent and misrecognize embodiment; it is to use embodiment theory as a method of exclusion.

Am I saying that rhetoric is disabled?

I am suggesting that disability is a material state and an identity, as well as a vital critical modality. This is not to say that we are all disabled, but instead to emphasize that no one is normal. Just as Butler argues that heterosexual identity is, in fact, always an elusive categorization, able-bodied identity, too, is an "inevitable impossibility" (McRuer 2007, 10).[21] This does not "answer" worries about the politics of disability identity, but it does offer useful pathways for thinking and moving through disability.

I am also advocating for the view that the body's partiality and incompleteness can be claimed as essential and generative. This is not to say that we are all disabled, or that rhetoric is disabled, but to embrace a

---

21. Along these lines, Robert McRuer notes an important gap in relation to disability that echoes Butler's differentiation of "virtually queer" and "critically queer" identities. He observes: "Everyone is virtually disabled, both in the sense that able-bodied norms are 'intrinsically impossible to embody' and fully in the sense that able-bodied status is always temporary, disability being the one identity category that all people will embody if they live long enough. What we might call a critically disabled position, however, would differ from such a virtually disabled position; it would call attention to the ways in which the disability rights movements and disability studies have resisted the demands of compulsory able-bodiedness and have demanded access to a newly imagined and newly configured public sphere where full participation is not contingent on an able body" (2007, 30).

nonnormative discourse/materiality, modestly proposing that such signifiers be tabled not as the natural inverse of a privileged wholeness in a
normative matrix, but rather as a valorization of alternative fleshing out
and potential resignification, a shift of meaning and value that might also
mitigate the oppression of bodies with disabilities.[22]

I do believe that, in understanding rhetoric through these dispositions, we all might more fully understand the ways normativity constrains
our available means of persuasion. We are asked to ignore our embodied
selves and constrain our expressions of subjectivity. But in the discordant
space between embodiment and normativity, we find ourselves and our
power to reinterpret rhetoric—as enabled by its prostheses, by the incoherence of its histories and the awkwardness of its postures—and we are
empowered to disruptively and subversively *become* ourselves.

I hope that such expansion of ideas about rhetoric and disability are
operative as I travel back into history, and as I make arguments about the
lingering impact of canonized theories of rhetorical normalcy and suggest
the ways we might amplify the tension that rocks their rigid formulations
of rhetorical facility.

22. Anita Silvers suggests that "human diversity must be seen as the product of creative human choice . . . as the extraordinariness of Van Gogh's manner is seen as being
meaningful." This is very similar to what I will suggest in this book, arguing that we can
"elevate otherness to originality" (2002, 242).

3

Imperfect Meaning

> [The prosthetic body] infirm or lacking, in need of the other, [is] not the
> exception but the paradigm for the body itself.
>
> —David Wills, *Prosthesis*

RHETORIC CAN BE SEEN as the function of power within language, and
I connect it to the body because the body is what has been traditionally
defined and (thus) disciplined by rhetorics of disability, while at the same
time our bodies speak back, insisting (prosthetically) upon the impossibility of a normative essence. Saying this, however, introduces static. Who
owns and what constructs—what owns and who constructs—the disabled
body? In order to assert that *all* bodily rhetoric is *mētis*, these questions
of power and agency must first (and continuously) be addressed. In this
chapter I will further examine ways that disability has been constructed
and defined, but more important I will make the crucial transition to proposing models and theories that situate disability as meaningful and as
meaning-making. I will move from surveying the construction of disability as deficit to theories of the unique, imperfect, powerful meaning that
disability generates.

Models of Disability

Within disability studies, there has been a relatively recent—and much
reflected upon and theorized through—split between social constructionist and materialist positions on disability identity. As Bonnie G. Smith
suggests in her introduction to the landmark collection *Gendering Disability*: "The term 'disability' is becoming increasingly polymorphous. . . . [I]t
can suggest a set of practices, kinds of embodiment, interactions with the

built environment, an almost limitless array of literary types, frames of mind and forms of relationships" (2004, 1). Indeed, disability (via this con-testation over meaning) puts the somewhat malleable rubber of construc-tionist theories to the road of lived experience. Through an observation of this tension, we also learn a lot about the split between biologism and sociologism across other discrete yet often convergent discussions—as it plays out in feminist, queer, and critical race discourses, for example. I want to show that a disability studies analysis of socio/material tension is a way to foreground these convergences—to recognize how race, gender, sex, sexuality, class, and ability are characterized by marked bodies. What these discourses do share, upon first glance, is that disability of some sort has been attributed to the minority or abjected group, most often pejora-tively. To interrogate the meaning of disability is to better understand all bodies and their discursive/corporeal markings, effacements, and rewrit-ings and to question the exclusions that underpin materialization.[1]

Disability studies as a political movement has been very much about claiming disability (see Linton 1993), owning disabled identity, and the right to define this lived experience. In the face of the medical model of disability, in which the individual was often reduced, via synecdoche, to the sum of her or his dysfunctional parts, disability rights has been an identity movement—a reclamation of the symbolic power of self-defini-tion. Disability rights activism is a direct challenge to the abbreviation of subjectivity. If there were an image for the medical model—a scene that I would never reproduce here—it would be a picture of an individual in which the head is out of frame, while the medical "abnormalities" of the body are centered, are the singular focus. Such images, unfortunately, fill the medical files of people with disabilities—as they fill the files of

---

1. As mentioned, a disability studies examination of embodied rhetoric takes up Judith Butler's argument that it is equally important to examine "how and to what end bodies are *not* constructed" (1993, 16; emphasis added). She argues that we gain power by questioning the normative conditions of the emergence of materiality (ibid., 10). Butler's vision is that "it will be a matter of tracing the ways in which identification is implicated in what it excludes, and to follow the lines of that implication for the map of future com-munity it might yield" (2000, 119).

anthropological studies of colonized Africa, as Londa Schiebinger (1993) and Robyn Wiegman (1995) show us. If there were a film to enact this image, it would be of a doctor lecturing to interns in front of the exposed body of a patient, named only by their disability, with this disability on display for the consumption of the student.[2] Obviously, I am responding to this model when, throughout this work, I try to position people with disabilities, in their own claimed bodies, as *makers* of meaning—rather than as surfaces reflecting the meanings of others, rather than as objects of knowledge.

While medical discourse couched disability in the negative and reductive terms of affliction, cavalierly applied the abstractions of pseudoscientific labels, and placed individuals in passive and disempowered roles, the disability rights movement said "label jars, not people." "The disabled" asked to be seen as people first, insisted on "nothing about us without us" and reclaimed formerly derogatory terms like *crip*, channeling their subversive meanings into subversive outsider critiques of societal norms and of an ableist culture. People with disabilities both reached out to and critiqued self-defined normals by labeling them "temporarily able-bodied." Essential to this movement was the message that disability is beautiful, that people who experience disability do not want to be cured, do not want to overcome their disabilities, and that they can and will lead very valuable lives in the face of oppression.

Yet as this activist identity evolved, and as people with disabilities and their allies took aim at society's discriminatory attitudes, exclusionary practices, and violent and eradicative actions, a new sense of the disabling impact of society itself emerged and took precedence. The protests that led up to the passage of the Americans with Disabilities Act in the United States, and other similar movements in other parts of the world, often centered around the message that exclusionary structures at least partially created disability, that if society and culture were more accessible, people with disabilities would face fewer barriers, their lived

2. In the canonical disability studies film *Vital Signs: Crip Culture Talks Back* (1997), this scene is critically reenacted twice, by Mary Duffy and by Cheryl Marie Wade.

experience would change. Adrienne Asch introduces this sentiment as a "possibly radical proposal" and then suggests that "instead of discussing which kinds of people have impairments or disabilities and which people do not, instead of saying that some members of society are disabled and others are not, we should consider which people cannot perform which activities in given environments and question how to modify the environments so they are not disabling" (2004, 16).

Another elaboration of this idea is that society actually creates barriers, in part because of a failure to imagine difference when designing structures (both physical and cultural), or perhaps to more consciously exclude. This idea reveals the tangle between disability as a material, lived experience and as a result of cultural constructions. To fully conceptualize disability, we must consider—as Asch and others argue—that disability is more than just a biomedical condition. Yet she qualifies that, "saying that disability is socially constructed does not imply that the characteristics are not real or do not have describable effects on physiological or cognitive functions that persist in many environments" (ibid., 18). Awareness of sociospatial constructions of disability could allow for an even greater awareness of the uniqueness and essential difference of physiological and cognitive functions if we think of sociospatial change in a slightly different way. That is, why not imagine that we could change the environment to minimize the constraining and impairing effects of intellectual and architectural structures, but also to emphasize and enable embodied differences to thrive? In this way we would move from synecdoche—the reduction of disability to an array of disabled parts that stand in for individuals—to disability as a generative asyndeton, the introduction of subversive gaps and reconfigurations of definitions that have been seen as natural and monolithic. Such a shift would advocate for a cultural logic of biodiversity in the face of the rhetoric of survival of the fittest, recasting *mētis* as what the (redefined) "fittest" employ. It is important to combat oppression and to eradicate violence—and living with a disability should not be made more painful or uncomfortable, even while we are wary of the push for cure. But how might we also transform environments so that instead of erasing disability we can value it, allow it to be seen and experienced as generative and essential to meaning, instead of as essentially negative and negatable?

How too can we think through the body, and of the body, without rein-scribing the abbreviations of the medical model, and do so in a way that *values* instability, change, partiality as multiplicity?

In the 1980s and 1990s, a British "social model" of disability also drew greater attention to the environment. The social model stood in opposi-tion to the individual and medical models of disability—which held that disability was located within the individual and that a disability held meaning only as pathology, defined entirely by its symptoms. The social model was of key importance politically, drawing attention to the oppres-sion of people with disabilities. That said, this was largely a materialist movement and suggested a clear bifurcation. This model posited that dis-ability is purely social, an oppression stacked onto people *on top of* their impairments, which are real. The view was that, as Michael Oliver wrote, "disablement is nothing to do with the body, impairment is nothing less than a description of the body" (1990, 34).

Asch's suggestion that there be a critique of cultural disablement that retains a synergistic view of cultures and bodies emerged from this model, suggesting that disability is socially constructed. Yet so-called postmod-ern disability studies also contradicts the British philosophy by suggesting that the strict separation of impairment and disability is a chimera (see Tremain 2002). The British model suggests the existence of both physical impairment and cultural disablement as engaged, yet independently sov-ereign, truths. The postmodern model blurs the lines between the two.

This postmodern model remains influential, often to the chagrin of disabled people who feel that their experiences of disability are under-mined. There certainly are dangerous implications for the issue of agency when a focus on individual empowerment and bodily reclamation cedes to discussions of social construction—particularly when a common assumption among "able-bodied" bigots is that people with disabilities are faking it anyhow, or that they should just try harder to overcome their impairment and cure themselves.[3]

---

3. For instance, Amy Vidali, through her extensive analysis of college application essays in which students claim (or do not claim) their disabilities, and her interviews with

In a more nuanced and perhaps even more sinister sense, this emphasis on social construction can often defuse the political power of an identity group. Social constructionism, in some ways, can be used as a method of silencing. Particularly, social construction can remove the focus on the particularity of differences of bodies and minds, a focus that I have been arguing is so important. If we are all disabled by an oppressive environment in some way, why does the disability perspective really matter? How is the embodied experience of disability any different from the norm? The final effect can often be just as oppressive as the reality that social construction serves to critique—without the solidarity and political unity that come with disability identity, it is very difficult to challenge the norm.

A cautious and rights-oriented social constructionist philosophy can interrogate the ways that bodies and cultures, biology and social structures—even texts—interact and cocreate one another. Much as Judith Butler (1993) has troubled the natural/cultural binary of sex and gender, this social model has troubled the notion of natural bodies, the very idea of a body curtained off from culture. Disability studies theorist Lennard Davis offers a rather radical interpretation of this postmodern constructionist stance: "The body is never a single physical thing as much as a series of attitudes towards it" (2002, 22). Yet Judith Butler's definition of a partial social construction of the body, from her introduction to *Bodies That Matter*, perhaps more subtly distills this idea: "To claim that discourse is formative is not to claim that it originates, causes, or exhaustively composes that which is concedes; rather, it is to claim that there is no reference to a pure body which is not at the same time a further formation of that body" (1993, 5).

But perhaps what is most important to remember is that social constructionism, although it may challenge some of the essentiality ascribed

---

these students, shows that "people with disabilities are regularly accused of 'faking it,'" and many people with disabilities then feel they must either clearly prove their impairment or completely hide it (2007, 632).

to disability, cannot be seen as somehow emancipating people with disabilities. In fact, it should be seen as a way to explain, most often, various forms of persistent social disable*ment*. Mary Jo Deegan offers an interesting deconstruction of the binary between physical and social factors of disablement: "Physical limits are often capable of being integrated into everyday life, but social limits are the most unstable, potentially humiliating, and dangerous factors emerging from physical disabilities. These social barriers are the most uncontrolled and vicious source of physical limitations" (2010, 45). The physical or somatic experience of disability can move to and from the "forefront of everyday life and consciousness," but social processes are most often what trigger these movements, and for many people with disabilities, these social factors continue to be the least predictable or controllable factors in an ableist world (ibid., 25).

Nirmala Erevelles further warns that "poststructuralism's attempts to fragment all social analyses into incommensurable parts" can offer new ways to interpret the social world, yet "continue[s] to uphold the economic structures that have produced [material] difference on a global scale." Further, it is disability that has been the "critical ideological category that is constructed so as to justify the exploitative relations that are implicated in the production of race, gender, class, and sexuality as well" (2011, 106). So although something like social constructionism may have "temporal usefulness" as a means of reinterpretation, it often fails to recognize or remedy "exploitative relations within the larger context of a social totality" (ibid., 107). And when disability itself is used as a means of justifying the exploitation of many other groups, the question of its materiality is centrally important.

Tobin Siebers explores the ramifications of a "strong social constructionism" for disability theory, suggesting that much "strong constructionism" fails to account for the pain and difficulty of disability, or presents the disabled body "in ways that are conventional, conformist, or unrecognizable" (2010, 57). He suggests that this strong constructionism needs to be tempered with a "restored sense" of (but not a solidified stand on) the "realism of the disabled body" in order to retain the political potential of disability and to ensure that the disabled body be seen as being "as capable of influencing and transforming social languages" as it is of being shaped by them (ibid., 67–68).[4]

Obviously, such blurring of boundaries between culture or discourse and the "pure body" is necessary to me, as well, to think through the rhetoric of embodiment, that crucial interweaving of body, power, and discourse; mythical sex and sexuality; corporeal rewritings; grammars of ability.

In this book, I will be speaking to what we might call a "cultural turn" in disability studies. Len Barton and others have suggested that such a turn engages with "phenomenology, psychodynamic, and poststructuralist ideas" that "privilege cultural and linguistic phenomena" (2006, 5). This turn "analyzes exclusion and oppression discourses, as well as the metaphorical and symbolic meanings historically assigned to specific impairments." The focus on "culture" may be slightly more specific than a focus on the "social," though cultural studies "do not neglect the political" (Joshua and Schillmeier 2010, 5). Importantly, like "postmodern" models of disability, a cultural turn does not deny the materiality of disability, yet it troubles the origins and sedimentations of this materiality. A cultural turn is not the "just right" alternative to tack onto the listing of individual or medical model, social model, and postmodern model. Instead, a "cultural turn" offers a range of strategies and foci through which disability can be studied as medicalizing, individuating, hinged, or unhinged from materiality or the social. Cultures and their expressions can be studied for their role in making bodies, and bodies and their expressions can be studied for their roles in making cultures. As you can see, my further nudge on the cultural turn is toward a specifically rhetorical sphere. Are bodies things made of language? Yes. But only insofar as languages are also things made by bodies. In the rest of this chapter, I will focus on some

---

4. Under this rubric, "bodies are linguistic effects driven, first, by the order of representation itself and, second, by the entire array of social ideologies dependent on this order" (Siebers 2010, 55). Yet Siebers argues that "the disabled body seems difficult for the theory of social construction to absorb: disability is at once its best example and a significant counterexample" (ibid., 57). There must be ways to view the disabled body as construct*ive*.

specific rhetorical locations of disability, and then I will explore more fully this latter idea: the ways that the body, in particular the disabled body, generates meaning.

Disability Semantics and Syntaxes

Tanya Titchkosky, David Mitchell and Sharon Snyder, Robert McRuer, and others have argued that it may be important for disability studies to move beyond just "policing" cultural representations of disability.[5] This "policing" might be exemplified by my chart of disability myths from earlier in this book. The chart urges us to see disability representation as a matter of political correctness—as something you get right or wrong. One way to push beyond this is to make the argument that representations of disability impact us all—the idea that disability's constructedness or rhetoricity reveals how all bodies are constructed. I have been making that argument, too. To affirm the disabled body is to affirm embodied rhetoric. This affirmation is important, politically, as well.[6]

Disability studies scholars have shown the many ways that disability meaning is circulated through narrative, through media, through law and policy, through economics, through architecture. Yet disability also (crucially at the same time) has a specifically linguistic and rhetorical dimension. Our words and the ways we use them are always already infused with disability meaning.

For instance, at the "micro" level of the rhetorical scene, disability is understood from top to bottom and side to side through metaphor. Words like *crip, idiot, moron, retard, psycho, schizo, mong, feeb,* and *spaz* are all metaphoric or metonymic, calling up supposed scientific truths that are themselves figurative, or attaching to bodies and contexts at a great distance from their original linguistic intentions. Medical *and* cultural labels for

5. See Titchkosky 2007; Mitchell and Snyder 2001a; and McRuer 2007.

6. Susan Wendell promises that "if disabled people were truly heard [without sentimentalizing], an explosion of knowledge of the human body and psyche would take place." She warns of the consequences of silence: "the oppression of disabled people is the oppression of everyone's real body" (1994, 274).

disability are synecdochic, neologistic, paranomastic, even onomatopoeic. For instance, almost all disability labels work through synecdoche, urging us to see the disabled person as their broken "part." Moreover, a word like *psycho* is both an abbreviation of the word *psychopathic* and an abbreviation (parts for the whole) of the embodied subjectivity of the labeled person. The word *moron* is a neologism invented to label an invented group, but was also intended to call up a classical (Greek) history and the connotation of "dullness" (as though minds need to be "sharp").[7] Paranomasia, or puns, often invoke disability, but words like *spaz* and *tard* and *mong*

7. The term *moron* was invented by Henry Goddard in 1910, and the classification was key to research he performed on immigrants at Ellis Island beginning in 1913. As Anna Stubblefield has argued, Goddard's invention of this term as a "signifier of tainted whiteness" was the "most important contribution to the concept of feeble-mindedness as a signifier of a racial taint," through the diagnosis of the menace of alien races, but also as a way to divide out the impure elements of the white race (2007, 173, 162). The moron was seen as, in the words of Goddard's contemporary Margaret Sanger, "the mental defective who is glib and plausible, bright looking and attractive." This person "may not merely lower the whole level of intelligence in a school or in a society, but may . . . increase and multiply until he dominates and gives the prevailing 'color'—culturally speaking—to an entire community" (1922, 210). The "moron," designated as a high-functioning feeble-minded individual, yet capable of "passing" as normal, being attractive to normals, highly sexualized, and thus an even greater menace to the gene pool, was a threat that created the need for greater diligence and surveillance, and inspection and worry, in the whole population and on the borders. Steven Gelb argues that it is important to also recognize the discourses that preceded Goddard's invention of this term, as well. As Gelb writes, "Henry H. Goddard first coined the term moron and applied it to mature persons who scored between eight and twelve years of mental age on the 1908 Binet-Simon test. His contemporaries argued that Goddard had actually discovered a milder type of deficiency than had been identified before, and this claim is still widely accepted. However, that belief is erroneous because it ignores the development of ideas about mild states of mental deficiency in the late eighteenth and nineteenth centuries which defined and shaped Goddard's work in 1910. This mythology sanitizes the modern construct by distancing it from earlier, scientifically discredited paradigms—including faculty and religious psychologies, phrenology, degeneracy theory, and criminal anthropology—in which its roots are planted" (1989, 360). Gelb's argument is that many have seen Goddard's coining of the term *moron* as the beginning of a modern and more valid paradigm of mental testing and classification, and he suggests we recognize the full pseudoscientific history as a way to challenge the validity of all later testing and classification.

and *feeb* are also puns with an onomatopoeic dimension—their "funny" sounds carry meaning.[8] The sibilance within the word *stuttering* twists the term itself into something cruel. The word *crippled* has impediment built into its consonants (in speech requiring the closure of the vocal tract and the use of the lips).[9] The word is also related to the Old English *creopan*, or *creep*, a word with slowness built into its vowels, but also a word that locates bodies, literally, in the dirt—moving with the belly on the ground. Of course, much more could be said about the ways disability is physicalized and defined through specific metaphors.

And, on the other hand, all metaphors are disabled. In positing one thing in terms of another, metaphors might be seen as bridges or ramps on the verbal map. Indeed, the Greek root of the word *metapherein* means "to carry across." What we might focus on here is not the carrying itself, but the need for it. *Meaning* itself can be metaphorized as immobile, "crippled," delayed, in need of assistance. As such, metaphor should be seen as the space within language where the breakdown of meaning is addressed not with correction or seamless substitution, but with something else: where the holes in language are plugged with squares and triangles, or where we recognize the inaccessibility of all meaning-making.

Historically, much violence has been committed in the name of many of the metaphors that are currently used to describe or to label disability. As James Trent wrote in *Inventing the Feeble Mind*, a violent history, one that has included eugenics and forced institutionalization, is "unavoidably manifest in the words (for disability) we now find offensive" (1994, 5). One particularly damaging metaphor is the word *retarded*, which, when we examine it, suggests that some people think more slowly than others, as though anyone has ever timed the speed of thoughts moving through

---

8. And/or their meanings urge speakers to utter them in "funny" ways. And by "funny" I simply mean through the accentuation of unique consonant sounds, for instance, or through patterns like the attachment of the suffix *o*—mongo, weirdo, sicko. The effect is further dehumanization.

9. The American Sign Language (ASL) sign for cripple also depicts the offset movement of "crippled" legs. Likewise, a spoken word like *spastic*, whether by coincidence or not, has a sibilance that seems to mirror the medical definition of stiffened joints and muscles.

the brain, or as though some people are arrested in their development. Despite this, the word *retarded* is given a reified and unquestioned status as a scientific term. But as rhetoricians, we can point out the ways that all scientific meanings are based on metaphor and use this to interrogate and challenge other negative medical definitions of disability, revealing when possible their pseudoscientific origins and the nastier intentions embedded in their rhetoric. Then, on the other hand, we can also develop new metaphors that conceptualize disability more usefully, perhaps positively. Julia Miele Rodas offers a tremendously useful overview of the rhetorical constructedness of disability in her essay "On Blindness," after listing dozens of metaphors and sayings invoking blindness:

> What does this word "blind" really mean? Is it descriptive of an established condition, a measurable physical disability, the lack of sight? Or is it, perhaps, the naming of an ambiguous and ephemeral category, a linguistic gesture, an attempt to restrict and to codify, to define and delineate an arena of sensation that ultimately cannot be disciplined? Perhaps the most significant thing about blindness is this: That blindness is ultimately about language and, for this reason, it exists as a reflection of the culture that describes it, rather than as a representation of the condition and identity it ostensibly names. (2009, 116)

Lakoff and Johnson write that "[it] is not just that we have bodies and that thought is somehow embodied . . . [but] that the peculiar nature of our bodies shapes our very possibilities for conceptualization and categorization" (1999, 19). In this way, metaphor can be seen as the available means for generating new embodied realities.[10] So, from one angle, disability has been metaphorized comprehensively and almost always

---

10. Similarly, Richard Gwyn writes that "the study and pursuit of metaphor is a means of questioning the assumptions, descriptions and definitions of a literalistic and constricting outlook on reality" (1999, 219). Donna Haraway suggests that "metaphors are tools and tropes. . . . [T]he point is to learn to remember that we might have been otherwise, and might yet be, as a matter of embodied fact" (1997, 39). Lakoff and Johnson write, "People in power get to impose their metaphors" (1980, 57). Susan Leigh Star states that "power is about whose metaphor brings worlds together" (1995, 52).

negatively, yet it can also be re-metaphorized. From another angle, we can also say that the metaphorical nature of all language situates disability at its discursive center.

From the semantic to the syntactic level, from word meanings to word orders, disability also already has a nearly frozen set of rhetorical meanings and roles. Rick Carpenter's work on disability as genre and as "socio-rhetorical action" shows us that disability is itself a "rhetorical convention used to construct and regulate human actions and interactions." Unfortunately, disability is invoked rhetorically with a "taken-for-granted" "use value" that is conventional—as something negative, something to be transcended or overcome (2011, n.p.). But more than just having a narrative role, disability has a more structural, rhetorical dimension. This rhetorical dimension generally fits within a simplified, transactional view of rhetoric. For instance, there are ways to view rhetoric itself as the "cure" whenever meaning breaks down, or as the normative force to plug in when opportunity arises. There are words and narrative structures of disability, but there are also rhetorical tools that might be seen as generated from disability.

One key term for rhetoricians—a term that might also help to speak to this normative or curative rhetoric—is *exigence*. Lloyd Bitzer defines *exigence* as "an imperfection marked by urgency; it is a defect, an obstacle, something waiting to be done, a thing which is other than it should be" (1968, 3). Exigence thus is a crucial aspect of *every* rhetorical move. A key term for defining the rhetorical situation, exigence is the issue or problem that compels us to speak, communicate, or write in response. Exigence has a temporal element—it arises at a particular point in time, and we have a certain window of time in which to address it. The nature of the exigence also impacts what we can say to respond to it—we need to address it according to its shape and nature. Exigence has been called a flaw, defect, imperfection, abnormality. In general, the rhetorician has been constructed as the person who can diagnose the shape and nature of the exigent flaw and then fix it. In this view of rhetoric, disability itself shadows the entire transaction, as the specter of rhetorical failure. Yet we can see the "defect" of exigence as something we neither can nor would want to "cure" and perhaps may want (and may even *have*) to accentuate, transfer, transpose, or enter into dialogue with.

The urge is to say that disability rhetoric should correct exclusions, suppressions, and oppressions. This could even be an important facet of *this* project. Yet disability rhetoric should also be seen as an alternative ontology. As Tobin Siebers suggests, "Disability offers a challenge to the representation of the body—this is often said. Usually this means that the disabled body provides insight into the fact that all bodies are socially constructed—that social attitudes and institutions determine, far greater than biological fact, the representation of the body's reality." But, further, "the disabled body changes the process of representation itself. Different bodies require and create new modes of representation." This represents to Siebers a possibly serious shift in "body theory as usual" (2010, 54). It is this shift toward disability's role in the *making* of meaning that I hope to follow now, as I also carry along a sense of the mythical, social, and rhetorical construction *of* disability. I will focus in the last part of this chapter on this idea of bodily rhetoricity, linking the rhetoric of the body to disability, and finally offering a new rhetoric of bodily expression: *prosthesis*.

Rhetoric, language, and bodies can all be seen as disabled, and they change when we view them through disability. I have been suggesting that language voices the body, but that this voicing or writing of the body is never a perfect, or even a nearly perfect, communication: to embrace the writing of the body is to embrace difference, in the Derridean sense—it is to continually fail to signify, when failing to signify is our only means of making meaning. Disability studies gives us a way to value this imperfection of meaning as we value our imperfect bodies, as we come to see the disabled body as meaningful. In this way, embodied rhetoric is always *prosthetic*. Through the theory of prosthesis, this connection between rhetoric, embodiment, and disability can be persuasively illustrated.

Prosthesis

I now turn to prosthesis as my key example of *imperfect meaning*. David Wills defines *prosthesis* as that which "makes explicit the very break that constitutes the human body" (1995, 246). The word *pros*thesis has been confused with the Greek-derived *pro*thesis, meaning to prepose or propose, or the setting forth or placing of something in view, as with food on a table. Aristotle and others referred to the *pro*thesis as one of the key parts of a speech, as the statement of the proposition—also a setting forth—followed by the pistis, prooemium, and epilogue (see chapter 13 of his *Rhetoric* [1991b]).[11] Others define prothesis as "when the orator amplifies the thing that he [*sic*] is discussing by bringing up its opposite" (Gibson 2002, 204). You will notice that the first section of this book has this title—"Prothesis"—and this is a nod to the term's history as a discursive or rhetorical element. As a definition of an ongoing feature of any text, prothesis might be seen as both the act of physically baring the structure of an argument, setting the table, and at the same time as potentially duplicitous or misdirecting; in either case, prothesis is about relief and contrast and visibility, the ways that the margin and the center interact and compose one another, even semantically.

As Wills has shown, the word *pros*thesis was first used in English in 1553 to refer to the addition of a syllable to the beginning of a word.[12] Only in 1704 was the word *prosthesis* first used to refer to the replacement of a missing part on the body. But this history reveals the ways that prosthesis fuses linguistic and corporeal supplementarity in our embodiment, as beings with a grammar and biology, an idiom and anatomy, overlapping both in something material and much that is ineffable—in, as Smith and Morra word it, *"the delicate dialectical situation in which we find ourselves"* (2005, 11; emphasis in the original). Prosthesis reveals our "relation to and dependence upon the inanimate, the artificial" (Wills 1995, 246). The prosthetic body, "infirm or lacking, in need of the other," is "not the exception but the paradigm for the body itself" (ibid., 137). Therefore, "every rhetorical form that comes into effect is a prosthetic transfer" (ibid., 14). The fragmentation and incompleteness of discourse mirrors the body, the

---

11. The term is also used in the Greek Catholic and Eastern Orthodox churches to refer to a liturgy of preparation and/or the altar where this takes place. The liturgy entails the preparation of wine and bread for the eucharist and, because it is done privately and quietly, also symbolizes the hidden years of Jesus Christ's life.

12. You will notice that the epilogue to this book is given the title of "Prosthesis," another nod to the term's linguistic history, the after-the-fact addition of a section or syllable, a new limb, or a limn that nonetheless also precedes and alters the previous "whole."

shifting of signification echoes the malleability of the body, yet this makes communication possible.

Wills writes that, every rhetorical move is a "running hither and thither," and communication is always "dealing with the sideways as well as the forward momentum." In this way, prosthesis reveals the *mētis* of discourse—think of Hephaestus's sideways-facing feet. Importantly, this movement is "perhaps not structurally different from a natural gait," "an explicit infraction upon or departure from the straits of linearity" (ibid., 25). In this way, our bodily imperfections are ineluctably tied to our embodied communication, our embodied knowledges. Even when we strive for the norm—of language or body—the meaning we convey is conveyed only prosthetically, but this is much closer to the "natural gait" of both body and discourse. Wills suggests that the very essential and natural disarticulation between the fragmentation and partiality of our body and our cognition and our idealization of an objective view and an objectively knowable world constantly interact as we stumble for meaning. Especially when the prosthetic is seen as an added part of the body (or as a discursive addition to the word or the speech), the prosthetic then revokes the surety of wholeness and naturalness as given. Prosthesis emphasizes the obliqueness of thought and suggests that the disabled body is the engine for the creation of meaning. All attempts to impose logic, to create a linear grammar, will necessarily fail.

Mitchell and Snyder are the disability studies scholars who introduced Wills's theory of prosthesis to the field. Applying Wills's theory, they suggest that "disability's representational fate is not so much dependent on a tradition of negative portrayals as it is tethered to the act of meaning-making itself" (2001a, 6). For instance, all of the disability myths that I listed are what Mitchell and Snyder call *narrative prostheses*, a term "meant to indicate that disability has been used throughout history as a crutch upon which literary narratives lean for their representational power, disruptive potentiality, and analytical insight" (ibid., 49). Mitchell and Snyder work to expose the "faulty, or at least imperfect, prosthetic function" of such myths: *"the effort is to make the prosthesis show, to flaunt its imperfect supplementation as an illusion. The prosthetic relation of body to word is exposed as an artificial contrivance"* (ibid., 8; emphasis added).

The basic argument is that such myths cannot be smoothly utilized and accepted within a narrative—they expose a gap in experience and understanding. Of course, all of the "disability myths" from my first chapter are examples of this narrative prosthesis—and perhaps *dis ex machina* is the example par excellence.

This type of interpretive complexity directly addresses and moves us beyond the role of disability studies as "police officer" surveilling cultural representations. This more complex perspective also responds to Siebers's suggestion that disability studies can make an important shift away from body theory as usual. Further, what Wills is directly writing about in *Prosthesis* is rhetoric. Despite this, few (if any) rhetorical scholars have taken up his work. Thus, the theory of prosthesis presents the interface between a critical disability studies view of bodily meaning and rhetorical theory.

Indeed, the repeated motif of Wills's book is the presence of disability at the site of creation: he writes of Derrida on crutches, composing and decomposing *The Post Card* (1987); he repeatedly mentions his own father's prosthesis; he mentions Freud's cancerous jaw and his later works as well as Roussel's drug use and his exaggeration of literary forms. In each case, the disability both drives meaning and changes its shape. In this way, every text is about disability, in the sense that it issues forth from the unsteady rhetorical stance of prosthesis, which always *"fails* to return the incomplete body to the *invisible* status of a normative essence" (Mitchell and Snyder 2001a, 8; emphasis added). Mitchell and Snyder write that "literary forms, like disabled ones, are discordant in their unwillingness to replicate a more normative appearance" (ibid., 9).[13] Disability tropes and myths like those I cataloged in my first chapter function prosthetically because they can never neatly and tidily connect disability with evil, or pity, or shame. Their "shorthand" fails.

13. Augusto Boal, in his *Theatre of the Oppressed*, also writes about the "prosthesis of desire" that connects the audience to the protagonist of any dramatic work and that "prosthetically implants in the spectator, the desires of the protagonist" (2000, xviii). For Boal, this is a trick, connecting us to an idealized but reductive self. The prosthetic relationship is a failed one, even as it creates the feeling of embodied connection.

The same can be said for any linguistic form. Margrit Shildrick suggests that the leakiness of bodies, as discursive constructions, also equates with the "inherent leakiness of meaning in the *logos*" (2002, 84). Wills himself wrote that "writing is prosthesis par excellence" (1995, 27). The body and word relate, not in direct reference but in a series of prosthetic poses, "constantly shifting relations" (ibid., 249). The fact that discourse needs prosthesis, needs supplementation, reveals an imperfection that might be valued as a reflection of our partial, leaky, abnormal bodies.

Ernst Knapp, one of the first philosophers of technology, wrote that tools and technologies are "organ projections," material extensions of the body (1877, 44). He suggested that "in the tool the human continually produces itself. . . . [A] wealth of spiritual creations thus springs from hand, arm and teeth" (ibid., 45). He described tools as coming from specific body parts, as a shovel looks like a bent hand, or a knife is a large tooth, and refused the line of distinction between the tool and the tissue. John Dewey also saw tools and technologies as extensions of the body and as capable of reaching into the body: "There are things inside the body that are foreign to it, and there are things outside of it that belong to it" (1934, 75).[14]

Yet, as Jennifer Bay has argued, "one of the reasons why many theories of embodied rhetoric have not addressed technology might be that technology poses a threat to the perceived organic unity of the body" (2004, 937). The idea of a relationship with the world mediated by technology might be acceptable, but the idea of the *incorporation* of technology as part of this process is less easily accepted. We resist the idea that we may allow technologies to trespass beyond the boundaries of our bodies; we will not admit that we all extend ourselves through our relationships with others and our use of tools. We will not admit that our knowing of the world is fragmented because our knowing of our bodies and therefore ourselves is fragmented—or, rather, relies on constant augmentation.

14. In media studies, prosthesis is also seen as both extending our bodies and "amputating": any extension of the body through media also leads to another connected "numbness or blocking of perception" (McLuhan 1994, 43).

This speaks to the normate belief in the organic unity and autonomy of the body: our bodies are essential things; they do not really change. Our culture is obsessed with agentive and often artificial physical change toward ideality and at the same time petrified of "organic" and inevitable bodily change. Fear of disability is in some shape this fear of change, the fear that we are only temporarily able-bodied, a fear that the body is not static, rational, and whole (or a text that readily yields to controlled cosmetic revision).[15]

Furthermore, this is related to a fear of interdependence.[16] What we finally come to understand, in a strange looping around from what we want to believe about embodiment to what we do not know about our bodies and through our bodies, is that embodiment is a phenomenology defined not by boundaries, but by openings. We rely not just on technological, prosthetic incorporation, but also on others. As Janet Price and Margrit Shildrick argue, it is "in an acknowledgment of the permeability between bodies and between embodied subjects that disability studies

---

15. Recognizing this fear as characteristic of normativity and ableism allows us to recognize the need for rhetorics, across marginalized groups, which at once seize some control of the representation of bodies and spaces and at the same time acknowledge some diminished authority over the material fate of the body. We can think through alternative accounts of embodiment, and we can interrogate the cultural logic and biopolitics that are so resistant to mixture and difference and transformation. As Rosi Braidotti writes, "The problem is not to know who we are, but rather what we want to become, how to represent mutations, changes and transformations, rather than being in its classical modes" (2002, 2). This calls for a totally transitional phenomenology—a *mētis* phenomenology.

16. As Lewiecki-Wilson argues, by delimiting rhetorical bodies, "we may also be revealing our general anxiety [and thus our desire] to hold back the undifferentiated physical and social flow of language" and revealing an "unwillingness to enter into caring and committed intersubjective dependency with others and with the material world" (2003, 160). As Gail Weiss writes, we need to "negotiate the turbulence of our corporeal existence, a turbulence that cannot and should not be abjected from our body images, since it is precisely what enables us to meet the vicissitudes of our bodily life" (1999, 56). This turbulence is also central to a rhetorical study of embodiment, as it likewise characterizes the vicissitudes of our corporeal life.

might move forward" (2002, 62).[17] Importantly, this doubleness and divergence of bodily understanding is not something easily toggled and controlled and in this way gains subversive power.[18]

Rod Michalko investigates this interaction through his application
of Hannah Arendt's concept of the "two-in-one" to his relationship with
his guide dog, Smokie. He analyzes this relationship as a way to view
intersubjectivity more broadly. He suggests that "the world we generate
springs from our communication in the midst of the world and from our
movement through it" (1999, 187). He writes that "as a blind person, I exist
in the midst of 'many blindnesses,' which are expressed in the multitude
of opinions and collective representations my society has of blindness.
I am grist for this opinion mill. I receive opinions about blindness from
professionals such as ophthalmologists and rehabilitators. My friends
and acquaintances give me their opinions. Strangers comment about my
blindness as Smokie and I move through the world. The mass media contribute to collective representations. I am certainly for others and clearly

17. For instance, Butler writes that "what I call my 'own' gender appears at times as
something that I author or, indeed, own. But the terms that make up one's gender are, from
the start, outside oneself, beside oneself in a sociality that has no single author" (2004, 1).
In this way, gender, sex, sexuality, and ability, when and how they are rhetorically constructed, are socially negotiated, collaborative. Margrit Shildrick also specifically links the
concept of intercorporeality to sexuality. She suggests that "sexuality is inherently about
intercorporeality, about a potential merging of bodies, wills, and intentions . . . a physical
contact that is neither wholly predictable nor decidable." She then also argues that "it is precisely because of the inherent risk of losing self-control and self-definition that the domain
of sexuality is so highly disciplined and regulated" (2009b, 129).

18. Margrit Shildrick suggests that the body is "an always insecure and inconsistent
artifact, which merely mimics material fixity" (1997, 13). When the body is ignored, or when
it is constructed via definitions of what it *is not*, this leads to "not only the protection of
one's own body from encroachments, but a denial of the leakiness between one's self and
others" (ibid., 179). Yet, as Shildrick writes, "vulnerability is not a debased condition of the
other, but the very condition of becoming" (2002, 133). To understand embodiment is neither
strictly to examine the body, the body image, or the thinking of the body. It is also to examine the shadows and scissions that differentially constitute embodiment.

not just one" (ibid., 185).[19] Michalko's experience then describes the ways that the disabled body—and any body—is not just made up of many open possibilities, but also made by culture and by relationships.

This understanding of other bodies—and of our own body—as being made up of others *both* is an apt description of the experience of the living body *and* likely comes across as terrifically foreign.[20] We are powerfully conditioned to cordon off our own bodies and minds. But perhaps rhetoric itself can help to make sense of this interdependence: we can understand the rhetorical utterance as something shaped not solely by an author or speaker. Maybe the same can be said of the body. As Barbara Couture has argued, "We are designed to think through attending to others. . . . [We are] always already directed toward what is *other than*" (1998, 221; emphasis added).[21] From this idea of embodiment as dialogic and rhetorical, we can

---

19. Commenting on the tension around social constructionist and materialist approaches to disability, Michalko elaborates: "Blindness is only one of many things that a society and its people have ideas about. It is only one idea among a plurality of ideas. It is in the midst of this plurality that I, and all other blind persons, live. Privileging one version of blindness over another does not destroy or escape this plurality. The fact that the modern age conceives of blindness as a physical condition does not mean that blindness cannot be seen otherwise. Blindness as a physical condition is just one of many possible interpretations" (1999, 186).

20. One thesis we might try on then is the idea that embodiment cannot fully separate "I" from "you." For Husserl, via kinesthesia (sensing our own movement, thus sensing change, moving through the continual abstraction of the lived body), we experience movement as we direct it. I would therefore assert that this is a sense in which embodiment is prosthetic—we never experience movement "purely," but rather sense our bodies both as movers *and* as movable. Husserl also suggests that the human "I" includes the living body, which includes the physical body *and* relations to other bodies, which, in turn, are related the same way. He writes that while only "I" can directly experience my own intentional movement, "I understand another physical body as a living body in which another I is embodied and wields" control over that body (1958, 2, 62).

21. Further, embodiment is rhetorically intersubjective: "Meaning evolves from continuous interaction." The movement of consciousness is "embodied through speaking [or discoursing] with others" (Couture 1998, 94). Couture concludes that rhetoric "is a conscious embrace of the Other . . . embody[ing] in language our shared consciousness of the world" (ibid., 95).

move on to think about embodiment and culture or society—and to frame these relationships in terms of norms, and in terms of both constraint and enablement. The shared word allows for the shared body, and vice versa. In this way discourse shapes embodiment (and the inverse). This shaping is rhetorical. Available means—discursive and material—are negotiated socially.[22] We are intercorporeal and concorporeal. Language is one of the key vectors of this contact and touch and exchange between bodies.[23]

It is not that disability rhetoric is always already intercorporeal: in fact, disabled bodies and minds are touched, shaped, manipulated by others far too much. This should be acknowledged so that, for instance, resistance to compulsory sociality can be recognized as a possible disability rhetoric, even in a world in which the individuating and isolating

22. The work of Silvan Tomkins offers another angle for approaching this idea of intercorporeality. Tomkins suggests that perceiving is "not partly some mediate process but entirely so" (1995, 144). For instance, Tomkins suggests that a sense like vision is an "intermittent source of stimulation for the body image because what is figural in vision is rarely one's own body." As Tomkins writes, "One looks out of [her own] body but rarely at it" (ibid., 248). This is the same sort of principle at work in body dysmorphia. This outward focus can lead to what we commonly call "negative body image"—it is the reason we can believe our bodies are abnormal, that we are too fat or too skinny because we literally *feel* skinnier or (more likely) fatter than we may be, "materially." Tomkins suggests that "the body image is, to begin with, usually an exaggeration of characteristics about which the individual is hyperaware with pride or shame or fear" (ibid., 250). These same characteristics are what we look for in others, and the constant comparison between our own bodies and those of others blurs the boundary between the two. We constantly re-create a feeling for our own body (in part) by referencing those around us. Clearly, this is a theory necessary to a reconsideration of disability—especially as it introduces a clear idea of how bodies are (partially) socially constructed. Looking at a disabled mind and body as *not mine* is a (negative) formulation of that other body as well as a (defensive) material formulation of your own body. This concept is also important to a rhetorical study of embodiment and to the creation of an embodied rhetoric.

23. Elizabeth Grosz suggests that "a body is produced from other bodies, and its cohesion and continued existence and integrity as a body are contingent on its ability to glean energy from other bodies" (2005, 192). In this way, "a body reproduces itself not only biologically but through its self-representations and the rigors of its practice" (ibid., 193).

construction of disability can be used against people with disabilities.[24] However, my argument is that all knowing arises out of disability, as does meaning. We *are*, only because language, rhetoric, and embodiment are communally not normal, not "able."[25] This essential imperfection often means that we do need others, or we need access to other modes and discourses of being, and this makes our existence essentially prosthetic.

Despite these rhetorical possibilities, the theorization of prosthesis, Vivian Carol Sobchack argues, "has become fetishized and 'unfleshed-out,'" *prosthesis* becoming a "catchword that functions vaguely as the ungrounded and 'floating signifier' for a broad and variegated critical discourse," emerging from the desire to disrupt the "traditional notion that the body is whole," while at the same time it "is predicated on a naturalized sense of the body's previous and privileged wholeness" (2004, 209–10). Sobchack's objections align with a disability studies perspective—as I said earlier, not just challenging the attribution of disability to marginalized groups, but challenging the construction of disability itself; challenging not just social norms, but the function of normativity.

In fact, actual prostheses, like those discussed by David Serlin in his influential book on the subject, *Replaceable You* (2004), have been viewed as compensating for a bodily lack and/or as a signal of lack itself. As mentioned in one of the snapshots of my introduction, after World War II, there were huge advances made in prosthetic technology. This signaled a shift

24. See, for instance, Julia Miele Rodas's "'On the Spectrum': Rereading Contact and Affect in *Jane Eyre*" in which she argues that "without the strength and will to resist the world and build a functional private space, the autistic individual is prone to imprisonment and extermination. Resistance to the encroaching world, and to tyrannical expectations of compulsory sociality, is necessary to autistic survival and self-determination" (2008, para. 20). This needs to be seen alongside the intersubjectivity and agentive interdependence that some other people with disabilities may need for survival.

25. Rosi Braidotti explains this nicely, suggesting that "language is not only and not even the instrument of communication but a site of symbolic exchange that links us together in a tenuous yet workable web of mediated misunderstandings. . . . [A]ll knowledge is situated, that is to say partial; we are all stuttering for words, even when we speak 'fluently'" (1994, 14).

in bodily attitudes—the "wounded hero" was to be incorporated back into society and made industrially productive. Yet more recently, "wounded warriors" from Iraq and Afghanistan have been represented much differently: their injuries and prostheses are often understood as symbols of unjust and ill-conceived missions. If we look back to my chart of disability myths, the injured World War II soldier was forced to overcome, while the Vietnam War vet with a disability or the current "wounded warrior" is viewed as a signifier of a social problem (still forced to overcome, but in many ways less "celebrated" because these recent wars have been more controversial).[26] Thus, it becomes dangerous to view prosthesis purely as a metaphor or trope—we can overwrite the real experience of people with disabilities. Yet we also come to understand, through the shifting cultural value of prosthetics, that the material and the rhetorical always interact.

I hope to show that these shifting prosthetic relations with respect to meaning, the body, and disability are the paradigm for rhetoric itself, the power of discourse always already generated from disability—not always directed toward a return to some innate biological state of purity and ability. Rhetoric "as disability" is useful so long as it disrupts this return, this tendency. To rephrase Sobchack and answer her objection, I am advocating for a sense of the body's partiality and incompleteness. This is not to say that we are all disabled, or that rhetoric is disabled, but to embrace a nonnormative discourse/materiality, modestly proposing that such signifiers be tabled not as the natural inverse of wholeness in a normative matrix, but rather as a valorization of alternative "fleshing out" and potential resignification, a shift of meaning and value that might also mitigate the oppression of bodies with disabilities. Kellner asks historians to get the story "crooked," by recognizing the rhetoricity of history. I suggest that this lesson can also reveal the generative crookedness of all discourse.

My definitions of rhetorical embodiment move between models of disability identity—perhaps in dangerous ways. Certainly, I want to

---

26. The term *wounded warrior* was actually created by these men who were injured in combat in recent wars—they did not want to be called disabled.

admit that many people in the disability community would reject, and rightly so, arguments that all bodies are fragmented, that affirming disability is a means of recognizing all of our real bodies and embodied experiences (in relation to norms), and that all rhetorical expression is prosthetic. Of course, I am not the only body out on this limb. Instead of shying away from the politics (or the phenomenology) of disability, I have tried to work *through* my (pros)theses about embodiment to show how these hard questions in fact clarify my project. I want to suggest that these positions on materiality, social construction, and agency do not have to clash, nor do they have to fuse together into a homogeneous compound, and thus negate the uniqueness and situatedness of the disabled body, or of each of our different bodies. Instead, there may be ways that perspectives on embodiment decenter the logic of equality, of a mean, ideal or normal embodiment, even if the final result can never be full autonomy. Indeed, I hope this examination calls into question the possibility and desirability of autonomy, proposing intercorporeality as a generative possibility. Perhaps, examining embodied knowledge might reveal how we rely upon disability to make sense of the world we move through—not disability as our inverse image, but disability as the fount of human creativity, erupting from those lines of subduction where our embodiment clashes with our desire to ignore it, reduce it, simplify it. I want to offer some uncertainty and ambiguity to you, to suggest this is something you might feel.

Generative Imperfections

Classical perspectives on the generative potential of imperfection can be read against the grain of our idealized, canonized, classical view of the rhetor. For instance, when the Homeric hero Odysseus is at his most cunning, it is when he begins a speech badly, when he appears as a "witless man," an *aphrona* (AFF-RONA) (Detienne and Vernant 1978, 22). We commonly read this as an example of a performance, a perhaps ironic, winking portrayal of what Odysseus is not. Yet this has also been read as an embodiment of the classical idea of *anmut*: "not a property of bodies and persons but a term for the effects they produce in interaction with others" (Humphreys 1999, 126). *Anmut* (AN-MUTT), as a concept, holds that bodily attitudes are mutable, socially constructed.[27] Odysseus did not have a perfect body, but he had *anmut*, the ability to make his body signify in relation to the bodies in his audience. In speeches he "act[ed] out an image of the common citizen," acting like a boor, hitching up his belt, in a physicalized claim to speak for the common man (ibid., 128). *Anmut* holds that bodies are not static things; they are the product of the interaction with other bodies. We have neglected this classical tradition—not just of valuing the rhetoricity of the body, but also of opening the sphere of bodily rhetorical values to include less overtly "able" formations of self.

Why can we not imagine that Odysseus is rhetorically successful because he has captured his audience, he has become consubstantial with the Greek polis in which, as Martha Rose, Fareed Haj, and Jacques Stiker remind us, disability was very common? I am willing to perform this retelling with some modesty, understanding that many will reject the possibility that a rhetor's mistakes are just as generatively rhetorical as his triumphs, that his inhabitation of "common" bodily positions resonates rhetorically. Certainly, in Homer, violence against characters with bodily flaws was significant. Yet, as I will show, the rhetorical plasticity of myth was also significant in its performed context. Whereas *aphrona* was likely pejorative, other terms for disability in the period are more flexible—suggesting not downward comparison but dynamic lateral association.

As mentioned earlier, Demosthenes, the most quoted orator in Hermogenes's *Art of Rhetoric*, widely esteemed as the greatest rhetorician of the period, if not of all time, was also disabled according to a narrow reading of the idea of ability. First of all, he was represented as soft and effeminate. Aeschines repeatedly labels Demosthenes a "queer," and as MacDowell argues, "there was also gossip about homosexual affairs."[28] He suggests

27. *Anmut* is also the German word for grace or graciousness.

28. Aeschines uses a Greek term that historians have now reconstructed as connoting something like the modern epithet *queer*. (See also Davidson 2009.) MacDowell suggests that Aeschines's insults were not common to Greek oratory: "It is not the case that all Athenian politicians are alleged by their opponents to be queers" (2009, 23). At the same time, as Nicole Loraux points out, the ancient Greeks took "delight in dividing humanity into womanly women, virile men, men-women, and women who act like men" (1995, 42). So,

that "perhaps Demosthenes really was bisexual. Alternatively he may have had an . . . effeminate manner, which made the accusations seem plausible even if they were untrue. On the available evidence we cannot decide between these possibilities" (2009, 23).

Importantly, in a connected but equally nebulous way, Demosthenes was represented as lame, a stutterer with a lisp and an inability to control his gestures. Yet as Martha Rose suggests, it is quite likely that Demosthenes's stutter was never a weakness. As Rose points out, we have latched onto Demosthenes's story as one of overcoming: we believe that through great labor, he overcame his impediment, training it out of his speech by walking up mountains declaiming with pebbles in his mouth.[29]

---

any consideration of the ancient rhetorical construction of the body might also and always examine ancient rhetorical negotiations of the "abnormally" sexed or gendered body. Both prefigure a limited range of rhetorical possibilities, yet also provide models that offer more critical and more flexible strategies for the rhetorical understanding of any body. This also allows us to follow the imperatives of feminists such as Mary McIntosh and Fausto-Sterling, who argue that it is important to show that "all forms of human sexuality have a history" (Fausto-Sterling 2000, 13). When I argue that Demosthenes's stutter may have been rhetorically useful and powerful, I am also arguing that his "effeminacy" could also have been rhetorically useful and powerful.

29. In her book *Bodily Arts* (2005), Debra Hawhee tells the story of Demosthenes twice and uses the story to argue that bodily impropriety *can* be overcome—and therefore implies that disability *should* be overcome—and that if it isn't, the rhetorical body is invalidated. Yet the possibility that Demosthenes's difference could have queered his bodily/rhetorical performance in a generative sense is not addressed—indeed, any such transgressive possibility is ignored. James Fredal, similarly, calls Demosthenes the "Orator Imperfectus" and suggests that, as illustrated by his flaws, "one crack in a well-constructed persona could be titanic" (2006, 220). While Fredal richly describes the layers of practice, action, and performance that go into crafting this embodied persona, and which Demosthenes employed to "overcome" his fears and deficiencies, he concludes that "because speech was also always action (delivery), no one with a speech defect, or who was 'soft' or lame could, by definition, be a good speaker" (ibid., 244). In these interpretations, despite the warnings of other classical historians like Rose, we are to read Demosthenes's "lame" body as something to overcome, never as something rhetorical, and never as something we might all identify with—these tensions are to be erased with labor. Thus, the norms are not challenged but reinforced as they are incorporated.

Craig Cooper summarizes stories from a range of classical sources when he writes that Demosthenes was believed to have "exercised his voice by discoursing as he ran, strengthened his breathing by reciting speeches is single breaths and practiced his gesturing before a mirror [as well as] even more bizarre practices: retiring to a cave, shaving half his head to shame himself into not coming out, and hanging a sword over his shoulder to correct a shoulder spasm" (2000, 226).

Yet Cooper and others, including Pomeroy, argue that "Demosthenes became a celebrated example of overcompensation for a physical handicap" (ibid., 173). These stories of compensation are "the romantic fictions of biographers . . . and there is little in their report that should be trusted" (ibid., 226). Martha Rose likewise reminds us that this narrative of overcoming has more than likely been imported into the past, a projection of our desire to see heroes overcome disability, rather than to understand disability heroically (2003, 2). In her unraveling of the stories of this orator, she points out that "the physical condition that barred people from oratory in Greece was that of being female, not necessarily that of having a speech impairment. . . . [A]ll men had the potential to speak well" (ibid., 63).

Of course, when we examine more closely, we understand that this is not altogether true either. Thanks to histories such as Joy Ritchie and Kate Ronald's *Available Means* (2001), we see that women such as Diotima, the female philosopher and tutor, may well have spoken. If they could not speak in public, they could speak very persuasively in private and to Athens's political and intellectual leaders in the fourth century BCE. Other women, such as Aspasia, whose name is mentioned in the writings of Plato, Xenophon, and Aristophanes, were instrumental in the composition of some of the period's most famous speeches (see Kahn 1963; Plato 1961c). These women played a key role in the instruction of the period's best orators, including Socrates himself (Ritchie and Ronald 2001, 1–15).

Regardless of this generalization about gender, Rose goes on to suggest "that Demosthenes would be known to the modern world for his rhetorical skills would no doubt have pleased him," but "that he would be known for stuttering would have surprised him" (2003, 65). In this example, we gain much from understanding the rhetorical constructions of disability, the stock and stereotypical stories that disability studies scholars have revealed and critiqued for their role in managing the fears of the (supposedly) able-bodied. Given the knowledge that "overcoming" is one of the most prevalent societal tropes of disability, we can question the veracity of this story, or at least we can understand its negative effect. Overcoming could be a demand *we* place on the *narrative*, as likely as it is to be a description of what Demosthenes actually did. The labored triumph over disability results in the final devaluation of disability. Holding on to stories like these also tells people with disabilities today to get to work eradicating their impairments. If disability is not overcome, this must be because the individual is lazy (see my chart of disability myths from chapter 1). Such narratives also assuage the fears of the supposedly able-bodied—if they are ever disabled, they will be able to overcome it.

The Greek word *pseilos* (SI-LOSS), most commonly used to describe Demosthenes's "impediment" and which we translate as "faltering speech," can also denote bad manners or, simply, the meaning behind written words. In the latter instance, the idea of a stutter suggests the deconstruction of rhetorical norms based on narrow customs (ibid., 57). Derrida would certainly agree that to communicate is to stutter—as would David Wills, suggesting that the stutter and the limp are analogous.

As Brenda Jo Brueggeman writes, "Throughout its history, rhetoric has . . . *itself* been denounced as a disabling pursuit . . . crippling an audience's ability to deliberate rationally or to follow the truth." In this way, a certain form of Platonist thinking suggests that it is rhetoric that is the very problem—that rhetoric is disabling. As Brueggeman argues, "The concern for rhetoric, from Plato forward, has been how the speaker "trips up" the audience" (2005, 23). But her argument (and mine) is that this "crippling" or "tripping up" also creates a complex and meaningful rhetorical relationship between orator and audience, one in which "disability critiques, even as it delivers" rhetoric; "disabilities [can] allow [speakers] to make [their] points even more persuasively" as a "compelling antispectacle" against perfection (ibid., 25). Demosthenes was not the only famous orator with a "speech impediment": Aristotle himself and Alcibiades were also said to speak with a lisp, and for every account that mocks this impediment, there are other historical accounts that argue this speech pattern was rhetorically effective.

Alcibiades's lisping speech in Plato's *Symposium* offers a particularly potent example of the rhetorical power of nonnormative and ambiguous ability *and* sexuality. He tells a story about his love for Socrates that leaves Socrates speechless—as Wohl argues, Alcibiades "flaunts the asymmetry of unrepressed sexuality and the irresolvable difference within—being *in* difference." He wears a strong feminine scent and celebrates the "holes, protrusions and paroxysms of the body" (1998, 30). Alcibiades's speech is most basically about his unrequited love for Socrates—the many ways he has tried to attract his attentions, even crawling up under his cloak and falling asleep, only to discover disappointedly that Socrates had not taken advantage of him. All of Alcibiades's praise for Socrates is tinged with the bitterness of these rejections. Importantly, he is not praising or defining love; he is narrating it, and not very appealingly. He swings into the conversation and refuses to allow the Hermaphrodite myth to whitewash sexual difference or to represent a lack of desire, instead performing a sexual role that leads to speechlessness, perhaps because the normative symbolic economy has been disrupted. As Kevin Ohi argues, this speech reveals "the homoerotic basis of [all] cultural transmission": "not to say its homoerotic content but its persistent understanding of transmission as synonymous with failed or thwarted transmission" (2011, 358). Alcibiades's speech is a wonderful, embodied, queer failure.[30]

---

30. The myth of Hermaphrodite is also taken up in the *Symposium*, and the story is used by Aristophanes to pose an original and essential, perfect fusion between men and women, two equal halves, symmetrical, a reduction to sameness. Aristophanes does not refer directly to Hermes or Aphrodite, but instead suggests that "human nature was originally one and we were a whole, and the desire and pursuit of the whole is called love. There was a time, I say, when we were one, but now because of the wickedness of mankind god has dispersed us" (Plato 1961f, 473). He suggests that, without much mention of the fate of women (except to say that women who took too much womanliness away in the division tended to be too much with other women), men tended in two directions away from the state of original unity. If they took away too much that was feminine from the union, they would never be satisfied; these individuals would be aimless and overly desirous. But if they took away enough man from the union, they might seek and find something akin to the pure union that they had fallen from. In the words of Aristophanes, these manly men,

In this way Alcibiades's or Demosthenes's *pseilos* becomes an important rhetorical ability or advantage. *Pseilos* is not unlike the word *apate* (AP-AT-AY), which Susan Jarratt suggests was also a term for the mysterious transfer of meaning from thought to expression, for the play of signification. *Apate*, in her definition, is an exploration of how probable arguments can cast doubt on conventional truths. Both *apate*, deception, and *ate* (AT-AY), human blindness, have nonpejorative meanings and roles in the making of meaning. *Apate* means "the emotional experience between reality and language" (1991, 55). *Ate*, then, is the human condition that locates us within that space. Blindness or stuttering, in these conceptions, serve to remind us of the partiality of rhetorical expression. Recall Derrida's statement that writing "has a blindness to do with it . . . hasn't a damn sight to do with it" (1981, 135). This is not a condemnation of

---

"being slices of the original man . . . hang about men and embrace them, and they are themselves the best of boys and youths, because they have the most manly nature" (ibid., 475). These manly men become statesmen, "uninfected" by femininity.

In this Platonic dialogue, Socrates then repeats a speech taught to him by Diotima, the famous female orator. The speech is read commonly as an origin myth that removes the maternal role of woman, renouncing the body. Socrates's assumption of Diotima's voice, and the message that this speech conveys, reinforces the elision of the feminine. The performance then stands in contrast to Aristophanes's posing of the perfect union, yet the speech seems to be in agreement with his conclusions—that masculinity impels virtue and even procreation, that femininity is too bodily and desirous (Wohl 1998, 28). Two stories, one removing procreative power from the feminine, one renouncing the feminine influence within the ambiguously gendered body, seem confluent in their rhetorical purposes. Yet the conclusions are disorienting—it is difficult to be sold on the efficacy of measuring manliness, especially as the rejection/abjection of femininity seems like a case of protesting too much. The effect is that the intersexual figure represents purity, while Hermaphrodite also represents what Wohl labels a "confusion at the origin of desire" (ibid., 19).

We cannot jump too quickly to the conclusion that these stories function only as grotesque threats of disfigurement aimed at the sexually improper, or as tales of compulsory heterosexuality, because the final speaker of the *Symposium*—Alcibiades—asks us to come to a different conclusion. These dialogues and mythologies then present some evidence of the rhetorical wrangling over the significance of the body, as well as the powerful use of the sexed and sexualized body rhetorically, and of the flaunting of the flaws of the body.

writing as sensorily deprived; it is an honest appraisal of the partiality *and* embodiment of communication. In this way, then, we move away from an idea of disability as deficit. Instead, disability is the very possibility (and concurrently the uncertainty) of human knowledge. It follows that in this world, people with disabilities can be more than just rhetorical symbols. This represents an important turn for disability studies theory, as it also provides a new paradigm for rhetorical theory.

A Repertoire and Choreography of Disability Rhetorics

THE GOAL OF *DISABILITY RHETORIC* is to instantiate an expanded sense and a more inclusive framework through which we might view the rhetorical body. In introducing terms like *aphrona*, *anmut*, *apate*, and *pseilos*, I am not trying to establish a new lexicon, but rather I am working to show that we could choose to view a history in which disability and rhetoricity were consubstantial, in which this connection was fully theorized, when we screen our stories again. In the next chapter I will expand on these enabling approaches to embodiment through the stories of *mētis*. But, as I promised at the beginning of the last chapter, I am also in the midst of a crucial turn to proposing models and theories that situate disability as meaningful and as meaning-making, and I want to further harness this momentum.

Thus far I have packaged a condensed overview of disability in antiquity, at the supposed "origins of civilization." But I am actually much more interested in establishing the body as the origin and epistemological home of all meaning-making. In the next chapter, I will look from prosthesis to *mētis*, the connected rhetorical concept that I situate as best affirming the body's meaningful and powerful partiality. But before I move on, I will create a parallel lexicon, a mirror litany to stand alongside my earlier chart of disability tropes or myths, the majority of which showcased the ways that a society can get disability "wrong." Here, I will propose a range of disability *rhetorics*: means of conceptualizing not just how meaning is attached to disability, but to view the knowledge and meaning that disability *generates*. In response to my archive of myths, I will offer a repertoire of rhetorics. Like the *Diagnostic and Statistical Manual*, this inventory labels a range of rhetorical conditions, yet frames them as potential rather than as deficit. Part of what I want to do with this list is to remind the reader that disability rhetoric, which may at times in this book seem like a historical or theoretical field, describes also the ways we move with and through and toward disability *all the time*. The list should cue us to the rhetorical power and possibility of these moves.

Jeanne Fahnestock defines all "rhetorical figures" as the departure from the expected order of words; Fontanier also claims that figurative language is a departure from "degree zero" language (Fahnestock 1999, 17; Fontanier 1977, 64). In this way, all rhetorical figures are nonnormative or "disabled": they are the abnormality that fires newness and invites novel and multiple interpretations. The rhetorical figures in this list are selected for their potential to generate nonnormative meanings. Lining these up in a list may seem terribly Aristotelian, may seem like a reduction or a limited schematics. But my hope is that instead, they are used as tools that readers will make their own, adapt, and activate. While the disability myths I listed might be seen as analogous to Mitchell and Snyder's "anatomy" of body genres, this inventory of rhetorics hopefully forms an accessible choreography.

My list of disability myths from the first chapter might have been read as policing all of the ways that we stereotype and stigmatize disability, challenging only the disablism that negatively constructs disability experience, and thus failing in some ways to interrogate ableism.[1] Yet that list was created in many ways to be held alongside this list of rhetorics (I was thinking sideways). These disability rhetorics do offer challenges to ableist normativity, challenges that range from overt to carefully nuanced. But they also offer available means and ways to move, ways to make meaning by recirculating power through the body.

I will first present the rhetorics in brief form in a chart, and then offer a lengthier exploration of the rhetorics to end this interchapter.

1. I borrow this distinction between disablism and ableism from Fiona Kumari-Campbell. Yet I would suggest that these rhetorics create what she calls "disability imaginaries," reconceptualizing knowing so that we might "think/speak/gesture and feel different landscapes not just for being-in-the-world but [also for the] conduction of perception, mobilities and temporalities" (2009, 15).

Rhetoric	Description	Example
Disability Forensic	Forensic or judicial rhetoric is one of three overarching genres of rhetoric identified by Aristotle, dealing with the truth or falsity of past events.	For disability studies, work in this rhetorical genre has largely taken the form of revisionist histories, or just historical work that addresses the ways that disability has been actively submerged or ignored. The scholarship covers a lot of ground, and continues to expand: from Stiker's and Rose's works on antiquity to powerful histories of more modern legacies like ugly laws, institutionalization, and sterilization (Schweik 2009; Trent 1994).
Disability Deliberation	Deliberative rhetoric (again one of Aristotle's genres) seeks to determine what actions should be taken in the future, and the most recognizable form of this genre is the political speech.	Perhaps the goal of disability deliberation is to search for and invoke disability futures that could be welcomed. In this way, we might see some of the science fiction novels of Philip K. Dick as forms of disability deliberation.
Disability Epideictic	The final of Aristotle's three genres, epideictic rhetoric deals with praise and blame through commemoration and celebration.	A contemporary genre of epideictic is the biopic: the biographical film. And there is perhaps no other film genre more highly populated by disabled characters. In this book I discuss *The King's Speech* and *The Iron Lady* at great length, but a long range of other (not

Rhetoric	Description	Example
		surprisingly award-winning) biopics are also disability epideictics: *A Beautiful Mind, My Left Foot, Ray, The Aviator, The Sea Inside,* and HBO's *Temple Grandin.* These films generally adhere to disability myths in order to assess the virtue and honor of their subjects.
Pseilos	The Greek word *pseilos,* which we translate as "faltering speech," can also denote bad manners or, simply, the meaning behind written words.	I have already detailed the rhetorical potential of the *pseilos* of Demosthenes and Alcibiades, and I will return to the rhetorical significance of the "stutter" in my final chapter on *The King's Speech.*
Apate and Ate	Both *apate,* deception, and *ate,* human blindness, have nonpejorative meanings and roles in the making of meaning. *Apate* means "the emotional experience between reality and language" (Jarratt 1991, 55). *Ate,* then, is the human condition that locates us within that generatively doubtful and thus creative space.	In the *Encomium of Helen,* Gorgias speaks specifically of *apate,* suggesting that that we cannot have perfect memory of the past, we cannot be completely present to ourselves, and we cannot foresee the future—thus we need poetry and art, words and images, and thus these things are powerful (Ijsseling 1995, 342).
Anmut	The classical idea of *anmut* is "not a property of bodies and persons but a term for the effects they produce	We have been told that Odysseus did not have a perfect body, but he had *anmut,* the ability to make

Rhetoric	Description	Example
	in interaction with others" (Humphreys 1999, 126).	his body signify in relation to the bodies in his audience and thus build his authority. *Anmut* offers a way to reconsider disability—not as something an audience will reject or stigmatize, but as something that a diverse audience is receptive to and accepting of.
Ekphrasis (*ECK-FRAY-SISS*)	Refers to the ways that one form of art can be used to illuminate and accentuate the properties of another. Most often, this happens when a visual medium is described with words. *Ekphrasis* is also an artistic process—as when a poem is used to describe a painting.	We should understand *ekphrasis* as a way to make visual mediums and information accessible to people with visual impairments, or, moreover, a way to add rhetorical value to images by using words to work through them. An example would be the "visual descriptions" used at art galleries and performances.
Sitpoint Theory	Standpoint theory is the idea that one's social positioning greatly influences their perspectives and that thus we could look to marginalized positions for forms of new knowledge and challenges to dominant norms. Rosemarie Garland-Thomson coined this neologism to make standpoint theory more accessible to disability (1997a, 21).	Sitpoint theory would show that knowledge creation is always rhetorical—a flow of power through bodies— and thus disability is both usefully and "naturally" at the center of a process of knowing. Garland-Thomson suggests that Nancy Mairs's unique perspective in her memoir, *Waist-High in the World* (1997), is a perfect example of sitpoint theory.

Rhetoric	Description	Example
Situated Knowledges	An elaboration of the concept of standpoint epistemology: "Subjugated standpoints are preferred because they seem to promise more adequate, sustained, objective, trans-forming accounts of the world" (Haraway 1991, 191).	One example of disability as "situated knowledge" offering a "transformative account" of the world is that many of the technologies developed first for people with disabilities (such as optical character recogni-tion, pagers, texting, or e-mail) have reshaped com-munication for all.
Dissoi Logoi (DISS-OY LO-GOY)	The Sophistic concept (often attributed to Protagoras) of *dissoi logoi* means, literally, "different words" and is interpreted, most commonly, as arguing from both sides or making the weaker argu-ment stronger.	On the most basic level, disability rhetoric can be about refusing the normate ordering of the world. Dis-ability rhetoric can also refuse to agree with any one story, version, explanation, or body. To make the weaker argument stronger, with respect to disability, is to begin by situating disability as desirable.
Least Dangerous Assumption	This idea has become para-digmatic within disability studies. In 1984 Anne Don-nellan proposed the prin-ciple of the "Presumption of Competence" as the "least dangerous assumption" that can be made about people with disabilities.	We can recognize how the least dangerous assump-tion might function in the sphere of education or in the workplace, where dangerous assumptions about ability structure access. Legislation like the Americans with Disabilities Act might even be considered to legally codify the least dangerous assumption.

Rhetoric	Description	Example
Most Generous Interpretation	The most generous interpretation can be viewed as related to the least dangerous assumption. I situate the most generous interpretation as a heuristic for responding to negative portrayals of disability, at least temporarily, by considering the "good intentions" that may have inspired them.	For instance, the pity and charity response to disability continues to be tremendously popular. In order to understand how to counteract that propensity, we might need to begin by allowing that those millions who give money to fund a cure for disability are well meaning, and we might harness these good intentions to convince them that it would be better to support the rights of disabled people than to eradicate them.
Defective Detectives	"Defective detection" should be understood as a disability rhetoric, something akin to a heretical heuristics or an interpretive noncompliance: what are the nonnormative ways to understand any given text? What are the nonnormative—or even the least normative—means to express yourself in any given situation?	As Hoppenstand and Browne (1983) have shown, the "defective detective" was a key presence in pulp fiction in the United States in the thirties. Sherlock Holmes and a number of Poe's characters can also be seen as "defective detectives," as they solved crimes through strange, unexpected, and unconventional means.
Strategic Ignorance	Strategic ignorance refers to "the ways expressions of ignorance can be wielded strategically by groups living under oppression as a way of gaining information, sabotaging work, avoiding	Those things that may seem to make us "abnormal" can also serve to confuse a context, set the world on its side, disarm, and this can then be used to our advantage. People with disabilities

Rhetoric	Description	Example
	or delaying harm, and preserving a sense of self" (Bailey 2007, 77). For people with disabilities, strategic ignorance can also be used as a refusal of forced forms of sociality and interaction.	might grab the momentum of society's push to pity them, infantilize them, or speak for them and reposition these oppressive views until they are themselves in a position of strength.

Disability Forensics

Forensic or judicial rhetoric is one of three genres of rhetoric identified by Aristotle, dealing with the truth or falsity of past events. For disability studies, work in this rhetorical genre has largely taken the form of revisionist histories, or just historical work that addresses the ways that disability has been actively submerged or ignored. The scholarship covers a lot of ground and continues to expand: from Stiker's and Rose's works on antiquity to powerful histories of more modern legacies like ugly laws, institutionalization, and sterilization (Schweik 2009; Trent 1994).

Mitchell and Snyder recognize the literary genre of "new historical" criticism, and I would suggest that they are also discussing forensics: "Historical revisionists argue that physical and cognitive difference was the rule rather than the exception of historical experience" (2001c, 205).

Forensics also includes *apologia* (defenses) and *kategoria* (accusations). Certainly, disability forensics both rescues and defends disabled figures and recognizes and impugns a long record of disablism, oppression, and persecution. But importantly, a disability forensics would not just offer "corrections" to the historical record, but would unearth the interestedness of the record keepers, never limiting the multiplication of meanings and archives. In short, disability forensics employs a sideways, skeptical, *mētis* approach to the truth and falsity of past events. As you will recognize from my analysis of the myths of Hephaestus and Metis in the next two chapters, and from my analysis of the film *The King's Speech* in the final chapter, disability forensics assumes that there are always hidden stories of disability, that there are many reasons these stories may have been hidden, and the job of the disability rhetorician is both to recirculate the hidden stories and to recognize values recalibrating through their submersion and their reinvocation. Disability rhetoric enables history to move differently.

Disability Deliberation

Deliberative rhetoric (again one of Aristotle's genres) seeks to determine what actions should be taken in the future, and the most recognizable form of this genre is the political speech. As the rhetorical genre that deals most specifically with the future, the role of disability in deliberative rhetoric is perhaps the most vexed. Simply, disability is seen as the very absence of futurity, or as the very least desirable future, and thus deliberative rhetoric invokes disability to characterize everything that was undesirable about the past, everything that the future must overcome.

In one of the most famous political speeches of the twentieth century, US President Warren Harding's 1920 speech "Readjustment," Harding used (or perhaps even invented) the term *normalcy* to describe an idealized state, attainable once America was again at peace and had closed its doors to foreigners (see Murray 1973). The rhetoric of an idealized American "normalcy" is what allowed Harding and others to paint the international world as irrational, crooked, impaired, while the new America would be straight and sure on its feet.[2] Harding suggested that America had been viewing the world with "vision impaired in a cataclysmal war. . . . Poise has been disturbed, and nerves have been racked, and fever has rendered men irrational." He concluded, "My best judgment of America's need is to

---

2. Although many believed the use of the word *normalcy* was a lexical mistake, the word perhaps nicely summed up a new system of making-normal. Of particular note is Harding's strong push for "not submergence in internationality but sustainment [*sic*] in triumphant nationality" (1920, n.p). He was referring here both to the end of war overseas and to the end of the stream of immigration into America as well. He promised to close the gates, and he did just that. As Roger Daniels and Otis Graham point out, his speech "served as a stimulus for congressional action on immigration restriction" (2001, 18).

steady down, to get squarely on our feet, to make sure of the right path" (1920, n.p.). Of course, looking at any deliberative speech might yield very similar disability tropes.[3]

In science fiction, as well, disability deliberation is used to associate disability with future dystopia. This said, we might see some of the science fiction novels of Philip K. Dick as forms of more positive disability deliberation—for instance, when he imagines a future planet populated by seven clans, with each clan representing a different mental "disability" in the novel *Clans of the Alphane Moon* (2002).[4]

Further, as Robert McRuer suggests, disability studies might "conjure up the disability to come" and welcome it (2007, 200). More specifically, McRuer defines this as "a crip promise that we will always comprehend disability otherwise and that we will, collectively, somehow access other worlds and futures" (ibid., 208). So the goal of disability deliberation is to search for and invoke disability futures that could be welcomed, that can retain the critical possibility to oppose normalcy and normativity. These futures can include not just new expressions, but also new forms of expression, and thus new embodied realities.

---

3. In my final chapter on *The King's Speech*, I will look at how the climax of the film is a deliberative speech, the speech in which King George VI prepares the British public to go to war again, now against Hitler. This speech does gesture to overcoming, but has a dark and realistic edge: "The task will be hard. There may be dark days ahead, and war can no longer be confined to the battlefield, but we can only do the right as we see the right, and reverently commit our cause to God. If one and all we keep resolutely faithful to it, ready for whatever service or sacrifice it may demand, then with God's help, we shall prevail" (2008, n.p). Of course, the king also "leaves in a few" stutters in the speech, placing it more closely in the realm of disability deliberation.

4. Thanks to Josh Lukin for making this point. As he wrote in a personal message when I asked him for examples of anti-ableist disability futures in sci-fi: "I'm gonna say there's some Philip Dick novels that fit the bill, most often with respect to intellectual or mental disability: Isidore in *Do Androids Dream of Electric Sheep?* and Bill in *The Transmigration of Timothy Archer* come to mind. Possibly the community of mental patients in *Clans of the Alphane Moon* and just maybe, in the context of its time, the autistic kid in *Martian Time-Slip*" (2012).

Disability Epideictics

The final of Aristotle's three genres, epideictic rhetoric deals with praise and blame through commemoration and celebration. As I have already discussed at great length, one of the requirements of *mētis* rhetoric is that we resist memorialization. Yet epideictic rhetoric is just this, a means of memorializing and celebrating. An epideictic speech assesses character and virtue, stacking up and measuring flaws and strengths. In this way, epideictic most closely resembles and forms a broad range of genres of normativity. Ableism itself is a valence for epideictics, a script that foregrounds flaws and abnormalities, using medical and scientific grammars. Thus, disability epideictics would recognize the interestedness of our arguments around bodily values.

Another contemporary genre of epideictic is the biopic, the biographical film. There is perhaps no other film genre more highly populated by disabled characters.[5] In this book I discuss *The King's Speech* and *The Iron Lady* at great length, but a long range of other (not surprisingly award-winning) biopics are also disability epideictics: *A Beautiful Mind*, *My Left Foot*, *Ray*, *The Aviator*, *The Sea Inside*, and HBO's *Temple Grandin*; I could go on and on. These films generally adhere to disability myths in order to assess the virtue and honor of their subjects: they are honorable to the degree that they overcome or compensate for their disability, flawed when the disability "causes" them to be angry, unreliable, unrelatable. These biopics are both created and read through ableism. For this reason, they are *bio*pics not just about an individual life; they are *biopolitical*. They are

---

5. As Alyx Vesey writes in *Bitch Magazine*, "In general, I'm weary of the biopic as a genre. For one, it unfairly singles out 'exceptional' people. We don't usually see films about 'regular' people, unless they struggle with a mental or physical disability. This of course makes them exceptional in a number of films, which is dehumanizing. . . . Thus I'm often left wondering two things when I finish a biopic: One, how well do I actually know the subject after watching a fictional film about them? Two, do biopics reinforce the myth of disability as an individual, treatable concern that only exceptional people can overcome?" (2013, n.p.).

narrated through the flaws of the body and mind, reinforcing but also sometimes resisting biopower.

As I will show in my final chapter on *The King's Speech*, and also through my epideictic chapters on Hephaestus and Metis, there are ways to resist normativity through disability epideictics: searching for the refusal of negative disability myths, praising and accentuating disability, restoring the virtue of the denigrated, and restoring the flaws of the venerated. This would only ever be *suspect* memorialization; this can be an affirmative biopolitics.

Pseilos

The Greek word *pseilos*, which we translate as "faltering speech," can also denote bad manners or, simply, the meaning behind written words. In the latter instance, the idea of a stutter suggests the deconstruction of rhetorical norms based on narrow customs (M. Rose 2003, 57). I have already detailed the rhetorical potential of the *pseilos* of Demosthenes and Alcibiades, and I will return to the rhetorical significance of the "stutter" in my final chapter on *The King's Speech*.

Pseilos alludes to the struggle for meaning that surrounds words. As Marc Shell has written, "Stuttering involves spiritually and physiologically inescapable ways of human articulation. At the same time, it pertains to the problem of the unspeakable or what remains unsaid" (2006, 2–3). David Wills, who would argue that the stutter reveals the prosthetic relationship between the body and the word, writes that communication is always "dealing with the sideways as well as the forward momentum" (1995, 25). In this way, the stutter as *pseilos* can oppose the idea that any communication happens smoothly or easily. The stutter can be viewed as amplifying that which is rhetorical in every utterance or movement, highlighting all struggle to make meaning.

Apate **and** Ate

Susan Jarratt suggests that *apate*, like *pseilos*, was a term for the mysterious transfer of meaning from thought to expression. *Apate*, in her definition, is an exploration of how probable arguments can cast doubt on conventional truths. Both *apate*, deception, and *ate*, human blindness, have nonpejorative meanings and roles in the making of meaning. *Apate* means "the emotional experience between reality and language" (1991, 55). *Ate*, then, is the human condition that locates us within that space. In the *Encomium of Helen*, the Sophist Gorgias speaks specifically of *apate*, suggesting that that we cannot have perfect memory of the past, we cannot be completely present to ourselves, and we cannot foresee the future—thus we need poetry and art, words and images, and thus these things are powerful (Ijsseling 1995, 342).

This positive role for *ate* is provocative, because blindness is most often rhetorically constructed as the very absence of understanding (or even morality) in a post-Enlightenment philosophical tradition. Though I try to avoid using the words *see* or *view* as analogues for knowing throughout *Disability Rhetoric*, these metaphors are nearly unavoidable. Negative representations are ubiquitous in popular narratives as well. The novel *Blindness* by Jose Saramago presents the disability of visual impairment as an expanded parable. As Liat Ben-Moshe argues, this "is not a story about people who are blind, but an ableist metaphor that appropriates blindness as its signifier." She suggests that blindness offers "an allegory about the breakdown of humanity and morality in modern societies" (2006, n.p.).

On the other hand, in the recent film *The Book of Eli*, blindness takes on a drastically different meaning. Throughout the film, the antagonist abuses a blind woman named Claudia, who has been blind since birth. The hero, Eli, is also blind, but was blinded by something called "the flash." The entire plot of the movie revolves around the fact that Eli is able to memorize the Bible and thus to pass it along to future generations, but also that (ironically, it turns out) Claudia can read braille—which is what the only extant Bible has been written in. In this rhetorical scheme, blindness serves as an extended parable, not as a symbol of debasement and evil, but as the very possibility of transmitting knowledge. (Further, I hope that we can resist the easy analogy of seeing, reading, and knowing *Disability Rhetoric* itself.)

Samuel Ijsseling suggests that *ate* and *apate* were seen by Gorgias as "essential for human beings and for culture, for rhetoric and literature, for each art form, and for politics" (1995, 342). Gorgias may have been thinking of *ate* specifically as a metaphor for "blinding" or deception and not as blindness itself. But what if the imperfection of all of our senses, of all of our bodies, were also recognized as a given? Moreover, what if we saw this imperfection as *necessary* and causally linked to all culture and communication? That is, if we could all "see" perfectly, we would not need rhetoric; we would not even need language (and what a shame that would be).

Anmut

When the Homeric hero Odysseus is at his most cunning, it is when he begins a speech badly, when he appears as a "witless man," an *aphrona* (Detienne and Vernant 1978, 22). At one point in the *Odyssey*, Athena also gives Odysseus the body of an old, weak beggar. In this section, inhabiting another body is intended to allow him to understand the lives and challenges of others more intimately. He literally becomes consubstantial with another body that lacks his strength. *Anmut*, as a concept, holds that bodily attitudes are mutable, socially constructed. Odysseus did not have a perfect body, but he had *anmut*, the ability to make his body signify in relation to the bodies in his audience. In speeches he "act[ed] out an image of the common citizen," acting like a boor, hitching up his belt, in a physicalized claim to speak for the common man (Humphreys 1999, 128). Both *aphrona* and *anmut* radically revise our accepted rhetorical tradition, in which we have come to believe that the more perfect a body is, the more perfectly it can speak or signify. *Anmut* offers a way to reconsider disability—not as something an audience will reject or stigmatize, but as something that a diverse audience is receptive to and accepting of.

Recent rhetorical studies of the speeches of Christopher Reeve (Brueggeman 2005) and Michael J. Fox (Quackenbush 2011) provide compelling arguments for the power of what I would call disability *anmut*. As Quackenbush argues, when he delivers a speech without having taken his Parkinson's medication, Fox "as a visibly disabled rhetor speaks both as stigma—because his rhetoric issues from and through his body as he experiences Parkinson's disease—and of stigma—because he performs disability not just to provide an exigency for research into cures but also to challenge the cultural norms that dehumanize the disabled subject" (2011, n.p.). I would argue that *Anmut* was also at work when, as Brueggeman writes, Reeve delivered a speech "between the pulses of his respirator-regulated breaths (roaring, perhaps oceanically, in his own ears) and powerfully performed, yet gestureless and expressionless as it was, from his quadriplegic body" (2005, 17). The supposed imperfection of these speakers could be easily seen as alienating the "able" bodies in the audience, yet *anmut* names the space where rhetor and audience might share nonnormative and imperfect, though profound, embodied rhetorical connections.

Ekphrasis

The concept of *ekphrasis* refers to the ways that one form of art can be used to illuminate and accentuate the properties of another. Most often, this happens when a visual medium is described with words. Socrates speaks of *ekphrasis* in the *Phaedrus*, it is an element of Aphthonius's *Progymnasmata*, and it appears in Virgil's *Aeneid*. But perhaps the most relevant example of *ekphrasis* from antiquity comes from book 18 of the *Iliad*, when Homer describes Achilles's shield at great, great length, crediting Hephaestus for its creation. *Ekphrasis* is central to poetry across eras and cultures, particularly in the romantic period, yet still prevalent today. And *ekphrasis* does not need to be isolated to relationships between visual art and writing—*ekphrasis* can occur between any two artistic mediums.

With all of the images and figures in this book, I am using a kind of *ekphrasis* to describe the visual in words, as descriptively as I can. Thus, we could understand *ekphrasis* as a way to make visual mediums and information accessible to people with visual impairments, or, moreover, a way to add rhetorical value to images by using words to work through them. We live in an ocularcentric culture—not just this, for we continue to center the Enlightenment idea that light and sight *are* knowledge. We live through the fantasy of perfect and monolithic clarity, despite the fact that most of us would have impaired vision without glasses or surgery and despite the fact that vision is always imperfect, that we all process visual information differently, at different speeds and depths, with differing interaction with our other senses. But *ekphrasis* offers a pause and a discursive delay between image and understanding, revealing the essential differentiation and overlap of sensory engagements.

Ekphrasis is also an artistic process—as when a poem is used to describe a painting. This then gives us ways to think about such things as

ASL interpretation, visual description, *alt tags* within websites, and other "accommodations" for people with disabilities as *adding* artistic and rhetorical value, not simply transposing or distilling meanings. Importantly, it is the spirit of *ekphrasis* that matters more than its accuracy: the works come to be understood as speaking in dialogue with one another, enhancing meaning reciprocally rather than having a one-to-one or transactional relationship.

Sitpoint Theory

This neologism was coined by Rosemarie Garland-Thomson. This theory "interrogates the ableist assumptions underlying the notion of standpoint theory" yet also (I would suggest) perhaps extends standpoint theory—which is the idea that one's social positioning greatly influences their perspectives and that thus we could look to marginalized positions for forms of new knowledge and challenges to dominant norms. Garland-Thomson asks, "What perspectives or politics arise from encountering the world from such an atypical position?" offering Nancy Mairs's "waist-high" position in a wheelchair as one example, citing Mairs's 1997 memoir *Waist-High in the World*. Garland-Thomson continues:

> Our collective cultural consciousness emphatically denies the knowledge of vulnerability, contingency, and mortality. Disability insists otherwise [and] is perhaps the essential characteristic of being human. The body is dynamic, constantly interactive with history and environment. We evolve into disability. Our bodies need care; we all need assistance to live. An equality model of feminist theory sometimes prizes individualistic autonomy as the key to women's liberation. A feminist disability theory, however, suggests that we are better off learning to individually and collectively accommodate bodily limits and evolutions than trying to eliminate or deny them. (1997, 21)

Obviously, this is a key to all of disability rhetoric. There are reasons to be cautious, however—as sitpoint theory could also simply replace dominant claims to truth with marginalized claims that are just as certain and inflexible. Sondra Harding, for example, has argued that standpoint theory can lead to "strong objectivity," a more objective understanding of the world that should not be confused with a more authoritative or "real" understanding—instead, standpoint theory should "center" "the relationship between knowledge and politics" (1993, 55). In short, then, sitpoint theory would show that knowledge creation is always rhetorical—a flow of power through bodies—and thus disability is both usefully and "naturally" at the center of a process of knowing.

Situated Knowledges

In her theory of "situated knowledges," Donna Haraway calls for a "doctrine of embodied objectivity," situated knowledges that accommodate both radical contingency and "made" meaning as well as "modest meaning," faithful, shared accounts of the world. She calls for "partial, locatable, critical knowledges sustaining the possibility of webs of connection called solidarity." In this scheme, "subjugated standpoints are preferred because they seem to promise more adequate, sustained, objective, transforming accounts of the world" (1991, 191). What is needed is "diffraction," "the production of different patterns" (1997, 268).

Utilizing situated knowledges as an extension of sitpoint theory, we might search for what Don Ihde calls a "nonfoundational phenomenology," a "perceptual-bodily-referentiality" that takes into account the idea that "our perspectives are multiple, refracted, and compound . . . simultaneously both deconstructive and yet structural" (1983, 6, 86). Lennard Davis suggests that "all groups, based on physical traits or markings, are selected for disablement by a larger system of regulation and signification" (2002, 29). Owing to this bodily subjugation, "the oppression of disabled people is the oppression of everyone's real body," to quote Susan Wendell (1994, 274). The experience of the limits of embodiment is universal, even while this experience is never identical. I would add that the experience of disability, then, allows for a more real (inherently unstable) perspective on embodiment and, through embodiment, a more real perspective on rhetoric and our cunning world. Rhetorics of disability can allow for the kind of partial, situated knowledge that is the only kind of knowing we can hope for. Also, once we recognize that, as Lennard Davis writes, "difference is what all of us have in common . . . identity is not fixed but malleable . . . technology is not separate but part of the body . . . dependence, not individual independence is the rule," then situated knowledges and partial perspectives are not all we can hope for, but rather the embodied tools for an expanding range of rhetorical expression (2002, 26).

Dissoi Logoi

The Sophistic concept (often attributed to Protagoras) of *dissoi logoi* means, literally, "different words" and is interpreted, most commonly, as arguing from both sides or making the weaker argument stronger (see Kent Sprague 1972). Disagreement offers subversive potential, particularly because people with disabilities have historically had their agency and authority taken away from them or constrained—disability has equated with weakness, rhetorically, yet through rhetoric disability might also be made "stronger."

On the other hand, disabled "disagreement" will continue to be framed as bitterness. And, at the same time, disability will itself be rhetorically constructed as disagreeable. That is, as Sarah Ahmed suggests, paraphrasing Deleuze, we continue to believe that solidarity and agreement require actual *bodies* that agree with one another (2010, 211). And, conversely, wherever we have disagreement, this disagreement is localized to "whatever" gets in the way—we blame disagreement on the disagreeing or disagreeable body. Yet then we are left with the subversive possibility that bodies simply will not agree—that an individual body is not a cohesive and agreeable whole, nor that our encounters with others will ever (or should ever) enact a harmony. On the most basic level, disability rhetoric can be about refusing the normate ordering of the world. Disability rhetoric can also refuse to agree with any one story, version, explanation, or body. *Dissoi logoi* can also mean that we are constantly seeking other stories and interpretations and explanations that, in a normative culture and society, will not be the most ready at hand, convenient, or easy to access.

Least Dangerous Assumption

This idea has become paradigmatic within disability studies. In 1984 Anne Donnellan proposed the principle of the "Presumption of Competence" as the "least dangerous assumption" that can be made about people with disabilities. This presumption is important because most often the assumptions that are made about people with disabilities are the opposite of this—they assume incompetence, incapacity; they are truly dangerous in that they stigmatize and they delimit the social roles of people with disabilities (see my list of disability myths).

Perhaps the most popular example of the "least dangerous assumption" can be found through the cultural stories of Helen Keller. All other overwritings aside, Keller was at first viewed as incapable of communication, unable to learn. The popular version of the story gives credit to Anne Sullivan as the "miracle worker" who found a way to reach Helen. A simple reading might suggest that Sullivan made the least dangerous assumption: that Helen would want to communicate and would find a way to do so. Or, perhaps if Keller had been viewed as capable and competent from the very beginning of her life, it might not have taken so long for the people around her to assist her in communicating.[6]

The power of the least dangerous assumption has also been channeled through popular films, memoirs, and novels such as *The Diving Bell and the Butterfly*, first an autobiography written by Jean-Dominique Bauby, who was paralyzed but developed a system of communication using his left eyelid. Keller and Bauby come to be represented as "super crips" who overcome their limitations and shock the world with their abilities. Yet these stories can also be held up as warnings that nobody should be assumed incapable of communication, intelligence, engagement, rhetoricity. On a slightly lesser scale, we can recognize how the least dangerous assumption might function in the sphere of education or in the workplace, where dangerous assumptions about ability structure access. What happens when all students are seen as fully capable of learning, when all citizens are seen as fully capable of contributing?

The nature of the "assumption" should also cue up embodied connotations: an assumption as a way of taking control and power and also as a means of "taking up" a body. Assumptions structure an assumer and

---

6. See Kim Nielsen's *Beyond the Miracle Worker* (2009) for more about the contradictions and complexities of the relationship between Keller and Sullivan.

an assumed. This should remind us that assumptions and values around ability and disability can reflect dangerous power relations and reach into bodies.[7]

Finally, the least dangerous assumption can also apply to our acts of interpretation—a dangerous assumption about Hephaestus or Demosthenes, for instance, or *mētis* more broadly, is that the failures, delays, reversals, and sidesteps of their rhetoric are simply duplicitous or unsophisticated schemes. But *mētis* should teach us to never assume that what may look on the surface like a "failure" does not contain genius and critique.

Most Generous Interpretation

The most generous interpretation can be viewed as related to the least dangerous assumption—although "assuming competence" is different than generosity—and in the disability paradigm, "generosity" often constructs people with disabilities as objects of pity and charity. Nobody wants to be condescended to. So I situate the most generous interpretation not as a simple way to read all texts and all bodies as inherently good, but as a heuristic for responding to negative portrayals of disability, at least temporarily, by considering the "good intentions" that may have inspired them.

I borrow this idea from one of my own favorite teachers, Kate Ronald. Paul Ricoeur has been seen as a champion of the "most generous interpretation" of texts that are ambiguous or obscure—as a hermeneutic strategy (see Reagan 1996). In disability studies, this can mean that we look for a generous way to interpret even the texts that seem the most negative and offensive. This does not mean that we are forced to *conclude* that all texts must come from a "good place," or that we forestall or rescind our right to speak truth to power and to recognize what is hurtful or oppressive. It just means that, while we expect our society to assume the competence (and even the potential genius) of all bodies, we must also, as part of a

---

7. Another important example: autism has also been rhetorically constructed (through the most dangerous assumption) as a lack of emotion and affect. However, scholars such as Melanie Yergeau (2010) and Julia Miele Rodas (2008) have refuted this construction and instead located the neuro-typicality of "empathy" and the possibility and power of irony as an autistic rhetoric.

rhetorical process of understanding one another, take the time to, at least temporarily, try on generous interpretations of cultural texts.

For instance, the pity and charity response to disability continues to be tremendously popular. In order to understand how to counteract that propensity, we might need to begin by allowing that those millions who give money to fund a cure for a disability are well meaning, and we might harness these good intentions to convince them that it would be better to support the rights of disabled people than to eradicate them.

In this book, I try on generous interpretations of a series of cultural texts, from the myths of Hephaestus to *The King's Speech*. The most generous assumption, then, becomes a disability rhetoric, part of the repertoire of *mētis*, one of the ways we can move sideways and backward through a range of meanings and readings.

Defective Detectives

As Hoppenstand and Browne have shown, the "defective detective" was a key presence in pulp fiction in the United States in the thirties. These detectives are "both incomplete and deliberately different," and they argue that when "the deformed hero . . . overcame his weaknesses and employed ingenuity and brute force to subdue the evils and injustices of the world," so too could society "overcome its deformities and return to normal" (1983, 2). Hoppenstand and Browne suggest that Odysseus was the very first defective detective, and they argue that this pulp fiction favorite continued "the motif of the [defective] mythological hero, thousands of years old" through to Poe and Sherlock Holmes (ibid., 7, 1). While their emphasis is on this archetype's compensation, there is also a way to suggest that the deliberate social abnormality, the strange habits, the sensory confusion, and even the extraordinary bodies of these detectives are what allow them to solve crimes, are the rhetorical vehicle for their acuity and perceptiveness. Sherlock Holmes and C. Auguste Dupin solve cases only once they stop thinking "normally."

For instance, in recent screen versions of Holmes—for instance, the Robert Downey Jr. Hollywood version or the BBC TV series—Holmes is depicted very clearly as being on the autistic spectrum. Yet the habits that may make his neighbors or his roommate view him as "strange" are the skills that allow him to solve mysteries. In the same way, "defective detection" should be understood as a disability rhetoric, something akin to a heretical heuristics or an interpretive noncompliance: What are the nonnormative ways to understand any given text? What are the nonnormative—or even the least normative—means to express yourself in any given situation?

Strategic Ignorance

Strategic ignorance refers to "the ways expressions of ignorance can be wielded strategically by groups living under oppression as a way of gaining information, sabotaging work, avoiding or delaying harm, and preserving a sense if self." Bailey views ignorance not as an accidental phenomenon, but as an "active social production" (2007, 77). Views of strategic ignorance are most commonly theorized as "epistemic blank spots that make privileged knowers oblivious to systemic injustices" but could also be recognized when, for instance, "people of color use ignorance strategically to their advantage" (ibid., 77, 78). For people with disabilities, strategic ignorance can perhaps be used as a refusal of forced forms of sociality and interaction or perhaps the right to choose when to call someone out on their ableism and when not to.

Strategic ignorance also has potentially important connections to *mētis* and to cunning intelligence. Strategic ignorance may at first seem to contradict the idea of disability activism or the strong position of disability rights. The term *ignorance* has most often insinuated cognitive lack for people with disabilities, as well, and not the action of ignoring. Yet a critical understanding of strategic ignorance warns against the selectivity of cunning: one might always be willfully ignoring the oppressive complications and implications of a way of doing or knowing. Yet, also, strategic ignorance, realized as at times a cunning strategy employed against oppression, opens up interesting possibilities, in fact skewing and subverting the view that, for instance, people with disabilities are unintelligent or naive. In this way, strategic ignorance connects intimately to the "least dangerous assumption"—even seeming "ignorance" can be a rhetorical move.

Further, strategic ignorance connects to the idea of "defective detection"—those things that may seem to make us "abnormal" can also serve to confuse a context, set the world on its side, disarm, and this can then be used to our advantage. People with disabilities might grab the momentum of society's push to pity them, infantilize them, or speak for them and reposition these oppressive views until they are themselves in a position of strength.

Strategic ignorance might also pose a highly rhetorical alternative to the myth that people with disabilities are "faking it" or that they can "drop" disability. As such, strategic ignorance might connect to what Tobin Siebers calls disability "masquerade": "Exaggerating or performing difference, when that difference is a stigma, marks one as a target, but it also exposes and resists the prejudices of society. The masquerade fulfills a desire to tell a story about disability, often the very story that society does not want to hear because it refuses to obey the ideology of able-bodiedness. It may stress undercompensation when overcompensation is required, or present a coming out of disability when invisibility is mandatory" (2004, 19).

For instance, in the MTV series *How's Your News?* and the preceding movie by the same name, a group of journalists with intellectual disabilities travels across the United States to report on the issues that matter to them. The reporters are directly addressing the ways that people with disabilities are excluded from participation in the mainstream news media and the ways that the news prescribes their roles in society. But they also use their disabilities to disarm the people that they interview in subtle ways. One of the last things any American expects as they go about their day is to be questioned by a person with an intellectual disability, holding a microphone. The *How's Your News?* crew knows this, flaunts it, and thus the insights they gain are significant.

When Tom Shales reviewed the show in the *Washington Post*, he wrote that "one of the stars of the group is Bobby Bird, a man with Down Syndrome who is in his 50s and who speaks in a private language that to others sounds very close to meaningless babble. He seems to know that's how people respond to him, however, and has fun with it, turning the tables in a way that makes a supposedly normal person feel isolated and out of it—ostracized, as mentally challenged [*sic*] people often are" (2009, n.p). Shales seems to recognize one of the key features of the show and one of the key, underrecognized modalities of disability rhetoric: twisting people's stereotypical reactions to your own advantage. This rhetoric reverses so many of the disability myths I listed previously—because a common feature of all of these myths is the idea that people (or characters) with disabilities are blank canvases upon which plot points, cultural values, and social institutions can make their marks. It is crucially important, from the perspective of disability rhetoric, to always recognize the agency and resistance of people with disabilities in these mythologizations. This resistance is not always direct and easy to read. Often, it is cunning.

This repertoire or choreography of rhetorics presents just a few possible moves—hopefully, the reader is inspired to think of and create many more. As I hope I have shown, these disability rhetorics often respond directly to negative disability myths. Yet these rhetorics are not limited to policing or curing representations; they are equipment for living in an ableist world. Further, *mētis* could be understood as the system or philosophy under which each of these disability rhetorics operates. In the next two chapters, I will be reading back into rhetorical history for early iterations of *mētis*, but this does not mean that we should not also continue to link *mētis* to a wide range of rhetorical possibilities available today—in fact, the opposite must be true. Like the *How's Your News* crew, disability rhetoric might show up anywhere, at any time.

4

Mētis

> Humans have always exercised the right to make choices about the
> anatomical features that they consider desirable or interesting, and, at
> times, these options have included rather than excluded women and
> men with disabilities.
>
> —Harlan Hahn, "Can Disability Be Beautiful?"

SO FAR I HAVE OFFERED a brief guided tour through rhetorical history,
a moving through and with the bodies of this history. I have suggested
that we can read embodied rhetoric and bodied rhetorical history as
powered by tension around normativity. I have also explored disability
myths and disability rhetorics. My argument is that disability has myriad
meanings, many of them positive and generative. *Mētis*, I will show, is the
craft of forging something practical out of these possibilities, practicing
an embodied rhetoric, changing the world as we move through it. The key
examplar of *mētis* is the disabled Greek god Hephaestus, and this chapter
will focus on his stories. Thus, *mētis* comes to us through myth, and (for
me) is disability rhetoric's epistemological home, capable of explaining
and activating a wide range of available means.

To ally disability and rhetoric, one must face the dismissive conclusions of other rhetorical historians: the idea that disability precludes
rhetoricity. The historical record seems to reinscribe this dismissal—and
we have few stories of orators or rhetors with disabilities. In my first
three chapters, I provided an inventory of representations of disability
in canonical rhetorical history while also bending our readings into the
apocrypha and forward toward contemporary myths. I also showed that
we could reclaim an expansive and expanding lexicon of disability rhetorics as available means and as ways to move.

In the subtext and the margins of the record, there is always much to learn about the center—understanding the impact of the persistent presence of norms, as well as recognizing the subtle, ghostlike presence of a desire for and an acknowledgment of the rhetorical role of disability. Tanya Titchkosky has suggested that cultural texts may preclude us from viewing disability as "a desired status" or "as a difference that the collective needs" (2007, 6). Instead, most often we are given negative portrayals of disability, such as those in my inventory of disability myths. But she argues that we can develop ways of reading disability differently: "As the space of provocation where we might begin to reread how culture puts our embodiment to text and textures all of our lives" (ibid., 9).

In this chapter I will validate and value the possibilities of the nonnormative body and thus create a more expansive machinery for understanding rhetorical embodiment. I will tell the stories of Hephaestus, a Greek god with a disability—a Greek god who embodied *mētis*, the cunning intelligence needed to adapt to and intervene in a world of change and chance. Hephaestus was the famed inventor, the trickster, the trap builder and machine creator of Greek myth. His body, despite being "crippled," was celebrated, as I will show.[1] I will suggest that Hephaestus's story has been neglected, but that we can now read it as a challenge to stories of rhetorical history that reinscribe normative ideas about rhetorical facility and about which bodies/minds matter. I will again use theory from the field of disability studies in order to analyze the function of such norms and to disrupt our acceptance of an ableist view of rhetorical history.

---

1. I recognize the problem posed by the use of the term *celebrate*. As Morris Young has pointed out (in comments on a very early version of this chapter), one of the dominant tropes for the recognition of marginalized groups by the majority is celebration. For instance, North Americans celebrate the novelty of Chinese New Year or hold "Taste of Thailand" fairs to celebrate cuisine, but these actions do not address other cultural exclusions, nor do they offer multifaceted cultural roles—the celebration is often a celebration of stereotypes, or of the Americanization of a foreign custom or food. But I will refer specifically to a particular celebration later in this chapter, and so I choose to use the word throughout.

Double or Divergent Orientation

Mitchell and Snyder suggest that there was just one Greek god with a disability, Hephaestus, and they use this evidence to argue for the centrality of bodily ideals in antiquity (2001c, 213). But, in fact, there was also Thersites, and there was Tiresias (whom I have discussed at length already). And, of the major Greek heroes, Achilles was also obviously and famously disabled.[2] But more than this, Olympus itself looks from one angle more like a hospital than a beauty parlor: the gods are continually maiming one another, transforming, failing. We think that having the "body of a Greek god" is an ideal, but these bodies were actually polymorphous, eminently vulnerable, and essentially flawed, each and every one of them.

But perhaps the point is that this "reality" has been ignored, submerged.

Hephaestus was a Greek god with a physical disability—a Greek god who embodied *mētis*, the cunning intelligence needed to act in a world of chance. Hephaestus was the famed inventor, trickster, craftsperson, the trap builder and machine creator of Greek myth. His body was celebrated, not despite his disability, but because of his embodied intelligence. Hephaestus's story has been neglected, but we can now read it as a challenge to stories that reinscribe normative ideas about rhetorical facility and about which bodies matter.

As discussed earlier, Hans Kellner urges historians to "get the story crooked!" He suggests that this entails "looking at the historical text in such a way as to make more apparent the problems and decisions that shape its strategies" (1989, vii). In his words, "The straightness of any story is a rhetorical invention" (ibid., xi). In this chapter, then, and in subsequent chapters, I will attempt to layer stories, to allow the reader to choose through interpretations, and I will also seek a variety of historical materials that might reveal the rhetorical complexity of a crooked history. Because Hephaestus was himself represented as "crooked," and because

---

2. See also my discussion of Odysseus—there are certainly ways to see him, and his actions, as distinctly nonnormative. The point is that when we really start looking, and resist the urge to dismiss disability, we recognize it everywhere.

this difference was valued, this mythical figure moves through this narrative as an ideal protagonist.

This chapter places bodily difference in the driver's seat. I argue that exclusion has been imported into the classical world. As a result, we have been left with a narrow view of the role disability may have played in the period. Telling the stories of Hephaestus allows me to recover a different rhetorical body. This is true both in the sense that he provides an image of disability as valued by ancient society, but also because *mētis* is a distinctly bodily intelligence. I want to elaborate upon this embodiment as I trouble mythological and rhetorical history. I will illustrate why we need to tell new stories, while I also show that we need to recognize *mētis* as a rhetoric, thus recognizing the body as rhetorical.

It is important to say that Hephaestus's role in the development of this particular rhetorical history—my own radical one and our accepted Western one—could be found elsewhere. Hephaestus's name may have come from an Egyptian word for the god Ptah, or Thoth, evidence of, at the very least, a connection to Africa (see Poe 1999). Sandra Blakely suggests that in fact, Ptah was an "Egyptian Hephaistos" (2006, 44).[3] Neal Walls (2007) also recounts the Sumerian origin myth of Enki and Ninmah, in which the third man created is born with paralyzed feet, and is thus appointed to be a silversmith.[4] The African Pan-Yoruba god Ogun was also a deity of metalwork and fire, and has both Old World and New World manifestations.

---

3. Blakely (2006) shows that when archaeologists recovered evidence of the cult of Ptah at Memphis, they discovered that this temple was called the "house of Hephaistos" in a Ptolemaic papyrus found there.

4. This is a particularly interesting disability myth: each of the humans fashioned out of clay by Ninmah has a particular disability. Enki then finds a vocation for each: the man with weak hands becomes a servant to the king, a blind man becomes a musician, an infertile woman becomes a weaver, a eunuch becomes (something like) a governmental aide to the king. I am condensing and simplifying the myth here. For more, see Walls 2007. The main point, however, is that in the myth, these are the *first* humans created, and the challenge is to prove that all can be valuable within Sumerian society. Thus, in the myth, we find value for disability at the "origin of the species." As Walls writes, "The Sumerian text recognizes the non-normative medical condition of these persons," but "rather than naming 'disability' as a means to exclude some persons . . . each becomes a functioning member

1. *Hephaestus (Vulcan) on a winged throne.* Red figure cup by the Ambrosius Painter. Attic, ca. 510 BCE. Late Archaic. Inv. F 2273. Destroyed in World War II. © Antikensammlung, Staatliche Museen, Berlin, Germany. Photo credit: bpk, Berlin/Staatliche Museen zu Berlin/Art Resource, NY.

Loki, a giant and enemy to the Norse gods, was also a god of fire and cunning (see Dumezil 1986). Kitsune is a shape-shifting trickster in Japanese mythology (see Radin 1956). Vulcan is the Roman version of Hephaestus,

---

within the social organization, and many are given technical skills and high social status consistent with their abilities" (2007, 19).

also often seen with a disability. The stories of other characters, like those of Hephaestus, would offer us insight into the ways disability, mythology, and rhetoric intersect.[5] I will explore some of these cross-cultural connections in the next chapter. The point is that, just as Greek myth is subject to interpretive forces from our own "modern" era, Greek myth was influenced by and cross-inflected myth from other traditions. To study Greek myth, then, is to study its multiple origins as well as its influences, to examine what the tradition has become but also what it might have been.

In our accepted Western tradition, Hephaestus was the Greek god of fire and metallurgy. In figure 1, Hephaestus appears able-bodied, yet he rides a proto-wheelchair, a chariot with wings. We see a side view of Hephaestus, in a seat with both a set of wheels and a set of wings. He holds his hammer over his shoulder. In vase paintings, sculpture, and written texts, Hephaestus is most often depicted as having a physical disability, his feet twisted around backward or sideways (see figure 2 below). In figure 1, because he holds his tools and he rides a chariot that he has crafted, his abilities as an artisan are also depicted, and these skills are valued. Homer repeatedly mentions that he is lame, god of the "dragging foot" (1999a, 18.371). But his disability also has positive connotations. Having feet that face away from one another does not necessarily entail impairment—it means he can move from side to side more quickly.

Marcel Detienne and Jean-Pierre Vernant, in *Cunning Intelligence in Greek Culture and Society* (1978), write that Hephaestus was symbolized by the crab and that his side-to-side movement had symbolic value. *Mētis*, as with other forms of intelligence, was associated with particular animals—the crab, the octopus, the cuttlefish. In Greek thought, these animal affiliations had vastly different meanings than those we might infer today—the animal world was not understood as separate from the human in the same distinct way. To a certain degree, Greek philosophers would have

---

5. Perhaps the most obvious connection to make here is to Jesus—Nancy Eiesland's book *The Disabled God: Toward a Liberatory Theology of Disability* argues that Jesus was disabled. She points to Luke 24:36–39: "In presenting his impaired body to his startled friends, the resurrected Jesus is revealed as the disabled God," she wrote—he is not cured and made whole; his injury is not divine punishment; it is a part of him (1994, 311).

agreed with contemporary "animal standpoint theorists" that "nonhuman animals have been key driving and shaping forces of human thought, psychology, moral and social life, and history overall" (Best 2009, 18). To think like a crab or an octopus was to incorporate modes of thinking/ moving that were highly valued, far from abstract.[6] In the classical world, Hephaestus's extraordinary body was positively allied with his cunning mind, and both were then further allied with the symbolic movements and strategies of specific animals. More recently, a conversation between animal studies and disability studies has pushed us to recognize such positive associations and cross-species understandings. Cary Wolfe notes that disability studies and animal studies are in ideal positions to pose "fundamental challenges" to "the liberal justice tradition and its concept of rights, in which ethical standing and civic inclusion are predicated on rationality, autonomy, and agency" (2009, 127). Both disability studies and animal studies could "explore the decentering of liberal humanist ability that prioritizes the organization and mastery of space by reframing this 'ability' as, actually, an impairment to connecting with and understanding the experiences of nonhuman animals" (ibid., 131). Shannon Walters

6. In my introduction, I alluded quickly (in a footnote) to the recent argument about the biological bases of rhetoric—arguments that could shed light on both rhetorical theory and disability studies. George Kennedy has argued that rhetoric is a "form of mental and emotional energy" that is "biologically prior to speech and to conscious intentionality" (1992, 3, 26). Diane Davis disagrees with the pure biological essentialism of Kennedy, even while she echoes the radical ontological point he is making: she instead argues for an "always prior rhetoricity, an affect*ability* or persuad*ability* that is due not to any creature's specific genetic makeup but to corporeality more generally, to the exposedness of corporeal existence" (2011, 89). Kennedy is arguing that rhetoric is not just discourse and that rhetoric is not just something possessed by humans—it is biologically a priori in all animals. ("This rhetorical energy," in the words of Debra Hawhee, "resides in places where human animals may not even tread" [2011, 85].) Davis is arguing that "rhetoric is not first of all an essence or property '*in* the speaker' (a natural function of biology) but an underivable obligation to respond that issues from an irreducible relationality" (ibid., 89). Both theorists link rhetoric to the body, however, and—importantly—for Davis, it is the vulnerability, exposedness, and incompleteness of any body that are rhetorically generative. In this way, we might even go so far as to say that it is the *mētis* of the "animal" that signals the rhetorical ontology of biology.

suggests that *mētis* is a "rhetorical strategy that draws productively on connections among humans, disability, and animals" (2010, 687).[7]

Like the crab, or other animals that he is associated with, including the fox, cuttlefish, and octopus, Hephaestus was recognized as having a "power . . . emphasized by his distinctive characteristic of being endowed with a double and divergent orientation." This ability allowed him to harness fire and to invent metallurgy. His disability was (and can again be) understood as that which allowed him to "dominate shifting, fluid powers such as fire and wind" in his work in the forge. In their version of the story, Hephaestus had to be "even more mobile and polymorphic than these [elements]" (Detienne and Vernant 1978, 273). Like a crab, Hephaestus's symbolic movement is not straightforward. Also, like any person who might build himself an extraordinary winged vehicle, like the one pictured above, he is crafty. These qualities also conform to, and shape, the particular form of intelligence that Hephaestus was said to symbolize: *mētis*.

Responding to an accepted rhetorical tradition that denies the body, and hoping to advance my thesis that extraordinary bodies should be *the* bodies of rhetoric, I have looked for other views of rhetorical facility in the classical period. Thus, the engine of this chapter, this book, and its reclamation project is *mētis*—cunning, adaptive, *embodied* intelligence.

The word *mētis* means wise and wily intelligence. As Debra Hawhee points out, *mētis* is always affiliated with crafty figures that "display a somatic cunning" or "bodily intelligence" (2005, 46). In the classical world, *mētis* is enacted as flair, forethought, subtlety of mind, deception, cleverness, opportunism, and experience. Hawhee's linkages between *mētis*

---

7. Yet Walters points out that *mētis* "has been recently revised as a rhetoric that focuses almost exclusively on its human potential" (2010, 687). Important connections have been ignored or dropped: "burgeoning studies of animality have largely ignored issues of disability" (ibid., 707), and because people with disabilities have been traditionally dehumanized and sometimes animalized in a negative sense, it has been tricky to negotiate between these three valences of human, disability, and animal. Walters point is that the animal nature of *mētis* should be seen as much more than metaphorical. The developing vocabulary of animal studies might afford the means of understanding this in a positive sense, while the connections between disability and the *de*human remain fraught.

and wrestling, and then between wrestling and rhetoric, provide an interesting image for this form of intelligence: "the corporeality of *mētis*" as "struggle" or "the swarming mass of cunning craftiness and flailing limbs" (ibid., 46, 45). As Lois Bragg suggests, *mētis* is an embodied rhetoric that "in contrast to the linear progress of rational thought, never goes forward in a straight line but is always weaving from side to side and looping back on itself" (2004, 32). John Peradatto adds that *mētis* is "intuitive power, the imaginative anticipation of probabilities [requiring] a knowledge of the indeterminate and coincidental" (1990, 47). In all of these ways, *mētis* both exemplifies rhetoric and redefines it.

Mētis should also be recognized as exemplifying and redefining disability, countering historical norms, but also the norms that inhibit difference in modern contexts. Michel de Certeau writes of *mētis* as a means to "obtain the maximum number of effects from a minimum of force" (1984, 82). *Mētis* is timely, flexible, and practical. *Mētis* is an embodied, responsive act that is the "instant of art"; therefore, it always introduces newness or "foreignness" (ibid., 85–86). *Mētis*, for Certeau, is the basis for his concept of "tactics"—those practices formed by the relatively weak in order to navigate the "strategies" of institutions and power structures. Tactics are a way of "making do" in any given situation, and Certeau suggests that it is "the discipline of rhetoric [that] offers models for differentiating among the types of tactics" (ibid., 481). It is my hope that this book begins this work of offering such models: laying out the rhetorical possibilities of *mētis* as intellectual and material movement against normativity.

Perhaps the most important way to understand *mētis* is to recognize that it is not an idea from another time, but is instead the best way to describe and enact forms of knowledge and tactics of communication in any uncertain situation—and if we approach our world as one of chance and change, then *mētis* becomes the best available means for us to move in hundreds of rhetorical situations every day. In the Greek context from which Certeau borrows these concepts, *mētis* was much more than an important term—it was the modus operandi for the entire mythical world, full of reversals and thus demanding resourcefulness. As James C. Scott argues, while typically translated as "cunning intelligence," this definition of *mētis* "fails to do justice to the range of knowledge and skills represented" by the concept. Instead, *mētis* should be "broadly under-stood" as a "wide array of practical skills and acquired intelligence in responding to a constantly changing natural and human environment" (1985, 313). *Mētis* "resists simplification into deductive principles" and instead "lies in that large space between the realm of genius, to which no formula can apply, and the realm of codified knowledge" (ibid., 316). In the further, perhaps strained, words of Françoise Lionnet, *mētis* "projects itself on a plurality of practical levels but can never be subsumed under a single, identifiable system of diametric dichotomies. It is a form of *savoir faire* which resists symbolization within a coherent or homogeneous con-ceptual system since it is also the power to undo the logic and clarity of concepts" (1989, 328). *Mētis* is slippery symbolically, but unendingly *useful*.

Mētis also aligns with Halberstam's "queer art of failure" in interesting ways, including her suggested three premises of this art: that we should resist mastery, privilege the naive or nonsensical, and suspect memori-alization (2011, 15). Halberstam suggests that "failure can be counted in that set of oppositional tools that James C. Scott called 'the weapons of the weak.'" In Scott's definition, "certain activities that look like indifference or acquiescence" are "'hidden transcripts' of resistance to the dominant order." Thus, "the concept of 'weapons of the weak' can be used to recat-egorize what looks like inaction, passivity, and lack of resistance in terms of the practice of stalling the business of the dominant . . . and as a form of critique" (ibid., 88). Of course, when Scott wrote about "weapons of the weak" in his 1985 book of the same name, the book that Halberstam is quoting here, he is discussing a concept that he will later explicitly link with *mētis* in his 1998 monograph, *Seeing Like a State.*[8]

---

8. In *Weapons of the Weak*, perhaps the most poetic description of these weapons comes from an inventory in the final sentence of the book. Weapons of the weak include "the tenacity in self-preservation—in ridicule, in truculence, in irony, in petty acts of noncom-pliance, in foot dragging, in dissimulation, in resistant mutuality, in the disbelief in elite homilies, in the steady, grinding efforts to hold one's own against overwhelming odds—a spirit and practice that prevents the worst and promises something better" (J. Scott 1985, 350). The reference to foot-dragging here is interesting, of course, as it seems to unintention-ally reinvoke Hephaestus and create a new category of embodied rhetoric.

Like the "weapons" or the *mētis* Scott conceptualizes, or that I discuss in this book, Halberstam explains that "as a practice, failure recognizes that alternatives are embedded already in the dominant and that power is never total or consistent; indeed failure can exploit the unpredictability of ideology and its indeterminate qualities" (ibid.). Halberstam understands that an argument for failure is a tricky one to make—and I agree. It might be especially fraught to ally queerness and/or disability with failure. Yet she argues that "failure is something queers do and have always done exceptionally well; for queers failure can be a style" (ibid., 3). When she makes this suggestion, however, she is challenging the very epistemology of "winning" or of success in a late-capitalist society.[9] And this is a cunning argument to make. Halberstam argues that "under certain circumstances failing, losing, forgetting, unmaking, undoing, unbecoming, not knowing may in fact offer more creative, more cooperative, more surprising ways of being in the world" (ibid., 2–3). I would argue that while history has written people with disabilities as losers and as weak, carefully working *with* these constructions might be a way to (1) recognize the oblique, surprising, lateral forms of knowledge these positions have always allowed; (2) recognize the cunning threat that these alternative knowledges have always posed, and thus to understand that nonnormative bodies and minds have been constructed as less than *because of* their threatening power; and (3) avoid the trap of replacing one type of normate

9. This also offers clear resonance with disability studies theory. Halberstam argues that "while failure certainly comes accompanied by a host of negative affects, such as disappointment, disillusionment, and despair, it also provides the opportunity to use these negative affects to poke holes in the toxic positivity of contemporary life"—the belief that "success happens to good people and failure is just a consequence of a bad attitude rather than structural conditions" (2011, 3). This is essentially a "social model" of failure, in opposition to an "individual model" (see my discussion of Oliver). For many people with disabilities, this belief also seriously impacts their lives in late-capitalist society. Neoliberalism in particular demands the triumph of the individual, boot-straps logic, and "survival of the fittest," even when this economy dictates that only the very few will "win." Disability itself is seen as a personality flaw, just like failure is, even though both are created in large part by social conditions. This then powers arguments against social programs and structural changes that might address inequality.

history with a "corrected" one just as straight as the old one. The bodies of *mētis* and of its stories have been represented as weak, as failed, yet they are also weapons of stylish and cunning undoing, embodying critique.

Peradatto goes so far as to suggest that *mētis* offers a paradigm-exploding version of selfhood: "a subtler ideology of self . . . a sense of self with depth . . . a secret base for open predication . . . a view of the self as capable, dynamic, free, rather than fixed, fated, defined" (1990, 169). No matter how seriously one chooses to invest in the power of *mētis* as an epistemology or hermeneutic, the concept introduces a tripping up or stuttering of the disembodied classical tradition. *Mētis* asks us to understand that "thought does not just happen within the body, it happens *as the body*" (Hawhee 2005, 58). *Mētis* is a way to recognize that all understanding and all communication is embodied. In the Greek context, *mētis* was more than the description of a form of action, it was a way to describe the world, a world powered by persuasion, differentiation, shifting contexts, and meaningful bodies. And in contemporary contexts, *mētis* can be a way to recognize the need for flexible, embodied, responsive rhetorical movement.

As Klaus-Peter Koepping and others have shown, in myth there has been a somewhat "restricted repertoire" of bodies, through which the "grotesquely extended body" has classically been aligned with "crooked thinking" and *mētis* is certainly a central part of this tradition (1985, 196). In most mythical interpretations, Hephaestus is represented, somewhat dismissively, as "just" a trickster—a crooked body that can be laughed at and should be distrusted. The easy interpretive route is to ally "bad" thinking with "bad" bodies. Yet a more complex recognition of the "grotesque" body across mythical traditions (from Greece to North American First Nations to the West African trickster, for instance) might lead to a view of the "hidden dimensions of the naked orifices under the clothing of civilized and rule-governed life" (ibid., 213). Karl Kerenyi calls the mythical trickster "the exponent and the personification of the life of the body"—a symbol both compact and unfolding (1955, 155). Robert Pelton then suggests that this trickster, "in juggling with his own body, in his manipulation of its parts . . . his confidence in its potencies, draws an icon of human openness to every world and every possible transformation"

(1989, 133). The quick default is to align *mētis* with deviant bodies and devious intentions. Yet there is also an alternative tradition of openness to the signification of these bodies. Here the extraordinary body is not a flawed part of an ordered world, but rather reveals the impulse toward "transgression, rebellion," a freeing from "that which, if not seen through, would oppress us." It is easy to stigmatize and abject the disabled body, but myth might encourage us to laugh "not about the body, but about its unruliness, while at the same time delighting in it" (Koepping 1985, 213). Further, "the features commonly ascribed to the trickster—contradictoriness, deceptiveness, trickery—are the features of the language" of myth itself. The disabled body in myth then, through the figure of the cunning trickster, like Hephaestus, reveals the "difference between, and the undecidability of, discourse and story, referential and rhetorical values, signifier and signified, a conventional mind and one that is open" (Doueihi 1984, 308). In this way, the trickster could be a "possibly paradigmatic expression" of the dissonant experience of language, symbolism, or any given social order—each of these "normative" orders itself an absurdity unraveled by the "anomaly/ambivalence" of the trickster (Koepping 1985, 196).

Of course, cunning can be used just as easily to deceive and dominate as it can be used to subvert and equalize. As Richard Heitman suggests, *mētis* "cannot be distinguished—except quite artificially—from deception and mendacity" (2005, 5). Yet Detienne and Vernant work diligently through their scholarship to show that *mētis* was a virtue in Greek society.[10] Further, as Jeffrey Barnouw argues, the *mētis* of Odysseus is "invariably in service of a larger purpose. He plays no tricks for their own sake." Barnouw suggests that more attention must be paid to the "anticipating and planning aspects of *mētis* . . . the overall and long view" (2004, 21).

---

10. Joseph Russo suggests, for instance, that "Detienne and Vernant distinguish between the positive *mētis* of Athena and Hephaestus, one of strategy and craftsmanship, and the ambivalent *mētis* of Hermes and Aphrodite, one of thieves and lovers" (2008, 263). The distinction is not actually that clear-cut—either in Detienne and Vernant or in the myths themselves. Yet Detienne and Vernant do work hard to recognize the centrality of *mētis* to Greek thought.

This is *mētis* as an "attitude toward life . . . expressly circumspect and concerned, taking care and taking precautions" (ibid., 63).

A broader view of *mētis* not as a label for a set of actions, but rather as an epistemology, also helps to rescue the term, though never completely. Letiche and Statler offer a useful summary of this seeming contradiction of *mētis*:

> *Mētis* can simultaneously be associated with the rhetoric of control and repression (found in Foucauldian discourses), while at the same time retaining a rhetoric of creativity and release (as found in more postmodern discourses). These two rhetorics appear contradictory and incompatible. On one hand, if *mētis* is portrayed in terms of deliberate and rationally self-interested interventions in social reality, it cannot sustain the image of the trickster or jackal that brings fresh possibilities. Yet on the other hand, if *mētis* is seen as improvised interventions on behalf of the otherwise powerless, it cannot be ignored as a source of creativity or innovation. (2005, 4)

This contradiction or doubleness at the heart of *mētis*, fittingly, disallows strict schematizations of *mētis*. It is impossible to argue that any individual can fully control or master *mētis*, or ever fully evade the control and mastery of others. Instead, as Letiche and Statler suggest, the only way to "learn" *mētis* is "through a willingness to be open to unexpected ideas and a sensitivity for unforeseen possibilities . . . a positive attitude towards serendipity. . . . [M]ētis thus assumes a partial abandonment of control—that is, it involves not assuming oneself to be the agent of every solution, or the cause of each decision" (ibid., 5). (This also offers an interesting warning to someone like me—the author of a book about *mētis*.)

Mētis, Tuchē, Kairos, Technē

The key to understanding and accepting *mētis*, then, is that one understand the complexity and contradiction of a world of *tuchē*. Detienne and Vernant define *tuchē* as that which "brings the indiscernible future within the realm of possibility." *Tuchē* (TWO-KAY) is luck, happenstance, metaphorized as the wind itself, calling for both navigation and artisanship, as the sailor must know when and how to change direction. *Tuchē* is both the wind on the water and the play of the tiller— it "stands for the opportunity to succeed" (1978, 223).[11]

One possible analogue is to define *tuchē* as Foucault defines power, as a "complex strategical situation," a "multiplicity of force relations immanent in the sphere in which they operate and which constitute their own organization" (1973b, 92). A world of *tuchē* is a world in which one is always implicated and tangled in power relations, never emancipated, mastered even in moments of mastery. Foucault saw power as omnipresent, in rulers and ruled, and entwined with all relations, never as pure opposition but always as symbiosis across points. Importantly, for Foucault, power is always linked to the "intensification of the body"—"its exploitation as an object of knowledge and an element in relations of power" (ibid., 107). When the body is recognized as always rhetorically invested and "controlled," and when the world is viewed as itself a "witty agent," then one tends to hold onto the ideal of a pure and schematic rhetoric less tightly. *Mētis* encourages this confusion and relaxation.

Importantly, it is the extraordinary body that we must position at the root of this epistemological view. If we actually experienced the world through an ideal, "normal" body, we might see it as predictable and ordered. Yet, as Rod Michalko suggests, "disability is precisely the turbulence . . . so necessary to those who [falsely, temporarily] understand and experience the world as a taken-for-granted, unified reality" (2002, 182). Disability asks and allows us to value the embodied *tuchē* of being in the world.

Mētis may not always be used for "good." Yet arguments that cunning intelligence most often leads to deceptive action tend to also connect to the denigration of *mētis* as rhetoric that evades schematizatioe. (Perhaps even more important, arguments against *mētis* also often further the supposed allegiance between *mētis* and undesirable bodies.) As James Scott argues, "One major reason why *mētis* is denigrated . . . is that its 'findings' are practical, opportune, and contextual rather than integrated into

11. There was also a Greek deity named Tyche (TY-KAY) who was the blind mistress of fortune.

the general conventions of scientific discourse." The assumption, when one suggests that *mētis* is deceptive and untrustworthy, is that scientific knowledge, *logos*, or rational philosophy are never interested, deceptive, or harmful themselves. In the end, like any rhetoric, *mētis* is impartial, prone to misuses, and gains its ethical character only through its applications and iterations, not through any inherent quality. As Scott says, "The litmus test for *mētis* is practical success" (1998, 323).[12]

That none of these definitions offers any comfortable ways to pin down *mētis*, well, that is sort of the point—and this discomfort is certainly essential to the power of the concept.

Addressing worry about the polymorphous quality of *mētis*, Detienne and Vernant define *mētis* as characterized by and embodying a "complex but very coherent body of mental attitudes and intellectual behavior," as "a type of intelligence and of thought, a way of knowing." *Mētis* manifests itself as flair, forethought, subtlety of mind, deception, resourcefulness, vigilance, opportunism, and experience acquired over the years (1978, 3). In Greek thought, through close alliance with *kairos*, *tuchē*, and *technē*, *mētis* interacts with and circumscribes the world of chance and opportunity—in effect, providing the very possibility of acting in a world characterized by the swirling winds of luck.

Tuchē, as described above, is said to match the ambivalence of *kairos* (KY-ROSS) (ibid., 223). The two terms, in fact, were often situated as a

12. Halberstam might qualify that as "weapons of the weak," these successes can also look a lot like failure, when "failure can exploit the unpredictability of ideology and its indeterminate qualities" (2011, 88). In short, when we are operating within a system of false certainly, false opportunity, and oppressive normativity, one of the most cunning things we can do within this system is to fail. Thus, the ingenuity of the artisan relies not on outward logics of success, but instead on trial and error, stumbling upon what works within the shifting instances of invention. *Mētis* is not pragmatism—not making the best of a reality. Indeed, Jose Esteban Munoz would actually argue that the queer art of failure is an outright "rejection of pragmatism" (2009, 30). The clarification here is that practicality is not pragmatism—pragmatism assumes that we can size up the reality at hand and make do. *Mētis* recognizes no such static or understandable reality and instead suggests that in making do, we also reshape context. As Munoz also points out, this is not a rejection of the American pragmatic philosophical tradition of Pierce, James, or Dewey (2009, 21).

pair. Detienne and Vernant argue that *kairos* was introduced after *mētis* and that it means navigating—looking ahead and seeing a "propitious moment" for steering or "crafting" a product—or an argument. Margaret Price suggests that "kairotic spaces" are those "less formal, often unnoticed, areas . . . where knowledge is produced and power is exchanged" (2011, 60). Eric Charles White writes that *kairos* entails a "conception of time as discontinuous occasions" (1987, 14).[13] He writes that in such a universe, "there can never be more than a contingent and provisional management of the present opportunity" (ibid., 13). *Kairos*, then, is one aspect of *mētis*, and *mētis* is likewise conceptually enfolded in *kairos*. *Kairos* is the "speculatively mobile form of interpretation" that White insists is necessary to act in the moment (ibid., 160). *Kairos* is an acknowledgment that we need to pay as much attention to the momentary, the impromptu, the local, and the interpersonal as we do to monolithic structures of power. On the level of interpretation, *kairos* reminds us that no meaning is static, fixed, or durable. *Kairos* is also the idea of invention only within shifting contexts, only in the world of *tuchē*—of the winds of chance. Thus, *kairos* requires *mētis*, a way to be even more mobile, polymorphic, and cunning than the world itself. Like an experienced sailor, the person with *mētis* perceives the world of *tuchē* (swirling seas), harnesses *kairos* (a prevailing wind), and has the ingenuity required to think of cutting and building the tiller itself, to steer the ship instead of simply being blown around the sea.

Further, the building of tillers as a form of folk knowledge and industry could be an example of utilizing *mētis* to create a *technē* (TECK-NAY). Janet Atwill writes at length about *technē*, and she suggests that "the significance of *technē* often lies in the power of transformation that *mētis* enables" (1998, 56). In her history, *technē* are all of the transformative arts

---

13. As Margaret Price shows, we can and should connect *kairos* to the idea of *crip time*: the "flexible approach to normative time frames" (2011, 62). Crip time has generally been interpreted as responsive: a way to impose critical delay through the refusal to follow strict schedules (schedules that might be normative, ableist, medically rehabilitative, and so on). Time marches on, and we can refuse to roll with it. But in arguing that a standard and obedient response to time and timing actually overlooks unique opportunities for making meaning, we can also situate crip time as an epistemology.

that *mētis* makes possible. As Atwill explains in *Rhetoric Reclaimed*, *technē*, when it is allied with *mētis* (as it is by the Sophists), "deforms limits in to new paths in order to reach—or, better yet, to produce—an alternative destination" (ibid., 69). Through their connections and interactions, then, without obsessing about their causal relationships, we can recognize how *kairos*, *tuchē*, *technē*, and *mētis* help to describe a certain worldview, as well as actions, habits, and arts.

Through the rest of this chapter, I will suggest that *mētis* is a powerful way for us all to move. *Mētis* is a way to think and also a way to think about thinking. Importantly, *mētis* values bodily difference as generative of meaning, as in the example of Hephaestus. Looking at the image of Hephaestus in his chariot, we might feel some ambivalence—he is a disabled god, a "crippled" craftsman, and we might assume that these things are mutually exclusive. One could suggest that he overcame his disability through hard work. Yet both his bodily difference and his craftsmanship are evidence of the particular form of intelligence that Hephaestus was said to symbolize: *mētis*. In this way, his disability *is* his ability.

There is evidence that, from the very beginning of recorded history, human culture has had a more inclusive, more generous perspective on ability. There is evidence that exclusion has been imported into the classical world, and therefore we have been left with a narrow view of the role disability may have played in the period. It follows that rhetoric, philosophy, history, and many, many bodies are the victims of this discrimination. Methodologically, then, I employ a movement that, instead of reinscribing a normative reading of history and rhetoric, challenges and expands both. The vehicle for this reading is *mētis*, and the protagonist of my stories is Hephaestus.

Mētis is specifically *not* identified with the strongest and the best, with the norm, with the unchanging, but rather with an artisan like the "lame" Hephaestus. *Mētis* represents a "revers[al of] the 'natural' outcome of the encounter." Detienne and Vernant state that in the Greek intellectual world, there was an understanding that "whatever the strength of god or man, there always comes a time when he confronts one stronger than himself" (1978, 13).

In a world full of such inevitable instances, *mētis* is what the "fittest" employ. I want to analyze Hephaestus's *mētis* in order to suggest that, as Martha Rose also argues, "the distortion inherent in contemporary beliefs about disability is reflected in the portrayal of ancient Greek notions of disability" (2003, 3). More simply, I want to argue that we have exported our own prejudice into the past. It is thus surprising (to many) to recognize that there was a very positive association between Hephaestus's body and his mind: his outward-facing feet and his lateral thinking were allied, and both became a metaphor for *mētis*, the ability to move from side to side like a crab, as opposed to the forward march of logic. Pushing this association further, we learn that the word *mētis* shared an association, from its very first usage, with the idea of a physical curve, with the idea of a body not composed in perfect ratio. The roots *gu* and *kamp* were often used in words that described *mētis*, and these roots denote "feet [that are] twisted round or are capable of moving both forwards and backwards" and "whatever is curved, pliable or articulated" (Detienne and Vernant 1978, 46). I hope to show that what seems like a simple metaphorical connection between bodily difference and cunning thought can be reclaimed as a means of challenging physical and intellectual norms.

The Greek Myths Of Hephaestus

> We do not know what exactly his disability was, or how it occurred . . .
> [B]ut that he is disabled and that his birth was special, we are sure.
> —Jacques Stiker, *A History of Disability*

Into this story moves (perhaps sideways or backward) Hephaestus, Greek god of metallurgy, god of fire, the forge, and engineering. As a god with a noticeable physical disability, Hephaestus obviously represents an important character as we consider the story of disability in the classical period. How Hephaestus was presented reveals much about how norms of Greek society were figured and refigured—every story, every sculpture, every vase depicting the god wove Hephaestus into the cultural context, as part of an artistic and rhetorical process of self- and societal understanding.

Reading of Hephaestus and writing his story, one might expect to witness difference, deformity, and silence "reaffirmed," to borrow Robert

Garland's words. But I want to suggest that these representations did not always reaffirm and reinscribe his difference as deficit. Hephaestus's role in myth yields an often contradictory picture—a complexity that challenges simple constructions, reductions, or dismissals of his important role in history. The confusion and the flexibility of norms, as applied to and embodied by Hephaestus, suggest that Greek society did not understand disability as simply as our history might suggest.

Sissa and Detienne suggest that, "all things considered, [the most] profitable method for analysis of myths is first to read all their different versions" (2000, 213). Suitably, as I hope to use my radical history to combat a canonical story with fragments and apocrypha, the stories of Hephaestus are loose and diffuse. He is the least represented of all of the Greek gods, at least in the myths, textual fragments, and artifacts we now have access to. Still, he can be found, even if there seems to be no cohesive or continuous narrative to discover. Hephaestus is stories, more than he is a story, in fact. The contradictions abound. With this in mind, I think it is worthwhile to create a forensic and epideictic inventory of many of the things Hephaestus has been, in the context of my own double and divergent narrative.[14]

Borrowing from the recorded words of Homer, Apollodorus, and Hesiod, I have been able to nail together a branch of stories, a tangle of representations, a variety of different forms that tell the myths of Hephaestus. I focused on the second book of Hesiod's *Homeric Hymns*, as translated by Evelyn-White. I read Frazer's version of the collected Apollodorus. I set Lombardo's and Murray's translations of Homer's *Iliad* and *Odyssey* side by side, recognizing that in different translations, the stories greatly diverge. Finally, I looked at some of the existent imagery, the iconography of Hephaestus, as found on vase paintings and in engravings. In this way, I have first looked to the traditional historical texts to find Hephaestus. Of

---

14. As I suggested in the last chapter, disability forensics employs a sideways, skeptical, *mētis* approach to the truth and falsity of past events. Disability epideictic searches for the refusal of negative disability myths, praising and accentuating disability, restoring the virtue of the denigrated, and restoring the flaws of the venerated as a genre of *suspect* memorialization and an affirmative biopolitics.

course, I have also worked to make this narrative curve and double-back, to avoid smoothing the story into flatness. So, the resultant collage may be hard to read, and it is even harder to understand or believe how this myth, or any other, could have functioned to strictly reinscribe a polarity with any hope of holding its charge.

Pausanias, in his *Description of Greece*, wrote that "the legends of Greece generally have different forms, and this is particularly true of genealogy" (1933, 8.53.5). As I hope to show, Hephaestus's genealogy was also double and divergent. Hephaestus is the son of Hera. He is born of Hera alone, a virgin birth. Or Hera invented this story to cover up an affair. Or Hephaestus is born of Zeus and Hera. In this version of the story, he is also the son of the goddess Metis, however, because she lives in Zeus's head. Zeus ate the pregnant Metis to consume the cunning intelligence that bears her name, and after this meal, all cunning must channel through Zeus. Because of this lineage, Hephaestus (and Athena) carry Metis's *mētis* and are thus a constant threat to Zeus's control of this, the most powerful form of intelligence.[15] We are sometimes told that Hephaestus's feet were crooked from birth. Consequently, he is sent away from Olympus—he is rejected by Hera, and by Zeus, because of his disability. Yet in other stories, Hephaestus is not crippled at birth, but is injured by Zeus, for coming to Hera's rescue when Zeus threatened or bound her. In this version, Zeus expels Hephaestus, and it is his long fall from Olympus that injures him. Or is it Hera who throws Hephaestus, hoping to hide his infirmity from Zeus? In any case, he finds himself tossed out of Olympus, his very godliness threatened, and as he lays on the ground we see him as very mortal—he has a crooked leg. And then the story gets weird. Hephaestus is rescued by the Nereids, sea nymphs who take him to their underwater caves. In seclusion, Hephaestus proves that he

---

15. I would argue that Hephaestus's disability also symbolizes his *mētis* to Zeus—the disability is a reminder of Metis and thus of the threat that her descendants pose to his sovereign power. I will explore these stories further in the next chapter. As I hope to show, it is impossible not to read Metis into the drama of Hephaestus's banishment. It would not be a stretch to say that, in the same way that Metis is eaten because she embodies *mētis*, Hephaestus is thrown because his disability is evidence of his cunning intelligence.

is crafty and creative. He is known as a trickster, but he also perfects the craft of metallurgy, utilizing his *mētis*. He builds two voice-activated tripods, what we would call robots, to help him with his work, and he befriends the Cyclops, teaching him to work with fire as well. Throughout these stories, he works with others, is a teacher, and often comes to the defense of friends. Descriptions of his bodily movements, while they may seem to us to clash with descriptions of his industry, become part of a whole—Hephaestus as *mētis* enacted.

The connection here between *mētis* and prosthesis is clear: recall Wills's suggestion that every rhetorical move is a "running hither and thither," and communication is always "dealing with the sideways as well as the forward momentum." Importantly, this movement is "perhaps not structurally different from a natural gait," "an explicit infraction upon or departure from the straits of linearity" (1995, 25).[16] In this way, our bodily imperfections are ineluctably tied to our embodied communication, our embodied knowledges. *Mētis*, and the sideways, ingenious movements of Hephaestus, then perfectly personify prosthesis. As such, Hephaestus and his rhetorical work are prosthesis enacted. In a variety of representations of him and his work, Hephaestus reveals our "relation to and dependence upon the inanimate, the artificial" (ibid., 246). Recall David Wills's suggestion that the prosthetic body, "infirm or lacking, in need of the other," is "not the exception but the paradigm for the body itself" (ibid., 137). Therefore, "every rhetorical form that comes into effect is a prosthetic transfer" (ibid., 14). Hephaestus's relationships and his tools are not compensatory, do not "correct" him. They are part of him, incorporated (see figure 3).[17]

16. While Hephaestus's "gait" is often accentuated to be ridiculed in myth, Adam Benjamin argues that "Hephaestus was not only a problem-solver and inventor, he was also in his time a famed dancer. His hobbling 'partridge dance' has accompanied the storytelling traditions associated with the art of metal work and is still found today as far afield as West Africa and Scandinavia" (2002, 24).

17. In her "cyborg manifesto," Donna Haraway also argued that "the boundary is very permeable between tool and myth, instrument and concept, historical systems of social relations and historical anatomies of possible bodies, including objects of knowledge. Myths and tools mutually constitute one another" (1985, 2). This has particular meaning for

Next is the story of his return from seclusion to civilization (Olympus). This becomes the tale most often told about Hephaestus. The story is commemorated in numerous works of art, celebrated by archaic vase painters. As Fineberg suggests, this scene was "most popular representations in attic vase paintings of the fifth and sixth centuries" (2009, 277). But again, there are many ways to tell this story. In some paintings, on some pottery, Hephaestus's disability is made glaringly obvious—for instance, he is shown riding a mule, his leg grotesquely twisted backward, as shown in figure 2. In this image, Hephaestus is depicted in his return to Olympus, seated on a mule. We view him from the side, and the foot in the foreground looks like a fist, with the toes pointed backward and the ankle twisted upward. These works may be meant to focus the viewers' attention solely upon his disability as an object of pity, or they may denote, in a kind of shorthand, his ability to think laterally.

It has also been said that, before the journey, Dionysius (who is depicted to the left of Hephaestus, holding a vessel, in the image above) gets Hephaestus drunk and that this is why he rides the mule—this story also makes a fool of Hephaestus. In some paintings, he is nearly falling from his mount. In others, his mule has an erection—is about to mount another mule and throw him. In fact, in one depiction, there is an amphora hanging from this erection. It is also noteworthy that in these depictions he is riding a mule, and not a horse; as J. Michael Padgett points out, "Donkeys and mules [in vase paintings] constituted the negative counter-model to the noble race of horses" (2003, 43). Yet in other depictions, he is on foot, a seeming contradiction to the symbolism of the mule as a token of his lameness (Fineberg 2009).

Figure 3 shows Hephaestus on a mule. The mule has a noticeable erection. Hephaestus's feet are not shown. He carries his tools prominently.

In depictions such as this one, Hephaestus's ride back to civilization is heroic. He is now the god of fire, a gifted craftsman. He has resumed his place in Olympus, and the other gods view him as *able* even if he

---

the myths of Hephaestus and the overlap between "forging" tools, weapons, and embodied rhetorical possibilities.

2. *Return of Hephaestus to Olympus*, Dionysos, Maenad. Black-figured Hydria from Caere, Ionic-Greek (525 BCE). Height 41.5 cm. Inv. IV 3577. © Photograph by Erich Lessing. Kunsthistorisches Museum, Vienna, Austria. Photo credit: Erich Lessing/Art Resource, NY.

has a disability—perhaps because of this disability. His inclusion in the pantheon then also subtly (or not so subtly) changes the way gods are viewed. In *The Daily Life of Greek Gods*, Sissa and Detienne suggest that there is a shift in perceptions of the gods' effort and industry (2000, 29, 50). Hephaestus describes himself as *achnumenoi*, affected by pain (ibid., 29). Hephaestus also sweats, proof that he engages in real labor (ibid., 50). As a worker, Hephaestus sets a new model for the lives of the gods. In figure 3, he is shown carrying his tools on this triumphant ride to Olympus. Figure 4 shows a close-up of the god. He is seated on a mule, though the image focuses on his head and upper body. Most notably, we once again see him carrying his hammer and tongs—the hammer slung

3. *Hephaestus, god of fire, bronzework, and craftsmen, returns to Olympus.* Black-figured Attic amphora, end of sixth century BCE. Terracotta. Height: 40 cm. Diameter 27.3 cm. Kunthistorisches Museum, Vienna, Austria. Photo credit: Erich Lessing/Art Resource, NY.

over his right shoulder, the tongs in his left hand. These outward signs of his industry clash with the general image of gods at leisure. That his body labors, and that this labor is itself cunning, challenges our modern impression of the gods as being lazy, as it changes the message that their stories convey, then and now.

Now back in Olympus, Hephaestus begins his new career. He appears throughout Homer's stories, making and extinguishing fire, distributing thunderbolts, building clever traps. He builds each of the gods a house (ibid., 44). He makes a golden breastplate for Heracles, armor for Achilles (Hesiod 1914b, 240; Auden 1976). Interestingly, Hephaestus is also said to have built a home and then a scepter for Zeus, his father

4. The Kleophon Painter (Greek, Attic), *Skyphos, Side A, detail of Hephaestus*, about 420 BC, wheel thrown, slip decorated earthenware, Height: 11 13/16 in. (30 cm). Diameter (rim): 13 1/16 in. (33.2 cm). Diameter (with handles): 18 13/16 in. (47.8 cm). Diameter (foot): 8 15/32 in. (21.5cm). Toledo Museum of Art (Toledo, OH), purchased with funds from the Libbey Endowment, Gift of Edward Drummond Libbey, 1982.88. Photo credit: Tim Thayer, Oak Park, MI.

(Homer 1999a, 2.100). He also builds a bronze man, or perhaps a bronze bull, another archetypal robot. In one particularly interesting, perhaps vexing, twist, Hephaestus is credited with creating women. He builds an army of females, golden women who are strong, smart, and able to speak their minds (Homer 1997, 18.417).[18] Or, in another version, he makes one

18. Through his Roman alter ego, Hephaestus appears in Flannery O'Connor's short story "Good Country People," here invoked as an artisan whose physical debility belies an artistic gift. O'Connor's story, as Nicole Markotic shows us, "depicts a woman [Joy], overeducated and unhappy, with one wooden leg" (2003, n.p.). The character of Joy later changes her name to Hulga, and she "had a vision of the name [Hulga] working like the ugly sweating Vulcan who stayed in the furnace and to whom, presumably, the goddess

woman, firing her from clay (Hesiod 1914b, 60). This woman is Pandora, and Hephaestus gives her a special jar that she is not to open. In these stories, we recognize that *mētis* was more than just an industry; it was a craft of innovation, however complicated. Hephaestus's *mētis* is at times an actual creation of bodies, while it is always an extension of the body. In a sense, *mētis* is an application of ingenious bodies to the problems the world presents, answering the shifting contexts of existence with shifting rhetorical, mechanical, and corporeal positions.

In less favorable stories, Hephaestus is said to have attempted to rape Athena who, it is said, never had a lover (Apollodorus 1921, 2.91).[19] Supposedly, Athena's son Ericthonius is born from Hephaestus's fallen seed. In this story, there is evidence of the conflation of Hephaestus's disability with a kind of predatory perversity (see the myth of sexual excess in my chart of myths in chapter 1). Yet the story is also used, curiously, to prove that Athenians are born of the earth, because Ericthonius later becomes king of Athens.

Hephaestus is also the one who bound Prometheus, with special chains that he made himself (Aeschylus 1970, 39).

In his lengthiest cameo appearance in *The Odyssey*, Hephaestus appears for comic relief. He has married Aphrodite, and he finds that she is having an affair with Ares, "who is handsome and clean-built," he says, "whereas I am a cripple" (Homer 2000, 8.267). Hephaestus fashions a trap for the adulterers and tricks them to have his revenge. He appears as a cuckold, yet he is also represented as crafty, smarter, and a "better man" than Ares, even though Ares supposedly has the superior body.

And so it goes, back and forth, from one story to the next. Hephaestus is never fully a hero, never fully a villain. He is represented reverently—as

---

had to come when called" (1983, 174). As Markotic shows, Joy "believes that, like Vulcan, she has a lame leg, but has the power to call forth great beauty, dedication, and love in another" (2003, n.p).

19. We see, then, that across myths, Hephaestus is constructed as asexual, a cuckold in some instances, and as excessively sexualized in other instances. This adheres to the "disability myth" of the poles of asexuality or excessive sexuality.

"renowned smith" (Homer 1999a, 18.463), "glorious Hephaestus" (ibid., 8.286, 8.287). Such images and honorifics deify *mētis* as it is performed by Hephaestus, embodied by him. Yet other times he is represented pityingly, reductively, objectively—"god of the dragging foot" (ibid., 18.371).

To summarize: It is true that, in comparison to the other Greek gods, we rarely see Hephaestus. When we do, the "eye" that beholds Hephaestus sometimes focuses wholly and negatively upon his disability—and these negative depictions often invoke disability myths. But sometimes the eye that beholds Hephaestus gazes positively upon his ability. His appearance and his movement send a message about the power of cunning intelligence. Yet there is no one essential Hephaestus. The inventory I have just recounted contains within it many contradictions. The way that he is figured is a matter of constant conflict. Of course, questioning the significance of these distinctions is worthwhile. I see the myths and images themselves as a sort of heuristic—a set of questions propelling a cycle of discovery and rediscovery. Here, then, I want to create an interpretive machine, expressed through the questions that matter to me. The trajectory of this vehicle can be determined by how you choose to discover answers and also via the questions you add. I hope that in emphasizing the partiality of my own interpretation I am not, as Xin Liu Gale suggests, doing so only to privilege the truths I do present and actually "excluding the competing truths" (2000, 372). My intention is to present multiple interpretations, as well as multiple questions and multiple interpretive openings.

Asking Questions

Lillian Eileen Doherty argues that the "interpretation [of mythology] is [always] an exercise of *mētis* (1995, 4). With this in mind, I want to provide a litany of questions and move sideways and backward through possible answers.

How are we to view Hephaestus's trade? In some ways, is he doubly marginalized because he is also "working class"? What does his prolific production signify? How is his craft specifically suited to his body? How does *mētis*, then, stand as an "accessible" intelligence, something one can develop, something that dovetails with one's abilities, something syncretic with the body, yet not in service of a normate image of the body?

What of the drama of his banishment and return? How does this symbolize the conflict between acceptance of and/or exclusion of people with disabilities or of the disavowal and/or acceptance of disability conceptually? How does this story comment on the cultural value of citizenship in Athens—that Athenians were not wanderers, like others, but were tied to their city (Jarratt and Ong 1995, 21)?[20]

What about the visual images of Hephaestus? Sometimes he is standing, sometimes seated, sometimes on a donkey, sometimes walking on foot, sometimes in his winged chariot or proto-wheelchair. For instance, he is sometimes on foot and sometimes on a donkey in the popular vase paintings of the "Return of Hephaestus." Stephen Fineberg argues that this represents an "iconographic inconsistency [that] expresses psychological conflict: when Hephaestus rides, he acknowledges Zeus's superior authority (indeed Zeus once before punished Hephaestus for allying with Hera against him), but when Hephaestus walks, he becomes the son his mother hoped for, a fully formed adult who can, literally and figuratively, stand up to Zeus" (2009, 275–76).[21] Fineberg even goes so far as to argue that the upright Hephaestus represented "the fantasy of a young man standing up in his mother's behalf and in defiance of the patriarchal order" and thus addressing "an anxiety felt by contemporary young Athenian men" who may have also been "female-identified" as Hephaestus was (ibid., 316).[22]

20. See my discussion about connections between *mētis* and *metics*, Athenian "foreigners," in the next chapter.

21. Fineberg elaborates: "In psychological terms, Hephaestus, a mythic representative of young men in the city itself, is negotiating a troubled passage to manhood expressed in mutually exclusive impulses that, under the aegis of Dionysus, finds open expression in the vase representations" (2009, 276).

22. Fineberg argues that this anxiety was "felt by contemporary young Athenian men as they moved from the company of the women to the society of men. . . . [T]he transition would have been dramatic and, as I argued, psychologically traumatic. Like Hephaestus, a male who was seen as female-identified was socially marginalized and subjected

What do these images say, then, about the importance of Hephaestus to this culture, the tangle between gender and ability norms, and the fantasy of overcoming?

Fineberg argues that in these "on foot" vase paintings of his return, Hephaestus walks "without apparent reference to his traditional deformity" (ibid., 277). And Garland argues that in most sculptures, his body is "normal" (1985, 113). Yet in other depictions, he stands with crooked feet—Brommer argues that in the majority of vase paintings, his disability is in fact drastically represented (1986, 159). Hephaestus is also said to have a very strong upper body, presumably as a symbol of his labor (Homer 1999a, 1.607, 14.239). So what are all of the significations of his body, and, together, what do they represent? What about the tools and prostheses he wields and crafts? Is his power contained in the tools, or in the hands that hold the tools, the body that labors around them, the mind that trains them upon his craft?

What about the repeated bullying of Hephaestus in myth? Were all people with disabilities the object of derision and mockery? Or in his role as fool, does he expose what is laughable about larger forces and ideas? Or should we understand his failures as "art," in the ways Halberstam suggests—as strategic and cunning responses to difficult or illogical situations?

How does Hephaestus reincarnate Metis herself? How does the consumption and usurpment of Metis by Zeus mirror the consumption and usurpment of *mētis* by the rhetorical and philosophical tradition? How does Hephaestus's story fit into this denunciation? (I will return to this question in the next chapter.)

Is Hera, his mother, truly ashamed of Hephaestus? The answer to this question would reveal much about the ways a mother regarded, or was encouraged to regard, a disabled child. If Hephaestus's return to civilization was indeed celebrated, he stands as a symbol of reversal—as Marie

---

to ridicule, and yet, if the figure of Hephaestus on foot offers us any indication, the fantasy of a young man standing up in his mother's behalf and in defiance of the patriarchal order could not be set aside" (2009, 316).

Delcourt and Henri-Jacques Stiker have written, there is some evidence from the period of the expulsion and exposure of children with disabilities. Does this story support the idea that expulsion was "not primarily a killing but a return to the hands of the gods"? That Hephaestus was expelled from the heavens may have represented "insecurity in the face of the divine, linked to the wrongdoing of men and anger from above" (Stiker 1999, 40). Were the disabled really understood as being sent from above as punishment? If Hephaestus is welcomed back by Zeus, the angriest of all the gods, how are the disabled only a "sign of the gods' anger and . . . also the reason for it" (Delcourt 1957, 39)? Does Zeus's acceptance of gifts from this disowned son, or Hera's change of heart, signal a change in the perception and valuation of his existence?

What about Hephaestus's "queer kinship" (Halberstam 2011, 72)? He is isolated and banished from Olympus, but this allows him to form alliances with the Nereids, the Cyclops, to create his own automatons. Does this alternative "family" reinforce "relations that grow along parallel lines rather than upward and onward [as a] queer form of antidevelopment" (ibid., 73)? Does his isolation actually lead him to develop new and different forms of interrelations, models for a more collaborative and interdependent society? Is there a politics to be read through the bonds he creates?

Does the fact that Hephaestus is very capable, very much able, very creative, allow people to overlook or ignore his disability? Does a valorization of his *mētis* negate his disability, or does it require it? Might this allow for an identity for the disabled that *incorporates* a variety of different roles? Is Hephaestus's presence in myth more about his ability than his disability? Is his cunning, not always used in service of good, a form of trickery, or a kind of crafty pragmatism? What of the tension between his role as a kind of "exceptional cripple" and his labor and sweat, which seem to be a symbol of the god's humanity? Is he a symbol of the weakness of gods, or of their common-ness? Is he a symbol of godliness in the common man? Or is he just Hephaestus, a true original?

With each question in my heuristic, we are offered a glimpse of the rhetorical power of the myth of Hephaestus, the challenge his body and his body of work represents. He certainly operationalizes every one of the disability "myths" from my chart in the first chapter. My questioning is consistent with a view of myth as a site of cultural conflict—conflict that travels back into the middle of the crowd that constituted its original audience. To be able to question Hephaestus in this way reveals his importance. Hephaestus is a rhetorical figure, and he represents the suasive power of myth and its cultural importance. He allows us to configure important questions about ability and disability and to recognize their coexistence with Greek rhetorical theory and a chosen "origin" of Western thought. This, in turn, uncovers the central importance of the question of normalcy to all of rhetoric and to our long-held ideas about knowledge, art, and industry.

James Fredal, the rhetorician and historian I looked to earlier for a definition of the role of the disabled in rhetorical history, points out that while some historians of rhetoric have been obsessing about the authority of texts, "important events, trends, places, terms and cultural conditions" have been overlooked. Fredal asserts that such overlooked cultural and societal practices and institutions can "replace the author as focal points for historical investigations" (2006, 592). With this in mind, I suggest that the study of Hephaestus, the recognition of the richness and complexity of his representation, would be a starting point for further historical study. I also suggest that the rhetorical nature of this study, and of the Hephaestus stories themselves, reveals the powerfully rhetorical nature of disability itself.

"Celebration"

I have been enabled by Fredal's call to "replace the author as [the] focal point of historical investigations" (2006, 592). I am also excited by the work of historian Harlan Hahn, who has suggested that there is archaeological evidence that disability was actually held in high regard in the classical period. He says that "the appearance of physical differences seemed to be associated with festiveness, sensuality and entertainment rather than loss, repugnance and personal tragedy" (1988, 31). Many historians have suggested that Hephaestus's "lameness, epic risibility, and limitations in

5. *Temple of Hephaestus.* © Adam Carr, Gnu Free Documentation License, September 24, 2004.

cult practice have been interpreted as part of a general disregard for crafts in Athens" (Blakely 2006, 23).[23] Yet in Periclean Athens, around 420 BCE, at a time when metalworkers were in great demand, Hephaestus became, briefly, one of the most popular of mythical figures. The city was being rebuilt on an epic scale after the Ten Years' War. Workers were needed. Disabled or not, if you were skilled, you were in demand. The norms were slightly recalibrated. We have been given a version of history that asserts

23. Sandra Blakely (2006) makes this statement based on the research of Garland (1985) and Burford (1972), both of whom I have discussed and problematized in this chapter, as well as a short 1912 archaeological article by L. Malten. She also makes this argument as a way to create a distinction between Hephaestus and the Greek Daimones, also mythical metallurgists and the subject of her book, whom she constructs as being represented in sophisticated and positive ways, while Hephaestus is simply made fun of.

that a person's physical ability to wage war was paramount. Yet as Periclean Athens emerged from the wreckage of war, this was not the case. There was real cultural value assigned to a citizen's technical ability as a craftsperson—different ways of knowing were valued.[24]

At this time, according to Alison Burford, "metal workers and miners were especially vulnerable to injury." However, "having acquired a physical impairment, [they] would have had no reason to stop working or change trades" (1972, 72). As William Ebenstein argues, "Hephaestus' workshop provides a mythic model for a utopian workplace that applies universal design elements, and incorporates technology and individualized accommodations to tap the creative energies of all workers, with and without disabilities" (2006, n.p.).[25] It is possible then that Hephaestus's ways of knowing and doing made the workforce more diverse and the workplace more accessible.

24. In David Serlin's *Replaceable You*, he studies a very similar shifting of values following World War II in America, something I reference in my introduction to the book. He suggests that the invention of prosthetics both was necessitated by and allowed for the revision of held views about disability and labor. Simply, many men were injured in the war—yet they were then needed as productive workers. He suggests that "at the end of the war, an amputated arm or leg may have provoked associations between anatomical dysfunction and a lack of reliability, sturdiness, fortitude, or commitment." But by the mid-1950s, prosthetics offered "a new kind of social prestige as well as a new model of masculine labor" (2004, 56). In this way, through both Athens and America, we see that cultural ideas about the productive and aesthetic values of disability have always been prone to shifts and reversals.

25. Ebenstein traces this cultural valuation from ancient Greece into the industrial era: "Over the centuries, in Western society, as communities transitioned from an agrarian to an industrial way of life, traditional craft guilds that may have accommodated individuals with disabilities began to disappear. The widespread use of coal fueled an industrial revolution and Hephaestus's modest workshop evolved into the modern factory. In England, as early as the 1700's, many social commentators and artists became disgusted by the ugliness, pollution and human suffering associated with the new factory system. Instead of being connected with progress and the rise of civilization. . . . [I]ndustrialization and machine technology were viewed by many as . . . evil," and thus Hephaestus's image began to take on less desirable meanings (2006, n.p.).

The celebration of Hephaestus as metalworker could have reflected the idea that this trade was actually one of the only inclusive trades in the culture. Or his image could have been "used" to attract people with disabilities to the trade, to get everyone working. But what if, instead of just being an emblem of surplus labor, a nonproductive disabled body, and instead of then being subsumed temporarily as necessary labor, Hephaestus might signal a shifting of "the standardized demands of human value," representing "forms of creativity that cannot be reduced to an economic value" (Mitchell and Snyder 2006, 184). What if the respect shown for Hephaestus was motivated by an acknowledgment of the ways a society relies upon a wide range of contributions as well as a sense that art transcends and sometimes subverts normative economies? For instance, James C. Scott suggests that the "impetus" for what he calls *mētis* in the development of local agricultural practices throughout the world often has been the "marginal status" of the people behind such innovations. In situations of vulnerability, *mētis* is the "mode of reasoning most appropriate to complex material and social tasks where the uncertainties are so daunting that we must trust our (experienced) intuition and feel our way" (1985, 327). In this "new" Athenian reality, in which many of the old norms were being recalibrated, Hephaestus became a symbol for difference and marginality, but also productivity and creativity. This Homeric hymn to Hephaestus expresses the societal adoration for the god quite clearly: "Hephaestus famed for inventions. With bright-eyed Athene he taught men glorious crafts throughout the world,—men who before used to dwell in caves in the mountains like wild beasts. But now that they have learned crafts through Hephaestus the famed worker, easily they live a peaceful life in their own houses the whole year round. Be gracious, Hephaestus, and grant me success and prosperity!" (Hesiod "Homeric Hymn XX to Hephaestus" 1914a, 2.1–7). This very similar Orphic hymn also captures this reverence:

Hephaestus
Your hammer and pincers
Master every art
Molten bronze and gold
Flow from your workshop.

Volcanoes, lava, flame from earth

Pure clean light of the shining sun,

That is all we see of you.

You are the heat and strength of fire.

Father of tribes, builder of shelter, inventor of cities we honor you.

Our strong bodies your handiwork.

Breathe upon us an even flame.

(T. Taylor 1969, 198)

Pausanias tells us that at this time, in Athens, a temple was built in Hephaestus's honor, an accolade reserved for only the most major gods (1933, 1.14.6). This temple is not notably different from any other temple in Athens: huge marble Doric columns along all four sides. But it is the best-preserved temple in the city. In figure 5, the temple is shown as it looks today—there are visitors around it, and a groundskeeper works in the foreground. In Periclean Athens, a large festival was also held, commemorating Hephaestus's return to Olympus and, figuratively, his presence in Athens. Historian Takahiro Saito suggests that this festival, called the "Hephaistia," served as a citizenship rite for Athenians, honoring Hephaestus and Athena as the parents of this great civilization (2006, para. 20–26). Walter Burkert (1985) writes that the festival also took place in the city of Hephaistia, on the isle of Lemnos, and incorporated rituals of rebirth by fire. The *Suidae Lexicon* reports on a similar festival, possibly the same one, calling it the Kalkeia (Stoa Consortium 2006, chi 36). The festivals, it seems, were designed to recognize Hephaestus as a parent of an emerging civilization, as a teacher, and as a hero. Burkert suggests that the festival on Lemnos was a way to recognize the craftsmen of the island, but also to celebrate the very invention of fire (1985, 3). He goes on to write that such festivals are a part of a worldwide tradition: "Festivals of the new fire are among the most common folk customs all over the world" (ibid., 4). But fire, in the Greek context, is "the triumph of Hephaestus," and his festival is a celebration of new life (ibid., 9). According to Saito, the festival in Athens also had the purpose of reminding citizens of their civic responsibilities: "When the 10 years-long war ended, Athens felt a need to tighten up and reintegrate her citizen body. It was the Hephaistia that was utilized for this purpose" (2006, para. 26). Saito writes that Athena and Hephaestus were situated as the parents of this new Athens.

In Aspasia's famous speech "Pericles' Funeral Oration," retold in Plato's *Menexenus* (1961c), she too mentions this role for Hephaestus and Athena. That the two are not specifically named is perhaps the result of some historical editing. Yet at the time of the speech, I would suggest Pericles's audience would know exactly to whom he was referring. He praises "the gods who ordered our lives, and instructed us, first of all men, in the arts for the supply of our daily needs, and taught us the acquisition and use of arms for the defense of the country" (Ritchie and Ronald 2001, 4).[26] Plato also mentions Hephaestus's fatherly role in his *Critias*, lamenting that over time (the time between his own and that of Periclean Athens), society had failed to recognize the importance of Hephaestus (2000, para. 7). Since then, unfortunately, he has been even more neglected.[27] Yet the festival of Hephaestus, at the time, was an important and unprecedented event. Sissa and Detienne suggest that his festival was one (unlike nearly all others) where Metics or foreigners were welcome, and not just the upper class celebrated (2000, 200). Norms of class, ability, and citizenship/ ethnicity were all challenged.

Clearly, Hephaestus's image in Athens, and on Lemnos, was not burdened by the stigma that historians like Garland suggest disability entails. I would go so far as to suggest that the stigma comes from a modern reading and writing of the history. Clearly, there are ways to view disability as something worth celebrating. Hephaestus was not expelled from the city; he was heralded as Athens's father. Hephaestus's disability is not his sole characteristic. The invention of fire is his triumph, evidence

---

26. Notice the parallelism between these words and those of the "Homeric Hymn" previously quoted ("he taught men glorious crafts throughout the world, men who before used to dwell caves in the mountains like wild beasts") as well as Hephaestus's role as metalworker, building arms for the gods.

27. Susan Jarratt and Rory Ong (1995) point out that Plato mentioned Aspasia as well, and despite this she has been largely ignored.

of his *mētis* as an embodied knowledge concomitant with his bodily difference.

In addition to Hephaestus's reputation for industriousness and ingenuity, Saito suggests that instead of stigmatizing physical difference, he actually deified it—his disability is not hidden, but becomes part of his godly image. Cicero wrote that "at Athens there is a much-praised statue of [Hephaestus] by Alcamenes, a standing figure, draped, which displays a slight lameness, though not enough to be unsightly. We shall therefore deem god to be lame, since tradition represents [him] so" (1955, 1.24). The positive perception of his mind, his craftiness, was balanced with—not negated or superseded by—the positive symbolism of his disabled body. Detienne and Vernant write that "the peculiar shape of his feet is the visible symbol" not of weakness, but of "his *mētis*, his wise thoughts and his craftsman's intelligence" (1978, 272). As I have suggested, *mētis* can be understood as a rhetorical framework, a way to move, rhetorically.[28] Thus, instead of reaffirming the unity of the hegemonic group based upon a narrow view of ability, Hephaestus may have dissolved it—he may have allowed the monologue of unity to morph into a polyphony. His body might stand as a symbol of power, artistry, ingenuity, rhetorical facility, godliness, disability—these terms might in fact be inclusive of one another.

If Hephaestus has so many stories, why should we believe that disability was silenced in ancient Greece? If Hephaestus was so respected and celebrated as a tradesman and an artist, why should we believe that craft and art, that rhetoric and expression, are exclusively the realm of the "able-bodied"? Hephaestus might become not just a model for alternative versions of agency, but also a model for the agency we might all have access to, once we are willing to consider reversing, moving sideways,

---

28. By "way to move" I mean not just a way to move our own bodies or make rhetorical moves, but also a way to move others—to make others feel, act, and physically move; a way to change minds and bodies, as well as attitudes about minds and bodies; a way to avoid staticity and stillness and reification.

facing traps. This is not to suggest that disability should be erased. Just because Hephaestus might symbolize the ways we all move, the rhetoric we all have access to, does not mean that we are all disabled, nor does it mean that disability does not exist. Instead, I want to suggest that the worlds we create partially construct disability. So perhaps it is now time to return to ancient Greece, guided by Hephaestus, father of this civilization, and to revise our perspective, addressing the exclusions we have applied over time. In the end, this is not about superimposing a new history over the old; it is instead about enlightening the many stories of Western civilization with the fire of an even flame.

In this chapter, Hephaestus allowed us to question some of the foundational concepts of rhetoric as we reviewed myths, art, and customs through the filter of the body and the critical lens of disability studies. This view of history allowed us to trouble the idea that rhetorical facility was and is only about controlled, measured bodies and speech. Hephaestus's *mētis* presents a way of thinking and moving that challenges the linear, the logical, and that separates the mind and the body. These myths speak to my inventory of considerations for bodily rhetoric: first, that the body is rhetorically invested, inscribed, shaped; second, that all rhetoric is embodied; and third, that because of the rhetorical construction of the body, and rhetorical invention *by* the body, all bodies must be read through a normative matrix—and bodily difference must be recognized as the engine for meaning-making.

The doubleness and divergence of these stories also force us to recognize history itself as cunning. Thus, we need to carefully examine the uses of rhetorical or mythical texts as histories. The celebration of Hephaestus, his craft, his cunning, his ability, as well as the deification of his disability are means of challenging held perceptions about the mythical character, but also about all of us—defined as we all are by concepts of ability, by rhetorics of normalcy. Telling Hephaestus's story makes a difference. As we retell it and reinterpret it, we need to use *mētis* ourselves. We then open up the possibility of situating disability as strength, as fit for a world that is also cunning, changing, and changeable. Instead of exporting modern biases into the past, we might import this possibility into the present.

Modern Myths

One example of this contemporary importation is that Hephaestus has become an important and recurring figure in a number of video games, science fiction films, and comic books. Hephaestus appears in some form in the video games *BioShock*, *God of War*, *Diablo*, *Soul Calibur*, *Tomb Raider*, and *Dragon Quest* (and I am certainly neglecting to mention many others). Hephaestus's video game role is unique: because of the armed-combat format of so many of these games, as well as their quest narratives, he is the perfect archetype to create weapons and assist players in completing their tasks, as a metalsmith. We might even say that in the "economy" and story world of the video game, artisans such as Hephaestus are highly valued. There is obviously more we could say both about the ableist visual world of video games, the idea of quantified "handicaps" and ability quotients, their violence and militarism and chauvinism, and also about the possibly enabling vectors of interaction games might allow. Within the iterative, ongoing, and increasingly modifiable mythical world of the video game, however, Hephaestus's presence, at the very least, ensures the generation of more stories.

He lives on in "genre" films and literatures as well: Hephaestus is visited by Baron Munchhausen in Terry Gilliam's canonical film *The Adventures of Baron Von Munchausen* and appears in the 1981 *Clash of the Titans* and the 1997 Disney version of *Hercules*. He appears as a character in the *Percy Jackson and the Olympians* series of books.[29] In almost all of these appearances, the creators stick to and recycle traditional stories, and he

29. In this series, Hephaestus is depicted as bitter and mad at the world, distrusting of others. He wears a leg brace and has a hunch. Interestingly, however, the major characters in these extremely popular books are all demigods, meant to represent heroes from Greek myth. The demigods know how to read Greek, but are labeled as having dyslexia when trying to read English; their physicality makes it very difficult to sit still, so they are also diagnosed with ADHD (attention deficit/hyperactivity disorder). In the school setting, they are "disabled" and then also suffer through remediations and punishments. But at Camp Halfblood, the demigods' training ground, which serves as a sort of inverse of the world of public school, those things that disable them in school are strengths.

plays just a bit part. Yet one particularly rich and interesting recent role for Hephaestus has been in the *Wonder Woman* comic book series.[30]

In the May 2012 DC Comics *Wonder Woman* #7, written by Brian Azzarello and drawn by Cliff Chiang, Hephaestus appears as an ogre with burned arms.[31] He is not in a wheelchair, but in one arresting image we see him jumping into the air, and we recognize a set of very modern-looking braces on his legs. He holds his hammer above his head, in midswing, and he seems intent on using it for violence. He is yelling, "AND I WON'T HAVE IT!" (Azzarello and Chang 2012, n.p.).

In previous iterations of the comic, we have learned that Wonder Woman is descended from the Amazons and that Hephaestus created Wonder Woman's lasso of truth, a sword that can cut the electrons right off an atom, and her armor (which we might recognize as one of the most iconic costumes of modern pop culture, but may have also struck viewers as being traditionally composed of much more Lycra than metal). In all of the armor and weapons Hephaestus creates, he intentionally includes a weakness, so that no user can become too powerful. His creations, then, become exemplary prostheses—in the sense through which prosthesis has been defined thus far in this book.

In this recent run of *Wonder Woman*, Hephaestus also plays a central role in the narrative, as the protector and father to a group of orphaned men, whose Amazon mothers have abandoned them. There is a clearly eugenic message here: the Amazon mothers mate with men only three times every century, and when they do so they discard all male babies to maintain their female-only island. Hephaestus saves these male children, ostensibly because his own mother discarded him, left him to die. In the

30. Hephaestus also appears in *Phoenix*, a long comic book series by Osamu Tezuka, acknowledged as the Japanese "god of manga" (Thiesen 2011, 60).

31. Wonder Woman's entire "backstory" places her in the world of Greek myth. Further, she is able to "astrally project" herself back into the worlds of myth—and what happens to her there impacts her physical body in the present. Wonder Woman has been around since the 1940s and was originally created to fight with love rather than violence—she has been a symbol for feminism, appearing on the original cover for Gloria Steinem's *Ms.* magazine.

6. Detail from Azzarello, Brian and Cliff Chiang. *Wonder Woman* #7 (May 2012). © 2012 DC Comics. All rights reserved. Used with permission.

most notable and affecting cell (see below), one of these men is shown holding Hephaestus, who has been tied up by Wonder Woman; he lies on the floor, looking forlorn and powerless. Wonder Woman, for her part, thought she was doing the men a favor by attacking and detaining Hephaestus—believing they were enslaved in his forge as free labor. But in the following cell, one of these young men kneels beside and attends to the injured Hephaestus, saying that "we owe the smith our lives. If it wasn't for him we would have been thrown in the tide—to drown, unloved." Hephaestus adds: "As my mother did to me . . . something I could never allow" (ibid.). Here, the idea that Hera threw her son from Olympus is

7. Detail from Azzarello, Brian and Cliff Chiang. *Wonder Woman* #7 (May 2012). © 2012 DC Comics. All rights reserved. Used with permission.

reinforced, but Hephaestus is given the opportunity to address this betrayal by caring for others, by being a father himself, a powerful and positive retelling of the classical story. In the forge, the other men work with him, and though he is not shown as able-bodied, his "impairments" do not impede his efficiency and craftiness in the forge.[32]

32. Further, as Franny Howes has written, the world of comics exists in a temporal dimension of "continuity" (2013, 17). This is much like the *kairos* as well as the landscape of myth: comics are strongly based on the real world, but also include myriad science fiction and fantasy concepts, overlaps between comic book universes (that is, DC and Marvel), mythologies from across cultures, moving back and forth freely through history yet also adhering only to the timing of storytelling, while causal relationships and chronologies float in and out of relevance through concepts like retconning, the multiverse, and numbered earths. Yes, like myth, comic books are *mētis* (and their interpretation also requires *mētis*). We can also see *mētis* through the ways in which comics and classics often work *together* to "use the past to make sense of the present" and to blur distinctions between "high" culture and "low" culture (Kovacs and Marshall 2011, ix).

Just as we might read Hephaestus's *mētis* as arising from and address-ing disability as a social and a physical process in ancient Greece, and just as we might understand Hephaestus's myths as rewriting cultural values around disability in the period, so too can we recognize *mētis* address-ing and rewriting disability in contemporary contexts, across genres and mediums and geographies.[33]

33. Another multivalent iteration of these myths might be found in the 2001 docu-mentary film *Mama Wahunzi*, in which we see modern echoes of Hephaestus's myths: *mama wahunzi* means "woman blacksmiths" in Swahili, and the film follows three African women in their quest to create their own wheelchairs. The protagonists are connected to *Women Pushing Forward*, an international initiative that offers metalworking training and wheelchair-making workshops to women. As Jennifer Croissant wrote in a review of the film, this organization provides "skill development, [as it also] lessens dependency on inter-national suppliers, thus lowering the cost, as well as providing wheelchairs designed for the activities of daily living in specific contexts" and environments. Instead of being forced to purchase chairs designed for urban environments at a high cost, the women make their own chairs for their own needs, for the social and physical geography of eastern Africa, as they also learn a valuable trade. The film also shows the ways that a specific mytho-logical history can confront current disparities in international development, health, and technology. As Croissant writes, "African metalworking has an ancient, and specifically mythologically gendered, history, and the film perhaps understates the radical potential for these women learning metalworking." The film thus "expresses a number of subtle, if important tensions between radical self-determination and neo-liberal agendas of normal-ization" (2006, n.p.).

5

Eating Rhetorical Bodies

Mētis is "the illegitimate offspring of language."
—Michelle Ballif, *Seduction, Sophistry, and the*
Woman with the Rhetorical Figure

THE CELEBRATION OF HEPHAESTUS, his craft, his cunning, his ability, as well as the deification of his disability are means of challenging held perceptions about the mythical character, but also about all of us—defined as we all are by concepts of ability, by rhetorics of normalcy. An epideictic and forensic exploration of his myths does not just martial praise or blame through his body or question the truth or falsity of rhetorical history; this rhetorical work should shift body values and roles, becoming a deliberation on embodied possibilities.

I have argued that rhetoric will not admit it has a body; I have then argued that rhetoric does indeed have a body, but that the shape and movement of this body have been normative; I have suggested that this narrow image limits our ability to recognize our own real bodies and their inevitable connection to our being in the world as thinking, persuading, collaborating subjects, as embodied selves. I have suggested that a tension thus always underlies the body, the tension of our anxiety about imperfection, our sublimated desires, our unsatisfied need, finally, to affirm our (incomplete) bodies and embodiments. So, celebrating Hephaestus is also a way to give rhetoric a body. And *mētis*, I have suggested, is an embodied knowledge, one that refuses the sexist, ableist body image of rhetoric, an image that we have *chosen* from our (Western, Greco-Roman) versions of history. There is work to be done here to explain just why, and how, *mētis* has been overlooked. So I want to spend some time with Metis, the Greek goddess who is named after this form of intelligence, because I believe her role in myth can be understood as an analogue for the role *mētis* has been relegated to in the rhetorical tradition. Most notably, the popular story of Zeus actually *eating* Metis will be used as an analogue and a point of entry for exploring other denunciations and usurpments of embodied rhetoric.

Hephaestus's and Metis's appearances in myth yield an often contradictory picture—a complexity that challenges simple constructions, reductions, or dismissals of the important role of *mētis* in history. The confusion and the flexibility of norms, as applied to and embodied by Hephaestus, suggest to me that Greek society did not understand disability as simply as our history might suggest. The idea that Hephaestus's physical disability could have had positive connotations seems contradictory to the modern reader. But I have argued that this is the result of an import of bias into the past—Hephaestus was robustly worshipped and celebrated in the Greek context, his bodily difference not necessarily fetishized or diminished, not just to be overcome or compensated for, but idealized. Disability, throughout history, has not always represented loss, punishment, perversion, and alienation, but has instead often been situated as an embodied reality, a physical eventuality, even a desirable human variation. The elision of Hephaestus and his *mētis* from our view of history is simply in keeping with a larger pattern of disavowals of Other bodies. But we could move through history differently.

Metis, perhaps no more so (and no less) than any other rhetorical figure, is body. In exploring this connection and in retelling these stories, I hope to further reveal the attachment between myth and rhetoric and to show that rhetoric is indivisible from embodiment. In this chapter I also examine a broad spectrum of mythical and rhetorical iterations of *mētis* myths—Helene Cixous's use of the Medusa myths, Trickster figures across a range of cultures, and finally Gloria Anzaldua's stories of *mestizaje*. I will suggest that there are useful similarities across geographies and eras, all linked by *mētis*. I also hope to inspire others to make their own further cunning connections.

Finally, I suggest that *mētis* is a way for us all to move. *Mētis* is a way to think and also a way to think about thinking. Because I understand history as shifting and fluid, and because I recognize our rhetorical interpretation of it as particularly powerful, I hope to pursue a reading inspired by *mētis*—mobile and polymorphic. When we reread history for evidence of different abilities—as both good rhetoricians and as anti-ableist historians—we will be drawn to double and divergent ways of knowing. History might be thought of as a forward march. My forensic and epideictic historiography moves differently—from side to side and in reverse. Donna Haraway suggests that "we exist in a sea of powerful stories . . . changing the stories, in both material and semiotic senses, is a modest intervention worth making" (1997, 45). In this sea I hope to move like a crab, like Hephaestus.

The Goddess Metis

The stories of the Greek goddess Metis urge their audiences (then and now) to consider who gets to be cunning, who gets to be rhetorical. The stories of Metis show how the struggle over bodily meanings and embodied meaning-making played out over a mythical geography. This sphere has relevance even far from its original iterations and illuminates a long legacy of attitudes and philosophical assumptions. *Mētis*, as an embodied intelligence, reveals a shadowy tangle of body values, body denials, and body power. I will address these relationships as I reconstruct a more inclusive story.

As I mentioned earlier, as Debra Hawhee points out, *mētis* is always affiliated with crafty figures that "display a somatic cunning" or "bodily intelligence" (2005, 46). I will show that because it is first and foremost a bodily intelligence, *mētis* has been subject to derogation. In Greek *mētis* means wisdom, wise counsel—but it also means cunning and connotes trickery. As Randy Lee Eickhoff points out, the form of the word itself is a kind of trick: the Greek words *me* and *tis* mean "no man" or "no one." But the two words put together label a particular someone: the sort of person whose identity can be elusive, who is unpredictable but resourceful and clever (2001, 404n4).[1] John Peradatto devotes an entire monograph to this

---

1. In Randy Lee Eickhoff's recent translation of the Odyssey, he points out that Odysseus, considered to be another exemplar of *mētis*, uses the name *me tis* or "no man" as a pun

"no-man-clature of the self," suggesting that it calls up also a new form of indeterminate selfhood, predicated on the flux and play of *mētis* (1990, 143). The term also has a disability modality, connoting blindness. Stephen Kuusisto has pointed out that "Odysseus called himself *noboday*, or no one, depending on the translation—his answer to strangers. In ancient Greece that was also the name of the blind beggar. Homer knew. Odysseus knew" (2012, n.p.).[2] I would add that thinking through *mētis* as *no one* could bring attention to the argument that we have no *one* body, never *one* body or subjectivity. As such, *me + tis* makes a radical phenomenological statement and poses a challenge to identity politics, centering the rhetorical nature of identity and embodiment. Rhetoric is what facilitates the communication and movement between bodies—our own bodies and those around us, our own bodies and the bodies we will become.

The ubiquity of *mētis* in Homer, for Peradatto, also suggests the presence of a cunning semiology at work in myth, and in turn in the classical world: no-man as "not simply nonbeing, but potentiality: what it means for the empty subject of any narrative to take on any predication or attribute . . . rich with the possibility of another beginning" (1990, 170). The word then serves as a useful pun for the body in the history narrated by the great philosophers and those who champion them, because in the accepted classical tradition the body is supposed to be both nowhere yet everywhere when we look for it. We choose to retain a chorus of bodily denunciations from Plato and Aristotle; we find *no body*, and we find the body negated. Yet we can search a bit further and find the body invoked in myriad ways in the classical period. In particular, we can find the unique embodiment of *mētis*. This chapter will confront the idea that

---

(2001, 404n4). John Peradatto's *Man in the Middle Voice* (1990) is a book-length exploration of this pun.

2. Kuusisto continues: "What it meant, then and now, is that Odysseus was dependent on the Greek code of sympathetic fortune, for the Greeks understood the capriciousness of luck" (2012, n.p.). Kuusisto goes on to link this to the shrinking of supports for people with disabilities—the destruction of Social Security disability and Medicaid, warning that, as in Greek society, without a social support system, Americans will be much more vulnerable to luck and chance.

no woman and no body exist in the histories of thought that we have canonized.

Focusing on the mythological role of *mētis*, and the character of Metis herself, I want to fire a fusion between mythology, rhetoric, and the body. I suggest that witnessing a rhetoric embodied in a mythological figure, though such personification may seem foreign, actually lays bare many of our assumptions about bodies and expression. In telling Metis's stories, I hope to show that Greek society may not have viewed women, the body, or rhetoric as simply as we may think, and thus that we need not limit our imagination of what rhetoric can be. *Mētis* provides a model for the ways we might repurpose tensions around bodily values, recognizing the stigmatization and effacement of bodily difference, yet also mobilizing new stories and new expressive possibilities.

The myth of Metis can be traced as far back as Hesiod's *Theogony* (1914b, ll. 886–900). Metis is known through Greek myth as Zeus's first wife, as the deity embodying, and naming, the cunning intelligence (*mētis*) that Zeus would claim for his own when he swallowed her whole. As the popular story goes, Zeus and Metis were married immediately following the victory of the Olympic gods over the Titans (Apollodorus 1921, 1.6). Metis herself had some Titan blood, and her role in this victory was central (ibid., 1.8). As Detienne and Vernant write, "Without the help of [Metis], without the assistance of the weapons of cunning she controls through her magic knowledge, supreme power could neither be won nor exercised nor maintained" (1978, 58). The form of intelligence that Metis is to represent, as a result of this mythical incarnation, and as explained through this story, was represented as dangerous, as Other, and as eminently powerful.

Mētis has always been associated with trickery—those with *mētis* can process and interpret the world slightly differently, can find opportunity to turn the tables on those with greater *bie*, or brute strength, than they have access to. Defeating the Titans, a race of giants, was possible only owing to superior cunning. That said, Zeus himself, before joining with and then consuming Metis, was pure *bie*. Because of her pivotal role in defeating the Titans, Zeus respected and feared Metis. He also foresaw the threat her children would be to him, having inherited her *mētis*—Metis is

8. *Athena issuing from the head of Zeus.* Attic black-figured amphora, fifth century BCE. Louvre, Paris, France. Photo credit:
Erich Lessing/Art Resource, NY.

pregnant with Athena, who Zeus knows could one day have the power
to usurp him. Zeus saw that Metis's wisdom and ingenuity were a threat
to his sovereign power, a power that he attained only with her aid. Not
content just to marry her, to learn from her, or to share power with her,
Zeus swallows the pregnant Metis and becomes, himself, *mētieta* (MAY-
TEE-ETA)—the "wise counselor" (Hesiod 1914b, 886; Apollodorus 1921,
1.20). Metis then lives on in Zeus as a voice in his head. After he consumes
Metis, thus evading the inevitable usurpment of his power, Zeus gets a
huge headache. In one version of the story, he asks Hephaestus to knock

a hole in his temple: Metis's daughter Athena springs out. This action is depicted in figure 8, in which a tiny Athena is seen emerging from the top of a seated Zeus's head. Yet despite this surprise, Zeus has successfully co-opted the power of *mētis*, channeling the cunning of Metis from within.[3]

Some versions of the myth insist that Metis continued to speak to Zeus from inside his head, an adviser only he could hear. In this way, though in Greek mythology there may have been a push for the substantiation of *mētis* as a rhetoric, *mētis* was also quickly appropriated in this story. *Mētis* was wrested from the feminine, its lineage became unofficial, and its uses were co-opted and controlled by Zeus. Below, I want to explore the ways that we have also allowed *mētis* to be subordinated in the rhetorical tradition we have chosen. In this way, we have also subordinated the bodies of Hephaestus and Metis, and in so doing, I would argue, we have subsumed the body of rhetoric.

Straightening *Mētis*

The overwhelming message we get from our reading of history is that the great philosophers also ate *mētis*. As Lisa Raphals suggests, "The abilities of *mētis* are not so much ignored as appropriated by the dominant philosophical viewpoints of . . . Greek philosophy." For instance, Plato "redefines certain qualities associated with *mētis* to suit his own epistemological priorities" (1992, 228). The *mētis* that embraces change and chance, that resists schematization, is *foreign* to Plato's view of wisdom, to the realm of Truth he idealizes. *Mētis* must be made to fit into an ordered world or rejected. Because it calls on changing opinions and positions,

---

3. Michael Davidson uses the mythical story of Athena being born from the head of Zeus as an example of male pregnancy, which, he further elaborates, might make Zeus, like other "pregnant men," a "figure feminized in his ability to bear children, queer in challenging traditional gender roles, disabled because pregnant" (2012, 209). Further, this represents, for Davidson, not just "a simple reversal of gestation from female to male body" but rather "a diaspora of sexual and gendered identities among differently abled bodies and cognitive registers" (ibid., 211). This reading goes directly against the grain of most feminist readings of Zeus's "pregnancy": readings that strongly emphasize instead the fact that, to become "pregnant," Zeus first violently consumes Metis.

Plato allied *mētis* with charlatanism and this with the pleasures of the body. For *mētis* to be acceptable, it had to be digested. Thus, in the words of Detienne and Vernant, we have followed Plato's lead and "pick[ed] out from the [cunning] skills of the artisan anything that . . . produces in the world of Becoming creations that are as real, stable and organized as possible" (1978, 4). More simply, as Fabienne Knudsen argues, "the Platonic truth that has kept haunting Western thought has discarded the kind of intelligence implied in *mētis*" (2005, 63). If *mētis* exists at all in Western thought, it is *mētis* with the cunning wrung out, placed into an ordered, proportional, hierarchized, and cerebral epistemology.

The allied concept of *technē* was similarly made practical by the rhetorical "tradition." As Janet Atwill explains in *Rhetoric Reclaimed*, *technē*, when it is allied with *mētis* (as it is by the Sophists), "deforms limits in to new paths in order to reach—or, better yet, to produce—an alternative destination" (1998, 69). Yet we now refer to *technai*, handbooks full of sets of rules and examples, when we think of *technē*.[4] It is also possible that Plato's own rivalry with his contemporaries, the Sophists, inflected his attitudes toward *mētis* and *technē*. William Covino argues that "reactions against the Sophists contributed to the establishment of rhetoric as *technē* without magic" (1995, 20). This distortion is similar to the attempt to ally *mētis* only with scientific, schematic forms of knowledge. Further, though Sophists such as Isocrates and Gorgias defended their teaching as *not* being formulaic and technical, but rather as being stochastic, and though Plato sometimes, opportunistically, positively defines moral knowledge through the terms of *technē*, there is a huge contradiction at the heart of these definitions. Mainly, we view Plato as denigrating the Sophists' teaching as *technē*, yet demanding that *mētis* be more predictable, more like what he sees as a "good" *technē* (see Roochnik 1996).

Much like Plato's oscillating uses of *technē* to criticize *mētis*, we have come to believe that Aristotle, as well, "displaced and devalued" *mētis* (Detienne and Vernant 1978, 5). Yet it could be argued that there is an

---

4. It is probably important to recognize that in creating a chart for my own examples of disability rhetorics, I may also have been converting *technē* into *technai*.

important connection between *mētis* and *phronesis,* a concept Aristotle explores at great length in his *Rhetoric* and in the *Nicomachean Ethics. Phronesis* (FRO-NEE-SIS) is roughly translated as "prudence," and when it is defined it shares adjectives (such as *acuity* and *acumen*) in common with *mētis* (Knudsen 2005, 63). When we act with prudence, we are cunning; when we are cunning, we act with prudence. *Phronesis,* however, has been generally separated from *mētis* with the explanation that *phronesis* is linked more closely to *episteme* (or scientific knowledge) and is regulated by habits of character with the goal of "truth" and wisdom, while *mētis* has the freedom to be less moral and seeks an isolated result. In this way, *phronesis* "rises above *mētis*" (Halverson 2002, 47). When defining *phronesis* in the *Nicomachean Ethics,* Aristotle never truly rules out the idea that one would need some form of cunning intelligence to have "prudence," and the version of *phronesis* he outlines is certainly an abstract form of knowledge. He suggests that to have prudence, one must understand particulars as well as universals. Yet the version of *phronesis* that was later adopted— for instance, as one of the four medieval cardinal virtues—sheds much of this uncertainty and avoids reference to cunning intelligence. This said, a more nuanced reading of Aristotle would likely make it difficult for the translator and interpreter to make this distinction so clear-cut or this elision so easy. Yet we have generally accepted the idea that *mētis* is "bad" *phronesis,* that cunning intelligence must be made more systematic and *epistemic* to be acceptable. This also requires a certain disembodiment of this form of intelligence, at least to the degree that its bodily entailments must also be made standard or tacit—not flexible and surprising (see Baumard 1999).

In another key section of the *Nicomachean Ethics,* Aristotle again mentions the stigma against *mētis,* stating that many believe that "some who are practically wise and clever are incontinent" (1985, 1037). The suggestion that lingers over this discussion is that some forms of thought (particularly scientific and philosophical thought) are continent, while others (like *mētis,* practical intelligence or cleverness) are linked with incontinence. Aristotle suggests that a soul can be disabled or incontinent. He asserts that, "exactly as paralyzed limbs when we intend to move them to the left turn on the contrary to the right, so it is with the soul; the impulses of incontinent people move in contrary directions." There is an interesting mirroring here of the double orientation of *mētis*, of Hephaestus and his curved body. An incontinent person cannot have virtues, as he is not "adapted to receive them," and the suggestion is that the cunning body is a broken body (ibid., 951). If *mētis* is not properly digested, if we accept *mētis* and rhetorical uncertainty, our very soul might be deformed. In turn, the obsessive categorization of what is broken, what is overly bodied, allows an ideal to be generated out of downward comparison (see also Aristotle's *Generation of Animals* [1944]). The body, *mētis*, and rhetoric are all at some point (often concurrently) the scapegoats of classical epistemology.

In some instances, when Plato and Aristotle speak of *mētis*, they recognize the value of practical intelligence, even while they would never embrace a conception of the world as windswept by chance, of thought as a matter of momentous (and embodied) inspiration, of logic as the curve and circle. But we have come away with an interpretation of their work that removes *mētis* from the body and digests it through philosophy.

Unfortunately, in the classical world, even those who embrace *mētis* qualify its uses and definitions. For instance, in Athens, defenders of *mētis* worked to respond to those who would label it *lepte* (LEP-TAY), light or airy. This defense is on one hand semantic, on the other hand symbolic. First of all, in insisting that *mētis* be *pukine* (PU-KEEN-AY)—"thought that is dense, rich and compressed," anchored and forward looking instead of light and airy—authors from Oppian and Homer, all the way up to Detienne and Vernant, erect a complex linguistic bulwark around the concept. Detienne and Vernant write that although "the man [*sic*] of *mētis* is always ready to pounce" and "acts faster than lightning," "this is not to say that he gives way to a sudden impulse." Detienne and Vernant insist that "in no way does [*mētis*] act lightly" (15). Key words for *mētis*, in this schema, are "informed prudence" and "vigilant premeditation" (ibid., 111). I would suggest that, even while *mētis* may be the inverse of an Aristotelian logic, even while the world of *tuchē* and *kairos* is foreign to Platonic Truth, one must stress the depth, the strength, and the practicality of *mētis* in order to save it from ridicule—it is not incontinent. This was necessary, perhaps, because *mētis* is specifically identified *not* with the strongest and the best, with the ideal, with the unchanging, but rather with an artisan like the "lame" Hephaestus. The fact that *mētis* represents a "revers[al of] the natural outcome of the encounter" may have been threatening. Naming *mētis lepte* or light was certainly pejorative. Yet, as mentioned, Detienne and Vernant state that, in the Greek intellectual world, there was an understanding that "whatever the strength of god or man, there always comes a time when he confronts one stronger than himself" (ibid., 13). In a world full of such inevitable instances, *mētis* is what the fittest employ, and therefore it is truly powerful. But labeling *mētis pukine* and not *lepte* was one way to defend it, another way to define it as being linked to the practical, another way, perhaps, to combat the stigma of disability.

It is worth noting that these ableist accents on the denunciation of *mētis* are also accompanied by a distinct ethnocentrism and even xenophobia. The associated word *Metic* meant immigrant in ancient Athens. The word is a compound of the words "change" (*meta*) and "house" (*oikos*) and literally meant someone who changed houses. Nicole Loraux suggests that the assumed Greek disposition toward Metics has been taken out of context and used as an "original model of discrimination" by Nazi Germany and other regimes in need of anti-immigration precedents, for instance (2000, 128). The French term *meteque* has become a pejorative for Mediterranean foreigners in contemporary France, for example. In Periclean Athens, Metics were subject to a special tax, and the killing of a Metic was recognized only as involuntary homicide or manslaughter. Yet at the same time, this society "had need of Metics for the many services they rendered the citizen-body" (ibid., 129). The Sophists were Metics, and they were successful educators. Some historical interpretations of the Athenian stance toward Metics, however, have been opportunistic to the extreme—have been used to justify xenophobia (and even genocide) by rooting it in a classical ideal.

Recall, however, that the festival of Hephaestus was one where Metics or foreigners were welcome and not just the upper class celebrated (Sissa and Detienne 2000, 200). There were times when Athens clearly needed and welcomed its foreigners (perhaps to help rebuild after the Ten Years' War, as in this particular instance). But we have now inherited a narrative that, as mentioned by Loraux, stands to mark both the Metic and the *mētis* out as foreign.

A Metic was a foreigner, and *mētis* has become foreign knowledge, in part as a process of exnomination. That is, in order to establish Athenian society as the fount of all knowledge and the seat of civilization, a foreign Other had to be constructed. Thus, the construct of the Metic establishes the claim of the Athenian citizen to the land, as the assumed foreignness of *mētis* establishes the epistemological preeminence of *logos* and philosophy (Loraux 2000, 130). In these ways, we can recognize that the establishment of any dominant "body" of knowledge requires the exclusion and denigration of a range of actual bodies.

I suggest that we recognize *mētis* as a rhetoric and that we connect it to embodiment and to the bodies I have illustrated: Metis and Hephaestus. We must always remember the strategies of the Metis myths, which forcibly masculinize this intelligence; we must always remember the rhetorical moves of Plato and Aristotle, legitimating only that which is Greek, denouncing *mētis* as foreign and alien; we should never forget their attempts to make *mētis* logical and proportional and to ally it with lightness and incontinence (and disability) when it is not. Michelle Ballif suggests that rhetorical history poses *mētis* "as the illegitimate offspring of language" (2001, 58). She suggests that an alternative tradition of *mētis*, like the one I have spun here, shows us that language is not for technicians but for artisans like Hephaestus (ibid., 189). Utilizing *mētis*, we might begin to write a new mythology that values partial and contextual knowledge and makes space for all of our real bodies.

Eating *Mētis*

Claiming a certain version of rhetorical history allows other forms of knowledge to "rise above" *mētis* or to convert *mētis* into a more logical, prudent, systematic and understandable form. This transcendence required that the body again be used as the negative ground against which an ideal could take form. In these ways, *mētis* was digested. And in these ways, the body of this rhetoric was consumed. In this selective reading of the rhetorical tradition, we find an analogue with Zeus's eating of the goddess Metis. From our point of view today, it is difficult not to learn a lesson from this story about the ways that certain bodies have been eaten, while other bodies have monopolized rhetorical power. It is also possible, then, to draw some inferences about why this consumption happened. My argument is that it is no coincidence that the bodies of a powerful woman and a man with a disability have been obscured.

As Lois Bragg writes, Hephaestus is represented as being "quasi-feminized" by his cunning intelligence; his "dependence on trickery and magic rather than brute strength" was the "very motivation and *modus operandi* that Greek mythology typically attributes to women" (2004, 32, 31). *Mētis* as a concept in ancient Greece is often referred to in shorthand as "feminine conduct." In this way, *mētis* is denounced because it calls up bodies, and specifically the wrong bodies: the unpredictable bodies of women (like Metis) and of the artisan (the disabled Hephaestus).

Further, the denunciation of *mētis* can be understood as reinforced by, and even connected directly with, the denunciation of rhetoric itself. As I have shown, both concepts are seen as too bodily, as irrational, as foreign. Rhetoric becomes philosophy's Other, soiled by its affiliation with the wrong bodies. As Michelle Ballif asserts, for Plato, "rhetoric, like *mētis*, is characterized by trickery and stratagem and remains a stochastic intelligence, not rational, ordered, nor measurable" (2001, 191). I would suggest that, as Karen Kopelson argues, the "obliteration of *mētis* is . . . fundamentally related to, if not one and the same with, the denunciation of rhetoric" (2003, 133). As I have shown, both denunciations are strongly propelled by a disparagement of the body and aimed in particular at feminized, disabled bodies. Thus, while Aristotle also strongly defended oblique forms of knowledge, as in the earlier discussion of *phronesis*, and while Plato was indeed a cunning rhetorician and concerned centrally with the body, we have inherited a tradition in which their denunciations of *mētis*, rhetoric, and the body echo loudly, informing future epistemologies while fixing a singular and exclusive view of the ancient intellectual world. A long view of this history asks us to view rhetoric, the body, and *mētis* as allied in disabling thought.

I am not the first person to suggest that the myth of Zeus's consumption of Metis might be seen as a metaphor for a different violence. Others have also used this myth to highlight the history of the digestion and reconstitution of women's knowledge by male philosophers and historians. Amy Richlin (1991) and Lillian Eileen Doherty (1995) both suggest that this metaphor mirrors the challenges feminist historians face. Doherty suggests that feminist historians now live inside the "belly" of a "prevailing andocentric ideology," and they must reread the past cunningly, in order to overcome normative forms of interpretation (ibid., 7). And Richlin addresses a classical history in which women's contributions have been overwritten, a sort of symbolic violence much like that perpetuated against Metis (1991, 160). I hope to learn from these warnings and also to extend the metaphor. I want to suggest that our histories have been particularly selective about which bodies to eat and that this selectivity threatens the rhetorical potential of all bodies. I also want to connect these calls for a cunning historiography to other efforts to remythologize.

What would rhetoric look like (and how would we teach it) if Metis and Hephaestus were the heroes of antiquity, if every move to historicize rhetoric was also a move to embody it differently? What if our inclination was not to align forms of knowledge against one another in order to champion a single story, but to move laterally between traditions as stories gain complexity? I suggest that the legacy of *mētis* can creatively unfurl along a surprisingly different trajectory than the narrative we have inherited. Looking quickly, but carefully, at a broader spectrum of mythical and rhetorical retellings—Helene Cixous's use of the Medusa myths, Trickster figures across a range of cultures, and finally Gloria Anzaldua's stories of *mestizaje*—I hope to suggest that there are useful similarities across geographies and eras, all linked by *mētis*. I also hope to inspire others to make their own further cunning connections. These mythologies illustrate and operationalize the power of *mētis* rhetoric to recognize the evasion of bodily epistemologies by certain traditions, and to counter the discursive disfigurement of corporeal Otherness. We can move sideways through multiple histories, reviving a range of *mētis* rhetorics.

Medusa

In the writing of Helene Cixous, we can find a similar manifestation of *mētis*, this time also very specifically mythologized through the story of Medusa. The link between Metis and Medusa is first of all etymological: *mētis*, the Sanskrit word *medha*, the Egyptian words *met* and *maat*, and Medusa all share the same root, and all denote female intelligence and wisdom.[5] Medusa, like *mētis*, also becomes a powerful symbol of "all that is obdurate and irresistible . . . a figure for a remarkable series of public virtues and private terrors: eloquence, fame and admiration; stupor, erotic temptation, and the confusion of genders" (Garber and Vickers 2003, 2–3). Medusa's body is particularly significant: as Fulgentius wrote (circa 500), Medusa's snakelike head was a direct symbol of her cunning, calling up the curving and polymorphism of *mētis* (1971, 61). More specifically, Medusa becomes a symbol of female embodiment and oftentimes a

5. Interestingly, Christopher Faraone and Emily Teeter, in tracing the Metis myths back to Egyptian roots through the stories of the Egyptian goddess Maat, suggest that in this earlier context, *maat* (clearly etymologically linked to *mētis*) was also seen as "both an abstract idea and as an anthropomorphized goddess" (2004, 179). Maulana Karenga defines *maat* as "the totality of ordered existence and represents things in harmony and in place" (2004, 7). He defines *maat*, simply, as *the* moral ideal of ancient Egypt. *Maat* also stands for truth and justice, and is the goal of all ancient Egyptian rhetoric—with this rhetorical consciousness attained "some 1500 years before the golden age of Greek rhetoric" (Fox 1983, 18, 21). As Denise Martin writes, *maat* is a "comprehensive construct that existed throughout ancient Egyptian civilization" (2008, 951). Martin and others suggest that this concept can be read across a range of African cultural locations and times.

Jan Assmann's hugely influential *The Mind of Egypt* explains *maat* as the principle of *connective justice*, that which "forms individuals into communities and that gives their actions meaning and direction by ensuring that good is rewarded and evil punished" (2003, 128). Most notable to Assmann are the political aspects of this epistemology—allowing him to argue against those historians who have characterized ancient African civilizations as unruly and chaotic.   Just how is it, exactly, that the concept of *maat* connects to the concept of *mētis*? *Maat* has been defined as "resistant to artifice and dissimulation" (Karenga 2003, 11). *Mētis* is often seen as exactly this, artifice and dissimulation. Yet the concepts of both *maat* and *mētis* suggest that individuals and communities must act to *shape* their world—the world is not ready-made but rhetorically constructed; specifically, it is intercorporeally constructed. Perhaps what is most interesting, then, in noting this connection, is to recognize that while an epistemology of *mētis* does surface across eras and times, it does not always surface in a standard form. This may be a curious way to create an inventory of *mētis* rhetorical traditions: suggesting that the *mētis* of classical Greece, while it may have borrowed from the stories of the ancient Egyptian goddess Maat, was a substantially distorted version of this earlier tradition. The point of writing these histories, however, is not to be smooth and consecutive. If *mētis* were somehow strictly archetypal, it would lose all of its power and possibility.

symbol of the stigma and confusion around, and the powerful, sometimes violent challenges to, women's embodied rhetoricity.[6]

Often, Medusa was used to symbolize "artful eloquence." For instance, Coluccio Salutati in the fourteenth century and Nancy Vickers in the twenty-first both argue for this reading. As Salutati suggests, the snakes on her head might be recognized as "rhetorical ornaments . . . instruments of wisdom" because snakes are "reported to be the most cunning" (2003, 55). In this interpretation, Medusa turns an audience to stone not because of her looks, but because of her rhetorical power—her audience "so convinced of what they have been persuaded that they may be said to have acquired a stony quality" (ibid., 56). Vickers goes further, sourcing this connection back to Plato (2003, 254). She also argues that Medusa's "stoning" be viewed as a rhetorical power, an ability to change the audience's state of mind, accompanied by a somatic effect. Finally, she suggests that Medusa's rhetorical power might represent the freezing of us all before the specter of the feminine—and she asks what we might do to reverse a legacy of neutralization and appropriation of the Other.

Yet the Medusa myth, as told in the poetry of Ovid and elsewhere, is most commonly read much more simply. The myth seems to warn that proud women, women who speak out, will be made ugly (Ovid 1986). As Cheryl Glenn writes, Cixous's rhetorical project is to write women and in so doing to "continue to resist received notions both of history and of writing history" (1997, 290). In her reclamation of cunning, Cixous confronts the tradition that has denigrated *mētis* and subjugated Medusa. She explains that men have "riveted us between two horrifying myths: between the Medusa and the abyss" (1976, 315). Women, as rhetors, can be either heretical or silent. The heretical option—to be Medusa—is to be monstrously bodied, discursively excessive, and thus corporeally oversignificant. See, for instance, figure 9 of a monstrous Medusa being beheaded

---

6. There also may have been a familial connection between Hephaestus and Medusa—in some myths, the two are sexual partners. Their child, Cacus, was said to be a fire-breathing giant. Cacus was said to eat human flesh and nail human heads to his door. Killing him was one of Heracles's twelve labors (Graves 1955, 158). This link is not made by all scholars, though the story shows up in Ovid and in Virgil's *Aeneid*.

9. *Perseus and Medusa*, mid-sixth-century BCE. In death, Medusa gives birth to Chrysaor and Pegasus whose father is Poseidon. Medusa holds her last-born in her arm. Metope from Temple C in Selimunte, Sicily, Italy. Museo Archeologico, Palermo, Sicily, Italy. Photo credit: Erich Lessing/Art Resource, NY.

by Perseus. Though it is impossible to see in this image, taken from the exterior of a temple, Medusa is giving birth to Chrysaor and Pegasus in this image. She is shown kneeling on one knee, with a very large head and a big, presumably scary grin. Almost all existing images of Medusa from this era look similar: an enlarged head and oversize body, a huge grin. Perseus holds her by the top of the head and slits her throat.

Yet Cixous implores her female listener to "write her self: [women] must write about women and bring women to writing, from which they have been driven away as violently as from their bodies" (ibid., 309). This driving away from the body resonates with Zeus's consumption of Metis and the condemnation of bodily intelligence (and of the bodies of cunning intelligence) encouraged by the tradition we have chosen. Zeus's usurpation is a symbol of exactly what Cixous means when she says that "writing has been run by a libidinal and cultural—hence political, typically masculine—economy; this is a locus where the repression of women has been perpetuated, over and over" (ibid., 311). Metis becomes a woman's voice in a man's head, the hidden body between the neat and ordered, rational and cerebral, deeply inscribed lines of a masculinist history.

Medusa's story is grisly. In the many translations of Ovid's *Metamorphoses*, with differing emphases, the story is much the same (see the translations of Dryden, Humphries, Mandelbaum, Melville, and More). Found worshipping in Athena's temple, Medusa either seduces or is raped by Poseiden—who is overcome by her beauty and cannot resist. Of course, it matters very much whether Medusa was raped. As Patricia Klindienst (1984) has argued, this rape has often been elided and responsibility for it shifted away from Poseiden to Athena. She suggests that this shifting of responsibility, essentially, excuses men's violence toward women, and thus silences women further.

When Athena finds out her temple has been desecrated by this act, she punishes Medusa. The beautiful Medusa is "disfigured," her head writhes with snakes, or perhaps the arms of the octopus. Detienne and Vernant (1978) write that *mētis* was often symbolized by the octopus. Thus, this connection to the octopus of *mētis* may not have been coincidental. Certainly, the original Medusa myth relied upon a reference to the dangerous, trapping "knot made up of a thousand arms" that the octopus represented and that conveyed a sense of the powerful double-ness and unpredictability of *mētis*.

Anyone who looked upon Medusa would thenceforth be turned to stone. According to Graves's retelling of the myth, Medusa was "once beautiful . . . but one night Medusa lay with Poseidon, and Athene, enraged . . . changed her into a winged monster with glaring eyes, huge teeth, protruding tongue, brazen claws and serpent locks, whose gaze turned men to stone" (1955, 127). As an example of the ways that myths crucially disagree with one another, we can recognize that in Homer's version of the story, Medusa comes into the world *with* her head of snakes. I think such differences reveal quite marked transitions in and contestations of signification. Yet while most of these versions of the myth tell a story of female jealousy, they also clearly describe male fears, fears that lead to violence against Medusa. Perhaps the central narrative thrust for all of these myths is the effort to defend or justify both the fear of and the violence toward women.

The myth always ends badly. In the image I have included, Perseus murders Medusa. Perseus also removes her head so that he can free his own mother from King Polydectes. In Graves's version, Poseidon kills Medusa to have her head to give as a sort of bachelor-party present—a totem of fertility and also women's persecution—to his friend Polydectes (ibid., 238). In this version, Athena flays Medusa and uses her skin as an *aegis*, as wings, perhaps in this way co-opting her power or channeling the cunning of both Medusa and Athena's own mother, Metis (ibid., 45). No matter the route, the story always ends with Medusa's decapitation. And just as Metis was eaten and imprisoned in Zeus's head, her wiles incorporated by him, even when Medusa was beheaded, her head retained a power harnessed by other bodies, or her killers used her blood for its magical powers (Ovid 1986, 4.618). Graves writes that vials of Medusa's blood were widely distributed: the blood had the power both to kill and to cure. There are many contradictory stories about who received the blood, who distributed it, and who used it for good, who for bad (1955, 175).

Although it is at first difficult to understand all of the motivations behind the "disfigurement" and decapitation of Medusa, Cixous provides a single disturbing interpretation, albeit with many complex consequences. Medusa is a dangerous, beautiful, intelligent woman, so she must die. The only remedy to the dangerous power of Medusa, made ugly because of her cunning, is murder. The Medusa myth communicates male fear of women's power, as does the story of Metis. The myth may also express a male fear of Medusa's *pro*creative power—she is so fertile that her children, Chrysaor and Pegasus, spring from her dead body (ibid., 127). In sum, when women are recognized as cunning, thus powerful, they can be recognized only as a threat and thus must be appropriated, silenced, slain. Cixous uses the myth to show how women have been forced to participate in discourse, and to shape and be shaped by language, based on the terms of a masculinist economy. This economy also leads to the consumption of the classical concept of *mētis*: it is symbolized by the feminized and incontinent body of Hephaestus, by the threatening female body of Metis; it must be straightened out, disembodied (brought into Zeus's head, for instance), made logical and systematic, or ignored. Of course, this economy is also reified in unique, and powerfully masculine and ableist, iterations by Freud and Lacan, the key targets of Cixous's critique. For the history of thought to maintain a disembodied masculinity as its frame, it must focus on the monstrosity of the female body, a perspective through which the male body need not ever come into focus. Any threat to this order must be consumed.

Cixous's historiography also reveals an important lineage, not just "modernizing" the Medusa story, but also connecting the Medusa *and* Metis myths to a much earlier history. According to Robert Graves, Medusa was a beautiful Libyan queen who led her troops into battle and was beheaded. Medusa has been linked to North African goddesses as far back as 1400 BCE (1966, 243; Pausanias 1933, 2.21.6). In this longer history, it actually becomes unclear whether Medusa and Metis can be separated, while it becomes quite likely that these two figures were conflated with Athena, the powerful African goddess who predated the Greek figure (see Bernal 1987). Ovidian variations of the Medusa myth trace the fall of Medusa as the descent of the great goddess religions and the ascent of the male gods Zeus and Poseidon (see Ovid 1986). It could be argued that Medusa's slaying (and Metis's consumption) is actually a symbol of the usurping of a long line of female goddesses, and the dying out of the cultures that worshipped them, to be replaced by masculine-headed, and oriented, culture. This leads Graves to lament the death of the female goddess and of female goddess culture and its replacement by patriarchal forms (1966, 322; see also Lerner 1986). Through the stories of Metis and

Medusa, symbolic consumptions and eviscerations of the female body accompany this transition and reinforce a silencing of the body.

Cixous, recognizing this vilification of the feminine, and of "bodied" expression, and refusing its legacy, asks us to reexamine the myth: "Look at the Medusa straight on," and you'll see that "she's not deadly. She's beautiful and she's laughing" (1976, 309). This point resonates in multiple ways. Looking, for instance, at two images of Medusa from the same period in Greece, one can recognize that sometimes Medusa is pictured as beautiful, sometimes as monstrous, at the same point in the same mythical narrative. The "monstrous" Medusa (figure 9) is shown with tusks and wings and a huge toothy grin, physically larger than Perseus, who chases her. Then we can compare this image to another rendering of Medusa, figure 10, in which she is a serene woman with wings, curly hair, her head resting peacefully on her hand.

But Cixous's point is also less cosmetic—she is suggesting that Medusa's beauty lies in her ability to threaten and shake up a male-dominated society, a normative society. Cixous suggests that Medusa's disruptive and evasive character is in fact where her "monstrosity" *and* beauty come from. The rhetorical joining of these two aspects, then, might be *both* threatening and lovely—challenging to those who have oppressed women and the body and beautiful to those who would reverse this legacy.

While the legacy connects back to Metis, it also connects forward in important ways. For instance, one very recent and specific example of the ways that the Medusa myth has been recognized for its subversive power and rhetorical possibility can be found in the 2011 artistic exhibition *Medusa's Mirror: Fears, Spells, and Other Transfixed Positions*, curated by Amanda Cachia at the PRO ARTS gallery in San Francisco and featuring prominent disability artists Joseph Grigely, Neil Marcus, Carmen Papalia, Katherine Sherwood, Laura Swanson, Sunaura Taylor, Sadie Wilcox, and Chun-Shan (Sandie) Yi, all "creating work addressing the disabled body." In the words of the gallery's promotional materials, "In Greek mythology, Medusa was viewed as a monster, and gazing directly upon her would turn onlookers into stone. Inspired by this myth, the artists in Medusa's Mirror address the able-bodied gaze upon the disabled subject—often viewed with fear, curiosity or wonder—by turning the gaze upon the

10. *Perseus beheading Medusa*, Polygnotos Vasepainter (fifth century BCE) (attributed to). Terracotta pelike (jar). Greek, Attic, ca. 450–440 BCE. Terracotta. Height: 18 13/16 in. (47.8 cm). Diameter: 13 1/2 in. (34.3 cm). Rigers Fund, 1945 (45.11.1). The Metropolitan Museum of Art, New York, NY. Image copyright © Metropolitan Museum of Art. Image source: Art Resource NY.

viewer. This shift allows the disabled subject to claim agency and gives cause for the able-bodied viewer to reflect on their own frameworks" (2011, n.p.).[7]

---

7. More from the exhibit's promotional materials: "The piercing gaze as interpreted through medicine are explored in Katherine Sherwood's mixed media paintings and Sadie

Cixous's message is that the body, alternately beautiful and monstrous, normal and abnormal, alive with significance and engorged and muted, gains power from this dynamism. Disability studies scholars (and artists) can easily find resonance in this duality and dynamism and understand the rhetorical power of the gaze—and of reversing it. What we need to flee from, following Medusa, are the appeals of certainty and sameness, whether rhetorical, historical, or corporeal. Cixous also more broadly refers to the act of embodied communication, which involves the individual always with the other, and instantiates within the body-changing and (at least partially) shared experiences of embodiment that challenge the norm, specifically phallogocentrism, thus being always double and divergent.

This incessant process of creation as change and exchange might be an example of the power of *mētis* as it is driven by Medusa, resuscitated and beautiful. This power, in some way, should also reconnect us all to a focus on embodiment as we write and communicate and make art; it should certainly remind us that Greek mythology, and then each version of rhetorical possibility that we create, potentially holds counternarratives, is full of other bodies, other tongues, and therefore so are we.

Tricksters

There are connections between the *mētis* of Hephaestus and Metis and the stories of Medusa, as well as a wide range of Tricksters—etymological,

---

Wilcox's examinations of the roles of patient, caregiver and doctor. The medicinal gaze is further skewed into the world of the sideshow in the work of Sunaura Taylor, articulating the point of tension in the gaze. Several works draw from the ruptures between the able-bodied and the disabled. Deaf artist Joseph Grigely's explores the ruptures and failures of communication, pointing to the rift between spoken and signed language. Blind artist Carmen Papalia's guided walking tours leads the closed-eyes participants to experience the world using their other senses—primarily sound and touch. Visual representations of the body and our relationship toward body image are thoughtfully explored in Chun-Shan (Sandie) Yi's latex sculptures and in the discomfort reflected in Laura Swanson's photographs. The body is further addressed in Neil Marcus's drawings, an extension of his performance practice, which grapples with mobility and movement as one with dystonia. The works in Medusa's Mirror bring to light the able-bodied gaze upon the disabled subject and in turn point to the vulnerabilities and fragilities commonplace with all human beings" (Cachia 2011, n.p.).

mythological, and also powerfully symbolic. As Hynes and Doty suggest, "For centuries, perhaps millennia, and in the widest variety of cultural and religious belief systems, humans have told and retold tales of tricksters, figures who are usually comical, yet serve to highlight important social values" (1993, 1–2). Hephaestus and Metis should be understood as connected to this tradition both as products and as producers of these tales. Making this connection is a way to place Greek myth within a continuum of mythologies, as it is a way to confuse the supposed ordering of this lineage. Perhaps even more important, connecting Metis and Hephaestus to figures such as the Zande trickster Ture or the Crow trickster Coyote (and its many other manifestations in Native American or First Nations culture, from the Nez Perce to the Yakama) is a way to interrogate the rhetorical power of these stories across diverse contexts.[8]

Just as female and feminized bodies have been eaten by the rhetorical tradition, Malea Powell argues that rhetoric ignores Native people: "Material Indian 'bodies' are simply not seen" (1999, 3). Qwo-Li Driskill concurs that "part of the colonial experience for Native people in the United States is that we are constantly disappeared through the stories that non-Native people tell, or don't tell, about us" (2010, 79). I draw connections to the trickster here in the spirit of making-material, of refusing to ignore or disappear rhetorical bodies. But I also draw the connections because once we begin to seek them, these stories begin to powerfully enliven what we know about *mētis* and how it might be used—what we know about rhetoric and what we do with it.[9]

---

8. I have covered some of these representations of the trickster previously in my discussion of Hephaestus, but many are worth repeating here. William Hynes and William Doty suggest that all tricksters are: ambiguous and anomalous; deceptive trick-players; shapeshifters; situation-invertors; messengers and imitators of the Gods; and sacred and lewd bricoleurs (1993, 33). In these tricks and reversals, we also see the skills of the artisan or inventor. For instance, Coyote is cunning enough to discover that fire can be created by rubbing two sticks together, just as Hephaestus invents fire for use in his forge. And in each of Hynes's six characteristics, we see descriptions of both actions and of bodies. Ture, for instance, is shown to be duplicitous, but his body is also half-animal (see Evans-Pritchard 1964).

9. One very material rhetorical example of the connection between the bodies and stories of *mētis*, and the bodies and stories of *un*seen native bodies, is the uncanny overlap

As Robert D. Pelton argues, "The trickster reveals that humans themselves are symbols"; the trickster "draws an icon of human openness to every world and every possible transformation" (1989, 133). The trickster has the ability "to turn on its head every idea and event . . . as he embodies the radically metamorphic character of humans and their imaginations" (ibid., 134). This ability then has a rhetorical effect on human epistemology: "The trickster shows that the task of imagining the real is an exercise in sacred irony, because the 'real' itself is more than incoherent dailiness or changeless sacredness." Further, the trickster "makes real the openness of each language to every other language [and] he makes all experience human experience as he reveals the point at which fluidity and structure, web and dance, become one" (ibid., 135). In short, building on the definitions we have explored so far in this book, the trickster has always worked to reveal the world as *mētis* and humanity as *metieta* (having *mētis*).

---

between the stories of Hephaestus and the stories of Sequoyah. Like Hephaestus, Sequoyah was a metalworker—a silversmith. Like Hephaestus, he was disabled—and, similarly, there is dispute about whether he was born with a disability or was later injured and disabled (and of course we know that the distinction does matter). His name comes from *siqua*, a Cherokee word meaning "hog," a word that also connotes disability or deformity—historians have suggested that the specific reference was to the pig's foot, suggesting that his own foot was deformed. He was the son of a white soldier and a Cherokee mother. Sequoyah is often mythologized reverently with the same "compensation" narratives attached to Hephaestus and common to all disability stories: "Because Sequoyah was physically limited, he developed other kinds of skills" (Basel 2007, 19). Indeed, Sequoyah became much more than a metal smith—he become a rhetorical artisan. His foremost accomplishment was that he invented the Cherokee syllabary, a system of representing the syllables of the Cherokee language. He is now legendary as "the only member of an illiterate group in human history to have single-handedly devised a successful system of writing" (Wadley 2013, n.p.). The syllabary has been recognized as having offered linguistic (and thus rhetorical) means to build solidarity in the face of genocide; it has also been since recognized as responsible for allowing Native political speeches and autobiographies to be retained and preserved.

In turn, Seqouyah has become a controversial figure, his stories the focus of debate and rhetorical negotiation. He has become a symbol system himself. But hopefully, the complicated history of Sequoyah as a progenitor of disability rhetoric will be further explored: there is much to learn here about the interconnection between bodies, languages, literacies, and cultures.

Karl Kerenyi has famously suggested that the trickster is the "exponent and the personification of the life of the body" (1955, 185). However, for Jung, the trickster "represents an archaic level of consciousness, an 'animal' or primitive self given to more intense expressions of libido, gluttony, and physical abuse" (Russo 2008, 243). This archetype of the trickster is difficult to shake and calls up many of the worst stereotypes about disability—disability as a lack of reason, as pure appetite and uncivilized impulse. Yet Joseph Russo suggests that while *mētis* can be recognized as something possessed by Greek trickster figures, "cunning resourcefulness is a talent widely admired throughout Greek culture and not one owned exclusively or primarily by the trickster" (ibid., 247). Thus, while Odysseus famously possessed *mētis*, and while he also possessed some trickster qualities, he is finally "a more fascinating, more mysterious figure" than any simple archetype would describe, perhaps because he personifies neither *mētis* nor the trickster reliably or with stability (ibid., 252).

The study of trickster figures has evolved greatly since Jung, and one distinguishing characteristic of recent trickster scholarship is this more humble insistence on the "diversity and complexity of the appearances of the trickster" and a reticence to encompass the trickster "as a single phenomenon" (Hynes and Doty 1993, 2). Further, just as *mētis* has come to be understood as a philosophical framework, scholars have begun to recognize that trickster stories "expose [underexplored] dimensions of human creativity," especially in terms of "real-world," practical intelligence (Hynes and Doty 1993, 8). As Anne Doueihi argues, the trickster can be viewed as "not *a* sacred being, but the way the whole universe may become meaningful" (1993, 201).

Doueihi suggests that "the features commonly ascribed to the trickster—contradictoriness, complexity, deceptiveness, trickery—are the features of the language of the story itself" (ibid., 193). Recall here Doherty's suggestion that Greek myth is also a manifestation of *mētis*. In these ways, trickster figures, just like figures with *mētis*, embody the malleability, play, and openness of the myth itself, indeed of all language. As "figures" with bodily flaws, with anomalies, and in constant material flux, trickster figures and *mētis* figures are "disabled" in the same generative sense as language is "disabled." Trickster figures also harness "weapons of the weak" (see Scott 1985) and the "queer arts of failure" (see Halberstam 2011). As mentioned earlier, the disabled body in myth, then, through the figure of the cunning trickster, like Hephaestus, reveals the "difference between, and the undecidability of, discourse and story, referential and rhetorical values, signifier and signified, a conventional mind and one that is open" (Doueihi 1993, 200). In this way, the trickster could be a "possibly paradigmatic expression" of the dissonant experience of language, symbolism, or any given social order—each of these "normative" orders itself an absurdity unraveled by the "anomaly/ambivalence" of the trickster (Koepping 1985, 196). Tricksters are prosthetic rhetoricians. This trickster rhetoric becomes a crucial way to view *mētis*: as the universal and timeless importance of *both* making *and* undoing language through the body.

Mestizaje and *Mestiza* Consciousness

As I have shown, there are important connections between *mētis* and other logics of "doubleness and divergence" from across quite different rhetorical traditions. Another example is the tradition of *mestizaje*, what Gloria Anzaldua refers to when she writes about *mestiza* consciousness. The French word *métis*, which has also been attached to North American (specifically western Canadian) Native populations of mixed lineage, is related to the Spanish word *mestizo*, both coming from the Latin word *mixtus*, the past participle of the verb *to mix* and connoting mixed blood. So this word, like *mētis*, also calls up the concept of biological and conceptual "miscegenation." As Daniel Heath Justice shows, the word should always call up "the history of Métis disenfranchisement and socio-political resistance," and its connection to "complications of identity . . . the tensions that blood quantum and the rhetorics of race have imposed on Aboriginal communities throughout North America" (2003, 49).

In Anzaldua's stories, the *mestiza* is linked to a colonial legacy in which such mixture was both often forced (through rape, invasion, usurpment) and almost always strongly stigmatized by the supposedly racially "pure" colonizer. More recently, the concept of *mestizaje* itself has been used as a way of erasing the Africanist presence in the Americas.[10]

Yet Anzaldua reclaims this word, and this identity, accentuating the generative power of this mixed identity. In response to antagonism and in the face of cultural forces that value "purity" and "coherence," Anzaldua recognizes the need for an identity and a language with "a malleability that renders us unbreakable" (1999, 64). As Diana Taylor writes, "The mestiza herself is a product of cultural memory; her body is mapped by racialized and gendered practices of individual and collective identity . . . along with the birth of the first mestizo comes a whole constellation of stories explaining gender, racial, ethnic, and national formation" (2007, 86, 94–95). The *Mestiza/Mestizo* race is a vision of modern *mētis* that, "rather than resulting in an inferior being, provides hybrid progeny, a mutable, more malleable species with a rich gene pool," resulting in an "alien consciousness" of the borderland, all cultures at the same time (Anzaldua 1999, 77).[11]

In contemporary critical theory, the concept of *mētissage* also locates and interrogates the ways that certain forms of knowledge have been relegated to the margins, and thus this concept links usefully to the stories I have been reanimating. *Mētissage*, obviously etymologically linked to *mētis*, and meaning "mixture" or "miscegenation," has been used as a critical lens through which one might observe issues of identity, resistance, exclusion, and intersectionality. Relying upon metaphors of mixture that are biological and cultural, this concept of *mētissage* both *is like* and *is* what Gloria Anzaldua refers to when she writes about *mestizaje* or *mestiza* consciousness. (See Kincheloe and Steinberg 1998; Hardt and Negri 2004; Gruzinski 2002; Glissant 1997.) As Serge Gruzinski writes, "*Mestizo* processes are mechanisms that occur on the edge of stable entities," as disorder imposed upon rationality (2002, 25). This language echoes the

---

10. See, for example, Debra A. Castillo's essay "Anzaldúa and Transnational American Studies": "*Mestizo*, in Mexico, is a nation-building concept, not a resistant one, and a concept that often resolves in racialist urges" (2006, 263).

11. See also Jose Vasconcelos's *La Raza Cosmica* (1997) as well as Diana Taylor (2007) and Susan Antebi's (2009) scholarship on this antieugenic project. Antebi's work, in particular, offers a disability studies-inflected perspective on Vasconcelos.

Greek idea of strength not through brute force (*bie*), but through cunning and adaptability (*mētis*). Edouard Glissant defines *metissage* as "the world's unforeseeable variations," emphasizing the importance of mixture and underscoring the idea that we live in a world of chance and change (1997, 288).

Mestiza consciousness similarly can counter an epistemology of purity, survival-of-the-most-normal. Diana Taylor also argues that *mestizaje* "takes into account the way culture is transmitted by/through/as embodiment . . . shaped ideologically as well as genetically" (2007, 108). Taylor argues that *mestiza* has been used both as a normalizing and as an essentialist concept and recuperated in service of postcolonial struggle.[12] Both Taylor and Anzaldua also, importantly, center the body within this theory of knowledge, refusing the "dichotomy between ideas and feelings" (Anzaldua quoted in Lu 2004, 24), focusing on other bodies, and suggesting that embodied difference is power. Taylor writes that *mestiza* "never quite frees itself from the bodies that live it," even while it is "never reducible to biology alone" (2007, 100). As Anzaldua says in an interview with Linda Smuckler, "I want to write from the body; that's why we're in a body" (Keating with Anzaldua 2000, 63).

Anzaldua herself rewrites and revitalizes mythologies, "putting history through a sieve" and effecting a "conscious rupturing and reinterpretation of history by using new symbols to shape new myths" (Foss, Foss, and Griffin 1999, 110). Most notably, she tells the stories of Coatlalopeuh, "she who has dominion over serpents" (1999, 49). For Anzaldua, Coatlalopeuh incorporates and enfleshes a threat to the colonial legacy and the ways that this history oppressed particular bodies, expressions, and ways of knowing. She is a subversive rhetorical figure. And Coatlalopeuh obviously looks and sounds a lot like the Medusa figure, and likewise the shared iconography of the snake could be seen to denote a connection

12. Alicia Arrizon, in *Queering Mestizaje*, also warns that we need to recognize the complex power relations behind the concept: "this also requires locating the racialized, ethnicized, and sexualized body: beginning in the late twentieth century, *mestizaje* has become a complex, ongoing negotiation that seeks to authorize hybrid sites of experience and empowerment" (2006, 7).

with cunning and with sexuality that is threatening to male patriarchy in both mythological semiotics (see Fulgentius 1971; Garber and Vickers 2003). For instance, we could reference figure 11, in which Coatlalopeuh is depicted as having a dress made of snakes, an inversion of Medusa's head of snakes, yet utilizing the same threatening, sexually subverting, cunning gravity. The image actually shows three separate views of the goddess: front, side, and back. She is shown with four hands in her front and two behind her, the aforementioned snakes around her waist, three clawed feet, and with skulls securing a belt in her front and back. Her head is also snakelike, with four noticeable fangs.

The argument inherent in my comparison between Medusa and Coatlalopeuh is that there is consonance between the words and the symbolic bodies of *mētis*, Medusa and *mestizaje*. There is also alignment through all of these stories of the themes of bodily oppression and derogation, and through their telling we enact a recovery and resuscitation of female goddesses, but also of maligned rhetorics and silenced rhetorical bodies. There is disability rhetoric at work.

The mode and power of the telling of such stories can also be recognized as echoing across my examples. The Coatlalopeuh myths come from Mexican Indigenous tradition, and Anzaldua consciously filters them through the Meso-American, Aztec, Spanish, and Roman Catholic traditions that rewrote them. (For instance, Coatlalopeuh later becomes conflated with the Virgin of Guadalupe after the Spanish Roman Catholic conquest of Mexico.) As I have tried to show with the stories of Metis, and as Cixous shows through the myth of Medusa, these narratives themselves lie within a larger cultural story of masculine domination and female disembodiment (and more violently through decapitation, flaying, swallowing). Anzaldua writes that "male-dominated Azteca-Mexica culture drove the powerful female deities [like Coatlalopeuh] underground by giving them monstrous attributes and by substituting male deities in their place" (1999, 49). As Irene Lara writes, in recovering and rewriting "Mexica histories and Mexica goddess figures from a feminist decolonial perspective," Anzaldua advocates for a return to the "gynecentric ordering of life" that used to exist (Lara with Anzaldua 2005, 44). There are parallels between this work and the ways that Cixous asks us to reevaluate

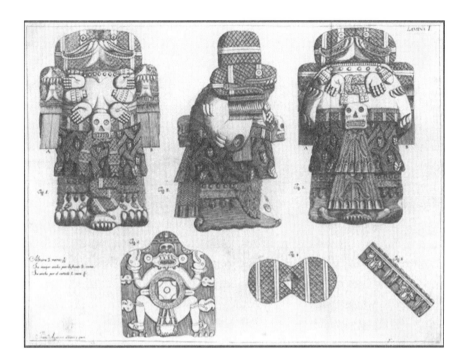

11. *Coatlicue*, Antonio de León y Gama, historical and chronological description of the two stones . . . , Mexico, 1792. Courtesy of the John Carter Brown Library at Brown University, Providence, RI.

Medusa, as well as the idea that the goddess Metis was once the most powerful Olympian.

Carrie McMaster also suggests that we might learn from Anzaldua's writing about her own bodily difference—having experienced congenital disease, chronic illness, disability—to "draw non-homogenizing parallels between various embodied identities" (2005, 103). In Anzaldua's own words, "Those experiences [with disability] kept me from being a 'normal' person. The way I identify myself subjectively as well as the way I act out there in the world was shaped by my responses to physical and emotional pain" (Keating with Anzaldua 2000, 289). From this identification, we might make some lateral suggestions about the epistemological entailments of *mestiza* knowledge—it comes from unique, never "normal," bodied experiences. The "leap" that should be encouraged, then, is to understand such situated knowledge as vital and perhaps even central to human experience. The "abnormal" body is not something given to women symbolically as a form of derogation.

These overlaps and links reveal a theme: the idea that rhetorics, across cultures, have been often animated by a spirit of *mestizaje* or *mētis*—can always be inherently subversive, embodied, powerfully Other modes of persuasion, even while they have most often been represented as the opposite.

Conclusions

All of these laterally aligned rhetorics, arising from Metis, *mētis*, Maat, *maat*, Trickster figures, Medusa, *metissage*, and *mestizaje* focus on rhetorical bodies. When I invoke this mixture, I am advocating for a more inclusive range of body images, an awareness of a legacy of negative body values, and a critique of the powerful discourses of silencing and delimitation that surround the body. I argue that we should look for what is beautiful in what we have been told is threatening (about ourselves and about others). This would mean admitting that the history of rhetoric is fully, strangely, and wonderfully bodied. It means admitting that rhetoric has a body—that rhetoric is perhaps best metaphorized and dynamized not by the proportionate and perfect body, but by a range of bodies fighting against imposed ideological limitations with true physical diversity, using cunning rather than brute force to defeat a Titanic tradition that has channeled oppressive strength to delimit rhetorical possibility. We fight against histories and cultures that consume and co-opt bodies, that eat rhetoric.

Through these stories we find further support for a *mētis* historiography and for *mētis* in contemporary rhetorical production—perhaps also for a *mētis* politics to address inequities and suppressions within contemporary cultural logics. *Mētis* asks us to both make and undo language, myth, and rhetoric through the body. These stories strongly advocate for the centrality of *mētis* across traditions and argue for a recognition of the power and importance of this way of thinking, recovering *mētis* not just as an idea from another era, but as a way to make and remake embodied meaning.

6

"I Did It on Purpose"

"The old psychology" of feeling the stutterclutter is of the earth is the
breaking down into the intestinal alimentary or reclamation of meaning back into the original "chaos of noises" since decomposed.

—Jordan Scott, *Silt*

THE RECENT OSCAR-WINNING FILM *The King's Speech*, because it focuses
on public speaking, on pedagogy, and on the body, is a movie about rhetoric. More specifically, the film is about disability rhetoric. Therefore, it is
an excellent space in which to try out many of the questions and ideas of
this book—and to thus argue that the questions have real, contemporary
significance. My method in this final chapter will be to employ *mētis* as I
explore not just how the film was actually made, or how it was popularly
received, but also how it has been argued over. In the crucial scene of
the movie, just when we expect the titular king to overcome his speech
impediment and deliver a perfectly eloquent speech, he stutters "on purpose." Likewise, in this final chapter I will be intentionally rolling and
falling between eras and approaches, moving laterally through many of
my previous arguments, and resisting the compulsion to conclude this
book neatly or normatively.

The first huge jump here is from ancient Greece, to *mestiza* borderlands
and decolonial legacies, to the empire itself, in wartime England. Yet, in
an early scene in the movie, as the future King George VI of England,
Prince Albert (Bertie) is undergoing speech therapy for his stutter, we are
transported back to antiquity. His doctor asks him to place five sterilized
marbles in his mouth, then to read from a book. His wife, Elizabeth, asks
the doctor what the purpose of the treatment is. "The classic approach

that cured Demosthenes," the doctor replies. "That was in Ancient Greece. Has it worked since?" Elizabeth asks. As Bertie struggles to read aloud, and to even keep the marbles in his mouth, the doctor demands that he "enunciate!" Bertie nearly chokes on the marbles (Seidler 2008, 5).

Like that failed therapy, this book now also has to ask: "Has it worked since?" I need to question whether any of this historical work matters, whether we really have access to disability rhetorics, or if the negative and limiting disability tropes and myths continue to be our only means of "treating" disability. I will argue that, as just one example, this film does offer the impetus for new rhetorical possibilities, in part because it *does not* work.

As the movie progresses, Bertie tries a variety of other methods to "cure" his stutter, and with the help of an innovative teacher, Lionel Logue, he has some success working through and around the stammer, which is important because as the king, he must speak publicly in a period of serious international crisis. The narrative arc is certainly conventional—one commentator called this "the Rocky of speech-therapy movies" (Oat 2010, n.p.). The focus here, however, is on the labor and the battle of overcoming a disability. Bertie's story might be understood simply as a myth that makes us feel good about the king's ability to eliminate his stutter and thus reassures us that with hard work, disability is something we can triumph over. The film then also might function as a reminder to people with disabilities that they had better work hard and seek a wide range of treatments, from the experimental to the masochistic. If they remain disabled, they probably just have not worked hard enough.

But fortunately, there are other ways to view the movie—as more than just a story of overcoming or compensation. In a later scene in which Bertie and his wife recall the episode with the marbles, Bertie angrily suggests that the doctor can "insert his own bloody marbles!" The movie script includes a note here that "when he speaks with his wife there's hardly any hesitation" (Seidler 2008, 6). Moments like these accentuate a divergence from the classical narrative, but also present alternative possibilities for interpretation and meaning. For instance, this scene shows that the movie, and the myth of King George VI from which it comes, might reveal a tension between medical and social models of disability: the stutter is defined and treated as a medical problem, yet the experience and expression of the "disability" changes between social contexts. Indeed, as Yaruss and Quesal (2004) argue, while in general stuttering has been treated as an impairment by speech pathologists, and seen as such by the public, the experience of stuttering may be much more like disability: many different factors can contribute to a speaker's experience of stuttering, including the speaker's reactions to the disorder as well as the reactions of those in the speaker's environment.[1]

It is also important to note that this popular contemporary representation of disability is linked so overtly to a very long tradition of disability myths, right back to Demosthenes. Recall that the great Greek orator Demosthenes was represented as a stutterer with a lisp and an inability to control his gestures. As Martha Rose (2003) argues, we have latched onto Demosthenes's story as one of overcoming. We believe that through great labor he overcame his impediment, training it out of his speech by walking up mountains declaiming with pebbles in his mouth: "Demosthenes became a celebrated example of overcompensation for a physical handicap" (Pomeroy 1997, 173). Jordan Scott's poem "Stuttering" from the epigraph to this chapter reinvokes these pebbles as "river stones" on the glottis, dividing the headwater of an "original 'chaos of noises'" from the "flowing out" of language, "a passage of force from subject to object" (2005, 58).[2]

Marc Shell suggests that Demosthenes, who specifically struggled with his *r* sounds—a *rhotacism*—practiced the tongue-twister (translated

---

1. The authors go on to suggest that "because there are so many internal and external factors that affect the individual who stutters, it is not surprising that different speakers can have vastly different experiences with their speech and speaking difficulties. This variability (both between and within speakers) is a fundamental aspect of the stuttering disorder that speech-language pathologists need to understand" (Yaruss and Quesal 2004, 35). It is important for me to retain an understanding of this variability throughout my discussion here as well.

2. Scott is an award-winning Canadian poet. About his work Scott says, "Having stuttered all of my life, [my poetry] represents a spelunk into the mouth of the stutterer, a trek across labial regions, a repel through the stalagmites of molars and canines, a lexical navigation into the cavernous poetics of what it means to stutter" (Apostolides 2009, n.p.).

as) "I have pronounced as a rhetor the rhetorical *rho.*" Practicing this phrase unstutteringly, Shell argues, was a way to also make the phrase come true, as being a rhetorician supposedly depended upon erasing the stutter (2006, 31). (One of Logue's chief therapeutic methods is also to have Bertie recite tongue-twisters like "I am a thistle-sifter.")

Yet Martha Rose argues "that Demosthenes would be known to the modern world for his rhetorical skills would no doubt have pleased him," but "that he would be known for stuttering would have surprised him" (2003, 65). The power of the myth, however, trumps the "reality" of Demosthenes's life: he becomes a model for ways to understand and treat stuttering (and perhaps other disabilities). His disability is a problem that requires intense effort to physically overcome—and if the disability cannot be overcome, then perhaps one is not trying hard enough. The idea that the disability could be easily overlooked, or that the disability could be a rhetorical signature with positive potential, is refused. In *The King's Speech*, this same message seems to be both reinforced and questioned. That is, there are ways to understand the film as a rehabilitative manual or ways to understand it as a celebration of imperfection. The trick with the marbles does not work, after all, and stands as an emblem of the futility and archaism of some forms of medical treatment—maybe even as a short-circuiting of the popular narrative of overcoming.

The King's Speech won four Oscars in 2010, continuing a long line of decorated films and award-winning film roles about disability—from *One Flew over the Cuckoo's Nest* to *Children of a Lesser God* to *Rain Man* to *My Left Foot* to *Scent of a Woman* to *The Piano* to *Forrest Gump* to *Shine* to *As Good as It Gets* to *Iris* to *A Beautiful Mind* to *Mystic River* to *Ray* to *Million Dollar Baby* to *Babel* to *Avatar* to *The Iron Lady* to *Silver Lining Playbook*.

Every year around Oscar season, in fact, you will find articles cynically describing the best ways to win an Academy Award: able-bodied actors are invariably encouraged to act disabled. The fact is that, for many people, disability is shaped and explained very strongly for them through film. It is no coincidence that in my list of disability myths and tropes from the first chapter, so many of these stereotypes arose from and gained reinforcement from the movies. Film is a contemporary mythical sphere through which ability and disability are rhetorically negotiated.

As mentioned earlier, many of the films from the above list are disability biopics and thus also biopolitical, narrated through disabled bodies/minds and speaking to social and cultural roles for people with disabilities (and all bodies) via disability myth and rhetoric. They are also epideictic, praising and blaming their subjects. Some may resist normativity; most do not at all. *The King's Speech* is an exemplary disability biopolitical biopic.

In turn, there are many ways to criticize the film and its disability troping, but, as Robert McRuer writes of the film:

> If I were to simply trash *The King's Speech*, I would essentially be identifying it as more of the same, as we have in fact learned to identify the "same old, same old" for a few decades now in disability studies. *The King's Speech*, that is, is an inspirational "overcoming" movie (meaning that it is clearly about the "triumph" *over* disability); it seems rather clearly designed for able-bodied consumption (disabled viewers have long critiqued the idea that one needs to "overcome" disability); it largely locates the problem not in the social context in which the disabled person finds himself but in his impairment (the problem is King George VI of England's stutter—or to use the more common British term, stammer); and it joins a very, very long list of films that present audiences with an actor (in this case Colin Firth) who is ultimately showered with awards for playing crip. (2013, 4–5)

Yet McRuer argues that *"The King's Speech* might be approached differently" (2013, 5). He points to BBC blogger Disability Bitch who reviewed the film: "I'm Disability Bitch. I'm supposed to be throwing popcorn at the screen in protest, I think. Instead, I merely shrugged and noted that there are informative articles about stammering in every single newspaper in the world this week. And I'm only slightly exaggerating" (2011, n.p.). McRuer notes that "disability identity thus *materialized* in both *The King's Speech* and in reporting around it." We should "signal its affirmation of disability identity," he suggests, even within a somewhat conventional representation (2013, 6). I will return to McRuer's critique later, but for now, let it suffice to say that however much the film replicates normative narrative structures, and however much the public has taken up the story of overcoming in standard ways, this easy (and ableist) reception of the film has also been refused.

These interpretations, refusals, and differing approaches only begin to reveal the rhetoricity of *The King's Speech*. As mentioned, my method in this chapter will be to employ *mētis* as I try out many of the questions and ideas of this book—and thus argue that the questions have real, contemporary significance.

He Stuttered

First of all, it is worth noting that a stutter is a particularly symbolic form of disability.[3] In the Bible, a small section of Isaiah 32 associates "the eradication of stuttering . . . with the redemption of the world" (Bobrick 1995, 24). The stutter contradicts biblical notions of speech as the light of the soul and then Renaissance notions of "the divinity of speech as a reflection of the soul" (ibid., 26). In Melville's *Billy Budd*, the protagonist's stutter is viewed as a curse—evidence that the devil always manages to "slip in his little card" (1924, 48). And then in modern linguistics, for instance via Chomsky, articulate speech is represented as that which distinguishes human from animal. But stuttering has not always been understood as the mark of evil or as an inversion of the soul or the human. As I have shown, in the ancient Greek context, the word *pseilos* was commonly used to describe Demosthenes's stutter. But the word also alludes to the meaning that lies ghostlike behind written words. As Martha Rose argues, a stutter implies a deconstruction of rhetorical norms (2003, 57). As Marc Shell has written, "The pan-global and pan-cultural phenomenon of the stutter 'literalizes' in the human body and spirit many of the key notions that humanists deal with—imitation, representation, doubling, synonymy, punning, inexpressibility, and metrics. . . . [S]tuttering involves spiritually and physiologically inescapable ways of human articulation. At the

---

3. See Joshua St. Pierre's "The Construction of the Disabled Speaker: Locating Stuttering in Disability Studies" (2012) for an excellent examination of the liminal status of stuttering within disability studies (2012).

same time, it pertains to the problem of the unspeakable or what remains unsaid" (2006, 2–3). Jordan Scott expresses this poetically:

> STUTTER in the gullet
>
> a blockage repetition replacement inadequate
>
> breath to language line. (2005, 57)

The poem then calls up David Wills, who would argue that the stutter reveals the prosthetic relationship between the body and the word and/or the word and meaning. Wills writes that communication is always "dealing with the sideways as well as the forward momentum" (1995, 25). Marc Shell also adds that "stumbling and stuttering are somehow the same is, of course, already established [etymologically] by most Indo-European languages" (2006, 33).[4] If language can be made syncretic with the body, this might be best understood through stuttering and stumbling. In this way, the stutter can itself symbolize the prosthesis and the *mētis* of discourse: as opposed to the linear and logical, or the idea that any communication happens smoothly or easily. I have mentioned that the sibilance within the word *stuttering* itself twists the term into something cruel. Yet the stutter can also perhaps be viewed as amplifying that which is rhetorical in every utterance or movement, highlighting all struggle to make meaning.

Of course, stumbling down this theoretical road also leads us away from the actual lived experience of the stutterer—who may in fact desperately seek a cure, may not at all agree that stuttering should be understood metaphorically. I do not want to ignore this worry—in fact, I am hoping that this worry, this critique of my own method in this chapter, encourages readers to maintain a very skeptical distance. Yet while the lived experience of the stutterer should be the central embodied concern at the root of any metaphorical extension, I am *also* writing here about that (connected) part of the disability that might be rhetorically constructed. As such, when the concept of the stutter can do rhetorical work to challenge

---

4. Shell writes that he himself is "a stuttering stumbler whose limbs were twisted by polio" (2006, 33).

oppressive norms, we might take the concept up cautiously and apply it subversively. The idea is that, as Mitchell and Snyder argue, every text is about disability, in the sense that it issues forth from the unsteady rhetorical stance of prosthesis, which always "fails to return the incomplete body to the invisible status of a normative essence" (2001a, 8). Further, rhetorical or "literary forms, like disabled ones, are discordant in their unwillingness to replicate a more normative appearance" (ibid., 9). *The King's Speech*, as well as the myths of King George VI, are perfect examples of narratives that cannot fully replicate a normative appearance, and this might be facilitated by the stutter itself.

As Isaac Chotiner writes, "By 1944, King George VI felt confident enough about his stammer to turn it into a verbal signature." In a speech disbanding the Home Guard, he "only stumbled over the 'w' in weapons. Afterwards, Logue asked him why this letter had proved a problem. 'I did it on purpose,' the King replied with a wink. 'If I don't make a mistake, people might not know it was me'" (2011, 5). In the film, this moment is actually wrapped into his famous 1939 speech declaring war on Germany, the key moment in the plot: "I had to throw in a few [stutters], so they'd know it was me," he says to Logue after the speech has been delivered (Seidler 2008, 89). So, the chronology is intentionally stuttered by the filmmakers. The moment is transposed into a definitively more *deliberative* speech—recall that deliberative rhetoric seeks to propose actions for the future; declarations of war by kings and politicians are *the* traditional exemplars of deliberative rhetoric.[5]

But more remarkably, the king's stutter is situated as a generative rhetorical device, part of his unique *ethos*. This is in its own small way a refusal of overcoming, of normative appearances.[6] The deliberation is

---

5. The deliberative moments of both *The King's Speech* and *The Iron Lady* in which Bertie and Thatcher deliver oratorically also accentuate the biopolitics of these biopics—we see groups of bodies arranged before radios, in the publics of Parliament, the church, a horse track. Indeed, the technologies of radio and TV are shown to disperse bodies, yet allow the speakers' rhetorical messages to reach even further than they ever have before.

6. And even if the king gains some fluency, the retention of some stuttering, as well, calls up what Judith Butler might call an undoing of normativity, wherein "the experience

not just over what England will do about Nazi Germany; it also becomes a deliberation on normalcy. The film refuses the "disability drop," and though we may be conditioned to expect the appearance of *dis ex machina* in the climax, it is resisted. Further, the idea that he could stutter "on purpose" or control how and when he "throws in a few" is somewhat ironic in this instance—there is no way to avoid an ambivalent reaction to this. If he really does have total control—enough control to stutter at will—then he is giving the finger to the normative imperative. Yet if he is just claiming control over the stutter, he subverts the normative demand just as powerfully: because then control of language might even be situated as the will or desire to stutter. Or perhaps he stuttered unintentionally, but claimed control in order to save face; or maybe he planned to stutter just in case he lost control, or planned to claim the intention regardless of what happened.[7] Unquestionably, it is impossible to know the truth, yet the insistence with which these questions arise is striking. And what would *The King's Speech* be without the gaps these questions rend in this most crucial moment of the film?[8]

The climax of the film is a deliberative speech, and about as "deliberative" as a speech can be—the speech in which Bertie prepares the British

---

of a normative restriction becoming undone can undo a prior conception of who one is only to inaugurate a relatively newer one that has greater livability as its aim" (2004, 1). That is, even though the effort to speak fluently might improve the king's life within a normative society, he neither escapes that normative pressure nor needs to denounce his former self.

7. In personal correspondence discussing an early draft of this chapter, Craig A. Meyer first asked this question about whether Bertie simply claimed control to save face.

8. I thank Craig E. Meyer for his critical reading of this chapter—he helped me to open up a more full range of meanings for the film. His input also proved that films such as this one can actually mean drastically different things to different people and reminded me that *mētis* methodology must always assume this multiplication. I also thank Joshua St. Pierre for his own tremendously insightful reading of a previous version of this chapter. Finally, I want to mention Amy Vidali's brilliant Society For Disability Studies presentation on her own father's stuttering and Vidali's general influence on all of the work in this manuscript, particularly her willingness to open up disability studies beyond "getting it" or not "getting it" and her reminder that our research can always (must always) help us create more accessible classrooms.

public to go to war again, now against Hitler. You will recall that deliberative rhetoric, one of the three main genres of rhetoric defined by Aristotle, seeks to determine the right future action and is perhaps best exemplified by political speeches. As I have shown, the role of disability in deliberative rhetoric is particularly vexed. Simply, disability is viewed as the very absence of futurity, or as the very least desirable future, and thus deliberative rhetoric invokes disability to characterize everything that was undesirable about the past, everything that the future must overcome. Recall that in American president Warren Harding's famous speech on "readjustment," post–World War I, the metaphorical focus is on returning the American body to "normalcy" and overcoming the disabilities of war and foreign immigration.

Bertie's speech does gesture to overcoming, but has an edge: "The task will be hard. There may be dark days ahead, and war can no longer be confined to the battlefield, but we can only do the right as we see the right, and reverently commit our cause to God. If one and all we keep resolutely faithful to it, ready for whatever service or sacrifice it may demand, then with God's help, we shall prevail" (Seidler 2008, n.p.). This invocation of darkness and difficulty is also a refusal of the tropes of overcoming the body. In fact, Bertie is indirectly reminding the audience that people will die and be injured, that their homes will be bombed. This, in combination with his stuttering, however intentional, places the speech more closely in the realm of *disability* deliberation than the more normative forms of the genre we might usually be given.

While Wills (1995) invokes stuttering as more than just a metaphor for rhetoric and for meaning-making, his mentions are rather minor. Gilles Deleuze, however, makes the argument for the stutter's linguistic and semiotic centrality more explicit: "Creative stuttering is what makes language grow from the middle . . . what puts language in perpetual disequilibrium" (1997, 111). Deleuze suggests that the inherent stutter of language makes meaning "take flight, send[s] it racing along a witch's line, ceaselessly placing it in a state of disequilibrium, making it bifurcate and vary in each of its terms, following an incessant modulation" (ibid., 109). Deleuze succeeds in not just "uncoupling the phenomenon of 'stuttering' from the negative clinical sphere, and presenting it as a critical-creative process, but also in seeing stuttering not as an aspect of speech but as an imminent quality of language itself" (Stalpaert 2010, 81). This is an important move for disability studies—challenging the priority of the medical definition of the stutter, and instead positioning it as a generative social and epistemological phenomenon.

This is also an important move for *rhetoric,* allowing the stutter to in a way "dismantle the logocentric paradigm and its rigid conception of language" (ibid., 80). As Deleuze (1997) shows, the stutter is a particularly meaningful rhetorical "device" or embodiment. Christel Stalpaert argues, via Deleuze, that stuttering is "the creative urge of the necessity to speak despite the short-circuiting effect of rigid language systems, it is a pronouncement of the unspeakable not despite, but thanks to the space for stuttering" (2010, 83). As Brenda Jo Brueggeman writes, the stutter is one way to figure how "disability critiques, even as it delivers" rhetoric; "disabilities [can] allow [speakers] to make [their] points even more persuasively" as a "compelling antispectacle" against perfection (2005, 25). The stutter has a particularly powerful *kairos*—it makes the audience recognize their tacit expectations in the pause and makes speaker and audience more directly aware of and present in the process of choosing or landing upon the available means of persuasion. Thus, we move away from an idea of disability as deficit. Instead, disability is the very possibility (and concurrently the uncertainty) of human communication and knowledge. Disability then also resituates rhetoric, not as the flawless delivery of pure ideas, but as the embodied struggle for meaning.[9]

9. Christopher Eagle also explores this generative possibility in his study of novels by Melville, Kesey, and Mishima, each featuring stuttering characters. He allows that in these novels, the stutter often functions as a simple and negative metaphor. Yet he also suggests another register: "The stutter as a symbol for everyday language's constant susceptibility to communicative breakdown. . . . By blurring rigid distinctions between stuttered and nonstuttered speech, these works remind us that the standard of purely direct speech is an impossible one, that all acts of language are prone to indirectness and susceptible to breakdown" (2011, 217).

As Nathan Haller writes in a review of *The King's Speech*:

> The stutterer's voice points towards a paradox of verbal culture: language was born of a need to communicate orally and in the moment, and yet, at its most influential, language is so little dependent on spontaneous speech that even someone permanently stymied on that front—a stutterer—can eke out a message that commands a nation. . . . [I]t affirms that there is more to public meaning and shared truth than smooth talk and rhetorical style. . . . The King's Speech champions a notion of the public voice as something impervious to glib manipulation. The difficulty of the stutterer's speech proves its good faith. (2011, 3)

Brueggeman (2005) suggests that the stutter parodies perfection. Haller (2011) suggests that the struggle of the stutter strips rhetoric of pretension. Shell (2006) and Deleuze (1997) show that the stutter can usefully atomize language. As Shell writes in the conclusion to his book *Stutter*: "Lack of closure and the concomitant desire or need for conclusion are exacerbated by prosaic rhythm, semantic meaning, and logical argument. These wants are a stutterer's burden—and, as we have seen, sometimes his peculiar boon" (2006, 217). What each of these theorists reveal is that the stutter (and the stutterer) is capable of subverting the dominance of *logos*—and in particular of subverting Aristotelian logic and its traditions. The stutter powerfully reminds the word of the body, the audience of the speaker, the utterance of its context, in spite of our efforts to forget them.

Same Old, Same Old

Haller suggests that there are ways to view *The King's Speech* as a "fantasy of voice, a fantasy about the nearly cosmic virtue of fighting to get the words out." He argues that it is "our cultural fantasy too," that "all has now been said: the language is pronounced, the meaning safeguarded in history" (2011, 7). If we view the film as a triumph *over* the stutter, then we might believe this fantasy is fulfilled.

    And this is what many disability studies critics have focused on in critiquing the film: the idea that this film, like many others, is about overcoming. Yet there are ways to view this theme of "overcoming" even within the critical move itself. That is, why is it that so much disability studies criticism seeks to "cure" cultural representations? Why is criticism so desirous of closure and conclusion? Isn't it just a way for disability studies, through the labor of critique, to overcome the social forces that hold it down or to point out the errors of others?

When McRuer references the "same old, same old" renderings of disability in culture, he is also referencing a "same old, same old" valence in disability studies critique: those negative representations we have "learned to identify . . . for a few decades now in disability studies" and I myself have cataloged in this book (2013, 4). Tobin Siebers also recognizes this tendency to police negative representations of the body, further suggesting that through such critique, "disability offers a challenge to the representation of the body—this is often said." Yet as with the underlying fatigue inherent in McRuer's "same old, same old," Siebers betrays this fatigue through the phrase "this is often said," labeling such challenges "body theory as usual." He then suggests that what would be new and revolutionary for disability studies would be the recognition of how "the disabled body changes the process of representation itself. Different bodies require and create new modes of representation" (2010, 54).

I would argue that these "same old" and "as usual" modalities of disability studies critique, as well as these new gestures toward a disability epistemology, actually need to be connected. It is important to say that the "as usual" modes of critique are still very important—and nobody seems to be arguing against them, or for their retirement. But a major problem with these modes is the idea that we can critique *any* representation as a full realization of the author's intention, or as a pure crystallization of a societal attitude. Disability studies should teach us that no meaning-making is ever that able. Simply, to critique *The King's Speech* as a narrative of overcoming would be to ignore its overt refusal to "replicate a normative appearance" through Bertie's retention of his stuttering style. But this critique would also strengthen the idea that *The King's Speech*, or any movie, could ever get disability representation "straight," no matter how straightened and normative the trope is, or how progressive and realistic. If every utterance is more like a stutter than any form of "pure" signification, if every rhetorical move limps or rolls a bit sideways, then even the most objectionable of ableist stories should not be reified even as they are critiqued; nor should we suggest that a more just representation is also inherently more real. A major problem with policing representations of disability is the assumption that we ever really control what we are doing when we represent the body in these fraught ways. To say that someone got disability representation "wrong" is important, for any number of ethical reasons. But this also assumes that these artists have full control over their art and its reception, that we can ever get a representation right. We must certainly be worried when criticism might serve as a form of reification. What is needed, then, is a mode of critique that can point out ethical problems but can also locate potential for new meanings wherever signification stumbles or trips.

Let's look for a moment at a lengthy article by the film's writer, David Seidler: "How the 'Naughty Word' Cured the King's Stutter (and Mine)" (2010). Seidler's article, in which he discusses his own stutter and its treatment, lends a feeling of clinical veracity to the film. Seidler suggests that he "knew a great deal about the standard techniques of the era" to treat stuttering because they had been used on him in his own speech therapy. He writes that "I remember almost choking when marbles were put in my mouth," and thus this scene from the film (and its invocation of Demosthenes) gains resonance (ibid., 8). Seidler also recalls having heard the king on the radio: "I remember his voice, high, and tense, with occasional pauses and hesitation. Yet the cumulative effect was marvelous: stalwart, staunch and stirring. Despite his stutter he was able to deliver glorious sentences that rallied the free world . . . [A]lthough everyone in the world, allies and enemies alike, listened critically to every syllable he uttered, he doggedly persevered" (2010, 2). Thus, when Seidler is inspired by the king, he is inspired because his stutter has clear rhetorical power. The film is in some ways a defense of stuttering, resistant to the push to cure or overcome or compensate.[10]

10. As I have argued repeatedly throughout the book, there are many examples of "stuttering" or other overtly recognizable disabilities having clear rhetorical power—from Demosthenes's stutter to Alcibiades's lisp. Recall as well that when the Homeric hero Odysseus is at his most cunning, it is when he begins a speech badly, when he appears as a "witless man," an *aphrona* (Detienne and Vernant 1978, 22). This can be read as an

Yet Seidler, and other commentators, also invoke their own narrative of cultural overcoming: "Today we've come a long way in our dealings with the handicapped," he writes. He suggests that for Franklin Delano Roosevelt, a "shriveled leg was a sign of weakness."[11] "So was a stammer," when Seidler was growing up, he recalls. At that time, perhaps because of negative media portrayals, he felt that if "you had a speech defect . . . thus you were a defective person" (2010, 5). Star Colin Firth also suggested, in a *Variety* interview discussing the film, that stuttering is "one of the last legitimately pastiched disabilities."[12] "You don't really get away with poking fun at people who are in wheelchairs," he said, "you know, or who are blind. I'm not saying we have to be po-faced about tragedy or hardship, but it's pretty rare, I think, that the issue's been dealt with as an issue" (Thielman 2010, n.p.). It is difficult to know exactly what Firth is getting at here, but one possibility is that he, like Seidler, is gesturing to the fact that society "gets" many disability issues, at least those that have become acceptable and visible, and that the success of the film signals a greater understanding of stuttering, which in turn advances societal sensitivity to a wider range of disabilities than before. He seems to be saying that people should really view stuttering as a full and representable disability, like other disabilities, and not as something that can be made fun of. The irony of this statement is that you would ever feel you have to justify a disability representation as being linked to a disability that is "real" enough to depict more than one-dimensionally. When the film is discussed, writ-

embodiment of the classical idea of *anmut*: "not a property of bodies and persons but a term for the effects they produce in interaction with others" (Humphreys 1999, 126). *Anmut*, as a concept, holds that bodily attitudes are mutable, socially constructed. Odysseus did not have a perfect body, but he had *anmut*, the ability to make his body signify in relation to the bodies in his audience.

11. The movie *Hyde Park on Hudson*, released in 2012, starring Bill Murray as FDR and based on a BBC radio drama of the same name, focuses on the 1939 visit to the United States by Bertie and Elizabeth, bringing Bertie and FDR together onscreen.

12. By pastiche, I am assuming that he means "a composition in another artist's manner, without satirical intent," and not a hodgepodge or medley of various ingredients, though I might want to retain some ambiguity between the two meanings (Gross 2010, n.p.).

ers (including Seidler) invariably invoke numbers: "One per cent of the population stammers. That's an awful lot of stuttering" (2010, n.p.). This quantitative tendency forces you to wonder how many people have to have a disability for it to be either socially or artistically acceptable and for it to be represented "as an issue."

Of course, the more cynical way to look at Seidler's comments is to think that movie producers are constantly on the lookout for the next disability "worth" depicting. Or that Firth has been keeping a checklist of the disabilities that have been successfully "pastiched"—and that maybe this list is getting dangerously close to the territory of disabilities that are unacceptable for film coverage, so he is happy to have found a disability to make his own.[13] In Barry Harbaugh's article "A History of Stuttering in the

---

13. The offensive but perhaps revealing joke of Ben Stiller's role in the film *Tropic Thunder* is that he plays a famous actor who is recovering from a film role in which he played a character with an intellectual disability as *too* disabled—or in the hateful lexicon of the film, he "went full retard." The film was attempting to lampoon other actors who have taken on roles as disabled characters and overly sentimentalized their depictions. Stiller himself admitted that "it's sort of edgy territory, but we felt that as long as the focus was on the actors who were trying to do something to be taken seriously that's going too far or wrong, that was where the humor would come from. [The joke is on] actors reaching for roles in terms of hopefully winning awards" (quoted in Adler 2008, n.p.). The negative reaction to the film from disability rights advocates may have even acknowledged this possibly incisive critique of the manipulation of disability tropes in film, but this could not compensate for the fact that the word *retard* itself was used dozens of times in the movie as the most direct kind of insult.

Further, while Stiller and the filmmakers may have been trying to make fun of other actors, they did so *through* disability, and to be oblivious to the idea that the staccato repetition of hateful words like *retard* and *moron* would somehow bypass the actual bodies that are most often targeted by those words is beyond naive. Of course, even amid this spectacular failure, there is some grain of truth to the satire here. The film also critiques what Firth has said—we are forced to question why "serious" movies about disability are so quickly connected, by the academy and by critical audiences, with acting genius. Stiller's character, "Simple Jack," is shown as a caricature of other disabled characters (notably a lampoon of Sean Penn in the film *I Am Sam*), and it is worth remarking that a pronounced stutter is supposed to be shorthand for his mental disability. Although it is not too generous to suspect that Firth is calculating upon the "disabledness" quotient of *The King's Speech*, it is also

Movies: It Hasn't Been Pretty" (2010), he offers an inventory of traditional disability roles in film, suggesting that on the whole, stutterers have been fools (see Tod Browning's *Freaks* or *A Fish Called Wanda*), violent criminals (see *Primal Fear*, the *Taking of Pelham 1-2-3*), abused or suicidal (see *One Flew over the Cuckoo's Nest* or Stephen King's *It*), or sexually blocked (see *Girl Shy*).[14] So perhaps what Firth is getting at is that, as with most depictions of disability, representations of stuttering have been "illegitimate" in the sense that they are one-dimensional, that they adhere too closely to common and insulting disability myths.

Harbaugh does suggest that the recent film *Rocket Science*, which, like *The King's Speech*, was written by a person with a stutter, is also "exacting in its portrayal of [the lead character's] mode of speech—we're often met by his interior monologue and are left to consider the divide between those thoughts and their (eventual) articulation." He concludes that, although rare, there are films in which a stutter "is used not as a lazy way of outlining a character but as an entry point into larger ideas. . . . In the face of everything we don't know about the condition, perhaps that's all, finally, we can ask for" (ibid., n.p.). Seidler concludes his own article by stating that "one percent of the population stammers . . . if this film brings hope to those afflicted, and understanding to their plight, I'll be very pleased" (2010, 14). The goals of both Harbaugh and Seidler seem to be the raising of awareness, for the benefit either of all of society or of the "afflicted."

In Seidler's article, Firth's interview, and Harbaugh's inventory, then, we are offered two imperfect but provocative means of understanding the film. The first possibility is that the film will be received as a sort

---

impossible to discount this calculus when other films like *Tropic Thunder* both raise this critique and at the same time represent disability so pejoratively. "Simple Jack" is not at all funny because of his disabilities, but his appearance in a Hollywood satire takes a cutting shot at the disability hierarchy in film and in culture more broadly (see my list of myths).

14. As Joshua St. Pierre (2012b) had pointed out, when commenting on an earlier version of this chapter, there is a character in the popular TV show *Glee* with a stutter. Tina Cohen-Chang is introduced as having a stutter in episode 9 of season 1. But we later find out she is faking the stutter to avoid having to speak in public—a textbook case of "disability drop."

of celebration of stuttering—as a refusal of the normative imperative to fully cure Bertie, an acknowledgment of stuttering as an integral (or even valued) part of his subjectivity. Certainly, many viewers understand the film this way. But just as surely, many do not: the trope of overcoming might be so powerful that it could overwrite any possible subversion. The visceral experience of watching the film might be seen to actually pattern the viewer's response to Bertie's stuttering in a way that encourages us all to root for his fluency. We zoom in on his tortured face as he speaks, hang on his stammers, endure his "therapy," desiring the release of *hearing* a perfectly formed sentence as much as we suppose Bertie wants to form one. (How the king's speech gets captioned, with the liberal use of ellipses, also lends to this patterning.) Harbaugh (2010) argues that too often, the film cuts away from these moments of pause and discomfort. Yet because *The King's Speech* (as well as *Rocket Science*) is focused also on a therapeutic relationship, every moment of hesitation reinforces a desire for cure in the audience. We want to hear fluency for Bertie, for Lionel, for the British public, and for ourselves. Perhaps this normative compulsion is too powerful for the film to subvert.

Yet if we are willing to assume that the film is not finally about cure, after all, then perhaps another way to understand the film is as a product of a time (our own) in which disability is more generously received or as a step toward a greater acceptance of people with disabilities. As McRuer suggests, even the blogger Disability Bitch seems willing to cede this point. Yet McRuer also suggests that this story could in fact be obscuring truly virulent forms of disability intolerance: the film won awards at the same time that, in England and elsewhere, austerity measures were removing key social supports for people with disabilities. Feeling good about how far society has come in its "dealings with the handicapped" because of this movie would be a dangerous thing to do. In fact, the feint toward disability "tolerance" or "acceptance" or even "celebration" seems like camouflage. The king becomes an acceptably disabled individual, because his disability cannot be cast as anything but "private"—and it is difficult to argue from *The King's Speech* for an expansion or protection of public programs for people with disabilities in the now. The king certainly paid for his own therapy, and though his job performance may have been at risk, his livelihood and security were not in jeopardy because of his disability. The same cannot necessarily be said for other people with disabilities—then or now. There are many ways to argue that contemporary society, despite a more politically correct stance toward disability, and perhaps hiding slyly behind this facade, does not "get" disability rights issues at all.

We seem to be offered a fairly simple binary for our interpretation: (1) the film, despite its best efforts, makes us desire normalcy, compels us to need a cure; or (2) the film resists this overcoming, subverts the trope slightly, but does so in ways that we can't be too quick to celebrate in an era of diminished disability rights.

Yet my point is that neither representation would really get anything "right." Likewise, neither the film's writer nor its stars can necessarily control either signification. In the same way, no critic should feel comfortable pinning the film down. Firth's use of the word *pastiche* is interesting, of course—because this also signals that a film starring a nonstutterer stuttering, that person being Firth himself, is just that, a pastiche; as it signals that the film combines the king's actual biography with popular disability myths and with Seidler's own life; as it signals that all film, and indeed all cultural stories, are pastiche, with meanings overlapping and pasted together, never an originary or received whole.

As Nathan Haller wrote disappointedly, "For a movie that's supposed to be about finding one's voice, *The King's Speech* raises more questions about life with the problem than it answers" (2011, 2). Of course, I do not find this disappointing at all—I find it unsurprising and maybe even edifying. If the movie were only about answering questions about a "problem," then what cultural (or rhetorical) value could it really have? I will argue that in fact the failures of signification in cultural texts about disability can and should (sometimes) be celebrated. As Judith Halberstam writes, "As a practice, failure recognizes that alternatives are embedded already in the dominant and that power is never total or consistent; indeed failure can exploit the unpredictability of ideology and its indeterminate qualities" (2011, 88). Disability studies as an epistemology should show us that meaning actually springs forth from gaps and flaws and mistakes. Halberstam asks, "Can we produce generative models of failure that do not posit" either "futurity and positivism" or "nihilism and negation"? (ibid.,

120). Disability studies might also ask, can we shape critical and rhetorical analyses that go beyond getting disability *right* or getting it *wrong*?

In the spirit of *mētis*, then, we might begin to layer some questions and conflicting interpretations. In the rest of this chapter, I will look at some of the multiple ways that the film has been received. I will also look at the alternative myths of King George VI, to examine and propose some of the other films that might have been made—alternative ways to narrate this life—a lateral array of interpretive possibilities beyond simple binaries.

Historically (In)Accurate (In)Articulation

One focus of reviews of the film has been a reinterpretation of "what really happened"—a quest for historical accuracy, a forensics. In his review, *"The King's Speech*: The Real Story" in the *Telegraph*, Nigel Farndale focuses on the irony of Bertie's stutter: "It was as if the gods, or Fates, were amusing themselves by toying with his mind, mocking his failings, reminding him that he was very much a mortal. . . . [E]ven crueler, his reign coincided with a revolution in mass communication. For the first time in British history, subjects could listen to their monarch addressing them through their wireless sets" (2011, 1). In the film, this new technology plays a central role—the microphone becomes almost a supporting actor in the plot, and in his "therapy" Logue also works with a new phonograph recording device to capture Bertie's voice and play it back for him. The technological context of the film is certainly important, and Bertie's prosthetic relationships with these technologies could have been an even-greater focus. His speeches take on a new biopolitical power. In an early scene in which the microphone is introduced, it is given almost phallic totemic value: it is carefully unveiled and polished and calibrated. A speaker is told by a technician to "let the microphone do the work," yet when Bertie is given the same advice, it does not work for him, and the microphone becomes his adversary rather than his friend.[15]

---

15. Joshua St. Pierre (2012b) offered an interesting elaboration on this point after reading an earlier draft of this essay. I reprint his comment here with his permission: "I think that the microphone 'becoming his adversary rather than his friend' has even more

But Farndale then goes on to place the film in the context not just of technological change, but also of British politics in the 1930s, suggesting that the movie defines an era for this empire. "The stammering that defined him," Farndale writes, "and the courage with which he tried to beat it, came to symbolize the vulnerability of the British people as they stood alone against the Nazi tyranny that had the rest of Europe in its grip. A certain solidarity emerged between monarch and subject." Farndale argues that the movie's thematic core is a coupling of Bertie's battle against stuttering and the British people's battle with Nazi Germany: "If he can get through his affliction . . . the British people can get through theirs [the Blitz]" (ibid., 2). In a review in the *Observer*, Dominic Sandbrook also concludes that "when war broke out in 1939," King George VI "became an unlikely symbol of national resistance, his mundane domesticity a reminder of what Britain was fighting for" (2011, n.p.). He argues that "when thousands applauded" the King's speeches, "they were not just acknowledging their monarch; they were applauding themselves" (2011, n.p.).

A review by Joe Neumaier in the *New York Daily News* even goes so far as to identify the stutter as a metaphor for "bridging the gap between classes, between who you are and who you need to be." This review focuses on the relationship between Bertie and Logue, who "delicately plays up and flouts the difference between King and subject," with the stutter itself serving analogically for the gulf between them, with its eradication as their shared goal—and the king's speeches as the means of uniting all of Britain (2011, n.p.). These reviewers appeal to the supposed

---

truth than you indicate. In the opening scene when Bertie is mounting the steps to make his inaugural speech, the POV [point of view] is focused fixedly on the microphone. For the stutterer, the microphone is an amplification not merely of one's speech, but (at least symbolically) is also a site of concentration of all the fears, worries and anxieties of being disabled. I think this may be because the microphone gives 'pure voice' and that is perhaps the thing a stutterer fears the most; being abstractly represented and identified solely as a stutter. I remember empathizing with Bertie really strongly in this scene because of the microphone. . . . Thinking of prosthesis in this way seems to be really interesting, because the prosthesis is totalizing (and threatens to be annihilating) for the stutter."

historical accuracy of the film in order to construct a feel-good story about the empire.

Not everyone agrees. (In fact, some commentators *really* disagree.) Christopher Hitchens, in a scathing review in *Slate*, also focused on historicism, wrote that *The King's Speech* "perpetrates a gross falsification of history." Hitchens argues that the movie offers a "bizarre rewriting" of the relationship between Churchill; Bertie's elder brother, Edward VIII, who abdicated the throne to Bertie; and Bertie himself. Churchill is shown in the film as the "consistent friend of the stuttering prince and his loyal princess and as a man generally in favor of a statesmanlike solution to the crisis of the abdication." But, "in point of fact, Churchill was—for as long as he dared—a consistent friend of conceited, spoiled, Hitler-sympathizing Edward VIII. And he allowed his romantic attachment to this gargoyle to do great damage to the very dearly bought coalition of forces that was evolving to oppose Nazism and appeasement." Hitchens situates the movie as participating in the "post-fabricated myth" of the royal family's role in "Britain's finest hour" when, "in fact, had it been up to them, the finest hour would never have taken place. So this is not a detail but a major desecration of the historical record—now apparently gliding unopposed toward a baptism by Oscar" (2011, n.p.).

In the *New Republic*, critic Isaac Chotiner called *The King's Speech* a "royal mess," suggesting that the film is "historically inaccurate, entirely misleading, and, in its own small way, morally dubious" (2011, 1). Chotiner also objects to the ways that the film sanitizes both Bertie's brother Edward's fascist sympathies as well as Churchill's support for Edward throughout the abdication. "Bertie ascended to the throne at the end of 1936. Three years later, he gives the speech of the film's title. In the time in between the two events, the British government notoriously blundered and appeased the Nazis" (2011, 2). The failure to act, to take a stand against Nazism, is never explored in the film, which presents a world of moral certitude. Chotiner thus argues that "the film fails . . . by implying that Bertie was staunchly anti-fascist from the start" (ibid., 2). "By the time the credits roll," Chotiner writes sarcastically, "Bertie has conquered his stammer, and the British people are well on their way to vanquishing fascism—the latter, naturally, having been aided by the former" (ibid.,

1). Yet the alternative that Chotiner implicitly constructs is that Bertie's hesitant speech, his slow and deliberate pace, not his fluency, might present the best metaphor for Britain's approach to Hitler, which was much more halting and uncertain than the film leads us to assume. So, instead of recognizing Bertie's overcoming of the stammer as a metaphor for the overcoming of fascism, the stutter might get posed as a metaphor for British moral ambivalence. Of course, the stutter is still viewed as negative, as the problem to be overcome. This construction also truly breaks down if we can recognize that a stutter actually never reflects a lack of intentionality—the stutter might get in the way of what one wants to say, but should not be mistaken for confusion or ambivalence.

It is possible to read *The Iron Lady* in a similar way. In my discussion of this film—in so many ways an analogue to *The King's Speech*—in the second chapter of the book, I mentioned that Thatcher's dementia might be read as "softening" the hard edges of her legacy or as a symbol of (or even a punishment for) her political failures. But in either sense, Thatcher's struggle with her disability serves as "narrative prosthesis" in the same way that Bertie's overcoming serves as "narrative prosthesis." If we really dig into this overcoming metaphor in the case of *The King's Speech*, then we recognize stuttering, in these metaphors, situated as fascism or as class division.[16] And we can quickly understand why the *use* of disabil-

16. One of the most compelling contemporary novels of dysfluency, David Mitchell's *Black Swan Green*, takes place against the backdrop of Thatcher's Falklands crisis, as well as the social conservatism and fiscal uncertainty of the time—"Thatcher's recession." Mitchell himself has what he calls a "stammer," and the novel is semiautobiographical. There are ways to read the struggle of being a stuttering teenager as a metaphor for England under Thatcher in *Black Swan Green*. Another way to say it is that in the novel "a child-like or immature [or, I would add, dysfluent] perspective is brought to bear on some of the main public and political questions of the period in a way that interrogates the founding assumptions of the dominant ideology" (Dix 2010, 31). The stutter, again, signifies through narrative prosthesis—perhaps simply or perhaps cunningly.

On the other hand, as Christopher Eagle has shown, stuttering is often used less ambiguously to explore political questions through novels. As Eagle writes, "In Philip Roth's *American Pastoral* (1997) and Gail Jones's *Sorry* (2007), the portrayals of stuttering in the female characters Merry Levov and Perdita Keene share a common conception of the

ity in this metaphorical way can be highly problematic. But this thematic observance is echoed in many other reviews—the popular reception of this movie is that Bertie's triumph is meant to be twinned with that of Britain, and his stuttering stands as a metaphor for fascism, or for the vulnerability of the British people to this force. In McRuer's essay, he also investigates how the film was received as a lesson for *modern* England: "The disabled figure in *The King's Speech* has been positioned by some commentators as an appropriate figure not only for the nation-in-crisis of 1939 (Britain in its 'fateful moment' of confrontation with fascism), but our own" (2013, 7). Indeed, commentators used the movie to paint King George VI as an idealized and sympathetic leader, capable of connecting with the public, albeit anachronistically, in ways that the current House of Windsor and British prime minister David Cameron had been unable to do. The Blitz and the London riots of the summer of 2011 were both situated as calamities that Bertie could solve: the movie was a reminder that, even postriots, "it's still a good time to be an Anglophile" (Petri 2011, n.p.).

As McRuer argues, "This is the [view] that I want to negate—any sort of disability exceptionalism that, *using disability as a vehicle*, both positions threats as external or simply elsewhere (because 'we' as a people, as a group, as a nation, are effectively and affectively united) and masks the redoubled, and internal, neoliberal threat to disabled or impaired bodies and minds" (2013, 8).[17] Of course, the threat to people with disabilities is at

---

stutterer as prone to violent, destructive behavior. . . . Roth and Jones deploy the stutter not only in gendered terms, as a symbol for the suppression of the female voice, but also as a broader symbol for the struggle to achieve political voice in the face of injustice" (2012, 17). Moreover, these stuttering women are held up as symbols of the failure to, respectively, oppose war and defend injustices against aboriginal peoples (ibid., 28).

17. Just as McRuer warns against using *The King's Speech* as a means of masking real disability inequities by overwriting them, he and many others would strongly challenge the tendency we might have to forget Margaret Thatcher's political legacy when we read *The Iron Lady* as a sympathetic disability text. This warning is particularly relevant in this current era of austerity measures and neo-Thatcherism in the UK and elsewhere. Yet at the same time, we would not necessarily want to see a film that uses disability to render Thatcher purely evil, nor would we necessarily want to see a film that elides the fact that Margaret Thatcher truly does suffer from dementia, nor would we really want this

once neoliberal *and* neoconservative—representing the loss of social programs and supports in the name of austerity, but also combined with the neoconservative increase of carceral power and "moral" regulation. These threats together have been "redoubled" in ways that disproportionately impact the lives of people with disabilities. Further, I would add that this resistance to using disability as a vehicle can extend backward and forward—the stutter "fails" as a neat metaphor for overcoming fascism in the 1930s and is suspect as an actual crip challenge to current inequities and threats. Thus, the meanings of the film should be much less confidently articulated, and through this caution the rhetorical potential of disability might in fact be mobilized.

Rhetorical Pedagogy

The King's Speech, as you might guess from the early scenes of "classical" speech therapy, is a film about rhetorical teaching. Interestingly, North American trailers for *The Iron Lady* positioned the film as a much more specific analogue to *The King's Speech*, focusing on the small part of *The Iron Lady* in which Thatcher is coached to change her own speech patterns to sound less feminine. This segment does, of course, lend a very interesting rhetorical angle to the film. Her feminine style is seen as a rhetorical disability to be overcome, and overcome she does, through a montage of exercises and transformations.[18] This rhetorical pedagogy is an even more central plot within *The King's Speech*.

Thus, the figure of Lionel Logue, Bertie's rhetorical teacher, played by Geoffrey Rush, offers some further interesting possibilities for interpretation. Theirs is the key relationship in the movie and the axis upon which

---

dementia to render her as a heroic, overcoming, figure—which *The Iron Lady* seems to resist doing.

18. Yet, in retrospect, because this part of the film was actually relatively minor, it seems that these North American trailers were intended to harness the popular public response to *The King's Speech* to create an audience for *The Iron Lady*. Much of the North American media that Streep did—for instance, her NPR *Fresh Air* interview—fixated on the speech lessons that both Thatcher and Streep had to take (as well as the dental prosthesis Streep had to wear to emulate Thatcher).

most of its themes orbit. As Christa van Kraayenoord writes, "The movie has many themes. They include: the socio-economic differences between the pair; the societal and family's reactions and responses to stuttering; the use of particular approaches to the treatment of stuttering; the relationship between 'client' and 'therapist' and the boundaries of such a relationship; and the possible causes of stuttering" (2011, 103). Logue's actual treatments took the form of eighty-two one-hour sessions over ten months (Farndale 2011, n.p.). In the film, the duration and intensity of the relationship are in a sense both protracted and attenuated through montage. We get to meet Bertie and Lionel both individually in their interactions with their families and then most powerfully in their extended scenes together.

Logue's official biography suggests that: "Using humour, patience and 'superhuman sympathy', [Logue] taught [his patients] exercises for the lungs and diaphragm, and to breathe sufficiently deeply to complete a sentence fluently. . . . [T]he fees paid by his wealthy clients enabled him to accept poorer patients without charge" (Edgar 2000, n.p.). In this short excerpt we are given the picture of an unconventional therapist—and we can only assume that he was seen as even less conventional for his own time. In the film, we are led to understand Logue's approach as the modern alternative to the antiquated and cruel therapy methods of Bertie's original doctors, such as the physician who forces him to fit the marbles in his mouth, à la Demosthenes. Of course, it is possible that Logue's techniques have much more in common with Demosthenes than we think. Back in ancient Greece, Demosthenes's training and rehearsal habits led some to liken him to an actor, even though many of his speeches denounced acting. Plutarch asserts that Demosthenes "never grew skilled enough to speak extempore, [instead] he remained dependent on his habits of diligent preparation and (actorly) rehearsal" (Plutarch and White 1966, 8). Of course, Logue was said to be "not only medically unqualified as a therapist, he was actually an actor by training" (Farndale 2011, 2). Logue's "unique and non-standard approaches should be seen in the context of his work as an actor and elocution teacher" (Kraayenoord 2011, 103). Seidler suggests that Logue used "mechanical exercises combined with therapy and friendship" with the king, and this is conveyed through his script (2010, 9). As we see in the film, Logue's acting ability aids him in developing the rhetorical aspects of his "therapy," allowing him to unite physical exercises with psychological techniques and to ground all that he does in his "friendship" with his patient Bertie. Further, as J. Hoberman points out, in an early scene in the movie, Bertie's father, George V, "complains that the new invention of radio has effectively transformed England's royal family: 'We've become actors!'" (2010, n.p.). I will return to the topic of Logue's acting in more detail later—but it is important to note that the theme of acting becomes a rhetorical engine for the movie. This also then throws into flux the tension of "acting disabled" for Firth, the concept of stuttering as a "pastiched" disability, the confluence of rhetorical pedagogy and performance, and the rhetorical construction of disability (locked in a dialectic with its physical experience).

What "medical" experience Logue had came from "treating 'verbally locked' and shell-shocked soldiers" in Australia (Edgar 2000, 2). Without a medical degree, but with a large group of needy patients in these soldiers, Logue was supposedly given the latitude to develop his unorthodox methods. As Hayhow notes, "The approach he pioneered was psychotherapeutic—the suspected the problem for stammerers was not simply physical, that there was something, usually a trauma, around the age of four or five, that created the condition" (quoted in Farndale 2011, n.p.). We are offered the impression that this trauma for Bertie may have been inflicted by his father, perhaps when he forced him to write with his right hand (a popular folk explanation for the development of a stutter) or perhaps through some other cruelty. In David Seidler's own memory of the development of his stutter, this trauma was caused by his emigration by boat across the ocean from England to America when he was a child.

The effect of this psychological emphasis is that, as Hayhow suggests, "in some ways Logue was treating the King as a child" (quoted in Farndale 2011, 4). The assumption, then, is that if a stutter is caused by a childhood trauma, the stutterer is also somehow blocked by this moment, not fully developed psychologically. Moreover, the role of the therapist is to somehow trick the patient into addressing this trauma, or into confusing one form of therapy with another—or, more simply, to trick the patient into simply speaking properly and "forgetting" that she or he cannot normally do so.

Utilizing this sleight-of-hand, Logue's approach was to blur the distinction between physical labor and psychological "therapy." While he was dealing with the stutter as a psychological issue, "part of [Logue's] technique was to make the Duke believe the opposite: that his condition was physical rather than psychological and could be cured by breathing exercises and saying tongue twisters" (Hayhow quoted in ibid., 2). Seidler suggests that he "knew from [his] own experience that mechanical techniques don't eliminate stuttering, although they're wonderful aids to fluidity of speech once an internal change has taken place" (2010, 8). In the film, this camouflaged emphasis on the mechanical comes through in Logue's focus on repetition and on Bertie's body. At one point, Logue suggests that Bertie has a "flabby tummy" and asks the queen to sit on his stomach as he talks. He also asks Bertie to sing. But even when Logue is engaging Bertie in a seemingly physical and linguistic exercise, he is digging deeper. From the script:

LIONEL: Know any songs?

BERTIE: "Swanee River"

LIONEL: Very modern.

BERTIE: Happens to be my favorite.

LIONEL: Sing it.

BERTIE: Certainly not.

> (fascinated by the plane repairs)
>
> May I help? Always wanted to build models. Father wouldn't allow
>
> it. I had to collect stamps. He collected stamps.

LIONEL: Only if you sing. Goes like this . . .

> (sings) "Way down upon the . . ."

BERTIE: I know the words!

> (sings) "Way down upon the Swanee River. . . ." Etcetera.

LIONEL: You didn't stutter.

BERTIE: Of course I didn't stutter, I was singing! One doesn't stutter

> when one sings!
>
> (realises) Oh . . .
>
> (then) Well I can't waltz around on State occasions warbling!

LIONEL: You can with me.

BERTIE: That's because you're peculiar.

LIONEL: I take that as a compliment.

In this exchange, Logue both spurs Bertie to a better physiological understanding of his stutter and begins to probe into Bertie's relationship with his father. He does this by positioning himself in the "peculiar" position of friend, confidant, *and* physician (more on this later).

This confluence of the physical and mental in approaches to rhetorical training harks back to the educational practices of the Sophists of ancient Greece.[19] As Hawhee shows, the sophist-athlete was trained concurrently in rhetoric and wrestling, with *mētis* as the "mode of knowledge-production, one that inform[ed] training practices for athletes and [rhetorical teachers] alike" (2005, 48). In Logue, we are given a manifestation of cunning through this very sophistic blurring of lines between training the mind and training the body. Logue is working with Bertie to move backward and laterally through the logics and physiology of the speech act itself but also through Bertie's own personal history. Logue teaches with and through *mētis*, and he teaches *mētis*.

His technique also strikes the modern viewer as psychoanalytical. Seidler, discussing his research for the film, wrote that "although I couldn't conclusively prove Logue had read Freud, I sensed he was using what became known as 'the talking cure'" (2010, 8). This talking cure is facilitated by a growing friendship between Logue and Bertie—Logue develops the trust of the king, and thus invites him to slowly open up. The exchange continues:

LIONEL: Tell me more about your storybook childhood. What was your earliest memory?

BERTIE: You asked that before.

LIONEL: This time I'd like an answer.

---

19. It is also important to note that there is a long history of the use of speech therapy to "cure" deaf people, just as there has been a long line of mechanical or technological interventions imposed. For more on this history from the perspective of disability rhetoric, see Brueggeman 1999.

BERTIE: Being born.

LIONEL: How can you remember that?

BERTIE: December 14th.

LIONEL: I don't understand.

BERTIE: "Mausoleum Day". Great Grandmamma hated me because
Prince Albert departed on that date. I was named Bertie to placate
Victoria. In return, she said it reminded her of her grief. (stutter
growing in intensity)
Let's stick to medical history please. I'm naturally left handed,
which was considered inappropriate.

LIONEL: And?

BERTIE: I was punished. Now I'm right handed.

LIONEL: Anything else?

BERTIE: Bandy legs. Also considered inappropriate.

LIONEL: waits.

BERTIE (CONT'D): Metal splints were made . . . worn night and day . . .
very painful. Now I have straight legs. This is so . . . tawdry! I need
your services as a Speech Therapist, not Grand Inquisitor. Are you
available?

Bertie here, for perhaps the first time in the film, allows himself to be
made vulnerable. Since birth, he has felt resented in the family, his very
identity a reminder of the premature death of his grandmother Queen
Victoria's beloved husband, Albert. His identity has also been shaped by
disability stigma, by his "inappropriate" body and tongue. His relationship with his father is also represented as somewhat abusive in the film,
and thus when he begins to admit this to Logue, the audience becomes
more convinced of the efficacy of a psychological intervention.[20]

Clearly, Seidler's version of Logue's version of Freudian analysis is
rather benign. But as Marty Jezer writes, "Psychoanalysts have done to

20. That Bertie's upbringing was somewhat abusive by today's standards, and that his
stutter might very well be connected to this abuse at either end of a causal chain, is likely.
For instance, Marc Shell suggests that Bertie's siblings were encouraged to tease him when
he stuttered (2006, 19).

stutterers with words what surgeons . . . used to do with knives"—that is, cut out the tongue (1997, 126). The suggestion is that psychoanalysis has actually disabled stutterers. In his capsule history of the Freudian treatment of stutterers, Jezer suggests that "neo-Freudians," employing none of the reticence and care of Freud himself, explained stuttering as a psychoneurosis related to "pre-genital oral nursing, oral sadistic, and anal sadistic" tendencies, "anal fixations," and finally "antisocial behavior" (1997, 126). In the 1950s and '60s, stutterers were placed "in the same category as feminists, homosexuals, radicals, and intellectuals" as persons who were "emotionally disturbed" and suffered from "mental illness" (ibid., 127, 135). Ironically, as a "talking cure," psychoanalysis has been traditionally extremely disempowering for people who stutter: "Listening to psychoanalysts catalog our neuroses . . . gives us a right to be angry, to be hostile even, and to demand some concrete proof that psychoanalysts know what they are talking about. But in traditional psychoanalysis the analyst always has the last word. Any expression of anger on the client's part only confirms the diagnosis" (ibid., 128). Jezer suggests that today's psychoanalysts and psychotherapists reject many of these earlier ideas, "but the old ideas persist in the popular culture and still do damage" (ibid., 135). It is this persistence of stigma and the continued ordainment of amateur neo-Freudians that inflects the reception of *The King's Speech*.

Yet in the above exchange, we see more of Logue's "peculiar" technique, but we also strongly sense Bertie's resistance. Bertie does feel that Logue is peculiar, he is uncomfortable, and he often tries to reinvoke his own authority when he feels he is losing control. He employs Logue. He is the king, and Logue is his subject. Yet the power dynamic between the two of them is decidedly shifting. Whether this therapy is physical, a Freudian talking cure, a Foucauldian confession (or Spanish inquisition), the relationship between the two exemplifies the fraught relationship and the power differential between doctor and patient, dynamics that disability studies scholars have long critiqued as inherent in the medical model of disability and that Jezer relates directly to the history of the treatment of stuttering. In the film, the flaunting of the doctor-patient power dynamic of the medical model, in addition to Logue's intentional confusion of physical and psychological techniques, positions Bertie's disability as not *only* an inherent condition that must be cured, but instead as in part social, subjective, relational. We might even cautiously label Logue's approach as postmodern, recalling the distinctions between models of disability that I discussed in chapter 3. In the film, Logue does seem to intentionally blur the distinction between physical impairment and cultural disablement. We cannot know whether that was his true approach or whether this less certain perspective on disability simply makes for better cinema. Regardless, the film does allow the viewer to challenge a fairly strict and dominant medical paradigm, and this opens up some daylight for less oppressive views of disability and its treatment. For instance, here is another excerpt from the script:

> LIONEL: Do you stutter when you think?
>
> BERTIE: Don't be ridiculous.
>
> LIONEL: One of my many faults. How about when you talk to yourself?
>
> BERTIE: I don't talk to myself!
>
> LIONEL: Come on, everyone natters to themselves once in a while, Bertie.
>
> BERTIE: Stop calling me that!
>
> LIONEL: Shan't call you anything else.
>
> BERTIE: Then we shan't speak!
>
>   Silence. The jug has boiled. Lionel makes himself a cup of tea.
>
> BERTIE: Must I pay for this?
>
> LIONEL: Loads. Now: when you talk to yourself, do you stutter?
>
> BERTIE: Of course not!
>
> LIONEL: Proving your impediment isn't a permanent internal fixture.
>
>   (Seidler 2008, 25–26)

In this exchange, we see first that Logue is not only subverting the standard doctor-patient dynamic in demanding that Bertie call him Lionel, but he is also subverting the royal protocol by calling the king by his nickname. Bertie attempts to reassert his authority, and when he tries to remind Lionel that what is happening is at base a financial transaction, Lionel responds dismissively. But the main point that Logue seems to want to make here, that the stutter is not a "permanent internal fixture," is also a direct challenge to the idea that this "impairment" is inherent and biological.

This challenge is also a rhetorical argument that Logue must continue to make to Bertie throughout the film: your impediment is not a permanent part of you. Logue might use his medical authority so that he does not have to explain any of his techniques—he may hide behind the mystique of science and medicine. Yet he also develops a friendship with Bertie to remove some of his defensiveness. Bertie is *made* vulnerable. In turn, Bertie is confused by these shifting roles: Are you a doctor who treats my body and mind objectively and scientifically, or are you a friend? Why can't the stutter be treated as my legs were—I wore metal splints, and now my legs are straight? Further, in spite of the fact that Bertie is royalty, his default subordination in the doctor-patient relationship tears down this identity and replaces it with a role defined by his disability or defect. Bertie's confusion crystallizes a much more general crisis in the medical model of disability: disability is not about a defective part of the body to be fixed through severe medical intervention, even if that route is often taken. Instead, disability can be much more often seen as an element of personal identity and subjectivity: psychological, social, intercorporeal.

This is an argument that the film must continually pose to the audience as well—whether intentionally or not. We have been powerfully habituated to read disability as deficit, and to link disability inherently to one flawed body, and not to either an evolving three-dimensional subjectivity or a social process or relationship. If disability does fire a link between the flawed outward sign and an inward quality, this inward quality is too often seen as flawed by association. As Nathan Haller has written, one of the chief worries of many stutterers is the idea that the stutter might be "taken as a window onto something like their personality" (2011, 6). I believe that this fear of diagnosis (or a recognition of its inevitability) is one of the things that Jordan Scott calls up in the poem "Stuttering," quoted in the epigraph to this chapter, when he references "old psychology" (2005, 57). The poem seems to me to comment on the ways a stutter is read and interpreted, as an outward sign of an inner failing or issue. The example of interpretation that Haller uses is that of Henry James—many have argued that his stutter somehow betrayed or explained his closeted sexuality (2011, 6). As you will recognize throughout this chapter, this sexual orientation guessing game is very much operant in the reception of *The King's Speech*, and of Bertie's life. Yet the compulsion to pin his personality down through his disability is part of a larger interpretive issue here. Not only *is* Bertie his stutter—the king's speech stands in as synecdoche for the king himself, he passes from subject to object—but the audience may also feel that the stutter, or any disability, must be traced back to some other perceived negative, be it a weakness of character, a trauma, or a closeted aspect of one's personality. Logue is not the only psychoanalyst, nor is he the only amateur doctor granted the power of medical authority. The audience is given (or naturally assumes) this stance as well.

The implications that the Logue-Bertie dynamic has for any rhetorical pedagogy are thus multiple. First, we should look in all teaching for the evidence of a medical model—all rhetorical teaching idealizes normative expression and normative bodies and the overcoming of any impairments. Yet in the "failure" of Bertie, we also see the perhaps subversive failure of Logue and of rhetorical pedagogy more broadly. Perhaps Logue "fools" Bertie not into overcoming his stutter, but into turning it into a signature; inversely, perhaps Bertie educates Logue into recognizing the stutter as an inherent, yet positive, part of Bertie's identity. Second, the film furthers my argument that all rhetorical teaching would blur distinctions between the physical and the mental or psychological—as rhetorical teaching of the sophistic period did, a period in which *mētis* was the mode of education. Finally, within the tense and shifting power dynamic between Logue and Bertie, and between any teacher and any student, we recognize that rhetorical pedagogy means a focus not just on teaching rhetoric, but also on the rhetorical nature of all teaching—as the circulation of power through discourse, through bodies.

Shakes

The King's Speech, like many cultural artifacts, like any myth, engenders a chain of guessing games. As mentioned, this film at times positions the audience as doctor, psychoanalyst, voyeur. Logue, who as detailed above has been trained as an actor, continues to harbor acting ambitions, and the film channels this theme into another diagnostic game. In one short scene, Logue is shown playing a game that he calls "Shakes" with his children. In this game, he performs a famous Shakespearean role, and his children have to guess the role and the play. This then also puts the children into a position that the audience has been placed into throughout the film: spot the Shakespearean intertext. As one commentator suggests, *The King's Speech* "has even more Shakespeare allusions than it has Corgies" (Bardfilm 2011, n.p.). There are allusions to *Othello*, *Hamlet*, *The Tempest*, *Macbeth*, possibly *King Lear*, and most notably *Richard III*.[21]

In one early scene in Logue's office, when Bertie is asked to yell into a microphone as loud music plays, he reluctantly recites Hamlet's most famous soliloquy at the top of his lungs before leaving Logue's office in frustration.[22] He listens to this recording only much later and realizes that it is a passable version of the speech. Yelling over top of the music allowed him to deliver the speech fluently. At this moment, he recognizes that Logue might be able to actually help him. There is a small irony here, however. Marc Shell argues that "several astute productions of Hamlet depict the Danish prince, whom his mother calls 'scant of breath' as a stutterer" (2006, 175). At one stage in the play, Hamlet asks the players, "Speak the speech, I pray you, as I pronounced it to you, trippingly on the tongue"— Shell suggests that the word *tripping* here has an "internal dialectic that relates to walking and talking," and means both light-footed and nimble

---

21. It is hard not to play this game when the film's cast also represents the cream of the British Shakespearean acting crop. Geoffrey Rush played Philip Henslowe in *Shakespeare in Love* and played the stereotypical fool Sir Andrew Aguecheek in the 1987 film of *Twelfth Night*, his first major movie role. (This character provides comedy through his slow speech.) Colin Firth also played Lord Wessex in *Shakespeare in Love*. Virtually every member of the supporting cast has appeared in a half-dozen major Shakespearean productions on stage and small and large screen.

22. There is a parallel between this technique and the apocryphal story that Demosthenes practiced speaking in a rowboat, so that he could not hear himself over the roar of the ocean, and thus he could remove any "blocks" that might have come from self-consciousness.

as well as tripping up (2006, 171–72).[23] In an important scene in *The King's Speech*, Bertie becomes angry at Logue and starts to swear. "See how defecation flows *trippingly* from the tongue?" Logue remarks (Seidler 2008, 55; emphasis added). Bertie begins to swear more: "bloody bloody bloody shit shit shit bugger bugger bugger fuck fuck fuck!" (ibid.).[24] Inspiration for the scene, we find out from Seidler himself, came from the writer's own experience:

> The naughty F-word is not in the scene to shock, nor for prurient interest. It is there because it demonstrates an important aspect of stammer therapy that I learned from my own stutter, and which all speech the therapists I've ever spoken to agree has validity. . . . I was 16 and my defect had not eased. I'd been told if a stammer doesn't disappear by the end of adolescence the chances of it leaving decreases dramatically. . . . Well, at 16, I got angry. . . . That flipped an internal switch. I said a naughty word. The stutter melted away. Two weeks later I was auditioning for the school play. (Seidler 2010, n.p.)

The repetition of the term *trippingly* here is interesting, as is the obtuse connection between Seidler' and Bertie's swearing and the scatological legacy of Shakespeare, whose work was a laboratory for swearing, profanity, and expletives (see Montagu 2001). Whether Seidler intended to draw some allusion to Hamlet's stutter or not is unclear. But in the spirit of the guessing game, even the unintentional parallel is worth remarking upon. While Shakespeare is held up as the exemplary master of language, his prose is at the same time nimble and awkward, clear and obscurant, common and elevated. To align *The King's Speech* with Shakespeare is

23. Shell also points out an interesting reference to a *mētis*-like "crab-walk" in Hamlet and catalogs "the problems of paralysis, both physical and verbal," that are "inescapable in Hamlet" (2006, 174).

24. In an extreme example of the analytical tendency of the audience, reviewer J. Hoberman even goes so far as to argue that an "elaborate Freudian explanation might link Bertie's retentive-expulsive speech patterns to his unconscious equation of words with feces" (2010, n.p.). You could push this notion further by examining the combined meaning of each of these four swear words, but I won't.

on the surface an appeal to an anglophile fantasy of language mastery, yet underneath this appeal lies a messier possibility: that the allusion to Shakespeare is to what is stuttering, disabled, tripping, and crip within this canon.

Further, in the scene in which Logue is shown playing "Shakes" with his children, Logue delivers a speech from *The Tempest* for his sons, and he seems to be playing Caliban with a hunchback. Even the name of Logue's game invokes disability, and Logue seems to enjoy not just acting, but acting disabled. Derek Jarman's version of *The Tempest* can also be recognized as a clear intertext here, whether intentionally or not. In that version of the play, Jack Birkett, a blind man, phenomenally played Caliban as a sighted man. Birkett's performance as Caliban was a "heady concoction of menace, petulance and camp." Adding camp to this character is also a bit like adding a hunchback: it makes his Caliban "so delightful that it is hard to square with the fairly conventional interpretation of him . . . as a 'baddy'" (Ohi 2011, 201). Jarman and Birkett were playing Caliban queer and crip—and perhaps Logue was too.[25]

As the blogger Bardfilm writes of the game "Shakes," Logue "seems to want to play Caliban as slightly deformed. The specific nature of that deformity ties Caliban to *Richard III*." This link is notable because Richard III is perhaps the most famous, archetypal disability figure in all of literature, Richard's disability being seen as a pure physical incarnation of his evil personality.[26] Thus, the disability critic pays particular atten-

---

25. Jarman saw his play as "a continuously changing mirror in which we can see ourselves reflected." As Kevin Ohi argues, "This labile, protean quality is appropriate to the many revisions and transformations Shakespeare's play has undergone over the last four centuries" (Ohi 2011, 195). Perhaps it is for this reason that the appearance of Caliban in *The King's Speech*, though very brief, can have real significance. Jarman had famously said that "the whole of the modern British state is founded on the repression of homosexuality" (quoted in ibid., 201). Thus, his version of *The Tempest*, in playing Caliban queer, was utilizing a common cultural currency for subversive purposes.

26. As Robert McRuer has argued, "From a certain critically disabled perspective, [Richard III is] one of the two most despised characters in literature." When we look for disability myths in culture, Richard III is one of the first archetypes to come to mind, his physical disability "shorthand" for his evil. As McRuer writes, his monstrous body is meant

tion when, in a notable scene, Logue auditions for the role of Richard III in a small theatrical production. In this scene he is shown holding his arm as though "he's about to make it act withered." He recites the opening soliloquy of the play: "Now is the winter of our discontent . . ." But he is quickly cut off by the audition committee, who say, "You don't look like a man suffering from a deformity who is scheming to be King of England," as Richard III was. Taking a step back, we can see that this evaluation also applies to Bertie, except that the emphases shift: Logue looks neither like a man with a deformity nor like someone scheming to be king. Yet Bertie might very well look like a man with a deformity, and he also might look to some to be scheming to be king. At least it is up to the film to ask these questions. Though his brother Edward at one point in the film, accuses Bertie of wanting to usurp him as king, when Logue asks Bertie about this possibility Bertie rejects the sentiment as treasonous. We come to view Bertie as "something of an anti-Richard. He is the reluctant king" (2011, n.p.). This is an important distinction for the development of Bertie's character—to develop as a sympathetic figure, this ambition needs to be removed.

The blogger Bardfilm goes on to reinforce this contrast. In his words, *The King's Speech* may "provide homage to" perhaps the most famous contemporary version of Richard III, Richard Loncraine's, "while simultaneously reversing the image that film provides." Loncraine cowrote the screenplay for this 1995 film version of *Richard III* with the gay actor Ian McKellen in the role of the king. For Bardfilm, importantly, Bertie's personality must be clearly distinguished from the ambitious and treacherous Richard III that McKellen depicts. In an important scene, Bertie "watches a black-and-white newsreel of his own coronation, as does Ian McKellen's Richard III [in that film]. But McKellen's Richard watches it while plotting to kill the princes who still have a claim to the throne"; Bertie watches

---

to "logically explain his monstrous deeds"—his "deformity," in other words, is generally causally connected to his evil machinations" (2011, 295). McRuer suggests that *Richard III* is despised by disability critics, not just by audiences, because this representation of disability is so objectionable. This character cues repulsion from audiences for the play, yet also cues a different repulsion within disability studies.

it with his family in a cute domestic scene. "McKellen's Richard has all the trappings of Nazism; Firth's George looks on in sorrow and horror as the newsreel continues to roll, showing Hitler rallying his people" (ibid.). Of course, the distinctions are likely nowhere near so neat, both because the depiction of Bertie (or any human) without ambition feels forced, but also because in fact King George VI has in the time since his reign been accused of being a Nazi sympathizer, and we can agree that he certainly favored the appeasement of Germany for much longer than he should have. Yet it is clear that, for the narrative of *The King's Speech* to function, Bertie must be situated as the anti-Richard and as clearly anti-Fascist.[27]

In Robert McRuer's essay "Fuck the Disabled," he also examines Richard Loncraine's film, but focuses on its "queer pleasures." Loncraine's version, "while retaining Shakespeare's plot and language, is stylized to evoke a proto-Fascist Britain in the 1930s" (2011, 294). Remarkably, this is the exact same setting as *The King's Speech*, no matter how much the film tries to excise this proto-Fascist background. Yet just as Loncraine and McKellen can position an old story about a prince scheming to be king to expose the nasty and complicated politics of 1930s England, so too should this recent film about a reluctant king be used to expose the same nasty and complicated politics. Further, both *Richard III* and *The King's Speech* should be read as commentaries on the contemporary drama of disability and normalcy.[28]

---

27. This controversy about the king's Nazi sympathies was revisited around the time of the Academy Awards in 2011—an e-mail circulated to Academy members asserting that Bertie had written a letter to Lord Halifax in which he advised that steps be taken to prevent Jews from leaving Germany for Palestine, despite clear knowledge of their persecution (see Bingham 2011).

28. A 2011 production of the play at London's Old Vic theater, directed by Sam Mendes and starring Kevin Spacey, transports Richard into the present day as a Gadhafi-esque dictator. Interestingly, though Spacey wears a leg brace and walks with a crutch, and though lighting choices as well as video screens that project his image certainly play up his disabilities, he has been criticized for not emphasizing the symbolic deceit of this disability. Spacey, as Richard, wore a modern black military outfit and crown, his leg often torqued and turned so that the audience could clearly see the steel of a very modern leg brace and cane and so that his shoulder would dip to reveal a hunch. As Quentin Letts wrote in a

As McRuer writes of McKellen's depiction of Richard, the pleasure and power of the performance lie in playing disability neither as an easy-to-read evil nor as sanitized and rehabilitated.[29] McKellen's Richard distills what Halberstam calls the queer art of failure. Without this tension, with a surfeit of sarcasm and camp and embedded critique, the performance might be seen as uninteresting and flat. There is some danger here that I am just flipping old criteria by arguing that a bit more inauthenticity actually makes this performance more "real" and successful. Yet the point is that it is the rhetoricity of disability that impels meaning in these embodiments, movements welded but not subordinated to authenticity or normativity.

Of course, there are ways to read *The King's Speech* through these tensions as well. Bertie's stutter is never fully represented as a manifestation of a fault of his character, as Richard III's deformity often has been. Instead, his disability is framed in part as a product of his family life, of stifling social expectations; if not a "pure" social construction, his disability is nevertheless something that should be seen sympathetically, and thus a corrective agenda is put forward. Yet his performance also might be read as a

---

Daily Mail review of the performance, "All the appurtenances of physical disability are there. Richard has a bulbous mound for shoulders. One leg is strapped and shriveled. His lopsidedness is there for all to see but maybe not to feel." He elaborates: "Spacey, normally so good, does not quite nail the part. He goes close but is ultimately undone by a surfeit of sarcasm and campness" (2011, n.p.). The suggestion here is that Richard III, post-McKellen, might be used as a surrogate to critique politics across eras, but that his disability should not be played straight.

29. Mitchell and Snyder read McKellen's depiction of Richard III as revealing that it is "not the individual, but an ableist society, that is responsible for Richard's evil" (2011, 296). McRuer suggests that this rereading might be seen as "disability studies 101" (2011, 297). He then argues instead for the queer and crip pleasures of the film: "the will to undo compulsory able-bodiedness" and "a positive, substantive, *authentic* alternative to able-bodiedness" (ibid., 296). In his words, the performance "present[s] audiences with faces of inauthenticity" appearing to "acquiesce to the normative, rehabilitative desire for a world without perversion." The pleasure audiences experience in the performance, however, "comes from the knowledge that 'irrefutable, organic and material deviance' nonetheless remains right below the surface" (ibid., 300; quote from Snyder 2001, 272).

refusal to perform normalcy "on purpose," a reticence to wear disability as deficit and a desire *for* disability, an example of failure as an art.

The Lost Prince

In McRuer's analysis of this film version of *Richard III*, he also reminds us that the setting of the film in the proto-Fascist 1930s should remind us that this was era of eugenics: "The fantasy of the healthy baby, made eerily literal through the 'healthy baby' contests that first emerged through the *actual* proto-fascist era of eugenics, is always threatened by the crip child who comes into the world scarce half made up" (ibid., 297). He suggests that this is part of the subversive power of setting the film of *Richard III* in this era. This should also stand as a reminder that *The King's Speech* must be read against the powerful influence of the eugenic era as well.[30]

Along these lines, we can continue to "read" around *The King's Speech* from a series of critical modalities, and in the spirit of *mētis*. What other movies might this have been? In what ways can we forget the film and instead analyze its ghosts—what Halberstam might calls its "shadow" archives (2011)?[31]

Figure 12 shows Prince John with all of his siblings. As I have discussed in previous chapters, not only is disability often edited out of

---

30. It is hard to avoid reading Rush's role as Logue against his 1996 Best Actor Oscar–winning crip role in *Shine*, where he played pianist David Helfgott. In this film, like Bertie in *The King's Speech*, Helfgott's manic mode of speech makes him very difficult to understand. He also has a domineering father who is obsessed with his winning local music competitions. His father disowns him when he eventually leaves for college. He later suffers a mental breakdown and spends years in institutions. This theme of institutionalization is also present in *The King's Speech*: the monarchy is also an institution with its own regimes of normalcy and its own locked doors (as I will explore more literally through the story of the "Lost Prince").

31. Halberstam would also advocate for some investigation of this film's "silly archives"—archives that allow us to make claims that are remarkably divergent from the claims made about high-culture archives (2011, 20). One "silly archive" of *The King's Speech* would have to be the cartoon canon of Daffy Duck, and Marc Shell does an excellent job investigating these films and their rhetorical importance to our understanding of stuttering as a disability and as a critical modality in his book *Stutter* (2006).

history, but the few versions of disability that are "memorialized" are often worthy of some suspicion. There are often more angles to be found. The focus on Bertie's stammer in the film might even distract us from the presence of other forms of disability in the film and in the "real" lives of its characters. As we saw from an excerpt from the script, Bertie admits that he was knock-kneed as a child and had metal splints. His wife, Elizabeth (the eventual Queen Mother), was also called the "bandy-legged queen" or "bow-legged Bess." This is not recognized in the film. Interestingly, right before Bertie is about to deliver his big speech, Winston Churchill also takes him aside and discloses his own speech impediment:

> WINSTON CHURCHILL: Good luck, Sir. I too dread this . . . apparatus.
>   Had a speech impediment myself, you know.
> BERTIE: I didn't.
> WINSTON CHURCHILL: Family secret. Tongue-tied. An operation
>   was considered too dangerous. I eventually made an asset of it.
>   (A moment of silent recognition between the two men.) (Seidler
>   2008, 85)

Bertie might also eventually "make an asset" of his impediment.

But Churchill's "family secret" is not the only family secret in the film. Bertie also had a brother, Johnny. When Lionel asks about him in the film, Bertie says that "Johnny was a sweet boy who died of epilepsy at 13." Johnny had some disabilities—"sweet" might be a euphemistic reference to this. Sir John Wheeler-Bennett, a biographer of George VI, wrote that John was "handsome and lovable, but unfortunately quite abnormal" (1958, 112). Denis Judd, another biographer of George VI, wrote that "no one has ever disclosed the precise nature of John's abnormality" (1983, 16). Through his entire (short) life, Johnny was kept from public view—as open a secret as a royal family could possibly have, a hidden prince. The fact that there is only casual mention of Johnny in the film is perhaps a case of, in the words of Gordy Slack, "one royal disability at a time, I guess" (2011, n.p.). Of course, Prince John was kept from public sight because of the possible stigma of his disability, yet Bertie's disability soon becomes very visible to the public. It is easy to infer that Bertie might have grown up with a fear that he too would be ostracized if his disability drew attention.

12. Prince Henry, Duke of Gloucester; Prince George, Duke of Kent; Prince John; Edward, Duke of Windsor; Princess Mary, Countess of Harewood; King George VI. © National Portrait Gallery, London. Artist: W. & D. Downey.

What we are not shown in the movie is that Bertie struggled through school as a result of his stutter, graduating last in his class from college, and he avoided almost all public functions, even reputedly employing a "look-alike friend to impersonate him at press conferences and speak on his behalf" when he was a naval cadet (Bobrick 1995, 146). Further, because of the open secret of his brother John's life and death, Bertie's stuttering took on added significance to the public when he was forced into service to the nation. As Slack suggests, following the abdication of Edward VIII, when Bertie took the throne, there were doubts about his ability to lead. These doubts were reinforced by the stutter, but the stutter may have signified more than just a speech impediment to the public: the Archbishop of Canterbury gave a radio address the day after the Duke of York became King George VI. For whatever reason, he mentioned the king's "occasional and momentary hesitation in his speech." As one biographer wrote, leading up to his coronation, "a wave of idle and malicious gossip" swept London, "which embraced not only on the general health of the King . . . but also on his ability to discharge his abilities as a sovereign." There was a "whispering campaign that the King was in such frail health" that the coronation would be postponed. This led to a public response, from the king's friend Reverend Robert Hyde, who gave a speech in which he said, "Never have I found any of evidence of those shortcomings, of physical and mental weaknesses, which notorious gossip has attached to him" (Wheeler-Bennett 1958, 309). The reverend then goes on to suggest that Bertie's stammer has been overcome. Yet Slack argues that the subtext here was not in fact just the stammer. People wondered, "Was the King an epileptic, like his youngest brother John (the deceased, 'lost prince')? Was he fit for duty?" (2011, n.p.). The king himself was quoted in *Time* as saying that "according to the papers, I am supposed to be unable to speak without stammering, to have fits, and to die in two years. All in all, I seem to be a crock!" (quoted in Judd 1983, 163). The elision of this part of the story from the film actually removes a crucial dimension from the social and rhetorical construction of Bertie's disability. The film relies concomitantly on the narratives of Bertie's developing self-identity and on the formation of his public identity. Both of these vectors were influenced significantly by the ghostly presence of Prince John. Erasing him from this story also removes much of the significance of disability both within the film and within this capsule history. This said, the quick mention of John in the film did create a fissure in the plot for me, and perhaps this gap was also noticeable for a broader audience.

Of course, the backdrop of the era of eugenics in *The King's Speech* should also remind us of the dangerous attitudes that led to John's banishment and may have shaped reception of the king—whose body was syncretic with the body politic. Not only does the editing out of the Fascist sympathies of the royal family rob the film of some of its political context, but the "forgetting" of the multiple dimensions of disability also robs the film of much of its embodied meaning, from a disability studies perspective. Bertie's leg braces, his early physical therapy, his wife's perceived disability, and of course the removal of his younger brother from the family all situate the story of the "real" King George VI as a revealing snapshot of the eugenics era and its influence on the shape of families and the individual bodies within them.

In figure 12, showing the royal children, Prince John is shown wearing a sailor's suit, in the front left of the photo. Albert (Bertie), Mary, and Edward stand behind him on a set of concrete stairs. Henry and George stand in the front row beside him. George also wears a sailor's suit. The children all look serious and stare directly at the camera—except for John, whose head is turned slightly to the side. The three older children in the back row rest their hands on the shoulders of their siblings.

Prince John was the subject of a 2003 BBC film, entitled *The Lost Prince* (Poliakoff 2003). Just as a visual focus of *The King's Speech* is Bertie's stuttering mouth, a focus of *The Lost Prince* is John in seizure, and both repeated visual foci are (perhaps intentionally) difficult to watch and command a visceral response. Gordy Slack's review of the film argues that it:

> Captures the remarkable resilience of children with epilepsy and the perspective they bring to those around them. As the royal family struts and wrings their hands over picayune protocol and the "horrors" of perceived and real slights, Prince John opts out and instead draws funny and incisive portraits of the family's follies. He is the only one brave enough to speak up when the emperor has no clothes. Having a child with epilepsy—and, in the case of John, learning disabilities as well—can bring a quick and corrective perspective shift in families. But that was a shift the royal family wasn't prepared to make. At least not until the death of the delightful young prince. (2011, n.p.)

Of course, this is a familiar "reading" of disability, that it exists to remind the able-bodied that their lives are not that bad or that it helps to develop empathy and thus make the nondisabled better people. But what is perhaps more remarkable here is the fact that even this specious "lesson" cannot be learned if the prince was never accepted as part of the family. And if we are willing to accept that the prince's inclusion in the family would "correct" some of the family's problems, then in what ways does his expulsion amplify what is broken?

The title of this film is curious for similar reasons: the prince was not really "lost"; he was hidden. Of course, this entails a real loss as well, for his family and for the public. But both are also to some degree implicit in this hiding. John was "lost" for many years before he died. As Judd wrote, "His segregation and 'abnormality' must have been disturbing to his brothers and sister" (1983, 17). One (perhaps ableist) way of looking at a quote like this is to say that John's disability could have upset the family as an embarrassment. Another way to look at it is that his brothers and sister would have been upset and disturbed that he had been taken away from them, just as would anyone who "lost" a sibling.

These seemingly semantic issues have real bearing on the very idea of disability in history. For instance, Hephaestus may have been "lost" to history, but he was also lost by historians, and maybe in some ways obscurantly rewritten, or hidden. The mythical figure of Metis has been lost, to a certain degree, but she was also eaten. And the entire early era of eugenics—especially its many preceding, very popular and virulent manifestations outside of Nazi Germany—has been lost from common memory, just as the legacy of Fascism was lost from *The King's Speech*. Every loss is also perhaps an intentional elision or excision, with attendant multiplying possibilities of human motivation and human cost.

Ben Summerskill writes:

> [John] was excluded from official family photographs [except for the photo I have included]. He was not allowed to be present at his father's coronation in 1911. Early in 1917, John was removed from any risk of public discovery forever. He was consigned—with a nanny and two robust male attendants to hold him down whenever he had fits—to Wood Farm, on a corner of the Sandringham estate. He was never to see his parents again. Two years later John died in his sleep. The King and Queen drove the three miles from the main house at Sandringham to view his body. (2000, n.p.)

Commenting on the controversial wall of silence surrounding one of the Queen Mother's sisters, Princess Alice, and her dementia, Ben Summerskill notes that "the royal family's refusal to acknowledge any human frailty is not new" and then recounts the story of John. But Summerskill goes on to write that "little appears to have changed since. In 1987 it emerged that Katherine and Nerissa Bowes-Lyon had been incarcerated in the Royal Earlswood Mental Hospital in Surrey for 46 years. The two women, nieces of the Queen Mother, had never been visited by a member of the royal family. When Nerissa Bowes-Lyon died in 1986, she was buried in Redhill cemetery. Her grave was marked with a plastic tag bearing a serial number and her name" (ibid.).

This practice was historically consonant with broader social trends of the institutionalization of people with disabilities, evidence of the persistence of eugenic ideology, and led to many other such family "secrets" throughout the twentieth century. This point drives home the reality that disability has been much more than theoretically "lost" or "hidden" historically. People with disabilities have been removed from their families and from society, allowing or forcing many to pretend that they do not exist at all.

As Slack writes, after the funeral of his "lost" brother, John, Prince Albert (Bertie), still a teenager, tells John's devastated nanny that his brother "was the only one of us who was really allowed to be himself" (quoted in Slack 2011, n.p.). This is a terribly ironic statement, seeing as John was actually removed from the family. Further, when John has a seizure in the film, his nanny removes him to a private room and tells him that "nobody will see this and tonight we will say our prayers twice and maybe there won't be another one for a very long time." She then tells John's mother that he has had a cold. The "self" that John was allowed to be did not include his epilepsy. But the young Prince Albert seems to be commenting on how difficult his own childhood was and in a way seeking to identify with John's experience.

In the film *The Lost Prince*, we are led to interpret John's behavior as at once perfectly "normal" for a young boy and at the same time as totally unacceptable for a prince. He wants to move his legs and sing along to a musical performance, he is curious about the live goldfish on a fancy birthday cake, he tells the truth when adults ask him questions, perhaps to a fault. This last characteristic leads his grandfather, King Edward VII, to call him "honest Johnny." But in the film, it is the life of a young prince that seems disabling. The filmmakers are clearly making an effort to suggest that it is the royal lifestyle that is irrational and unhealthy, and not young John's behavior. All of the clocks in the royal home are set a half hour ahead of time, "and nobody knows what time it is." The queen (his grand-mother) is obsessed with miniature glass animals; his father is obsessed with stamps. All of the adults smoke incessantly. King Edward VII drinks liberally from a flask. The world John grows up in is both stiflingly boring and overstimulating—he is expected to be on display at lavish parties, to sit still one moment and to perform the next. The desires and interests of a young boy are contrasted with those of the adults: though they act like children, he is punished for doing the same.

When King Edward VII (John's grandfather) is drunk, he is shown to be as honest as John: "That boy is always right," he says, after Johnny sug-gests to the drunken monarch that he cannot shoot as well as he used to because he is old. A relationship seems to be developing between the two. But in the next scene, the king dies. Prince George, the second youngest of the five children (not to be confused with Bertie, who is barely heard from in the movie),[32] upon hearing the news, asks his younger brother, John, "Do you know what this means Johnny?" "You are the son of the King now," John replies. "We both are, we both are Johnny," George says (Poliakoff 2003, n.p.).

Right before the funeral, John sneaks off by himself and has a violent seizure. His nanny later tells his mother about the episode. She is herself dealing with the loss of the king, but also the stress of becoming queen. This seizure sets off a string of medical interventions. What follows are a series of scenes depicting mental and physical tests that the prince fails. This failure seems easy to understand to the viewer, as the tests seem non-sensical—nevertheless, they confound Johnny. "It is clear his brain has not continued to grow as it should," a doctor tells the new queen. "Showing it must have suffered some damage at some stage . . . the brain is very

32. When Bertie is heard, in one very short scene, he does not have a stutter. Just as Johnny was a spectral presence in *The King's Speech*, so too is Bertie barely there in *The Lost Prince*. It is worth saying again, in the words of Gordy Slack, who reviewed *The Lost Prince*: "one royal disability at a time, I guess" (2011, n.p).

unlikely to develop any further." "I assure you gentlemen that Johnny is not an imbecile," the queen replies. "The brain is damaged, ma'am, whatever label we use," the doctor replies. "We are recommending complete isolation" (ibid.). The doctor then alludes to the trauma that anyone witnessing a fit would experience, and thus suggests that this isolation would be best for the child *and* for the family (and perhaps the public).

Curiously, Edward and Bertie are not really shown at all in the film, and it is as though they do not exist—although George and John are shown together frequently, and George is shown to be as capable, knowledgeable, fluent, and worldly and John is not. George is shown reciting French, practicing famous British speeches for small audiences of dignitaries: in one scene, he recites the famous St. Crispen's Day speech from Shakespeare's *Henry V*, with emphasis on the famous lines "We few, we happy few, we band of *brothers*," played for somber effect as his real brother John listens secretly from a hiding spot. George then sneaks into Johnny's room and tells him. "Don't worry, I will always be here. . . . I will never let them send you away" (ibid.). Of course, the "cottage" that John now lives in adjacent to the family home, with its windows boarded, with the strict decree of no visitors, is clearly a sort of prison. And it is not long before John is sent away from the family for good.

At this cottage and later in seclusion, Johnny does work on impressive gardens, albeit while tethered to a rope, a rope that is not shown in the movie. John shows an interest in his family history and is shown memorizing the royal family tree that he was later, in some versions, erased from (Wilson 2008, n.p.). But his schooling is shown to be a failure in the film, and his teacher is shown to be quick to anger and upset with his assignment of Johnny as his lone pupil. The focus of the film is on John's segregation and the threat of his being discovered. He is lonely and seems (understandably) to jump at any possibility of human contact beyond his teacher and his nanny.[33] In one scene, John is shown crashing a garden

33. Simon McShannon suggests that "although it is often commented that John was a lonely child, this has often been discredited. John's companionship came in the form of Winifred Owen, a Yorkshire girl, who had been sent to live in the country with her aunt and

party, a party including the prime minister, and he proceeds to make an embarrassing speech—embarrassing because, once again, he speaks the truth about his family. His father, King George V, nervously apologizes that "each of my children have their strange ways" (Poliakoff 2003, n.p.). But his significant discomfort and anger are clear, and the message is that, despite the somewhat sympathetic treatment by his family, there is "good reason" for John to be locked away.

Inciting the king's anger clearly has dangerous consequences within the family. As Christopher Wilson writes, "As a result of [the king's] parental brutality, Edward developed an eating disorder and starved himself." We already know about George's leg braces and how he was forced to write right-handed. Further, "of his two other sons, Henry and George, one became a famous drunk and the other a promiscuous chaser of both men and women. All had allowed themselves to be subjugated to the King's ferocious will—only John got away with it" (2008, n.p.). The causal relationships here are only inferred, and can be accepted or dismissed, but by all accounts King George V did have a violent temper and imposed very strict standards upon his children. This treatment is in many ways at the center of both *The King's Speech* and *The Lost Prince* and becomes one of the hinges upon which the audience's amateur Freudian analysis hangs. It also becomes, at the same time, one of the hinges upon which disability swings: we are led to believe that Bertie's stutter may in some way have been caused by his father's treatment, and John's banishment is in part "blamed" on King George V, while other characters are shown to be more sympathetic. In both cases, the construction of disability as somewhat pitiable relies upon the creation of the father as villain, and the agency of the characters with disabilities is constructed (or deconstructed) in relation to the powerful will of King George V as father figure.

In the climax of *The Lost Prince*, Johnny travels to London and excels in a mental examination in front of his doctors, naming prominent members

---

uncle, due to suffering from asthma" (2001, n.p.). The film does not depict this relationship. This omission then reinforces the idea of disability as an isolated experience and as socially isolating, which then justifies exclusion and isolation.

of his family and where they are from. This time, unlike in the previous failed tests, even when he challenges the script of the testing, he is shown to do so cleverly. At one point he is seemingly distracted by the decorations in the room, yet he recovers by identifying a stuffed "spiny anteater" on a mantle. The doctors are flustered when he picks it up to examine it; he has successfully subverted the exercise. But at this point, history takes over as deus ex machina, as the country is shown stumbling toward World War I. John then suffers another major seizure. Despite John's educational progress, which we are led to believe will convince his family of his human worth, the queen is shown to be seriously worried by the most recent seizure. His father, King George V, for his part, is consumed with his new role as a bumbling monarch doing all that he can to avoid war with Germany. Despite the fact that most commentators believe that John was quite summarily sent away, the film constructs the family as sympathetic, and the blame rests upon his epilepsy, perhaps obscuring both the social norm of segregation and the family's responsibility for his banishment. We are supposed to feel that it is neither John's fault nor his family's fault, nor is it even a reflection of common practice that he must be sent away; it is the epilepsy. Specifically, we are led to believe that the epilepsy makes John a danger to *himself,* and thus a victim of his own body, despite some veiled allusion to the fact that the seizures were also seen as potentially publicly embarrassing and distracting to the royal family.

In the final scene of the film, John is driven away in a car, ostensibly back to his cottage, as the rest of the family remains in London preparing for war. He receives a fond good-bye from his brother George, who once again promises that he will never let "them" send Johnny away. And the movie simply ends. We are left with George's tragic assurance that Johnny will never be sent away—but, of course, he is, at the age of twelve. He dies two years later. We do not see his death or funeral, and the audience is not given any real clue by the film that he will die. But, of course, he does. Perhaps the assumption is that the audience truly knows both of these things—that he will be immediately sent away and that he will soon die. This may be because the British public has always known those parts of the story—and his banishment and death have always both been open and obvious secrets. Or this elision of the nastier parts of John's story

13. Prince John. © National Portrait Gallery, London. Artist: Vere (or Vera) Temple.

may be evidence of the ghostly presence of narrative prosthesis: we have been given such stories of disability so many times that we can fill in the blanks. Disability myths have such a strong and intuitive narrative power that they need not even be fleshed out—we know how they work, and thus we know how the story will end.

Figure 13 depicts John, alone in his garden, a small bouquet of purple flowers in his left hand, a cane in his right. He wears a white coat and an elaborate white hat.

The Queen wrote in her diary, shortly after John's death:

Lalla Bill [John's nanny] telephoned from Wood Farm, Wolferton, that our poor darling Johnnie had died suddenly after one of his attacks. The news gave me a great shock, though for the little boy's restless soul, death came as a great release. I brought the news to George & we motored down to Wood Farm. Found poor Lalla very resigned but heartbroken. Little Johnnie looked very peaceful lying there. . . . For him it is a great release as his malady was becoming worse as he grew older and he has thus been spared much suffering. I cannot say how grateful we feel to God for having taken him in such a peaceful way, he just slept quietly . . . no pain, no struggle, just peace for the poor little troubled spirit, which had been a great anxiety for us for many years ever since he was four. (Pope-Hennessy 2000, 511)

At the same time, his eldest brother, Edward, said brutally that "the animal" had died and bemoaned the fact that the family had to mourn him (Alderson 2003, n.p.). These contrasting reactions nicely distill the contradictions of the film *The Lost Prince* and the contradictions at the heart of *The King's Speech*: even when we are led toward perhaps more positive views of disability, there is always something more sinister on the underside; for everything we are shown, something else is hidden. These are key modalities of the forensic genre of disability rhetoric, employing a sideways, skeptical, *mētis* approach to the truth and falsity of past events.

The Lost King

Of course, the focus on what is hidden in *The King's Speech*, according to most commentators, is the Fascist sympathies of the royal family, most notably Edward's. Yet Edward's entire story is a compelling and a queer one for many reasons, not least of which are those Nazi sympathies that the movie glosses over. According to *The King's Speech*, and according to many popular accounts, Edward abdicates the throne because of a forbidden love. His relationship with Wallis Simpson, an American divorcee, was scandalous at the time and unacceptable to the church and to the royal family. Forced to choose between Wallis and the throne, we are led to believe that he chose love. Madonna's 2011 movie *W. E.* tells the story according to this romantic script. But the entire picture might be much more cloudy. Simpson has been painted by many as a sort of dominatrix. Many commentators have suggested that Simpson's hold over the king was purely sexual. As one biography suggests, "Having been brought up in a repressed and inhibited household, displaying a whole range of nervous tics and mannerisms, it was unlikely that the Prince of Wales would have turned out to be a confident and accomplished lover. . . . None of his mistresses, apparently, had ever satisfied him as fully as Mrs. Simpson. Society gossips speculated that she was able to use techniques which led him to experience physical love to the full for the first time" (Judd 1983, 126). Yet official biographer Philip Zeigler disagrees that sex was the only reason for the attraction: "That Wallis Simpson provoked in him profound sexual excitement is self-evident. That such excitement may have had some kind of sado-masochistic trimmings is possible, even likely." But "Wallis Simpson's sexual allure may have gained the Prince's attention, quickened his interest, engaged his passionate commitment, but it could not have retained him for a lifetime" (Zeigler 1992, 237).

Guy Pearce, who plays Edward in the film, has had his own take on Edward's sexual leanings, as has Colin Firth, who has alluded publicly to the idea that Edward may have been gay. In an interview, Gregory Ellwood asked Pearce if he thought the rumors that Edward were gay were true.

> Look, I wouldn't be surprised by any of it. At some level he's a very simple character. . . . I think the relationship both boys had with their parents lead to all sorts of difficulties. . . . [B]eing such a sensitive kid, he really resented the fact that the only relationship he had with his father was through the guise of royalty. There was no real love expressed there and I think [he] really missed that. I think what [he] found with women in his life. . . . I think he was looking for someone to break the rules with him. I'm not sure about any sort of sexual orientation, but there are certainly things alluded to in various books that the sort of the physical relationship with him and Wallis Simpson was rather sordid and rather extreme from a sexual level. I think he was looking for things outside of the box. (2011, n.p.)

To many viewers of *The King's Speech*, Pearce seems to be playing his role "foppishly," his uncertainty and impulsiveness as code for both his unsuitability for the throne and his sexual orientation. Pearce seems to believe that whatever Edward's sexual proclivities were, they too may have been caused by his relationship with his father—as we have been led to believe Bertie's stutter and John's banishment might be blamed on King George V. Again, this urges the viewer to play at psychoanalysis, sets up the apparatus for pity, and also constructs homosexuality and disability as things for which someone must be blamed, instead of as inevitable and common aspects of our culture and dimensions of subjectivity.

I will admit that there is an urge here to firmly attach perceived subtexts to the movie. This might fall along the lines of disability studies work "as usual" or the "same old, same old," even if the analysis folds in more nuanced intersectional analysis of sexuality and disability. But here we recognize that this is more than just a disability studies proclivity: all cultural analysis of disability desires diagnosis. Often, the diagnoses are offensive: stutterers are effeminate or gay; homosexuality is the result of childhood trauma. Other times, the diagnoses are more empathetic or generous. But the desire to tie disability to a root cause and then to a static symbolic consequence remains. *Mētis* disability studies, rhetorical disability studies, might offer something much less sure and reassuring.[34]

For instance, we might suggest that Edward's abdication is "queer," as is Bertie's reluctance to become king. Halberstam argues that "de-linking the process of generation from the force of historical process is a queer kind of project: queer lives seek to uncouple change from the supposedly organic and immutable forms of family and inheritance; queer lives exploit some potential for a *difference in form* that lies dormant in queer collectivity not as an essential attribute of sexual otherness but as a possibility embedded in the break from heterosexual life narratives" (2011, 70; emphasis in the original). We cannot really say the royal family is not the exemplar of generational progression. But perhaps especially because of this rigidity and the ways it is held up as a heteronormative standard, Edward's and Bertie's unsuitability and resistance—as well as the royal

---

34. We might label this disability epideictic: searching for the refusal of negative disability myths, praising and accentuating disability, restoring the virtue of the denigrated, and restoring the flaws of the venerated.

"forgetting" of undesirable members—shows that the process of generational progression can itself be "disabling." Halberstam calls instead for "relations that grow along parallel lines rather than upward and onward. This queer form of antidevelopment requires healthy doses of forgetting and disavowal and proceeds by way of a series of substitutions" (ibid., 73). In these ways Wallis and Edward, John and George, George and his "promiscuous chasing of both men and women," Bertie and Elizabeth, and Bertie and Logue all present parallel relations or broken branches that might be recognized as challenges to the heteronormative family tree (and even its eugenic roots).

Building on the symbolic potential of this break, we might recognize the sexual tension within the friendship between Lionel and Bertie as the driving force of the film's meaning. (It may not be, as we have been led to believe, all about overcoming threats to the unified family and nation.) We have already discussed the homosocial nature of this relationship. Add to this the ways that Edward is played by Pearce in the film, and there is a subversive sexual energy. As McRuer argues, "Disability identity is also forged in the film through a particular kind of queerness," manifestations that are "not *necessarily* deployed solely in the service of an apotheosis of compulsory heterosexuality and able-bodiedness." This "non-homophobic homosociality is played up not only onscreen, but off, in public appearances with Firth, Rush, and [the film's director Tom] Hooper, who now-famously spoke in his acceptance speech at the Oscars about the 'triangle of man love' responsible for the film's success" (2013, 6). The question remains whether this nonhomophobic homosociality might ever interface with a nonableist or crip sensibility and whether either stance can ever be more than a temporary and token acceptance.

One interesting and perhaps unintentionally parodic assumption of this energy comes from the inevitable porn articulation of the film, *The King's Piece*. The film's trailer, which itself is AA-rated and readily available online, remaps the narrative of the film across the common story of erectile dysfunction. Logue is recast as a female dominatrix whose teachings coax Bertie toward (overtly heterosexual) sexual performance. As an over-the-top parody, the film still gets the dynamic between teacher and student, doctor and patient, right in many ways, even as it gets the relationship essentially wrong. Logue and Bertie's relationship and the trajectory of their therapy are both all too easy to transpose onto pornography like *The King's Piece*. Bertie is coached by this dominatrix to lose his stutter and "get it up" at the same time, as though the two things are connected. And these things may very well be implicitly wed by Bertie's biographers anyhow. Supposedly, Bertie's first proposal to his future wife, Elizabeth, was delivered through a messenger, and when she demanded that he propose in person, he handed her a note (Bobrick 1995, 147). His difficulty communicating is mythologized as also impacting his romantic life. *The King's Speech* certainly does not cast Elizabeth and Bertie's relationship sexually—he is shown as a great father and family man and a good husband, but she comes across as much more of a mother to him than a wife or lover. We first really meet Elizabeth as she is setting up an appointment for Bertie with Logue, just as other mothers do for Logue's mainly adolescent patients. That in real life Elizabeth is now known mainly as the "Queen Mum" perhaps also overwrites her role. And again, we cannot discount the simplified Freudian archetype here, wherein Bertie is shown to fear his father, identify with the figure of the mother, and thus align with the Freudian development of the male homosexual, creating a "peculiar" triangle with Elizabeth and Logue (see Kosofsky-Sedgwick 1985, 23).

In the film, we also come to see that Bertie's sexual identity might very well be linked to his stutter, and this would be consonant with other popular depictions of disability as emasculating or desexualizing. Recall that as far back as Demosthenes, a speech impediment was linked with effeminacy. But Bertie's desexualization seems to pertain only to his relationship with his wife. It would be impossible to say that because in the film there is no sexual spark between Bertie and Elizabeth, then this film is without sexual tension—that tension is between Bertie and Logue, and instead of being positioned as somehow deviant, it instead secretly drives the plot.

It is perhaps unsurprising that the porn version of *The King's Speech* gets remapped onto heterosexuality. In fact, the porn film gets mapped onto *excessive* heterosexuality, as it seems that the "climax" of *The King's Piece* is a scene involving the king and approximately a half-dozen women.

But, as Judith Butler would argue, for the viewer of the original film, this heterosexual iteration can really only be a parodic performance. As Butler states so nicely, "Heterosexuality offers normative sexual positions that are intrinsically impossible to embody, and the persistent failure to identify fully and without incoherence with these positions reveals heterosexuality itself not only as a compulsory law, but as an inevitable comedy . . . a compulsory system and an intrinsic comedy, a constant parody of itself" (1990, 155). The hyperbole of this king's heterosexual performance serves only to underline the clear homosocial dynamic of the original film.

Further, while *The King's Speech* borrows from films like *Rocky*, it also borrows from the genre of the romantic drama. Lionel and Bertie meet, their first few encounters are awkward, and then they develop a bond. Both men have flaws, yet come to understand that even these flaws are shared. For instance, we know that in his real life, Logue worked hard to hide his own Australian accent (Edgar 2000, 116). Yet at one point in the movie, Bertie loses his temper with Logue and mocks this accent— reminding Logue of the class and "ethnic" gulf between them. Logue also fails in an audition for a role in a Shakespearean play because his Australian accent is apparent. In these moments, the movie seems to want to clearly show that Logue has his own "speech impediment." We are also encouraged to recognize that the relationship between the two men makes them both vulnerable, and makes them both better, as they lower their defenses. The atmosphere of Logue's office also insulates the two men from the outside world—from their wives and families and responsibilities—so they are able to develop their relationship under their own terms. Following its Oscar win, it came out that the setting for Logue's office in the movie had previously been the set of a gay porn movie.[35] Reports strangely scandalized this coincidence, yet this feigned shock in fact prob-

35. Ben Child wrote in the *Guardian* that the room's "distinctive decaying wallpaper and Palladian windows made it an atmospheric double for speech therapist Lionel Logue's 1930s treatment rooms in bromantic Oscar front-runner *The King's Speech*. Yet that was not the first time the property at 33 Portland Place, London, has caught the eye of film-makers. Reports confirm that in 2008 it was also used as a location for a gay porn film, *Snookered*." Child called the phone number listed for the address, and an employee "said they were

ably reinforces how natural that overlap might be. When *The King's Piece* was later filmed at this same location, this became a selling point for the porn film, completing the loop. Of course, regardless of this coincidence, it can (and should) be argued that Logue's office is both a clinical setting and a romantic setting in the film, allowing the two main characters to develop a relationship that might be "peculiar" rather than purely professional, but is also romantic in a manner that is fairly plain and generic.

In *The King's Speech*, just as he did with Bridget Jones or Elizabeth Bennet after a promising romantic beginning, Colin Firth's character gets into a fight with his coprotagonist, Logue, and storms off to brood with the accompaniment of dark orchestral music and a driving rain. When Bertie discovers that Logue is not actually a licensed doctor, he reacts angrily and cuts off his treatment. Logue defends his nonmedical approach by saying he only advertises "speech defects" on his shingle, and all he wants to do is give patients "faith in their own voice." It is fortuitous that part of his technique is to address patients personally (Bertie) and to have patients address him by his name, because they cannot call him a doctor—because he is not a doctor. Yet this confusion and Bertie's angry reaction are not only an interruption—perhaps formulaically romantic—in the development of Bertie and Lionel's relationship, but also an interruption in the audience's expectations for the doctor-patient relationship.

Of course, like any good romantic drama, we know that *The King's Speech* will end with Logue and Bertie together, and it does. In the climax of the film, the day war was declared, September 3, 1939, the king has to deliver a speech. Logue is in a small closet-like room with Bertie (just the two of them and a huge microphone) and tells the king to "forget everyone else and just say the speech to me, as a friend" (Farndale 2011, 4). Melissa Wiginton argues that because of moments like this, the film is "a story of men dealing with difficulty through mutual vulnerability" (2011, n.p.). McRuer responds to this analysis by adding that the relationship is "structured in part through a playful embrace not only of vulnerability, but also

---

unable to confirm whether a porn shoot took place there, but added: 'Everything goes on at Portland Place—it's a fairly wild house'" (2011, n.p.).

of the libidinal energy passing between the men" (2013, 6). The other connected angle here is rhetorical: the relationship shapes the speech act, challenging the centrality and autonomy of the individual speaker, figuring instead the speech as an intercorporeal process.[36]

When Bertie throws in a stutter, "so they'd know it was me," he is also perhaps failing so that he can win—so that he can retain an identity outside of his role as monarch—and so that he can win a continued relationship with Logue, who would become expendable to a cured king. In McRuer's words, "this 'positive representation' of disability might be read through and not against homoerotics and new masculinities" (2013, 6). Whether the broad audience for the film engages in such a reading is up for debate. Yet the rhetorical power of the film can be recognized not in the possibly tidy conclusions we might draw from it, but instead from the ghosts and parodies and allusions that orbit it, the ways that the film and Bertie continue to fail to replicate a normative appearance.

Conclusions

Whether *The King's Speech* places its viewer in the role of psychoanalyst or doctor, encourages us to be a historical editor, involves us in a Shakespearean guessing game, successfully or unsuccessfully elides the other movies that might have been made or the cultural backgrounds that may have been switched out, or invokes disability and sexuality subtexts in subversive, token, or normative ways, regardless of all of these possibilities, *The King's Speech* is an excellent example of the complexity and messiness of disability rhetoric.

First of all, the film clearly locates disability at the very level of the word, the utterance. Not only does disability manifest itself through myths and rhetorics, narratives and tropes, but it is always there at the very center of the act of meaning-making. *The King's Speech* also reveals the tension between "models" of disability—disability as a felt, material process, and disability as also in part a cultural or rhetorical construction.

---

36. Here I cannot help but think of Mikhail Bakhtin's suggestion, in defining heteroglossia, that "the word in language is half someone else's" (1992, 294).

Through these constructions, we also recognize that norms of ability can never be detached from other embodied norms—gender, sex, and sexuality, for instance.

As part of a long, selectively Western and Westernized rhetorical tradition, the stories of King George also characterize the normative force of rhetoric, with its submersion and discipline of the body, with its specific elision of specific bodies. Yet this story also harnesses power through the subversion of this tradition. In positioning King George, Prince Albert, Hephaestus, Metis, Hermaphrodite, or any other mythical figure at the center of a rhetorical tradition, we should open up the possibility for further *mētis*, instead of just adding new heroes to the canon.

This film also crystallizes many of the useful conflicts of disability studies—revealing the rhetorical nature of the very act of defining the work of the field. Just as the concern with whether the film gets the story of King George VI "right" betrays a penchant for critical historicism, only at times incorporating the more reflexive tendencies of *new* historicisms, so too is interpretation of this film hooked on biographical criticism. This biographical bias is why we love to link the film to Seidler and why we might flinch when a nonstuttering actor wins an award for the film. But just as new historicists urged readers to recognize that "every act of unmasking, critique and opposition uses the tools it condemns and risks falling prey to the practice it exposes," we should also unveil the ways that disability studies relies on certain interpretive tendencies (Veeser 1989, xi). When Haller (2011) suggests that the stutterer worries about this disability being read as an internal flaw, we can understand that this is an interpretive fallacy that all of disability studies argues against. As "author" of the stutter, the individual should nonetheless be viewed separately from the disability, or at least the stigma of the disability should not be read right across the author's entire subjectivity. Yet at the same time, disability studies scholars tend to read cultural artifacts as though they directly betray the intentions of an ableist author (this looks like biographical criticism or psychoanalysis) or the ableist culture from which it comes (this looks like historicism), with a penchant for trying to correct (this looks, perhaps ungenerously, like new historicism).

Early in this book, when discussing my list of disability myths, my litany of the ways that our culture gets disability "wrong," I also defended this mode of "negative critique" as itself containing generative and positive potential. The myths lay out a range of ways that disability is "not this, not this, and not this"—and my critique of *The King's Speech* engages at times in the same dynamic. I admitted that this series of critical interpretive moves might feel a bit rote to many disability studies scholars and students, or a bit trenchant to those individuals who are new to the field. But I also argued that laying out these disability *wrongs* generates a range of possible awarenesses, critical tools, and disruptions.[37] The fact that disability is so naturally and habitually associated with negativity in our society means that we cannot neglect to question these natural habits, and we cannot forget that the pause, reflection, and reconsideration we might engender will themselves be critical *and* creative opportunities. Further, as I hope my analysis of *The King's Speech* shows, and as I hope my disability rhetoric throughout the book evidences, suggesting that disability is "not this, not this, and not this" means also resisting the impulse to isolate disability tropes. When we say disability is "not this" negative quality, we also need to remember that disability is "not only this" critical move: for instance, *The King's Speech* is *not just* about the one foregrounded disability (stuttering); it is underpinned by other networks of relations structured upon disability and also gender and class and sexuality. And when I suggest that the stories of Hephaestus or Metis are "not this" limited repertoire, I am also open to the idea that others will find many more meanings than I have.

37. I borrow from Elizabeth Povinelli's *Economies of Abandonment* for this description. Povinelli defends "negative critique" against the claims that such critique "lacks a direction around which a practical politics could be built . . . is parasitical on a given normative world [and] reflects the precritical political positions of the author" (2011, 189). In response, she suggests that "not this" "makes a difference even if it does not produce a propositional otherwise" because it "makes the world unready-at-hand for those for whom it has worked smoothly" (ibid., 191, 192). This point should serve as an excellent model for the critical work of disability studies, even when a focus is on "policing" ableism and normativity by arguing that disability is "not this" or that stigma, "not this" or that degraded position.

Another reason to resist moving entirely beyond the "negative critique" model of disability studies is that the alternative can seem to be a form of poststructuralism or postmodernism that also views disability too metaphorically—as when Deleuze or Wills labels all communication a stutter and a stumble. The disability studies theorist recognizes such analogies and is compelled to circle back to Disability Studies 101, but for good reason, because if all language is disabled, how can we recognize oppression? And then what if acceptance of disability in fact camouflages oppression? I have certainly used all of these "moves" in this book.

But I also hope that we could introduce a critical modality that, without discarding any of these interpretive vectors, instead recognizes cultures and individuals, as well as any interpretive act itself, as essentially disabled, prosthetic. Perhaps this is just a way to avoid the hard questions. Yet my hunch is that disability studies should be leading rhetoricians and cultural critics away from singular answers and instead layering myths and meanings.

The King's Speech, as well as the myths of King George VI, could be examples of narratives that fail to replicate a normative appearance. Finally, the king's speech and the pedagogical relationship between Logue and Bertie should also be recognized for their potential as exemplars of disability rhetoric: delivering difficulty and deferring normativity. The film might open up the rhetorical possibility of being subversively disabled and the general impossibility of being in rhetorical control. The film also places the nonnormative body at the center of all rhetorical and dramatic energy, exactly where it should be. Instead of being an incomplete expression of language (or of subjectivity, or of humanity), instead of being an unsuitable vehicle for rhetoric, disability should be understood instead as the very possibility of meaning.

Prosthesis

When we thought we were at the point of concluding, the frontiers of the domain we were claiming to explore receded before us.
> —Marcel Detienne and Jean-Pierre Vernant,
> *Cunning Intelligence in Greek Culture and Society*

This message will self-destruct.
> —Inspector Gadget

I BEGAN THIS BOOK with three moments, three spaces: Periclean Athens, following the Ten Years' War; in the aftermath of World War II; and here, today. I suggested that now, as in these historical spaces, bodies continue to change, as do attitudes about them, and the rhetorical entailments of these bodily transformations continue to be negotiated. I argued, deliberatively, that a "futuristic" disability studies will not be about eradication of disability, but about new social structures and relations, made possible by new rhetorics. Somewhat ironically, these disability futures, I hope I have shown, can be made possible through disability historiography.

Hopefully, this book has changed your view on all three of these spaces and the bodies within them. But most vitally, *mētis* needs to have transformed where you can go from here and how you will get there.

I have argued that tension around the body exists, first, because efforts to define rhetoric have so often denied and denigrated the body; second, because this denial has always been laughably impossible; third, because modern body values and anxieties have always been mapped back across history; and finally because studying any culture's attitudes and arguments about the body always connects us intimately with attitudes and arguments about rhetorical possibility. That is, to care about the body is to care about how we make meaning.

In my second chapter, I worked through an inventory of arguments about rhetoric and the body, I returned to these arguments throughout the book, and I will revisit these again, as a means of mapping where we might go next, and how.

One: The body is invested rhetorically. The body has always been a rhetorical product or experiment, even as bodies have always been insistently material.

Two: Rhetoric is always embodied. The body has traditionally been rhetorical equipment and a rhetorical instrument, but it has also always been a rhetorical engine. The body is rhetorical—it communicates and thinks.

Three: Disability shapes our available means of persuasion. Embodied difference can actually be read as the very possibility of meaning.

These three positions then shape how we learn through the body, but also *who* can learn. As I conclude this book, I want to return to these points and relate them specifically to learning, as a gesture toward future applications of *mētis*. My argument, in parsing through the classical debate, was that we have always worried about bodies, and this worry always centers around and never resolves the desire to exclude difference and thus to create categories of disability. Unfortunately, debates about education have also always utilized logics of exnomination—an obsession about who cannot learn, a cataloging of deficiencies. Underneath these explorations is always the notion that differences in aptitude are "natural." I believe that, finally, the great potential of *mētis* rhetoric is to challenge these beliefs about how we learn and about who can learn.

A *mētis* epistemology holds that we all, intercorporeally, shape realities. This is the inverse of an educational scheme in which bodies are containers for information, with some bodies better adapted to hold these contents than others. *Mētis* is a model for adaptation, change, critique, uniqueness, prosthesis, recursivity, invention, intercorporeality, ambiguity, and abstraction. What if these were our central educational values (instead of accumulation, retention, comprehension, compliance reproduction)?

Mētis should also offer a constant reminder of the exclusions (and consumptions) of the past and present, a machine for interrogating the interests and investments of the normative. Taking this rhetoric seriously in the modern classroom, we would create space for embodied knowing, advocate a heightened respect for all bodies, and perhaps even seek to endorse and enhance bodily difference—creating educational exchanges against the grain of the normative. How exactly this can be achieved is a matter for debate. But the possibilities and potentialities are exciting to consider. There is much work to be done. The future of disability rhetoric (and perhaps also *all of* disability studies *and* rhetoric) lies not just in developing tools for reinterpretations of culture, but in developing new cultures and new social relations. This process of creation will work through and toward positive conceptions of disability. I promise to pick up this thread in my own future work, moving more directly into the contemporary classroom.

As mentioned repeatedly in this work, the contradiction or doubleness at the heart of *mētis*, fittingly, disallows a clear understanding of *mētis*. In this way, for many readers, the book may seem to be a failure, finally—an attempt to fit an evasive concept into a historical and theoretical world that most believe can and should be ordered and schematized. But as Letiche and Statler suggest, the only way to "learn" *mētis* is "through a willingness to be open to unexpected ideas and a sensitivity for unforeseen possibilities . . . a positive attitude towards serendipity. . . . [M]ētis thus assumes a partial abandonment of control" (2005, 5). So, finally, the true test of a book about *mētis* is not how often it is read, but how useful it becomes, and the final judgment of the author of such a book should not be how clearly and authoritatively she has explored the concept, but how open and apprehensive she has been about her agency and control.

This book tells several important stories about the rhetorical body—not all stories, not the *most* important stories, certainly not well-known stories, and definitely not stories that can be easily confined to these pages. In fact, these bodies and ideas hopefully have the momentum, power, and multiplicity to exceed the restraint of being written. In locating spaces and moments in which tension around the body is most pronounced, my desire has been to amplify and recirculate this tension. My deliberations, hopefully, point us toward a desire for disability.

My hope is that the method of writing this book—layering myths and proposing interpretations, troubling accepted stories, and proposing new ones—allows and invites further and unforeseen uses and beginnings. This book, like the "even flame" of Hephaestus's metallurgy, might offer some illumination and heat. But it is up to you to forge and to adapt your own tools.

Bibliography

Index

Bibliography

Adler, Shawn. 2008. *"Tropic Thunder* Director/Star Ben Stiller Says Disability Advocates' Planned Boycott Is Unwarranted." *MTV News*, Aug. 11. http://www.mtv.com/news/articles/1592544/ben-stiller-planned-tropic-thunder-boycott-unwarranted.jhtml.

The Adventures of Baron Munchausen. 2009. 20th anniversary ed. Directed by Terry Gilliam. Sony Pictures Home Entertainment.

Aeschylus. 1970. *Prometheus Bound.* Edited by Herbert Weir Smyth. Cambridge, MA: Harvard Univ. Press.

Agamben, Giorgio. 1998. *Homo Sacer: Sovereign Power and Bare Life.* Stanford, CA: Stanford Univ. Press.

Ahmed, Sara. 2010. *The Promise of Happiness.* Durham, NC: Duke Univ. Press.

Alaimo, Stacy. 2010. *Bodily Natures: Science, Environment, and the Material Self.* Bloomington: Indiana Univ. Press.

Alcoff, Linda Martin. 2001. "Toward a Phenomenology of Racial Embodiment." In *Race*, edited by Robert Bernasconi, 267–83. Malden, MA: Blackwell.

Alderson, Andrew. 2003. "Tender Letters from the *Lost Prince.*" *Telegraph*, Jan. 12. http://www.telegraph.co.uk/news/uknews/1418632/Tender-letters-from-the-Lost-Prince.html.

Almassi, Ben. 2010. "Disability, Functional Diversity, and Trans/Feminism." *International Journal of Feminist Approaches to Bioethics* 3 (2): 126–49.

Antebi, Susan. 2009. *Carnal Inscriptions: Spanish American Narratives of Corporeal Difference and Disability.* London: Palgrave-Macmillan.

Anzaldua, Gloria. 1999. *La Frontera/Borderlands.* New York: Consortium Books.

Apollodorus. 1921. *Apollodorus, the Library.* Translated by Sir James George Frazer. Cambridge, MA: Harvard Univ. Press.

Apostolides, Marianne. 2009. "Jordan Scott Interview." *Bookninja Magazine.* http://www.bookninja.com/?page_id=4938.

Aristotle. 1944. *Generation of Animals*. Translated by A. L. Peck. Cambridge, MA: Harvard Univ. Press.

———. 1985. *Nicomachean Ethics*. Translated by Terence Irwin. Indianapolis: Hackett.

———. 1991a. *Politics*. Translated by George Kennedy. Oxford: Oxford Univ. Press.

———. 1991b. *Rhetoric*. Translated by George Kennedy. Oxford: Oxford Univ. Press.

Arrizon, Alicia. 2006. *Queering Mestizaje: Transculturation and Performance*. Ann Arbor: Univ. of Michigan Press.

Asch, Adrienne. 2004. "Critical Race Theory, Feminism, and Disability." In *Gendering Disability*, edited by Bonnie G. Smith and Beth Huchinson, 9–44. New Brunswick, NJ Rutgers Univ. Press.

As Good as It Gets. 2003. Directed by James L. Brooks. Sony Pictures Home Entertainment.

Assmann, Jan. 2003. *The Mind of Egypt*. Translated by Andrew Jenkins. Cambridge, MA: Harvard Univ. Press.

Atwill, Janet. 1993. "Contingencies of Historical Representation." In *Writing Histories of Rhetoric*, edited by Victor Vitanza, 98–111. Carbondale: Univ. of Illinois Press.

———. 1998. *Rhetoric Reclaimed: Aristotle and the Liberal Arts Tradition*. Ithaca, NY: Cornell Univ. Press.

Auden, W. H. 1976. "The Shield of Achilles." In *Collected Poems of W. H. Auden*. London: Verso.

Austin, Gilbert. 1806. *Chironomia*. London: T. Cadell and W. Davies.

Avatar (Original Theatrical Edition). 2009. Directed by James Cameron. 20th Century Fox.

The Aviator. 2005. Directed by Martin Scorsese. Warner Home Video.

Azzarello, Brian, and Cliff Chiang. 2012. *Wonder Woman #7*. New York: DC Comics.

Babel. 2006. Directed by Alejandro González Iñárritu. Paramount Pictures.

Bailey, Alison. 2007. "Strategic Ignorance." In *Race and Epistemologies of Ignorance*, edited by Shannon Sullivan and Nancy Tuana, 77–94. Albany: State Univ. of New York Press.

Bakhtin, Mikhail. 1992. *The Dialogic Imagination: Four Essays*. Austin: Univ. of Texas Press.

Ballif, Michelle. 1992. "Re/Dressing Histories; or, On Recovering Figures Who Have Been Laid Bare by Our Gaze." *Rhetoric Society Quarterly* 22 (1): 91–99.

————. 1997. "Seducing Composition: A Challenge to Identity-Disclosing Pedagogies." *Rhetoric Review* 16 (1): 76–91.

————. 1999. What Is It That the Audience Wants? or, Notes Toward a Listening with a Transgendered Ear for (Mis)Understanding." *JAC: A Journal of Composition Theory* 19 (1): 51–70.

————. 2001. *Seduction, Sophistry, and the Woman with the Rhetorical Figure.* Carbondale: Southern Illinois Univ. Press.

Barber, Jonathan. 1831. *A Practical Treatise on Gesture, Chiefly Abstracted from Austin's Chironomia: Adapted to the Use of Students, and Arranged According to the Method of Instruction in Harvard University.* Cambridge, MA: Hilliard and Brown.

Bardfilm. 2011. "Shakespeare in *The King's Speech.*" Jan. 4. http://bardfilm.blogspot.com/2011/01/shakespeare-in-kings-speech.html.

Barnes, Julian. 2011. *The Sense of an Ending.* New York: Alfred A. Knopf.

Barnes, Sandra T., ed. 1989. *Africa's Ogun: Old World and New.* Bloomington: Indiana Univ. Press.

Barnouw, Jeffrey. 2004. *Odysseus, Hero of Practical Intelligence: Deliberation and Signs in Homer's "Odyssey."* Lanham, MD: Univ. Press of America.

Barthes, Roland. 1972. *Mythologies.* New York: Hill and Wang.

Barton, Len. 2006. *Overcoming Disabling Barriers: 18 Years of Disability and Society.* London: Routledge.

Basel, Roberta. 2007. *Sequoyah: Inventor of Written Cherokee.* Minneapolis: Compass Point Books.

Batman Chronicles. 2013. Vols. 1–12. New York: DC Comics.

Baumard, Phillipe. 1999. *Tacit Knowledge in Organizations.* London: Sage.

Bay, Jennifer. 2004. "Screening in Formation: Bodies and Writing in Network Culture." *JAC: A Journal of Composition Theory* 24 (4): 929–46.

Baynton, Douglas C. 1997. "Bringing Disability to the Center: Disability as an Indispensable Category of Historical Analysis." *Disability Studies Quarterly* 1: n.p.

————. 2001. "Disability and the Justification of Inequality in American History." In *The New Disability History: American Perspectives,* edited by Paul K. Longmore and Lauri Umansky, 33–57. New York: New York Univ. Press.

A Beautiful Mind. 2006. Directed by Ron Howard. Universal Studios.

Bechdel, Alison. 2008. *The Essential Dykes to Watch Out For.* Boston: Houghton Mifflin Harcourt.

Benjamin, Adam. 2002. *Making an Entrance*. Routledge: London.

Ben-Moshe, Liat. 2006. "Infusing Disability in the Curriculum: The Case of Sara-mago's *Blindness*." *Disability Studies Quarterly* 26 (2): n.p.

Berlin, James. 1994. "Revisionary Histories of Rhetoric: Politics, Power, and Plural-ity." In *Writing Histories of Rhetoric*, edited by Victor J. Vitanza, 112–27. Car-bondale: Southern Illinois Univ. Press.

Berlin, James, et al. 1988. "Octolog: The Politics of Historiography." *Rhetoric Review* 7: 5–49.

Bernal, Martin. 1987. *Black Athena: The Afroasiatic Roots of Classical Civilization*. Vols. 1–2. New Brunswick, NJ: Rutgers Univ. Press.

Best, Steve. 2009. "The Rise of Critical Animal Studies: Putting Theory into Action and Animal Liberation into Higher Education." *State of Nature*: 9–54.

Bierlein, J. F. 1994. *Parallel Myths*. New York: Ballantine.

Bingham, John. 2011. "'Nazi' Smears on George VI Threaten Colin Firth's Oscar Hopes." *Telegraph*, Jan. 16. http://www.telegraph.co.uk/culture/film/oscars/8262814/Nazi-smears-on-George-VI-threatens-Colin-Firths-Oscar-hopes.html.

Bitzer, Lloyd F. 1968. "The Rhetorical Situation." *Philosophy and Rhetoric* 1: 1–24.

Blakely, Sandra. 2006. *Myth, Ritual, and Metallurgy in Ancient Greece and Recent Africa*. London: Cambridge Univ. Press.

Boal, Augusto. 2000. *Theatre of the Oppressed*. London: Pluto.

Bobrick, Benson. 1995. *Knotted Tongues*. New York: Simon & Schuster.

Bogdan, Robert, and Steven Taylor. 1988. "Toward a Sociology of Acceptance: The Other Side of Human Deviance." *Social Policy* 13: 32–35.

The Book of Eli. 2010. Directed by Albert Hughes. Warner Home Video.

Bordo, Susan. 1993. *Unbearable Weight: Feminism, Western Culture, and the Body*. Berkeley: Univ. of California Press.

Bourdieu, Pierre. 1990. *The Logic of Practice*. Stanford, CA: Stanford Univ. Press.

Bragg, Lois. 2004. *Oedipus Borealis: The Aberrant Body in Old Icelandic Myth and Saga*. Madison, NJ: Fairleigh Dickinson Univ. Press.

Braidotti, Rosi. 1994. *Nomadic Subjects: Embodiment and Sexual Difference in Contem-porary Feminist Theory*. New York: Columbia Univ. Press.

————. 2002. *Metamorphoses: Towards a Materialist Theory of Becoming*. Cambridge: Blackwell.

Breaking Bad: The Complete Fifth Season. 2011. Directed by Bryan Cranston. Sony.

Brisson, Luc. 2002. *Sexual Ambivalence: Androgyny and Hermaphroditism in Graeco-Roman Antiquity*. Berkeley: Univ. of California Press.

Broderick, Alicia A. 2011. "Autism as Rhetoric: Exploring Watershed Rhetorical Moments in Applied Behavior Analysis Discourse." *Disability Studies Quarterly* 31 (3): n.p.

Brommer, Frank. 1986. *Heracles: The Twelve Labours of the Hero in Ancient Art and Literature.* Translated by S. J. Schwarz. New Rochelle, NY: A. D. Caratzas.

Brueggemann, Brenda Jo. 1995. "The Coming Out of Deaf Culture and American Sign Language: An Exploration into Visual Rhetoric and Literacy." *Rhetoric Review* 13: 409–20.

———. 1999. *Lend Me Your Ear: Rhetorical Constructions of Deafness.* Washington, DC: Gallaudet Univ. Press.

———. 2005. "Delivering Disability, Willing Speech." In *Bodies in Commotion*, edited by Carrie Sandahl and Philip Auslander, 17–29. Ann Arbor: Univ. of Michigan Press.

Brueggeman, Brenda Jo, and James Fredal. 1999. "Studying Disability Rhetorically." In *Disability Discourse*, edited by Mairian Corker and Sally French, 129–35. Philadelphia: Open Univ. Press.

Buell, Lawrence. 2001. *Writing for an Endangered World: Literature, Culture, and Environment in the U.S. and Beyond.* Cambridge, MA: Belknap.

Bulwer, John. 1644. *Chirologia and Chironomia.* London: Tho. Harper.

Burford, Alison. 1972. *Craftsmen in Greek and Roman Society.* Ithaca, NY: Cornell Univ. Press.

Burke, Kenneth. 1969a. *Language as Symbolic Action: Essays on Life, Literature, and Method.* Berkeley: Univ. of California Press

———. 1969b. *Rhetoric of Motives.* Berkeley: Univ. of California Press.

Burkert, Walter. 1970. "Jason, Hypsipyle, and New Fire at Lemnos: A Study in Myth and Ritual." *Classical Quarterly* 20 (1): 1–16.

———. 1985. *Greek Religion.* Cambridge, MA: Harvard Univ. Press.

Butler, Judith. 1990. *Gender Trouble: Feminism and the Subversion of Identity.* New York: Routledge.

———. 1993. *Bodies That Matter: On the Discursive Limits of "Sex."* New York: Routledge.

———. 2000. *Contingency, Hegemony, Universality: Contemporary Dialogues on the Left.* London: Verso.

———. 2004. *Undoing Gender.* London: Routledge.

———. 2006. "Undiagnosing Gender." In *Transgender Rights*, edited by Paisley Currah, Richard M. Juang, and Shannon Price Minter, 274–98. Minneapolis: Univ. of Minnesota Press.

The Cabinet of Dr. Caligari. 2004. Directed by Robert Wiene. Kino Video.

Cachia, Amanda, curator. 2011. *Medusa's Mirror: Fears, Spells, and Other Transfixed Positions.* Pro Arts Gallery, San Francisco, Nov. http://proartsgallery.org /exhibitions/2011_medusa.php.

Cameron, Colin. 2009. "Tragic but Brave or Just Crips with Chips? Songs and Their Lyrics in the Disability Arts Movement in Britain." *Popular Music* 28 (3): 381–96.

Canguilhem, Georges. 1991. *The Normal and the Pathological.* New York: Zone Books.

Carpenter, Rick. 2011. "Disability as Socio-rhetorical Action: Towards a Genre-Based Approach." *Disability Studies Quarterly* 31 (3): n.p.

Castillo, Debra A. 2006. "Anzaldúa and Transnational American Studies." *PMLA* 121 (1): 260–65.

Certeau, Michel. 1984. *The Practice of Everyday Life.* Berkeley: Univ. of California Press.

Chen, Mel Y. 2012. *Animacies: Biopolitics, Racial Mattering, and Queer Affect.* Durham, NC: Duke Univ. Press.

Child, Ben. 2011. "His Majesty's Pleasure . . . *The King's Speech* Sets Used for Gay Porn." *Guardian,* Feb. 24. http://www.guardian.co.uk/film/2011/feb/24/kings -speech-gay-porn-tom-hooper.

Children of a Lesser God. 1986. Directed by Randa Haines. Paramount.

Chotiner, Isaac. 2011. "Royal Mess." *New Republic,* Jan. 6. http://www.tnr.com /article/film/80948/the-kings-speech-film-royal-mess.

Cicero, Marcus Tullius. 1955. *De Natura Deorum.* Translated by Arthur Stanley Pease. Cambridge, MA: Harvard Univ. Press.

———. 2003. *De Oratore.* Bks. 1–3. Translated by *Augustus S. Wilkins.* Bristol, UK: Bristol Classical Publishing.

Cixous, Helene. 1976. "The Laugh of Medusa." Translated by Keith Cohen and Paula Cohen. *Signs* 1 (4): 875–93.

Cixous, Helene, and Catherine Clement. 1986. *The Newly Born Woman.* Translated by Betsy Wing. Minneapolis: Univ. of Minnesota Press.

Clark, E. Culpepper, and Raymie McKerrow. 1998. "The Rhetorical Construction of History." In *Doing Rhetorical History: Concepts and Cases,* edited by K. Turner, 33–46. Tuscaloosa: Univ. of Alabama Press.

Clash of the Titans. 1981. Directed by Desmond Davis. Warner Video.

Cohen, Leonard. 1992. "Anthem." On *The Future.* New York: Columbia Records.

Cooper, Craig. 2000. "Rhetorical Reputation in Antiquity." In *Demosthenes: States-man and Orator,* edited by Ian Worthington. New York: Routledge.

Corker, Marian, and Tom Shakespeare, eds. 2002. *Disability/Postmodernity: Embodying Disability Theory.* New York: Continuum Press.

Couser, G. Thomas. 2011. "Conflicting Paradigms: The Rhetorics of Disability Memoir." In *Embodied Rhetorics: Disability in Language and Culture*, edited by James C. Wilson and Cynthia Lewiecki-Wilson, 78–91. Carbondale: Southern Illinois Univ. Press.

Couture, Barbara. 1998. *Toward a Phenomenological Rhetoric.* Carbondale: Southern Illinois Univ. Press.

Covino, William A. 1995. *Magic, Rhetoric, and Literacy: An Eccentric History of the Composing Imagination.* Albany: State Univ. of New York Press.

Croissant, Jennifer L. 2006. "Mama Wahunzi." *Disability Studies Quarterly* 26 (1): n.p.

Crowley, Sharon. 1994. "Let Me Get This Straight." In *Writing Histories of Rhetoric*, edited by Victor J. Vitanza, 1–19. Carbondale: Southern Illinois Univ. Press.

———. 1999. "Afterword: The Material of Rhetoric." In *Rhetorical Bodies*, edited by Jack Selzer and Sharon Crowley. Madison: Univ. of Wisconsin Press.

Crutchfield, Susan, and Marcy Joy Epstein. 2000. *Points of Contact: Disability, Art, and Culture.* Ann Arbor: Univ. of Michigan Press.

Daniels, Roger, and Otis Graham. 2001. *Debating American Immigration, 1882–Present.* Lanham, MD: Rowman and Littlefield.

Dark Victory. 1939. Restored ad remastered ed. Directed by Edmund Goulding. Warner Home Video.

Davidson, James. 2001. "Dover, Foucault, and Greek Homosexuality: Penetration and the Truth of Sex." *Past and Present* 170: 3–51.

———. 2009. *The Greeks and Greek Love.* New York: Random House.

Davidson, Michael. 2012. "Pregnant Men: Modernism, Disability, and Biofuturity in Djuna Barnes." *Novel: A Forum on Fiction* 43 (2): 207–26.

Davis, D. Diane. 2011. "Addressing Animals." *Philosophy and Rhetoric* 44 (1): 88–94.

Davis, Lennard J. 1995. *Enforcing Normalcy: Disability, Deafness, and the Body.* New York: Verso.

———. 2002. *Bending over Backwards: Essays on Disability and the Body.* New York: New York Univ. Press.

Deal, Mark. 2003. "Disabled People's Attitudes towards Other Impairment Groups: A Hierarchy of Impairments." *Disability and Society* 18 (7): 897–910.

Deegan, Mary Jo. 2010. "'Feeling Normal' and 'Feeling Disabled.'" In *Disability as a Fluid State*, edited by Sharon N. Barnartt. Bingley, UK: Emerald Group.

Delcourt, Marie. 1957. *Héphaistos; ou, La legende du magicien*. Paris: Belles Lettres Press.

———. 1961. *Hermaphrodite: Myths and Rites of the Bisexual Figure in Classical Antiquity*. Translated by Jennifer Nicholson. Paris: Belles Lettres Press.

Deleuze, Gilles. 1997. "He Stuttered." In *Essays Critical and Clinical*, translated by Daniel W. Smith and Michael A. Greco. Minneapolis: Univ. of Minnesota Press.

Demand, Nancy H. 1994. *Birth, Death, and Motherhood in Classical Greece*. Baltimore: Johns Hopkins Univ. Press.

Derrida, Jacques. 1973. *Speech and Phenomena, and Other Essays on Husserl's Theory of Signs*. Evanston, IL: Northwestern Univ. Press.

———. 1976. *Of Grammatology*. 1st American ed. Baltimore: Johns Hopkins Univ. Press.

———. 1981. *Dissemination*. Translated by Barbara Johnson. Chicago: Univ. of Chicago Press.

———. 1984. "Deconstruction and the Other." In *Dialogues with Contemporary Continental Thinkers*, edited by Richard Kearney. Manchester: Manchester Univ. Press.

———. 1987. *The Post Card: From Socrates to Freud and Beyond*. Chicago: Univ. of Chicago Press.

———. 1998. "Plato's Pharmacy." In *Literary Theory, an Anthology*, edited by Julie Rivkin and Michael Ryan. Malden, MA: Blackwell.

———. 2000. "Where a Teaching Body Begins." In *Revolutionary Pedagogies: Cultural Politics, Instituting Education, and the Discourse of Theory*, edited by Peter Pericles Trifonas. New York: Routledge.

———. 2005. *Paper Machine*. Stanford, CA: Stanford Univ. Press.

Detienne, Marcel, and Jean-Pierre Vernant. 1978. *Cunning Intelligence in Greek Culture and Society*. Translated by Janet Lloyd. Chicago: Univ. of Chicago Press.

Dewey, John. 1934. *Art as Experience*. New York: Capricorn Books.

———. 1938. *Experience and Education*. New York: Collier Books.

Diagnostic and Statistical Manual of Mental Disorders: DSM-IV-Tr. 2000. 4th ed. Washington, Dc: American Psychiatric Association.

Dick, Philip K. 1968. *Do Androids Dream of Electric Sheep?* New York: Ballantine Books.

———. 1982. *The Transmigration of Timothy Archer*. New York: Timescape Books.

———. 1995. *Martian Time-Slip*. New York: Vintage Books.

———. 2002. *Clans of the Alphane Moon*. New York: Vintage.

Dickens, Charles. 1983. *A Christmas Carol: In Prose, Being a Ghost Story of Christmas*. New York: Holiday House.

Diels, Hermann, and Rosamond Kent Sprague. 1972. *The Older Sophists*. 1st ed. Columbia: Univ. of South Carolina Press.

Disability Bitch. 2011. "Disability Bitch Isn't Angry at Colin Firth." *BBC Ouch! Blog*, Jan. 13. http://www.bbc.co.uk/ouch/opinion/b1tch/db_isnt_angry_at _colin_firth.shtml.

The Diving Bell and the Butterfly. 2007. Directed by Julian Schnabel. Miramax.

Dix, Hywel Rowland. 2010. *Postmodern Fiction and the Break-Up of Britain*. London: Continuum Press.

Doherty, Lillian Eileen. 1995. *Siren Songs: Gender, Audience, and Narrators in the Odyssey*. Ann Arbor: Univ. of Michigan Press.

Dolmage, Jay, and Bill DeGenaro. 2005. "'I Cannot Be Like This Frankie': Disability, Social Class, and Gender in *Million Dollar Baby*." *Disability Studies Quarterly* 25 (2): n.p.

Donnellan, Anne. 1984. "The Criterion of the Least Dangerous Assumption." *Behavioral Disorders* 9 (2): 141–50.

Doueihi, Anne. 1993. "Inhabiting the Space between Discourse and Story in Trickster Narratives." In *Mythical Trickster Figures: Contours, Contexts, and Criticisms*, edited by William Hynes and William Doty, 193–201. Tuscaloosa: Univ. of Alabama Press.

Dowden, Ken. 1995. "Approaching Women through Myth: Vital Tool or Self-Delusion?" In *Women in Antiquity: New Assessments*, edited by B. Levick and R. Hawley, 44–57. London: Routledge.

Driskill, Qwo-Li. 2010. "Double-Weaving Two-Spirit Critiques: Building Alliances between Native and Queer Studies." *GLQ: A Journal of Lesbian and Gay Studies* 16 (1–2): 69–92.

duBois, Page. 2010. *Out of Athens: The New Ancient Greeks*. Cambridge, MA: Harvard Univ. Press.

Duffy, John. 2007. *Writing from These Roots*. Honolulu: Univ. of Hawaii Press.

Dumezil, Georges. 1986. *Loki*. Paris: Flammarion.

Dunning, Stefanie. 2004. "Brown Like Me." In *Mixing It Up*, edited by SanSan Kwan and Kenneth Spiers. Austin: Univ. of Texas Press.

Durbach, Nadja. 2010. *Spectacle of Deformity*. Berkeley: Univ. of California Press.

Eagle, Christopher. 2011. "Organic Hesitancies: Stuttering and Sexuality in Melville, Kesey, and Mishima." *Comparative Literature Studies* 48 (2): 200–218.

———. 2012. "'Angry Because She Stutters': Stuttering, Violence, and the Politics of Voice in American Pastoral and Sorry." *Philip Roth Studies* 8 (1): 17–30.

Ebenstein, William. 2006. "Toward an Archetypal Psychology of Disability Based on the Hephaestus Myth." *Disability Studies Quarterly* 26 (4): n.p.

Edbauer, Jennifer. 2005. "Meta/Physical Graffiti: 'Getting Up' as Affective Writing Model." *JAC: A Journal of Composition Theory* 25 (1): 131–60.

Edgar, Suzanne. 2000. "Logue, Lionel George." In vol. 15 of *Australian Dictionary of Biography*. http://adb.anu.edu.au/biography/logue-lionel-george-10852.

Eickhoff, Randy Lee. 2001. *"The Odyssey": A Modern Translation of Homer's Classic Tale*. New York: Doherty.

Eiesland, Nancy L. 1994. *The Disabled God: Toward a Liberatory Theology of Disability*. Nashville: Abingdon Press.

Elioma, Joshua, and Michael Schillmeier, eds. 2010. *Edinburgh German Yearbook: Disability in German Literature, Film, and Theater*. Vol. 4.

Ellwood, Gregory. 2011. "The Forgotten King: A Conversation with Guy Pearce." *Hitfix*, Jan. 13. http://www.hitfix.com/blogs/awards-campaign/posts/the-forgotten-king-guy-pearce.

Enos, Richard. 1993. *Greek Rhetoric before Aristotle*. Prospect Heights, IL: Waveland.

Erevelles, Nirmala. 2011. *Disability and Difference in Global Contexts: Enabling a Transformative Body Politic*. New York: Palgrave Macmillan.

Evans-Pritchard, E. E. 1964. "Four Zande Tales." *Anthropological Quarterly* 37 (4): 157–74.

Fahnestock, Jeanne. 1999. *Rhetorical Figures in Science*. New York: Oxford Univ. Press.

Faigley, Lester. 1992. *Fragments of Rationality: Postmodernity and the Subject of Composition*. Pittsburgh: Univ. of Pittsburgh Press.

Faraone, Christopher, and Emily Teeter. 2004. "Egyptian Maat and Hesiodic Mētis." *Mnemosyne* 57: 177–208.

Farndale, Nigel. 2011. *"The King's Speech:* The Real Story." *Telegraph*, Jan. 5. http://www.telegraph.co.uk/culture/film/8223897/The-Kings-Speech-the-real-story.html.

Fausto-Sterling, Anne. 1993. "The Five Sexes: Why Male and Female Are Not Enough." *Sciences* (Mar.–Apr.): 20–24.

———. 2000. *Sexing the Body: Gender Politics and the Construction of Sexuality*. 1st ed. New York: Basic Books.

Fiedler, Leslie. 1996. Foreword to *Freakery: Cultural Spectacles of the Extraordinary Body*, edited by Rosemarie Garland-Thomson, i–xv. New York: New York Univ. Press.

Fight Club. 2002. Directed by David Fincher. 20th Century Fox.

Fineberg, Stephen. 2009. "Hephaestus on Foot in the Cerameicus." *Transactions of the American Philological Association* 139 (2): 273–322.

A Fish Called Wanda. 1988. Directed by John Cleese. MGM.

Fiske, John. 1987. *Television Culture.* London: Routledge.

Fontanier, Pierre. 1977. *Les figures du discours (1821–27).* Edited by G. Genette. Paris: Flammarion.

Forrest Gump. 1994. Directed by Robert Zemeckis. Paramount.

Foss, Karen A., Sonja K. Foss, and Cindy L. Griffin, eds. 1999. *Feminist Rhetorical Theories.* Thousand Oaks, CA: Sage.

Foucault, Michel. 1965. *Madness and Civilization: A History of Insanity in the Age of Reason.* Translated by Alan M. Sheridan-Smith. New York: Pantheon Books.

———. 1973a. *Birth of the Clinic: An Archaeology of Medical Perception.* Translated by Alan M. Sheridan-Smith. New York: Pantheon Books.

———. 1973b. *History of Sexuality.* Vol. 1. Translated by Alan M. Sheridan-Smith. New York: Pantheon Books.

———. 1979. *Discipline and Punishment: The Birth of the Prison.* Translated by Alan M. Sheridan-Smith. New York: Vintage Books.

———. 1980. "Body/Power." In *Power/Knowledge: Selected Interviews and Other Writings, 1972–1977*, edited by C. Gordon. New York: Pantheon Books.

Fox, Michael V. 1983. "Ancient Egyptian Rhetoric." *Rhetorica* 1: 9–22.

Freaks. 2004. Directed by Tod Browning. Warner Home Video.

Freccero, Carla. 2006. *Queer/Early/Modern.* Durham, NC: Duke Univ. Press.

Fredal, James. 2002. "Herm Choppers, the Adonia, and Rhetorical Action in Ancient Greece." *College English* 64 (5): 590–612.

———. 2006. *Rhetorical Action in Ancient Athens: Persuasive Artistry from Solon to Demosthenes.* Carbondale: Southern Illinois Univ. Press.

Fulgentius. 1971. *The Mythologies.* Translated by Leslie George Whitbread. Columbus: Ohio State Univ. Press.

Gale, Xin Liu. 2000. "Historical Studies and Postmodernism: Rereading Aspasia of Miletus." *College English* 62 (3): 361–86.

Garber, Marjorie, and Nancy J. Vickers. 2003. Introduction to *The Medusa Reader*, 1–9. New York: Routledge.

Garland, Robert. 1985. *The Eye of the Beholder: Deformity and Disability in the Graeco-Roman World*. Ithaca, NY: Cornell Univ. Press.

Garland-Thomson, Rosemarie. 1996a. *Extraordinary Bodies: Figuring Physical Disability in American Culture and Literature*. New York: Columbia Univ. Press.

————, ed. 1996b. *Freakery: Cultural Spectacles of the Extraordinary Body*. New York: New York Univ. Press.

————. 1996c. "From Wonder to Error: A Genealogy of Freak Discourse in Modernity." Introduction to *Freakery: Cultural Spectacles of the Extraordinary Body*, edited by Rosemarie Garland-Thomson. New York: New York Univ. Press.

————. 1997a. "Integrating Disability: Transforming Feminist Theory." *NWSA Journal* 14 (3): 1–33.

————. 1997b. "Integrating Disability Studies into the Existing Curriculum: The Example of Women and Literature at Howard University." *Radical Teacher* 47: 15–39.

————. 1999. "The New Disability Studies." *ADFL Bulletin* 31 (1): 49–53.

————. 2002. "Politics of Staring." In *Disability Studies: Enabling the Humanities*, edited by Sharon L. Snyder, Brenda Jo Brueggemann, and Rosemarie Garland-Thomson. New York: Modern Language Association of America.

Gartner, Alan. 1987. *Images of the Disabled, Disabling Images*. New York: Praeger.

Gelb, Steven A. 1989. "'Not Simply Bad and Incorrigible': Science, Morality, and Intellectual Deficiency." *History of Education Quarterly* 29 (3): 359–79.

Gencarella, Stephen. 2007. "Korax and the Art of Pollution." *Rhetoric Society Quarterly* 37 (3): 251–73.

Gibson, Craig A. 2002. *Interpreting a Classic: Demosthenes and His Ancient Commentators*. Berkeley: Univ. of California Press.

Girard, René. 1986. *The Scapegoat*. Translated by Y. Freccero. Baltimore: Johns Hopkins Univ. Press.

Girl, Interrupted. 2003. Directed by James Mangold. Sony Pictures Home Entertainment.

Girl Shy: The Harold Lloyd Comedy Collection. 1924. Vol. 1. Directed by Harold Lloyd. New Line Home Video.

Glee: The Complete First Season. 2009. Directed by Ryan Murphy. 20th Century Fox.

Glenn, Cheryl. 1985. "Remapping Rhetorical Territory." *Rhetoric Review* 13: 287–303.

————. 1997. *Rhetoric Retold: Regendering the Tradition from Antiquity through the Renaissance*. Carbondale: Southern Illinois Univ. Press.

Glissant, Edouard. 1997. *Poetics of Relation*. Translated by Betsy Wing. Ann Arbor: Univ. of Michigan Press.

Goddard, Henry H. 1917. "Mental Tests and the Immigrant." *Journal of Delinquency* 2: 243–77.

Golding, William. 1962. *Lord of the Flies*. New York: Coward-McCann.

Gorgias. 1982. *Encomium of Helen*. Bristol, UK: Bristol Classical Press.

Gran Torino. 2009. Directed by Clint Eastwood. Warner Home Video.

Graves, Robert. 1955. *The Greek Myths*. Vols. 1–2. London: Penguin.

———. 1966. *White Goddess: A Historical Grammar of Poetic Myth*. New York: Farrar, Straus, and Giroux.

Gross, John. 2010. *The Oxford Book of Parodies*. Oxford: Oxford Univ. Press.

Grosz, Elizabeth. 1994. *Volatile Bodies: Toward a Corporeal Feminism*. Bloomington: Indiana Univ. Press.

———. 1996. "Intolerable Ambiguity." In *Freakery: Cultural Spectacles of the Extraordinary Body*, edited by Rosemarie Garland-Thomson, 55–68. New York: New York Univ. Press.

———. 2005. "Naked." In *The Prosthetic Impulse: From a Posthuman Present to a Biocultural Future*, edited by Marquard Smith and Joanne Morra, 187–202. Cambridge: MIT Press.

Gruzinski, Serge. 2002. *The Mestizo Mind: The Intellectual Dynamics of Colonization and Globalization*. New York: Routledge.

Gustafson, Diana L. 1999. "Embodied Learning: The Body as an Epistemological Site." In *Meeting the Challenge: Innovative Feminist Pedagogies in Action*, edited by Maralee Mayberry and Ellen Cronan Rose, 249–74. New York: Routledge.

Gwyn, Richard. 1999. "Captain of My Own Ship: Metaphor and the Discourse of Chronic Illness." In *Researching and Applying Metaphor*, edited by Lynne Cameron and Graham Low, 219. Cambridge: Cambridge Univ. Press.

"Habitus." 1989. In *The Oxford English Dictionary*. 2nd ed. Oxford: Oxford Univ. Press.

Hahn, Harlan. 1988. "Can Disability Be Beautiful?" *Social Policy* (Fall): 26–31.

Haj, Fareed. 1970. *Disability in Antiquity*. New York: Philosophical Library.

Halberstam, Judith. 2011. *The Queer Art of Failure*. Durham, NC: Duke Univ. Press.

Hall, Alice. 2012. *Disability and Modern Fiction*. New York: Palgrave Macmillan.

Haller, Nathan. 2011. "The Stutterer: How He Makes His Voice Heard." *Slate*, Feb. 22. http://www.slate.com/articles/news_and_politics/assessment/2011/02/the_stutterer.single.html.

Halperin, David M., John J. Winkler, and Froma I. Zeitlin. 1990. *Before Sexuality: The Construction of Erotic Experience in the Ancient Greek World*. Princeton, NJ: Princeton Univ. Press.

Halverson, Richard. 2002. "Representing Phronesis: Supporting Instructional Leadership Practice in School." PhD diss., Northwestern Univ.

Haraway, Donna Jeanne. 1985. "A Manifesto for Cyborgs: Science, Technology, and Socialist Feminism in the 1980s." *Socialist Review* 80: 65–107.

———. 1991. "Situated Knowledges." In *Simians, Cyborgs, and Women: The Reinvention of Nature*, by Donna Haraway. New York: Routledge.

———. 1997. *Modest-Witness@Second-Millennium.FemaleMan-Meets-OncoMouse: Feminism and Technoscience*. New York: Routledge.

Haraway, Donna Jeanne, and Thyrza Nichols Goodeve. 2000. *How Like a Leaf: An Interview with Thyrza Nichols Goodeve*. New York: Routledge.

Harbaugh, Barry. 2010. "A History of Stuttering in the Movies: It Hasn't Been Pretty." *Slate*, Dec. 9. http://www.slate.com/articles/arts/culturebox/2010/12 /a_history_of_stuttering_in_the_movies.html.

Harding, Sondra. 1993. "Rethinking Standpoint Epistemology." In *Feminist Epistemologies*, edited by Linda Alcoff and E. Potter, 49–82. New York: Routledge.

Harding, Warren G. 1920. "Back to Normal: Address before Home Market Club." Boston, May 14, 1920. In *Rededicating America: Life and Recent Speeches of Warren G. Harding*, edited by Frederick E. Schortemeier, 223–29. Indianapolis: Bobbs-Merrill.

Hardt, Michael, and Antonio Negri. 2004. *Multitude: War and Democracy in the Age of Empire*. New York: Penguin Press.

Hauser, Gerard. 1986. *An Introduction to Rhetorical Theory*. New York: Harper.

Havelock, Eric. 1982. *Preface to Plato*. New York: Belknap Press.

———. 1986. *The Muse Learns to Write: Reflections on Orality and Literacy from Antiquity to the Present*. New Haven, CT: Yale Univ. Press.

Hawhee, Debra. 2005. *Bodily Arts*. Austin: Univ. of Texas Press.

———. 2011. "Toward a Bestial Rhetoric." *Philosophy and Rhetoric* 44 (1): 81–87.

Hayles, N. Katherine. 1999. *How We Became Posthuman: Virtual Bodies in Cybernetics, Literature, and Informatics*. Chicago: Univ. of Chicago Press.

Heitman, Richard. 2005. *Taking Her Seriously: Penelope and the Plot of Homer's "Odyssey."* Ann Arbor: Univ. of Michigan Press.

Hercules (Gold Collection). 2004. Directed by John Musker. Walt Disney Studios Home Entertainment.

Hermogenes. 1987. *Hermogenes on Types of Style*. Chapel Hill: Univ. of North Carolina Press.

Hesiod. 1914a. *The Homeric Hymns and Homerica*. Translated by Hugh G. Evelyn-White. Cambridge, MA: Harvard Univ. Press.

————. 1914b. *Theogony*. Translated by Hugh G. Evelyn-White. Cambridge: Harvard Univ. Press.

————. 1978. *Works and Days*. Translated by M. L. West. Oxford: Clarendon Press.

Hippocrates. 1994. *Volumes I–IX*. Translated by Wesley D. Smith. Loeb Classical Library. Cambridge, MA: Harvard Univ. Press.

Hitchens, Christopher. 2011. "*The King's Speech*: Good Movie, Very Bad History." *Slate*, Jan. 24. http://www.slate.com/articles/news_and_politics/fighting _words/2011/01/churchill_didnt_say_that.html.

Hoberman, J. 2010. "*The King's Speech*: How Therapy Saved Monarchy." *Village Voice*, Nov. 24. http://www.villagevoice.com/2010-11-24/film/the-king-s -speech-how-therapy-saved-monarchy/.

Holmes, Morgan. 2008a. *Intersex*. Danvers, MA: Rosemont.

————. 2008b. "Mind the Gaps: Intersex and (Re)productive Spaces in Disability Studies and Bioethics." *Journal of Bioethical Inquiry* 5 (2–3): n.p.

Homer. 1997. *The Iliad*. Translated by Stanley Lombardo. Indianapolis: Hackett.

————. 1999a. *The Iliad*. Translated by A. T. Murray. Cambridge, MA: Harvard Univ. Press.

————. 1999b. *The Odyssey*. Translated by A. T. Murray. Cambridge, MA: Harvard Univ. Press.

————. 2000. *The Odyssey*. Translated by Stanley Lombardo. Indianapolis: Hackett.

Hoppenstand, Gary, and Ray Browne, eds. 1983. *The Defective Detective in the Pulps*. Bowling Green, OH: Bowling Green Univ. Popular Press.

Horace. 1926. *Satires, Epistles, and Ars Poetica, with an English Translation*. London: W. Heinemann.

Howes, Franny. 2013. "The Superhero and the Supercrip: An Interrogation of Disability in Superhero Discourse." Unpublished article.

How's Your News? 2008. Directed by Arthur Bradford. Shout Factory Theatre.

Hughes, Karen, Tom Shakespeare, Christopher Mikton, Ellie Mccoy, Lindsay Eckley, Geoff Bates, Sara Wood, et al. 2012. "Prevalence and Risk of Violence against Adults with Disabilities: A Systematic Review and Meta-analysis of Observational Studies." *Lancet* 379 (9826): 1621–29.

Humphreys, S. C. 1999. "From a Grin to a Death." In *Constructions of the Classical Body*, edited by James I. Porter. Ann Arbor: Univ. of Michigan Press.

Husserl, Edmund. 1958. *Ideas: General Introduction to Pure Phenomenology*. London: Allen & Unwin.

Husserl, Edmund, et al. 2002. *Husserl at the Limits of Phenomenology: Including Texts by Edmund Husserl, Maurice Merleau-Ponty.* Evanston, IL: Northwestern Univ. Press.

Hyde Park on Hudson. 2012. Directed by Roger Michell. Focus Features.

Hynes, William J., and William G. Doty, eds. 1993. *Mythical Trickster Figures.* Tuscaloosa: Univ. of Alabama Press.

I Am Sam. 2002. New Line Platinum Series. Directed by Jessie Nelson. New Line Home Video.

Ihde, Don. 1993. *Postphenomenology: Essays in the Postmodern Context.* Evanston, IL: Northwestern Univ. Press.

Ijsseling, Samuel. 1995. "Power, Language, and Desire." In *From Phenomenology to Thought, Errancy, and Desire: Essays in Honor of William J. Richardson, S.J.,* edited by William J. Richardson and Babette E. Babich, 334–53. Dordrecht: Kluwer Academic.

Inception. 2010. Directed by Christopher Nolan. Warner Home Video.

Iris. 2002. Directed by Richard Eyre. Miramax.

The Iron Lady. 2011. Directed by Phyllida Lloyd. Weinstein.

Irwin, Jones. 2010. *Derrida and the Writing of the Body.* London: Ashgate Press.

It. 2002. Directed by Tommy Wallace. Warner Home Video.

Jacobs, Amber. 2007. *On Matricide: Myth, Psychoanalysis, and the Law of the Mother.* New York: Columbia Univ. Press.

James, William. 1907. *Pragmatism, a New Name for Some Old Ways of Thinking: Popular Lectures on Philosophy.* New York: Longmans, Green.

Jameson, Frederic. 1985. *Marxism and Form.* Princeton, NJ: Princeton Univ. Press.

Jarratt, Susan C. 1991. *Rereading the Sophists: Classical Rhetoric Refigured.* Carbondale: Southern Illinois Univ. Press.

Jarratt, Susan C., and Rory Ong. 1995. "Aspasia: Rhetoric, Gender, and Colonial Ideology." *Reclaiming Rhetorica: Women in the Rhetorical Tradition,* edited by Andrea A. Lunsford, 9–24. Pittsburgh: Univ. of Pittsburgh Press.

Jezer, Marty. 1997. *Stuttering: A Life Bound Up in Words.* New York: Basic Books.

Jirasuradej, Lawan. 2001. *Mama Wahunzi.* Distributed by Women Make Movies. New York.

Johansson, Warren, ed. 1990. *The Encyclopedia of Homosexuality.* London: Taylor and Francis.

Johnson, Mary. 2003. *Make Them Go Away: Clint Eastwood, Christopher Reeve, and the Case against Disability Rights.* Louisville, KY: Advocado Press.

———. 2006. "Terri Schiavo: A Disability Rights Case." *Death Studies* 30 (2): 163–76.

Johnson, Robert R. 1998. *User-Centered Technology*. Albany: State Univ. of New York Press.

Jones, Gail. 2007. *Sorry*. New York: Europa Editions.

Judd, Denis. 1983. *King George VI, 1895–1952*. New York: Franklin Watts.

Justice, Daniel Heath. 2003. "Renewing the Fire: Notes toward the Liberation of English Studies." *English Studies in Canada* 29 (1–2): 45–54.

Kahn, Charles. 1963. "Plato's Funeral Oration: The Motive of the Menexenus." *Classical Philology* 58: 220.

Karenga, Maulana. 2003. "Nommo, Kawaida, and Communicative Practice." In *Understanding African American Rhetoric*, edited by Ronald L. Jackson II and Elaine B. Richardson, 3–22. New York: Routledge.

———. 2004. *Maat: The Moral Ideal in Ancient Egypt*. Thousand Oaks, CA: Sage.

Kastrup, M. C. 2011. "Cultural Aspects of Depression as a Diagnostic Entity: Historical Perspective." *Medicographia* 33: 119–24.

Keating, AnaLouise, with Gloria E. Anzaldua. 2000. "Last Words? Spirit Journeys." In *Interviews/Entrevistas*, edited by AnaLouise Keating, 281–92. New York: Routledge.

Kellner, Hans. 1989. *Language and Historical Representation*. Madison: Univ. of Wisconsin Press.

Kennedy, George. 1992. "A Hoot in the Dark: The Evolution of a General Rhetoric." *Philosophy and Rhetoric* 25 (1): 1–23.

Kent Sprague, Rosamond, trans. 1972. "Dissoi Logoi." In *The Older Sophists: A Complete Translation by Several Hands of the Fragments in Die Fragmente Der Vorsokratiker*, edited by Hermann Diels-Kranz. Columbia: Univ. of South Carolina Press.

Kerenyi, Karl. 1955. *The Trickster: A Study in American Indian Mythology*. Philadelphia: American Folklore Society.

Kermode, Frank. 1967. *The Sense of an Ending: Studies in the Theory of Fiction*. New York: Oxford Univ. Press.

Kincheloe, Joe L. 1998. *White Reign: Deploying Whiteness in America*. 1st ed. New York: St. Martin's Press.

Kincheloe, Joe L., and Sheri Steinberg. 1998. "Addressing the Crisis of Whiteness: Reconfiguring White Identity in a Pedagogy of Whiteness." In *White Reign: Deploying Whiteness in America*. New York: St. Martin's Press.

"Kinesthesis." 1989. In *The Oxford English Dictionary*. 2nd ed. Oxford: Oxford Univ. Press.

Klindienst, Patricia. 1984. "The Voice of the Shuttle Is Ours." *Stanford Literature Review* 1: 25–53.

Knapp, Ernst. 1877. *Grundlinien einer Philosophie der Technik*. Braunscheig: G. Westermann.

Knudsen, Fabienne. 2005. *Seamanship and Anthropoship: Reflecting on Practice*. Arbejds: og Maritimmedicinsk Publikationsserie. Rapport nr. 11.

Koepping, Klaus Peter. 1985. "Absurdity and Hidden Truth: Cunning Intelligence and Grotesque Body Images as Manifestations of the Trickster." *History of Religions* 24 (3): 191–214.

Kopelson, Karen. 2002. "Dis/Integrating the Gay/Queer Binary: 'Reconstructed Identity Politics' for a Performative Pedagogy." *College English* 65 (1): 17–19.

———. 2003. "Rhetoric on the Edge of Cunning; or, The Performance of Neutrality (Re)considered as a Composition Pedagogy for Student Resistance." *CCC* 55 (1): 115–46.

Kosofsky-Sedgwick, Eve. 1985. *Between Men: English Literature and Male Homosocial Desire*. New York: Columbia Univ. Press.

Kovacs, George, and C. W. Marshall. 2011. Introduction to *Classics and Comics*, edited by George Kovacs and C. W. Marshall. New York: Oxford Univ. Press.

Koyama, Emi. 2006. "From 'Intersex' to 'DSD': Toward a Queer Disability Politics of Gender." http://www.intersexinitiative.org/articles/intersextodsd.html.

Kraayenoord, Christa van. 2011. "Movies and Disability: Positive Impact or Harm?" *International Journal of Disability, Development, and Education* 58 (2): 103–6.

Kriegel, Leonard. 1982. "The Wolf in the Pit in the Zoo." *Social Policy* 13: 16–23.

———. 1987. "The Cripple in Literature." In *Images of the Disabled, Disabling Images*, edited by A. Gartner and T. Joe, 31–46. New York: Praeger.

Kumari Campbell, Fiona. 2009. *Contours of Ableism: The Production of Disability and Abledness*. London: Palgrave Macmillan.

Kuppers, Petra. 2011. *Disability Culture and Community Performance: Find a Strange and Twisted Shape*. Houndmills, Basingstoke, Hampshire: Palgrave Macmillan.

Kuusisto, Stephen. 2012. "Odysseus, Paul Ryan, and Disability." *Planet of the Blind*, Apr. 3. http://www.planet-of-the-blind.com/2012/04/odysseus-paul-ryan-and -disability.html.

Lakoff, George, and Mark Johnson. 1980. *Metaphors We Live By*. Chicago: Univ. of Chicago Press.

———. 1999. *Philosophy in the Flesh*. New York: Basic Books.

Laqueur, Thomas. 1990. *Making Sex: Body and Gender from the Greeks to Freud*. Cambridge, MA: Harvard Univ. Press.

Lara, Irene, with Gloria E. Anzaldua. 2005. "Daughter of Coatlicue: An Interview with Gloria Anzaldúa." In *Entremundos/Among Worlds*, edited by AnaLouise Keating, 41–46. New York: Palgrave Macmillan.

Lee, Harper. 1960. *To Kill a Mockingbird*. Philadelphia: Lippincott.

Lerner, Gerda. 1986. *The Creation of Patriarchy*. New York: Oxford Univ. Press.

Letiche, Hugo, and Matt Statler. 2005. "Evoking Metis: Questioning the Logics of Change, Responsiveness, Meaning, and Action." *Culture and Organization* 11 (1): 1–16.

Letts, Quentin. 2011. "Richard III: Showmanship Supreme but, Alas, Spacey Is Hardly Olivier." *London Daily Mail*, June 30. http://www.dailymail.co.uk/tv showbiz/article-2009719/RICHARD-III-Showmanship-supreme-alas-Spacey -hardly-Olivier.html.

Lévi-Strauss, Claude. 1979. *Myth and Meaning*. New York: Schocken Books.

Lewiecki-Wilson, Cynthia. 1994. "Teaching in the 'Contact-Zone' of the Two-Year College Classroom: Multiple Literacies/'Deep Portfolio.'" *Teaching English in a Two-Year College* 2: 267–76.

———. 2003. "Rethinking Rhetoric through Mental Disabilities." *Rhetoric Review* 22 (2): 154–202.

Lindgren, Kristin. 2004. "Bodies in Trouble: Identity, Embodiment, and Disability." In *Gendering Disability*, edited by Bonnie G. Smith and Beth Huchinson, 145–65. New Brunswick, NJ: Rutgers Univ. Press.

Linton, Simi. 1993. "Reassigning Meaning." In *Claiming Disability: Knowledge and Identity*, 8–33. New York: New York Univ. Press.

Linton, Simi, Susan Mello, and John O'Neill. 2000. "Disability Studies: Expanding the Parameters of Diversity." In *Education Is Politics: Critical Teaching across Differences*, edited by Ira Shor, 178–92. Portsmouth, NH: Boynton/Cook.

Lionnet, Françoise. 1989. *Autobiographical Voices: Race, Gender, Self-Portraiture*. Ithaca, NY: Cornell Univ. Press.

Longmore, Paul K. 1987. "Screening Stereotypes: Images of Disabled People in Television and Motion Pictures." In *Images of the Disabled, Disabling Images*, edited by Alan Gartner and Tom Joe, 65–78. New York: Praeger.

———. 2003. Why I Burned My Book, and Other *Essays on Disability*. Philadelphia: Temple Univ. Press.

———. 2005. "The Cultural Framing of Disability: Telethons as a Case Study." *PMLA* 120 (2): 502–10.

Loraux, Nicole. 1995. *Experience of Tiresias: The Feminine and the Greek Man*. Translated by Paula Wissing. Princeton, NJ: Princeton Univ. Press.

————. 2000. *Born of the Earth: Myth and Politics in Athens*. Translated by Selina Stewart. Ithaca, NY: Cornell Univ. Press.

Lost in Translation. 2004. Directed by Sofia Coppola. Universal Studios.

Lu, Min-Zhan. 2004. "Composing Post-colonial Studies." In *Crossing Borderlands: Composition and Postcolonial Studies*, edited by Andrea Lunsford and Lahoucine Ouzgane, 9–32. Pittsburgh: Univ. of Pittsburgh Press.

Lukin, Josh. 2012. E-mail correspondence with author. Sept. 30.

Lunsford, Andrea, ed. 1995. *Reclaiming Rhetorica: Women in the Rhetorical Tradition*. Pittsburgh: Univ. of Pittsburgh Press.

————. 2000. "Toward a Mestiza Rhetoric: Gloria Anzaldúa on Composition, Postcoloniality, and the Spiritual." In *Interviews/Entrevistas*, edited by AnaLouise Keating, 251–80. New York: Routledge.

Lysias, and S. C. Todd. 2000. *Lysias*. 1st ed. Vol. 2. Austin: Univ. of Texas Press.

Mabe, Catherine. 2011. "Actor with Cerebral Palsy on *Breaking Bad*." *Disaboom.com*. http://www.disaboom.com/television/actor-with-cerebral-palsy-on-breaking -bad.

MacDowell, Douglas Maurice. 2009. *Demosthenes the Orator*. London: Oxford Univ. Press.

Mairs, Nancy. 1997. *Waist-High in the World: A Life among the Non-Disabled*. Boston: Beacon Press.

Malten, L. 1912. "Hephaistos." *JDL* 27: 232–64.

Markotic, Nicole. 2003. "Re/presenting Disability and Illness: Foucault and Two 20th Century Fictions." *Disability Studies Quarterly* 23 (2): n.p.

Martha Marcy May Marlene. 2011. Directed by Sean Durkin. 20th Century Fox.

Martin, Denise. 2008. "Maat and Order in African Cosmology." *Journal of Black Studies* 38 (6): 951–67.

Martin, Emily. 2007. *Bipolar Expeditions: Mania and Depression in American Culture*. Princeton, NJ: Princeton Univ. Press.

May, Vivian M., and Beth A. Ferri. 2005. "Fixated on Ability: Questioning Ableist Metaphors in Feminist Theories of Resistance." *Prose Studies* 27 (1–2): 120–40.

Mazzeo, Joseph Anthony. 1962. "St. Augustine's Rhetoric of Silence." *Journal of the History of Ideas* 23 (2): 175–96.

McAdon, Brad. 2004. "Plato's Denunciation of Rhetoric in the *Phaedrus*." *Rhetoric Review* 23 (1): 21–39.

McLuhan, Marshall. 1994. *Understanding Media: The Extensions of Man*. Cambridge: MIT Press.

McMaster, Carrie. 2005. "Negotiating Paradoxical Spaces: Women, Disabilities, and the Experience of Nepantla." In *Entre Mundos/Among Worlds: New Perspectives on Gloria Anzaldúa*, edited by AnaLouise Keating, 101–8. London: Palgrave Macmillan.

McRuer, Robert. 2004. "Composing Bodies; or, De-composition: Queer Theory, Disability Studies, and Alternative Corporealities." *JAC: A Journal of Composition Theory* 24 (1): 47–78.

———. 2007. *Crip Theory*. New York: New York Univ. Press.

———. 2011. "Fuck the Disabled." In *Shakesqueer*, edited by Madhavi Menon. Durham, NC: Duke Univ. Press.

———. 2013. "The Crip's Speech." Draft of essay shared with the author.

McRuer, Robert, and Abby Wilkerson. 2003. "Cripping the (Queer) Nation." *GLQ: A Journal of Lesbian and Gay Studies* 9 (1–2): 1–23.

McShannon, Simon. 2001. "World War One: The Tragedy of Prince John." Mar. 16. http://smnmcshannon.hubpages.com/hub/World-One-War-The-Royal-Tragedy-of-Prince-John.

Melnick, Jeffrey. 2007. "Immigration and Race Relations." In *A Companion to American Immigration*, edited by R. Ueda, 255–67. Oxford: Blackwell.

Melville, Herman. 1924. *Billy Budd*. London: Constable.

———. 1942. *Moby Dick; or, The White Whale*. New York: Dodd, Mead.

———. 1954. *The Confidence-Man: His Masquerade*. New York: Hendricks House.

Memento. 2001. Directed by Christopher Nolan. Sony Pictures Home Entertainment.

Merleau-Ponty, Maurice. 1965. *Phenomenology of Perception*. London: Routledge and Kegan Paul.

Mialet, Hélène. 2012. *Hawking Incorporated: Stephen Hawking and the Anthropology of the Knowing Subject*. Chicago: Univ. of Chicago Press.

Michalko, Rod. 1999. *The Two-in-One*. Philadelphia: Temple Univ. Press.

———. 2002. "Estranged-Familiarity." In *Disability/Postmodernity: Embodying Political Theory*, edited by Mairian Corker and Tom Shakespeare. London: Continuum Press.

Million Dollar Baby. 2010. Directed by Clint Eastwood. Warner Home Video.

The Miracle Worker. 2001. Directed by Arthur Penn. MGM.

Mitchell, David. 2006. *Black Swan Green: A Novel*. New York: Random House.

Mitchell, David, and Sharon Snyder, dir. and prod. 1997. *Vital Signs: Crip Culture Talks Back*. Marquette, WI: Brace Yourselves.

———. 2001a. *Narrative Prosthesis: Disability and the Dependence of Discourse*. Ann Arbor: Univ. of Michigan Press.

———. 2001b. "Re-engaging the Body: Disability Studies and the Resistance to Embodiment." *Public Culture* 13 (3): 367–89.

———. 2001c. "Representation and Its Discontents: The Uneasy Home of Disability in Literature and Film." In *Handbook of Disability Studies*, edited by G. L. Albrecht, K. D. Seelman, and M. Bury, 195–218. Thousand Oaks, CA: Sage.

———. 2006. *Cultural Locations of Disability*. Chicago: Univ. of Chicago Press.

Montagu, Ashley. 2001. *The Anatomy of Swearing*. Philadelphia: Univ. of Pennsylvania Press.

Morrison, Toni. 1977. *Song of Solomon*. New York: Alfred A. Knopf.

Munoz, Jose Esteban. 2009. *Cruising Utopia*. New York: New York Univ. Press.

Murderball. 2005. Directed by Dana Adam Shapiro. Velocity / Thinkfilm.

Murphy, James J. 1983. "The Origins and Early Development of Rhetoric." In *A Synoptic History of Classical Rhetoric*, edited by James J. Murphy. Davis, CA: Hermagoras Press.

Murray, Robert K. 1973. *The Politics of Normalcy*. New York: W. W. Norton.

My Left Foot. 1989. Directed by Jim Sheridan. Miramax.

Mystic River. 2010. Directed by Clint Eastwood. Warner Home Video.

Neel, Jasper P. 1988. *Plato, Derrida, and Writing*. Carbondale: Southern Illinois Univ. Press.

Neumaier, Joe. 2011. "*The King's Speech* Reigns Supreme." *New York Daily News*, Feb. 28. http://www.nydailynews.com/blogs/showandtell/2011/02/the-kings -speech-reigns-supreme.

New, Maria I. 1993. "Pope Joan: A Recognizable Syndrome." *Transactions of the American Clinical and Climatological Association* 104: 104–22.

Nielsen, Kim. 2009. *Beyond the Miracle Worker: The Remarkable Story of Anne Sullivan Macy and Her Extraordinary Friendship with Helen Keller*. Boston: Beacon Press.

No Country for Old Men. 2008. Directed by Ethan Coen. Walt Disney Video.

Norden, Martin. 1994. *The Cinema of Isolation: A History of Physical Disability in the Movies*. New Brunswick, NJ: Rutgers Univ. Press.

Oat, Zach. 2010. "*The King's Speech*: The Rocky of Speech Therapy Movies." *Television without Pity*, Nov. 30. http://www.televisionwithoutpity.com/mwop /moviefile/2010/11/the-kings-speech-the-rocky-of.php.

O'Connor, Flannery. 1983. "Good Country People." In *A Good Man Is Hard to Find*, 169–96. New York: Harcourt Brace.

Ohi, Kevin. 2011. "Forgetting *The Tempest*." In *Shakesqueer*, edited by Madhavi Menon. Durham, NC: Duke Univ. Press.

Oliver, Michael. 1990. *The Politics of Disablement: A Sociological Approach.* London: St. Martin's Press.

One Flew over the Cuckoo's Nest. 2002. Directed by Milos Forman. Warner Home Video.

Ong, Walter J. 1982. *Orality and Literacy: The Technologizing of the Word.* London: Methuen.

Ott, Katherine. 2005. "Disability and the Practice of Public History: An Introduction." *Public Historian* 27 (2): 11–24.

Ovid. 1717. *Metamorphoses.* Translated by John Dryden et al. Edited by Samuel Garth. London.

———. 1922. *Metamorphoses.* Translated by Brookes More. Boston: Cornhill.

———. 1955. *Metamorphoses.* Translated by Rolfe Humphries. Bloomington: Indiana Univ. Press.

———. 1986. *Metamorphoses.* Translated by A. D. Melville. New York: Oxford Univ. Press.

———. 1993. *Metamorphoses.* Translated by Alan Mandelbaum. New York: Harcourt, Brace and Company.

Padgett, J. Michael. 2003. *The Centaur's Smile: The Human Animal in Early Greek Art.* New Haven, CT: Yale Univ. Press.

Pausanias. 1933. *Description of Greece.* Translated by W. H. S. Jones and H. A. Ormerod. Loeb Classical Library. Cambridge, MA: Harvard Univ. Press.

Pelton, Robert. 1989. *The Trickster in West Africa.* Berkeley: Univ. of California Press.

Peradatto, John. 1990. *Man in the Middle Voice: Name and Narration in the Odyssey.* Princeton, NJ: Princeton Univ. Press.

Petri, Alexandra. 2011. "London Riots: It's Still a Good Time to Be an Anglophile." *Washington Post,* Oct. 8. http://www.washingtonpost.com/blogs/compost/post/london-riots—its-still-a-good-time-to-be-an-anglophile/2011/08/09/gIQA2ybc6I_blog.html.

Pfeiffer, David. 2002. "The Philosophical Foundations of Disability Studies." *Disability Studies Quarterly* 22 (2): 1–20.

The Piano. 1998. Directed by Jane Campion. Lions Gate.

Plato. 1894. *Republic.* Translated by Benjamin Jowett. London: Ayer Press.

———. 1961a. *Critias.* In *The Collected Dialogues of Plato,* edited by Edith Hamilton and Huntington Cairns. Princeton, NJ: Princeton Univ. Press.

———. 1961b. *Gorgias.* In *The Collected Dialogues of Plato,* edited by Edith Hamilton and Huntington Cairns. Princeton, NJ: Princeton Univ. Press.

————. 1961c. *Menexenus*. In *The Collected Dialogues of Plato*, edited by Edith Hamilton and Huntington Cairns. Princeton, NJ: Princeton Univ. Press.

————. 1961d. *Phaedo*. In *The Collected Dialogues of Plato*, edited by Edith Hamilton and Huntington Cairns. Princeton, NJ: Princeton Univ. Press.

————. 1961e. *Phaedrus*. In *The Collected Dialogues of Plato*, edited by Edith Hamilton and Huntington Cairns. Princeton, NJ: Princeton Univ. Press.

————. 1961f. *Symposium*. In *The Collected Dialogues of Plato*, edited by Edith Hamilton and Huntington Cairns. Princeton, NJ: Princeton Univ. Press.

————. 1961g. *Timaeus*. In *The Collected Dialogues of Plato*, edited by Edith Hamilton and Huntington Cairns. Princeton, NJ: Princeton Univ. Press.

————. 1997. *Gorgias*. In *Plato: Complete Works*, edited by J. M. Cooper and D. S. Hutchinson. Indianapolis: Hackett.

————. 2000. *Critias*. Translated by Benjamin Jowett. Vol. 3. New York: Modern Library.

Plutarch and John S. White. 1966. *Plutarch's "Lives."* New York: Biblo and Tannen.

Poe, Richard. 1999. *Black Spark, White Fire*. New York: Prima Lifestyles.

Poliakoff, Stephen. 2003. *The Lost Prince*. London: Methuen.

Pomeroy, S. 1997. *Families in Classical and Hellenistic Greece*. Oxford: Oxford Univ. Press.

Pope-Hennessy, James. 2000. *Queen Mary, 1867–1953*. London: Phoenix Press.

Possessed. 1995. Directed by Curtis Bernhardt. Warner Home Video.

Povinelli, Elizabeth. 2011. *Economies of Abandonment*. Durham, NC: Duke Univ. Press.

Powell, Malea. 1999. "Blood and Scholarship: One Mixed-Blood's Story." In *Race, Rhetoric, and Composition*, edited by Keith Gilyard, 1–16. Portsmouth, NH: Boynton/Cook.

Press, B. 2007. "The Sad Legacy of Jerry Falwell." *Milford Daily News*. http://www.milforddailynews.com/opinion/x1987843539.

Price, Janet, and Margrit Shildrick. 2002. "Bodies Together: Touch, Ethics, and Disability." In *Disability/Postmodernity: Embodying Political Theory*, edited by Mairian Corker and Tom Shakespeare, 62–75. London: Continuum Press.

Price, Margaret. 2011. *Mad at School: Rhetorics of Mental Disability and Academic Life*. Ann Arbor: Univ. of Michigan Press.

Primal Fear. 1998. Directed by Gregory Hoblit. Paramount.

Progymnasmata: Greek Textbooks of Prose Composition and Rhetoric. 2003. Atlanta: Society of Biblical Literature.

Pryal, Katie Rose Guest. 2011. "The Creativity Mystique and the Rhetoric of Mood Disorders." *Disability Studies Quarterly* 31 (3): n.p.

Quackenbush, Nicole. 2011. "Speaking of—and as—Stigma: Performativity and Parkinson's in the Rhetoric of Michael J. Fox. *Disability Studies Quarterly* 31 (3): n.p.

Quandahl, Ellen. 1989. "What Is Plato?" *Rhetoric Review* 7 (2): 338–48.

Quayson, Ato. 2007. *Aesthetic Nervousness: Disability and the Crisis of Representation.* New York: Columbia Univ. Press.

Quintillian. 1965. *On the Early Education of the Citizen-Orator.* Edited by James L. Murphy. New York: Bobbs-Merrill.

Radin, P. 1956. *The Trickster.* New York: Philosophical Library.

Rain Man. 2004. Directed by Barry Levinson. Santa Monica, CA: MGM Home Entertainment.

Ramsey, Eric. 1999. "A Hybrid Technē of the Soul? Thoughts on the Relation between Philosophy and Rhetoric in *Gorgias* and *Phaedrus.*" *Rhetoric Review* 17: 247–63.

Raphals, Lisa Ann. 1992. *Knowing Words: Wisdom and Cunning in the Classical Traditions of China and Greece.* Ithaca, NY: Cornell Univ. Press.

Ray. 2005. Directed by Taylor Hackford. Universal Studios.

Reagan, Charles E. 1996. "Philosophical Essays: Personal Identity." In *Paul Ricoeur: His Life and His Works*, 74. Chicago: Univ. of Chicago Press.

Richlin, Amy. 1991. "Zeus and Metis: Foucault, Feminism, Classics." *Helios* 18 (2): 160–80.

The Ringer. 2008. Directed by Barry W. Blaustein. 20th Century Fox.

Riordan, Rick. 2010. *Percy Jackson and The Olympians: The Complete Series.* New York: Disney/Hyperion Books.

Ritchie, Joy, and Kate Ronald, eds. 2001. *Available Means: An Anthology of Women's Rhetoric(s).* Pittsburgh: Univ. of Pittsburgh Press.

Rocket Science. 2008. Directed by Jeffrey Blitz. HBO Home Video.

Rocky: The Undisputed Collection. 2009. Directed by Sylvester Stallone. MGM.

Rodas, Julia Miele. 2008. "'On the Spectrum': Rereading Contact and Affect in *Jane Eyre.*" *Nineteenth-Century Gender Studies* 4 (2): n.p.

———. 2009. "On Blindness." *Journal of Literary and Cultural Disability Studies* 1 (2): 115–30.

Roochnik, David. 1996. *Of Art and Wisdom: Plato's Understanding of Techne.* State College: Pennsylvania State Univ. Press.

Rose, Martha L. 2003. *The Staff of Oedipus: Transforming Disability in Ancient Greece*. Ann Arbor: Univ. of Michigan Press.

Rose, Nikolas. 2007. *The Politics of Life Itself*. Princeton, NJ: Princeton Univ. Press.

Roth, Philip. 1997. *American Pastoral*. Boston: Houghton Mifflin.

Rowling, J. K. 1999. *Harry Potter and the Chamber of Secrets*. New York: Arthur A. Levine Books.

Russo, Joseph. 2008. "A Jungian Analysis of Homer's *Odysseus*." In *The Cambridge Companion to Jung*, edited by Polly Young-Eisendrath and Terence Daws. 2nd ed. Cambridge: Cambridge Univ. Press.

Saito, Takahiro. 2006. "The Decree of the Hephaistia in 421 BC and the Athenian Demos." *Journal of Classical Studies* 47 (1999). http://www.bun.kyoto-u.ac.jp /classics/CSJ/47_1999.html.

Salutati, Coluccio. 2003. "Medusa as Artful Eloquence." In *The Medusa Reader*, 54–56. New York: Routledge.

Samuels, Ellen Jean. 2006. "Fingerprinting the Nation: Identifying Race and Disability in America." PhD diss., Univ. of California at Berkeley.

Sandbrook, Dominic. 2011. "*The King's Speech:* How George VI's Simple Domesticity Made Him the King His Country Needed in Time of War." *Observer*, Jan. 2. http://www.guardian.co.uk/film/2011/jan/02/the-kings-speech-george-vi.

Sanger, Margaret. 1922. *The Pivot of Civilization*. New York: Brentano's Press.

Saramago, Jose. 1999. *Blindness*. London: Panther.

Scent of a Woman. 1992. Directed by Martin Brest. Universal Studios.

Schiebinger, Londa L. 1993. *Nature's Body: Gender in the Making of Modern Science*. Boston: Beacon Press.

Schweik, Susan M. 2009. *The Ugly Laws: Disability in Public*. New York: New York Univ. Press.

The Score. 2003. Directed by Frank Oz. Paramount.

Scott, James C. 1985. *Weapons of the Weak*. New Haven, CT: Yale Univ. Press.

———. 1998. *Seeing Like a State*. New Haven, CT: Yale Univ. Press.

Scott, Jordan. 2005. *Silt*. Vancouver, BC: New Star Books.

The Sea Inside. 2011. Directed by Alejandro Amenabar. New Line Home Video.

Sedgwick, Eve Kosofsky. 1990. *Epistemology of the Closet*. Berkeley: Univ. of California Press.

Sedgwick, Eve Kosofsky, and Adam Frank, eds. 1995. *Shame and Its Sisters: A Silvan Tomkins Reader*. Durham, NC: Duke Univ. Press.

Seidler, David. 2008. *"The King's Speech" Script*. London: Bedlam/See Saw Films.

———. 2010. "How the 'Naughty Word' Cured the King's Stutter (and Mine)." *London Daily Mail*, Dec. 20. http://www.dailymail.co.uk/femail/article-1339509 /The-Kings-Speech-How-naughty-word-cured-King-George-VIs-stutter.html.

Serlin, David. 2004. *Replaceable You: Engineering the Body in Postwar America*. Chicago: Univ. of Chicago Press.

Shakespeare, William. 1955. *The Tempest*. New Haven, CT: Yale Univ. Press.

Shakespeare in Love. 1998. Directed by John Madden. Miramax Lionsgate.

Shales, Tom. 2009. "TV Preview: MTV's *How's Your News?* Gives Disabled Reporters Spotlight." *Washington Post*, Feb. 5. http://www.washingtonpost.com/wp -dyn/content/article/2009/02/04/AR2009020404010.html?nav=rss_opinion /columns.

Shapiro, Joseph. 1993. *No Pity: People with Disabilities Forging a New Civil Rights Movement*. New York: Random House.

Shell, Marc. 2006. *Stutter*. Cambridge, MA: Harvard Univ. Press.

Sherlock: Season One. 2010. Directed by Coky Giedroyc. BBC Worldwide.

Sherlock Holmes. 2009. Directed by Guy Ritchie. Warner Bros.

Shildrick, Margrit. 1997. *Leaky Bodies and Boundaries: Feminism, Postmodernism, and (Bio)ethics*. New York: Routledge.

———. 2002. *Embodying the Monster: Encounters with the Vulnerable Self*. London: Sage.

———. 2009a. *Dangerous Discourses of Disability, Subjectivity, and Sexuality*. Basingstoke: Palgrave Macmillan.

———. 2009b. "Prosthetic Performativity." In *Deleuze and Queer Theory*, edited by C. Niagianni, 115–34. Edinburgh: Edinburgh Univ. Press.

Shine. 1997. Directed by Scott Hicks. New Line Home Video.

Shutter Island. 2010. Directed by Martin Scorsese. Paramount.

Siebers, Tobin. 2004. "Disability as Masquerade." *Literature and Medicine* 23 (1): 1–22.

———. 2010. *Disability Theory*. Ann Arbor: Univ. of Michigan Press.

Silvers, Anita. 2002. "Disability, Ideology, and the Aesthetic." In *Disability/Postmodernity: Embodying Political Theory*, edited by Mairian Corker and Tom Shakespeare. London: Continuum Press.

Sissa, Giulia. 1999. "Sexual Bodybuilding." In *Constructions of the Classical Body*, edited by James I. Porter, 147–67. Ann Arbor: Univ. of Michigan Press.

Sissa, Giulia, and Marcel Detienne. 2000. *The Daily Life of the Greek Gods*. Translated by Janet Lloyd. Stanford, CA: Stanford Univ. Press.

Slack, Gordy. 2011. "*The Lost Prince:* Epilepsy on Screen." *Brainstorm.* Jan. http://
    gordyslack.blogspot.com/2011/01/lost-prince-epilepsy-on-screen.html.

Slatkin, Laura M. 1996. "Composition by Theme and the *Mētis* of the Odyssey." In
    Reading the Odyssey, edited by Seth L. Schein, 223–38. Princeton, NJ: Princeton
    Univ. Press.

Smith, Bonnie G. 2004. Introduction to *Gendering Disability,* edited by Bonnie G.
    Smith and Beth Huchinson, 1–8. New Brunswick, NJ: Rutgers Univ. Press.

Smith, Marquard, and Joanne Morra, eds. 2005. *The Prosthetic Impulse: From a Post-
    human Present to a Biocultural Future.* Cambridge: MIT Press.

Smith, S. E. 2011. "*Breaking Bad* and the Adjustment Period." *This Ain't Livin'.* http://
    meloukhia.net/2011/07/breaking_bad_and_the_adjustment_period.html.

Smuckler, Linda. 2000. "Turning Points." In *Interviews/Entrevistas,* edited by
    AnaLouise Keating, 17–70. New York: Routledge.

Snyder, Sharon. 2001. "Unfixing Disability in Byron's *The Deformed Transformed.*"
    In *Bodies in Commotion,* edited by C. Sandhal and P. Auslander. Ann Arbor:
    Univ. of Michigan Press.

Sobchack, Vivian Carol. 2004. *Carnal Thoughts: Embodiment and Moving Image Cul-
    ture.* Berkeley: Univ. of California Press.

Solmsen, Friedrich. 1983. "Plato and the Concept of the Soul (Psyche): Some His-
    torical Perspectives." *Journal of the History of Ideas* 44 (3): 355–67.

Somerville, Siobhan. 2000. *Queering the Color Line: Race and the Invention of Homo-
    sexuality in American Culture.* Durham, NC: Duke Univ. Press.

Sophocles, and Mark Griffith. 1999. *Antigone.* Cambridge: Cambridge Univ. Press.

Spoel, Phillipa M. 1998. "The Science of Bodily Rhetoric in Gilbert Austin's *Chi-
    ronomia.*" *Rhetoric Society Quarterly* 28: 5–27.

St. Pierre, Joshua. 2012a. "The Construction of the Disabled Speaker: Locating
    Stuttering in Disability Studies." *Canadian Journal of Disability Studies* 1 (3):
    1–21.

———. 2012b. E-mail correspondence with author. May 12.

Stalpaert, Christel. 2010. "The Creative Power in the Failure of Word and Lan-
    guage." *Arcadia* 45: 77–93.

Star, Susan Leigh. 1995. "The Politics of Formal Representations." In *Ecologies of
    Knowledge: Work and Politics in Science and Technology,* edited by Susan Leigh
    Star. Albany: State Univ. of New York Press.

The Station Agent. 2004. Directed by Tom McCarthy. Echo Bridge Home
    Entertainment.

Steinbeck, John. 1953. *Of Mice and Men.* New York: Viking Press.

Stevens, Bethany. 2011. "Interrogating Transability: A Catalyst to View Disability as Body Art." *Disability Studies Quarterly* 31 (4): n.p.

Stevenson, Jennifer L., Bev Harp, and Morton Ann Gernsbacher. 2011. "Infantilizing Autism." *Disability Studies Quarterly* 31 (3): n.p.

Stiker, Jacques. 1999. *A History of Disability*. Ann Arbor: Univ. of Michigan Press.

Stoa Consortium. 2006. *Suda Online*. http://www.stoa.org/sol/.

Stockton, Kathryn Bond. 2009. *The Queer Child: Growing Up Sideways in the Twentieth Century*. Durham, NC: Duke Univ. Press.

Strage, Mark. 1980. *The Durable Fig Leaf: A Historical, Cultural, Medical, Social, Literary, and Iconographic Account of Man's Relations with His Penis*. New York: Morrow.

Stryker, Susan. 2004. "Transgender Studies: Queer Theory's Evil Twin." *GLQ: A Journal of Lesbian and Gay Studies* 10 (2): 212–15.

Stubblefield, Anna. 2007. "Beyond the Pale: Tainted Whiteness, Cognitive Disability, and Eugenic Sterilization." *Hypatia* 22 (2): 162–81.

Summerskill, Ben. 2000. "Princess the Palace Hides Away." *London Observer*, July 23. http://www.guardian.co.uk/uk/2000/jul/23/queenmother.monarchy.

Superman Chronicles. 2013. Vols. 1–10. New York: DC Comics.

Take Shelter. 2011. Directed by Jeff Nichols. Sony Pictures Home Entertainment.

The Taking of Pelham One Two Three. 1974. Directed by Joseph Sargent. Palomar Pictures.

Taxi Driver. 2006. Directed by Martin Scorsese. Sony Pictures.

Taylor, Diana. 2007. *The Archive and the Repertoire: Performing Cultural Memory in the Americas*. Durham, NC: Duke Univ. Press.

Taylor, Thomas, trans. 1969. "Hymns of Orpheus." In *Thomas Taylor the Platonist*, edited by Kathleen Raine. London: Harper, RKP.

Taylor, Timothy F. 1997. *The Prehistory of Sex*. London: Fourth Estate Press.

———. 2007. "Origins of Human Sexual Culture." *Journal of Psychology and Human Sexuality* 18 (2–3): 69–105.

Temple Grandin. 2010. Directed by Mick Jackson. HBO Films.

Terry, Jennifer. 1994. "Theorizing Deviant Historiography." In *Feminists Revision History*, edited by Louise Shapiro, 276–304. Edited by New Brunswick, NJ: Rutgers Univ. Press.

Tezuka, Osamu. 2003. *Phoenix*. Reissue. New York: Viz.

Thielman, Sam. 2010. "Talk of the Town: Colin Firth Discusses *Speech* Impediments." *Variety*, Nov. 11. http://www.variety.com/article/VR1118027301?ref CatId=13.

Thiesen, Nicholas A. 2011. "Declassicizing the Classical in Japanese Comics." In *Classics and Comics*, edited by George Kovacs and C. W. Marshall. New York: Oxford Univ. Press.

Thomson, Pat. 1992. "Disability in Modern Children's Fiction." *Books for Keeps* 7.

Titchkosky, Tanya. 2007. *Reading and Writing Disability Differently*. Toronto: Univ. of Toronto Press.

———. 2011. "The Becoming Crisis of Disability Studies." Disability Studies Summer Institute Keynote Address, July 18, Univ. of Toronto, Canada.

Tomkins, Silvan. 1995. *Shame and Its Sisters: A Silvan Tomkins Reader*. Edited by Eve Kosofsky Sedgwick, Adam Frank, and Irving E. Alexander. Durham, NC: Duke Univ. Press.

Tommy. 2004. Directed by Ken Russell. Sony Pictures Home Entertainment.

Torok, Maria. 1994. *The Shell and the Kernel: Renewals of Psychoanalysis*. Chicago: Univ. of Chicago Press.

Tremain, Shelley. 2002. "On the Subject of Impairment." In *Disability/Postmodernity: Embodying Political Theory*, edited by Mairian Corker and Tom Shakespeare, 32–47. London: Continuum Press.

Trent, James W., Jr. 1994. *Inventing the Feeble Mind: A History of Mental Retardation in the United States*. Berkeley: Univ. of California Press.

Twelfth Night. 1987. Directed by Neil Armfield. Umbrella Entertainment.

The Usual Suspects. 2002. Directed by Bryan Singer. MGM.

Valentine, David. 2002. "'We're Not about Gender': The Uses of 'Transgender.'" In *Out in Theory: The Emergence of Lesbian and Gay Anthropology*, edited by Ellen Lewin and William L. Leap, 222–45. Urbana: Univ. of Illinois Press.

Vasconcelos, Jose. 1997. *La Raza Cosmica*. Translated by Didier T. Jaen. Baltimore: Johns Hopkins Univ. Press.

Veeser, H. Aram, ed. 1989. *The New Historicism*. London: Routledge, Chapman, and Hall.

Vesey, Alyx. 2013. "Bechdel Test Canon." *Bitch Magazine*, May 15. http://bitch magazine.org/blog/3416.

Vickers, Nancy J. 2003. "The Face of Medusa." In *The Medusa Reader*, 232–37. New York: Routledge.

Vidali, Amy. 2007. "Performing the Rhetorical Freak Show: Disability, Student Writing, and College Admissions." *College English* 69 (6): 615–41.

Virgil. 1891. *Virgil's Aenied*. Book 1. Edited by John Henderson. Toronto: Copp, Clark.

Wadley, Ted. 2013. "Sequoyah." In *The New Georgia Encyclopedia*, May 10. http://www.georgiaencyclopedia.org/nge/Article.jsp?id=h-618&sug=y.

Walls, Neal H. 2007. "The Origins of the Disabled Body." In *This Abled Body*, edited by Hector Avalos, Sarah J. Melcher, and Jeremy Schipper. Atlanta: Society of Biblical Literature.

Walters, Shannon. 2010. "Animal Athena: The Interspecies *Mētis* of Women Writers with Autism." *JAC: A Journal of Composition Theory* 30 (3–4): 683–711.

Watson, J. S. 1887. "Critical Notes." In *Quintilian's Institutes of Oratory; or, Education of an Orator, in Twelve Books*, by Quintilian and J. S. Watson. London: Bell.

W. E. 2012. Directed by Madonna Ciccone. Weinstein.

Weiss, Gail. 1999. *Body Images: Embodiment as Intercorporeality*. New York: Routledge.

Welton, Donn. 1998. Introduction to *Body and Flesh: A Philosophical Reader*, edited by Donn Welton, 1–23. Malden, MA: Blackwell.

Wendell, Susan. 1989. "Toward a Feminist Theory of Disability." *Hypatia* (4): 104–24.

———. 1994. *The Rejected Body: Feminist Philosophical Reflections on Disability*. New York: Routledge.

Wheeler-Bennett, John. 1958. *King George VI: His Life and Reign*. London: St. Martin's Press.

White, David A. 1993. *Rhetoric and Reality in Plato's "Phaedrus."* Albany: State Univ. of New York Press.

White, Eric Charles. 1987. *Kaironomia: On the Will-to-Invent*. Ithaca, NY: Cornell Univ. Press.

Wiegman, Robyn. 1995. *American Anatomies: Theorizing Race and Gender*. Durham, NC: Duke Univ. Press.

———. 1999. "Whiteness Studies and the Paradox of Particularity." *Boundary 2* 26 (3): 115–50.

Wiginton, Melissa. 2011. "*The King's Speech* and Feminism." *Call and Response*, Mar. 4. http://www.faithandleadership.com/blog/03-04-2011/melissa-wiginton-the-king's-speech-and-feminism.

Willard, Nancy, and Barry Moser. 1992. *Beauty and the Beast*. San Diego: Harcourt Brace Jovanovich.

Williams, Linda. 1991. "Film Bodies: Gender, Genre, and Excess." In *Feminist Film Theory: A Reader*, edited by S. Thornham, 267–81. New York: New York Univ. Press.

Williams, Patricia. 1997. *Seeing a Color-Blind Future*. New York: Farrar, Straus, and Giroux.

Wills, David. 1995. *Prosthesis*. Stanford, CA: Stanford Univ. Press.

———. 2005. "Techneology; or, The Discourse of Speed." In *The Prosthetic Impulse: From a Posthuman Present to a Biocultural Future*, edited by Marquard Smith and Joanne Morra, 237–64. Cambridge: MIT Press.

Wilson, Christopher. 2008. "The Lost Prince: Written Out of History." *Daily Mail*, Nov. 15. http://www.dailymail.co.uk/femail/article-1085728/The-lost -prince-Written-royal-history—Prince-Johns-friend-recalls-happy-joker-sent -away-die-isolation.html.

Wilson, James C., and Cynthia Lewiecki-Wilson. 2001. "Disability, Rhetoric, and the Body." In *Embodied Rhetorics: Disability in Language and Culture*, edited by James C. Wilson and Cynthia Lewiecki-Wilson. Carbondale: Southern Illinois Univ. Press.

Wohl, Victoria. 1998. *Intimate Commerce: Exchange, Gender, and Subjectivity in Greek Tragedy*. 1st ed. Austin: Univ. of Texas Press.

———. 2006. "Impossible Metonymy: Lysias for the Cripple." Presentation, Miami Univ., Apr. 15.

Wolfe, Cary. 2009. *What Is Posthumanism?* Minneapolis: Univ. of Minnesota Press.

Yaruss, J. Scott, and Robert W. Quesal. 2004. "Stuttering and the International Classification of Functioning, Disability, and Health (ICF): An Update." *Journal of Communication Disorders* 37 (1): 35–52.

Yergeau, Melanie. 2010. "Circle Wars: Reshaping the Typical Autism Essay." *Disability Studies Quarterly* 30 (1): n.p.

Yergeau, Melanie, and John Duffy. 2011. "Guest Editors' Introduction to Special Issue on Disability and Rhetoric." *Disability Studies Quarterly* 31 (3): n.p.

Yergeau, Melanie, and Paul Heilker. 2011. "Autism and Rhetoric." *College English* 73 (5): n.p.

Young, Iris Marion. 1990. *Throwing Like a Girl, and Other Essays in Feminist Philosophy and Social Theory*. Bloomington: Indiana Univ. Press.

Zarefsky, David. 1998. "The Four Senses of Rhetorical History." In *Doing Rhetorical History: Concepts and Cases*, edited by Kathleen J. Turner. Tuscaloosa: Univ. of Alabama Press.

Zeigler, Philip. 1992. *King Edward VIII*. New York: Random House.

Zeitlin, Froma I. 1996. *Playing the Other: Gender and Society in Classical Greek Literature*. Chicago: Univ. of Chicago Press.

Index

Italic page number denotes illustration.